Protecting Genetic Privacy in Biobanking through Data Protection Law

Protecting Genetic Privacy in Biobanking through Data Protection Law

DARA HALLINAN

OXFORD
UNIVERSITY PRESS

OXFORD
UNIVERSITY PRESS

Great Clarendon Street, Oxford, OX2 6DP,
United Kingdom

Oxford University Press is a department of the University of Oxford.
It furthers the University's objective of excellence in research, scholarship,
and education by publishing worldwide. Oxford is a registered trade mark of
Oxford University Press in the UK and in certain other countries

First Edition published in 2021

Impression: 1

Published in the United States of America by Oxford University Press
198 Madison Avenue, New York, NY 10016, United States of America

British Library Cataloguing in Publication Data
Data available

Library of Congress Control Number: 2020948072

ISBN 978–0–19–289647–6

DOI: 10.1093/oso/9780192896476.001.0001

Printed and bound in the UK by
TJ Books Limited

Contents

Abbreviations

BCR	Binding Corporate Rules
BGB	Bürgerliches Gesetzbuch (Germany)
CoE	Council of Europe
CJEU	Court of Justice of the European Union
CNIL	Commission Nationale de l'Informatique et des Libertés
DPA	Data Protection Authority
DPIA	Data Protection Impact Assessment
DPO	Data Protection Officer
ECHR	European Convention on Human Rights
EctHR	European Court of Human Rights
EDPB	European Data Protection Board
EDPS	European Data Protection Supervisor
FFPE	Formalin-Fixed, Paraffin-Embedded
GDPR	General Data Protection Regulation
GWAS	genome-wide association study
HGP	Human Genome Project
MTA	Material Transfer Agreement
NHS	National Health Service (UK)
OECD	Organization for Economic Co-operation and Development
PGP	Personal Genomes Project
REC	Research Ethics Committee
RFID	Radio Frequency Identification
SGB	Sozialgesetzbuch (Germany)
SNP	single nucleotide polymorphism
SMEs	small and medium-sized enterprise
StPO	Strafprozessordnung (Germany)
UNESCO	United Nations Educational, Scientific and Cultural Organization
WMA	World Medical Association

Table of Cases and Legislation

COURT OF JUSTICE OF THE EUROPEAN UNION CASE LAW

EUROPEAN COURT OF HUMAN RIGHTS CASE LAW

NATIONAL CASE LAW

INTERNATIONAL INSTRUMENTS

EUROPEAN UNION INSTRUMENTS

NATIONAL INSTRUMENTS

1
Introduction

Over the past two decades, genomic research has become an increasingly significant approach to medical research. This results from its scientific and practical promise for human health. In the first instance, genomic research provides a methodological approach suited to reveal new information about a great number of diseases and, in particular, about diseases with particularly high instance—and therefore social significance—in modern societies. In turn, the approach supports the stratification of populations and the identification of the biomarkers essential for personalised medicine. As much as genomic research holds promise for human health, however, it is resource-intensive. Genomic research requires the availability, and capacity for distribution, of large stores of biological samples and associated data. The entities which function in this storage and distribution capacity, and which sit at the centre of the genomic research endeavour, are biobanks.

As genomic research has grown in significance as an approach to medical research, biobanks and biobanking have grown in significance as support infrastructure for medical research. With this increased significance, however, biobanks have also come under ever-increasing ethical and legal scrutiny. In particular, the novelty of biobanks as significant entities in medical research, and the novelty of the type of research they support, have given rise to new questions as to the rights engaged by the biobanking process and as to how these rights should be effectively protected. One right which has been the focus of much discussion and uncertainty is the right to privacy. It is not that the right to privacy is novel to medical research. Rather, the specifics of the biobanking process have meant that the meaning and value of privacy has needed to be considered in novel ways.

From a fundamental perspective, the fact that genomic research relies on the processing of large quantities of individuals' genomic data has raised new questions as to which forms of privacy right are engaged by research, and as to which privacy rights holders are engaged by research: questions of genetic privacy. For example, previously, discussion of privacy in research had focused on questions of bodily privacy and the restriction of third-party access to research subject data. Yet, the deep interrogation of a genome can reveal novel information about research subjects, of which they may not be aware, raising questions as to whether privacy rights may be engaged concerning the return of this information—rights to know and not know. Equally, previously, discussions of privacy rights in research focused predominantly on the research subject. Yet, as genomic data is hereditary, the processing of this data raises questions as to whether genetic relatives and genetic groups may also have privacy rights engaged.

Protecting Genetic Privacy in Biobanking through Data Protection Law. Dara Hallinan, Oxford University Press (2021). © Dara Hallinan.
DOI: 10.1093/oso/9780192896476.003.0001

In turn, the novel institutional, and actor, constellations involved in biobanking and genomic research have raised novel questions as to how to effectively and proportionately balance the need to protect genetic privacy rights with the need to promote other legitimate interests engaged by biobanking and genomic research—in particular interests tied up with the conduct and outcome of research. For example, previously, discussions of protecting privacy in research had predominantly focused on questions of clinical research involving live subjects. As biobanking and genomic research engage with biological samples and associated data sets, as opposed to live individuals, questions are raised as to the degree to which approaches to protect privacy in clinical research should also apply to data-based research involving little, if any, interaction with subjects' bodies.

Ordinarily, one might look to the law to provide some clue, or image, as to which genetic privacy rights are worthy of protection and as to what an effective and proportionate approach to their protection should look like. In this regard, a brief look at the legal landscape relevant to biobanking in Europe reveals a great quantity of legislation apparently relevant for the protection of genetic privacy in biobanking. Relevant instruments appear at international, EU, and at national level. Despite the quantity of relevant legislation, however, criticism has been, and continues to be, voiced as to the suitability of available approaches. Criticism appears concerning the structure of frameworks—for example, concerning their complexity and contradictions in relation to international biobanking activity.[1] Criticism also appears concerning the level of substantive protection provided.[2]

Since 25 May 2018, Regulation 2016/679—the General Data Protection Regulation (hereafter the GDPR or Regulation)—has applied, and now constitutes the keystone of European data protection law.[3] The GDPR aims to provide a comprehensive system of protection for individuals' rights engaged by data processing, applies to the processing of almost all personal data and, as a Regulation is, in principle, directly applicable in all European states in which it applies—including in all EU states. There is no doubt the GDPR applies to biobanking. There is also no doubt that the GDPR now occupies a significant place in the European legal framework relevant for the regulation of biobanking. As a result, over the past few years, there have been several works considering the applicability and consequences of the GDPR for biobanks and

[1] See, for example, Mahsa Shabani and Pascal Borry, 'Rules for Processing Genetic Data for Research Purposes in View of the New EU General Data Protection Regulation' (2018) *European Journal of Human Genetics* 26 149, 149–56; Gauthier Chassang, 'The Impact of the EU General Data Protection Regulation on Scientific Research' [2017] *Ecancermedicalscience* 11(709) <https://www.ncbi.nlm.nih.gov/pmc/articles/PMC5243137/> accessed 11 December 2019; Edward Dove and Jiahong Chen, 'Should Consent for Data Processing Be Privileged in Health Research? A Comparative Legal Analysis' (2019) *International Data Privacy Law ipz023* 1, 3–5; Michael Morrison, Jessica Bell, Carol George, et al., 'The European General Data Protection Regulation: Challenges and Considerations for iPSC Researchers and Biobanks' (2017) *Regenerative Medicine* 12(6) 693, 693–703.

[2] See, for example, Susan Gibbons, 'Mapping the Regulatory Space', in Jane Kaye, Susan M. C. Gibbons, Catherine Heeney, Michael Parker, and Andrew Smart (eds.), *Governing Biobanks: Understanding the Interplay between Law and Practice* (Hart 2012), 51, 53.

[3] Regulation (EU) 2016/679 of the European Parliament and of the Council of 27 April 2016 on the protection of natural persons with regard to the processing of personal data and on the free movement of such data, and repealing Directive 95/46/EC (General Data Protection Regulation) [2016] OJ, L 119/1.

biobanking.[4] Somewhat surprisingly, however, there remains little extensive analysis of the capacity of the GDPR—indeed of European data protection law generally, even prior to the GDPR—as a framework for the protection of genetic privacy in biobanking.

In light of the above, this book takes an in-depth look at the function, problems, and opportunities presented by the GDPR as a framework for the protection of genetic privacy in biobanking in Europe. In doing so, the book presents the following argument: European data protection law, under the GDPR, can and ought to be looked at to play a central role in the protection of genetic privacy in biobanking. The book argues that the substantive framework presented by the GDPR already offers an admirable baseline level of protection for genetic privacy. The book further argues that whilst numerous problems with this standard of protection are indeed identifiable, the GDPR offers the normative flexibility to accommodate solutions to these problems, as well as the procedural mechanisms to facilitate the realisation of solutions.

It might be argued that looking to the GDPR to play a role in the protection of genetic privacy in biobanking is obvious. Close inspection, however, reveals this argument is far from cut and dried. Three types of uncertainty emerge. First, whilst EU data protection law has historically had a close link with the protection of privacy, the precise nature of this link, and accordingly, the capacity of the GDPR as a framework for the protection of privacy, remain ambiguous and the subject of much academic discussion.[5] The right to data protection under Article 8 of the Charter of Fundamental Rights is a separate right to the right to respect for private and family life under Article 7 of the Charter and has been argued to have a separate function.[6] Equally, the GDPR, as second-order EU data protection law, at no point specifically mentions the protection of privacy in its stated goals—Article 1(2) states the GDPR seeks to protect: 'fundamental rights and freedoms of natural persons'.

Second, even if the function of the GDPR in relation to privacy generally were clear, uncertainty remains in relation to the degree to which the GDPR can function to protect genetic privacy. At a fundamental level, there remains uncertainty as to which genetic privacy rights, and genetic privacy rights holders, deserve protection under European law and as to the form of protection these rights deserve. Equally, issues of genetic privacy played little role in discussion leading up to the adoption of the GDPR. As a result, at no point in the GDPR is specific provision made for the protection of genetic privacy. There is no express reference, for example, to protection for genetic privacy rights to know and not know novel information produced via genetic analysis. Nor is there express reference to the protection of the genetic privacy rights of genetic

[4] See, for example, Marion Albers, 'Rechtsrahmen und Rechtsprobleme bei Biobanken' (2013) *Medizinrecht* 31(8) 483, 486.

[5] See, for a discussion: Orla Lynsky, *The Foundations of EU Data Protection Law* (Oxford University Press 2015) 89–131.

[6] Charter of Fundamental Rights of the European Union [2012] OJ C 326/391, Articles 7 and 8.

See, for example, the argumentation by De Hert et al. concerning the difference between privacy and data protection: Paul De Hert and Serge Gutwirth, 'Privacy, Data Protection and Law Enforcement. Opacity of the Individual and Transparency of Power', in E. Claes, A. Duff, and S. Gutwirth (eds.), *Privacy and the Criminal Law* (Intersentia 2006) 61, 61–104.

relatives or genetic groups.[7] There is thus little basis on which to assume the law will function optimally in relation to genetic privacy.

Third, uncertainty appears as to the degree to which the GDPR provides a suitable framework for the protection of genetic privacy in biobanking. In the first instance, there are other relevant legal frameworks in operation around Europe—some of which have a much longer pedigree in relation to the regulation of medical research than the GDPR. It remains unclear as to whether, and if so how, European data protection law under GDPR can provide a superior approach to these frameworks. In turn, the GDPR was designed as omnibus legislation—legislation applicable across many contexts in which personal data are processed. There are only a few references to the specifics of the research context in the GDPR, and not one of these refers to biobanking or genomic research. As a result, there remains doubt as to the extent to which the provisions of the GDPR can strike the right balance between protecting genetic privacy rights and promoting other legitimate interests in biobanking.[8]

In this regard, the book begins, in the next two chapters, by providing background to the subject of study. Chapter 2 provides an overview of the concept of genetic data and how this data may be used to produce socially significant information. The chapter considers, in particular, the range of types of genetic data, the range of socially relevant information which might be produced from these data, the modalities of production of socially relevant information, and the range of parties to whom this information might relate. Chapter 3 then provides an overview of the current European biobanking landscape. The chapter starts with a brief overview of the history and function of genomic research. The chapter then provides a working definition for the concepts of 'biobank' and 'biobanking' and an overview of the variety of types of activities and organisational structures constituting the modern European biobanking landscape. The chapter finally highlights a set of trends likely to define European biobanking in future.

The book then continues, in Chapter 4, by looking at how the concept of genetic privacy unpacks in the biobanking context. The chapter begins by providing a definition for the concepts of privacy and of genetic privacy. Next, the chapter maps the range of genetic privacy rights held by the research subject in biobanking as well as the range of other parties—specifically genetic relatives and genetic groups—which might also claim to have genetic privacy rights engaged by biobanking. As genetic privacy rights in biobanking do not exist in a vacuum, the chapter then moves to map the range of other legitimate interests engaged by the biobanking process—including interests tied up with the conduct and outcome of research supported by biobanking, and third-party non-research interests tied up with access to biobanking substances. Finally, the

[7] See, for example, the criticism of the protection provided by data protection law in relation to genetic privacy in: Mark Taylor, *Genetic Data and the Law: A Critical Perspective on Privacy Protection* (Cambridge University Press 2012) 101–98.

[8] See, for example, the criticism of the GDPR in this regard in: David Peloquin, Michael DiMaio, Barbara Bierer, et al., 'Disruptive and Avoidable: GDPR Challenges to Secondary Research Uses of Data' [2020] *European Journal of Human Genetics* 28 697, 697–705.

chapter provides a schematic for the way in which genetic privacy rights and other interests in biobanking relate to one another.

Next, in Chapter 5, the book sketches a baseline level of protection for genetic privacy rights in biobanking, against which legal systems—including the GDPR—might be compared. This baseline level of protection is provided via identifying principles dealing with the protection of all types of genetic privacy rights, and rights holders, in biobanking in the international framework. Two types of international principles are identified: common international principles—principles identified in a majority of all biobank-relevant international instruments; and emerging international principles—principles identifiable in a majority of biobank-specific international instruments. Finally, the chapter engages in a critique of the international framework and the set of identified principles constituting this framework. This critique aims not to undermine the legitimacy of regarding identified international principles as offering a baseline level of protection, but rather to highlight that the protection provided has flaws, and thus should not be regarded as definitive, or perfect.

Chapter 6 then considers a question which must be answered before any detailed consideration of European data protection law under the GDPR can be undertaken: is there any need to consider European data protection law as a framework for the protection of genetic privacy in biobanking at all? The chapter answers this question by engaging in a thought experiment. In this regard, the chapter begins by mapping the protection provided to genetic privacy in biobanking by the EU's, and three European states'—Estonia, Germany, and the UK—legal systems *excluding* through data protection law. The chapter then engages in a critical analysis, highlighting the significant inadequacy of the protection provided by these systems *excluding* data protection law. The chapter then finishes by showing why, generally, European data protection law under the GDPR looks a viable solution to address the problems displayed by other approaches.

On the back of the work in Chapter 6, the book subsequently moves, in the next three chapters, to offer a detailed elaboration of how European data protection law under the GDPR will apply to biobanking. Chapter 7 describes when the GDPR will apply, *rationae materiae*, to biobanking—considering, in particular, the key questions as to whether biological samples can fall within the scope of the GDPR, and which types of biobanking substances will qualify as identifiable. Chapter 8 describes how the key classification systems in the GDPR—the actor classification system and the personal data classification system—classify the biobanking process. Chapter 9 finally describes how the GDPR's substantive provisions apply to biobanking. The chapter breaks provisions down into seven groups—oversight, legitimate processing, data subject rights, data controller obligations, international transfers, sanctions, and derogations—and provides a detailed analysis of the applicability of provisions in each group in turn.

Finally, Chapter 10 shows the utility of the GDPR as a framework for the protection of genetic privacy in biobanking. In this regard, the chapter outlines twenty-three problems concerning the standard of protection offered by the GDPR. Problems are outlined in relation to: the structure of the GDPR; the range of types of genetic privacy rights protected; the range of types of genetic privacy rights holders protected; the standard of substantive protection offered—in relation to the genetic privacy rights and rights holders which are protected; the technical suitability of the GDPR's substantive provisions in relation to biobanking; the disproportionate impact of substantive provisions on other legitimate interests engaged by biobanking; the practical applicability of the GDPR's substantive provisions to biobanking; and the degree to which the GDPR harmonises protection across Europe.

The chapter also, however, considers the degree to which each problem casts doubt on the efficacy of the GDPR as a framework for the protection of genetic privacy in biobanking. In this regard, the chapter considers whether there are factors evident which are likely to mitigate the severity of the impact of each problem, as well as whether each problem is subject to resolution—either through the GDPR's internal interpretation and adaptation mechanisms or through external legislation operating in tandem with the GDPR. The analysis shows that the great majority of problems are not as severe as they initially seem and, as a result, do not call into question the efficacy of the GDPR as a framework for the protection of genetic privacy in biobanking. The analysis also shows that all problems which either require a solution, or would benefit from a solution, can be resolved via the GDPR's internal mechanisms or via external law operating in parallel with the GDPR, or both.

2

Genetic Data, Genome Understanding, and Socially Relevant Information

A. Introduction

Genetic privacy concerns rights engaged by the collection and processing of genetic data to produce socially relevant information. This chapter thus provides a background to the analysis in the rest of the book by providing an overview of the relationship between genetic data, genetic analysis of genetic data—based on scientific understanding of the structure and function of the genome—and the production of socially relevant information. In particular, the chapter provides an insight into the complexity and variations in the relationships between genetic data, genetic analysis, and socially relevant information.

The chapter begins by providing a basic typology of the range of data which might be subject to genetic analysis: genetic data (section B). The chapter then highlights the types of socially relevant information which might be extracted, via genetic analysis, from these types of data (section C). Next, the chapter discusses two significant modalities of genetic data: that genetic data may be subject to multiple analyses; and that the results of genetic analyses may not always produce accurate information (sections D and E). Finally, the chapter looks at the range of parties about whom socially significant information may be produced (section F).

B. Types of Genetic Data

Scientific understanding of genes and their relationship with human heredity, development, and phenotypes, can be used to subject certain types of data to genetic analysis to produce socially relevant information. We might call these types of data genetic data. There are a variety of different types of genetic data. Four are particularly important:

1. The genomic sequence
2. Phenotype information
3. Inheritance information
4. Ostensibly non-genetic data connected to genome expression.

Protecting Genetic Privacy in Biobanking through Data Protection Law. Dara Hallinan, Oxford University Press (2021).
DOI: 10.1093/oso/9780192896476.003.0002

The genomic sequence: this is the core form of genetic data and may exist in both computerised and biological form. Whilst the gene concept may still lack defined edges in the biological sciences, the genome remains firmly at its core. There is no doubt that the genome plays a central role in organismal heredity, development, and eventual phenotype. Thus, the sequence of the genome can always be subject to genetic analysis to produce socially relevant information.

Phenotype information: this becomes relevant when the relationship between genotypes and phenotypes is understood. The genotype plays a role in the construction of the phenotype. Therefore, data about a certain phenotype may be subject to genetic analysis to reveal information about the genotype. Usually, if the phenotype is already known, there will be no use in knowing the genotype. Certain aspects of genetic architecture, however, may play a role in multiple biological functions. Accordingly, deducing a genotype in relation to one phenotype may allow further genetic deductions which reveal other likely phenotypes or likely future phenotypes. As Visscher et al. observe: 'Multiple lines of evidence are consistent with widespread pleiotropy for complex traits … [for example] studies have reported genetic correlations between traits, implying that a number of the same [genetic] variants affect two or more traits in the same direction.'[1]

Inheritance information: this becomes relevant when genetically defined inheritance patterns are understood. If the genetic inheritance patterns of a phenotype are known, it is possible to infer information about an individual's genetic architecture from relevant information related to inheritance. For example, family health records can reveal information about an individual's propensity to contract a disease if the genetic inheritance patterns for that disease are clear. Indeed, such genetic inheritance inferences are even possible without direct knowledge of the specific genetic architecture of inheritance—if a trait displays genetic inheritance patterns, then, in certain cases, the form of these patterns can be known without knowing the specifics of the genetic architecture involved. For example, the genetic inheritance patterns of the disease alkaptonuria have been researched since 1902. It was only in 1996, however, when the specific genetic architecture was isolated—abnormalities in the gene 'HGD'.[2]

Ostensibly non-genetic data connected with genome expression: this becomes relevant when the influence of external factors on gene expression is understood. Gene expression in final phenotypes is highly dependent on external factors—such as environmental factors. Accordingly, such non-genomic information may also be subject to genetic analysis to provide information as to how an individual's genetic architecture will eventually express. For example, As McPherson et al. observe, susceptibility to breast cancer may be partially determined by genetics, but it may also be influenced by

[1] Peter Visscher, Naomi Wray, Quan Zhang, et al., '10 Years of GWAS Discovery: Biology, Function, and Translation' (2017) *American Journal of Human Genetics* 101(1) 5, 8 (hereafter Visscher, Wray, Zhang, et al., '10 Years of GWAS Discovery').

[2] J. M. Fernández-Cañón, B. Granadino, D. Beltrán-Valero de Bernabé, et al., 'The Molecular Basis of Alkaptonuria' (1996) *Nature Genetics* 14(1) 19, 19–24.

environmental factors.[3] Thus, an individual's environmental information could be analysed to shed light on the likelihood with which identified genetic architecture related to breast cancer is likely to express in terms of contracting the disease.

Against this background, it is now possible to move to consider the content of socially significant information which can be extracted via genetic analysis.

C. Types of Socially Significant Information Revealed via Genetic Analysis

The range of socially significant information which can be revealed through genetic analysis is broad. Six types of such socially relevant information are particularly important:

1. Identity information
2. Biological relationship information
3. Ethnicity and ethnic heritage information
4. Physical appearance information
5. Health information
6. Social and behavioural trait information.

Identity information: the unique characteristics of an individual's genome makes it a near-perfect biometric identifier. Genetic analysis producing identification information might be done in several ways. Two are noteworthy. First, through cross-matching of genomic data. Data extracted from a biological sample—a genetic profile—can be compared with an existing database in which an individual's genetic profile has already been stored together with identifying information. This is how genetic databases for law enforcement work. They rely on the matching of genetic profiles found at crime scenes, with profiles stored in existing databases.[4] Second, a variation of the above process relying on other forms of genetic data is also possible—even if data has supposedly been anonymised and there is no comparator sample. For example, Gymrek et al. have shown it to be possible to use genealogy information as a proxy to identify specific individuals from genomic data sets.[5]

Biological relationship information: the inherited nature of the genome means it can be used to identify familial genetic relationships. Genetic analysis producing relationship information might happen in three ways. First, the genetic relationship between any original genome, or genetic profile—a reduced section of the genome—and

[3] K. McPherson, C. M. Steel, and J. M. Dixon, 'Breast Cancer: Epidemiology, Risk Factors and Genetics' (2000) *British Medical Journal* 321(7261) 624, 624–8.

[4] Nuffield Council of Bioethics, The Forensic Use of Bioinformation: Ethical Issues (Report, 2007) 8–11 (hereafter Nuffield Council of Bioethics, 'The Forensic Use of Bioinformation').

[5] M. Gymrek, A. L. McGuire, D. Golan, et al., 'Identifying Personal Genomes by Surname Inference' (2013) *Science* 339(6117) 321, 321–4.

another genome, or genetic profile, can be determined by comparing the quantity of genetic architecture shared.[6] Such matching procedures are used, for example, by law enforcement. If a sample found at a crime scene does not show any clear matches in a police database, a familial search might be performed to find relatives in the database. Second, matching can also happen using other forms of data potentially subject to genetic analysis as a proxy for genome data. Such matching procedures can be used, for example, by individuals trying to track down relatives. In 2005, Kramer used a combination of his own genetic data and genealogy records to track down his anonymous sperm-donor father.[7] Finally, genetic analysis of genome data can be used to establish infertility problems and can be used to disprove the existence of a genetic relationship originally presumed to exist.[8]

Ethnicity and ethnic heritage information: genetic relationships between those who share ancestry can be analysed to reveal ethnicity information. Certain ethnic groups display tendencies towards possession of certain genetic architecture and certain phenotypic traits.[9] If an individual has certain architecture or displays certain phenotypes, then their ethnic origin might be inferred via genetic analysis. It should be noted, however, that ethnicity analysis is problematic.[10] Three problems present. First, as Collins observes, ethnicity is as much a social and political concept as a genetic concept.[11] Producing clearly definable objective genetic categories relating to ethnicity is thus difficult. Second, the Nuffield Council of Bioethics points out that, whilst ethnic inferences may be more or less specific, inferences will never be completely exact—largely due to the fact that global mobility has led to considerable mixing.[12] Finally, ethnic genetic inference can be socially problematic. For example, with particular reference to police databases in the UK, the Nuffield Council further observe: 'In the light of the social factors and policing practices that lead to a disproportionate number of people from black and ethnic minority groups being stopped, searched and arrested by the police, and hence having their DNA profiles recorded ... there are concerns that inferring ethnic identity from biological samples risks reinforcing racist views of propensity to criminality.'[13]

Physical appearance information: genetic analysis can reveal information about physical appearance. That aspects of physical appearance are genetically determined has been known for over a century. There is thus much data on genetic determinants of physical appearance. Traits known to have genetic determinants include eye colour,

[6] Nuffield Council of Bioethics, 'The Forensic Use of Bioinformation' (n. 4) 19–20.

[7] Rob Stein, 'Found on the Web, with DNA: A Boy's Father' *Washington Post* (Washington 13 November 2005) available at <http://www.washingtonpost.com/wp-dyn/content/article/2005/11/12/AR2005111200958.html> accessed 27 November 2019.

[8] Nuffield Council of Bioethics, 'The Forensic Use of Bioinformation' (n. 4) 20.

[9] A. L. Lowe, A. Urquhart, L. A. Foreman, et al., 'Inferring Ethnic Origin by Means of an STR Profile' (2001) *Forensic Science International* 119 17, 17–22.

[10] Nuffield Council of Bioethics, 'The Forensic Use of Bioinformation' (n. 4) 80–3.

[11] Francis Collins, 'What We Do and Don't Know about "Race", "Ethnicity", Genetics and Health at the Dawn of the Genome Era' (2004) *Nature Genetics* 36 513, 513.

[12] Nuffield Council of Bioethics, 'The Forensic Use of Bioinformation' (n. 4) 20.

[13] Nuffield Council of Bioethics, 'The Forensic Use of Bioinformation' (n. 4) 20.

hair colour, and skin colour.[14] Looking into the future, it has even been suggested that the recreation of an image of an individual's bodily and facial appearance could be accurately generated from genome analysis. There are reports of the use of such analysis in law enforcement. However, these are limited.[15] In practice, the science is not anywhere near ready for broad deployment in any sector.[16] Despite such predictions, it should be recalled: not only are the precise genetic determinants of many physical features not yet known, but it is also thought that most physical characteristics result from the interaction of genetic and environmental factors.

Health information: genetic analysis can be used to reveal significant information about an individual's health. If a health condition is known to be genetically influenced, genetic analysis of genetic data can reveal information about an individual's status in relation to that condition. For example, whether an individual suffers from Down syndrome can be confirmed either through analysing their genome or through analysing their phenotype—sufferers of Down syndrome usually have one extra chromosome, forty-seven rather than forty-six, and tend to have a distinctive facial phenotype.[17] As an individual's genome plays a role in future development, genetic analysis in relation to health is often used to extrapolate information about the likelihood of future health status. This is particularly the case in relation to the genome and in relation to hereditary information. For example, as Ford et al. observe, genetic analysis of the genome in relation to mutations in the BRCA1 gene can be used to make predictions as to the likelihood of the onset of breast cancer.[18]

Social and behavioural trait information: the field of behavioural genetics suggests genetic analysis may reveal social or behavioural traits. The field suggests a great many social and behavioural traits may be—at least partially—genetic. For example, it is suggested there are genetic determinants for aggression. Gronek et al., for example, observe aggression may, at least in part, be determined by 'genes located on chromosome Xp11.3'.[19] A sub-field of behavioural genetics is psychiatric genetics, which seeks to locate the genetic basis of psychiatric illnesses. For example, several genes related to neural pathways have been cited as related to alcohol dependence. Morozova et al., for example, cite the significance of CHRM2, CHRNA5, and COMT.[20] However, it should

[14] See, for example, on eye colour: Jonas Mengel-From, Terence Wong, Niels Morling, et al., 'Genetic Determinants of Hair and Eye Colours in the Scottish and Danish Populations' (2009) *BMJ Genetics* 10 88, 88.

[15] Andrew Pollack, 'Building a Face, and a Case, on DNA' *New York Times* (New York, 23 February 2015) <http://www.nytimes.com/2015/02/24/science/building-face-and-a-case-on-dna.html> accessed 27 November 2019.

[16] M. Kayser and P. M. Schneider, 'DNA-Based Prediction of Human Externally Visible Characteristics in Forensics: Motivations, Scientific Challenges, and Ethical Considerations' (2009) *Forensic Science International Genetics* 3(3) 154, 154–61.

[17] See: Genetics Home Reference, 'Down Syndrome' (*Genetics Home Reference*) <https://ghr.nlm.nih.gov/condition/down-syndrome#genes> accessed 27 November 2019 (hereafter Genetics Home Reference, 'Down Syndrome').

[18] D. Ford, D. F. Easton, M. Stratton, et al., 'Genetic Heterogeneity and Penetrance Analysis of the BRCA1 and BRCA2 Genes in Breast Cancer Families' (1998) *American Journal of Human Genetics* 62(3) 676, 676–89.

[19] Piotr Gronek, Dariusz Wieliński, and Joanna Gronek, 'Genetic and Non-Genetic Determinants of Aggression in Combat Sports' (2015) *Open Life Sciences* 10 7, 13.

[20] Tatiana Morozova, David Goldman, Trudy Mackay, et al., 'The Genetic Basis of Alcoholism: Multiple Phenotypes, Many Genes, Complex Networks' [2012] *Genome Biology* 13(239) <http://genomebiology.com/content/pdf/gb-2012-13-2-239.pdf> accessed 27 November 2019.

be noted that the difficulties in clearly defining behavioural, social, or psychiatric traits as subjects of genetic analysis, combined with the multiple environmental and genetic influences which need to be taken into account, have limited the number of scientifically irrefutable claims in this field.[21] In turn, claims that social, behavioural, or psychiatric characteristics are rooted in genetics can have eminently political implications. Such claims thus require a high degree of scrutiny.[22]

This section provided an overview of the types of socially significant information which might be revealed through genetic analysis of genetic data. Yet, a mere consideration of the types of information which might be extracted from a genome ignores important modalities of these types of information. Two such modalities are particularly significant.

1. Genetic data may be subject to a range of genetic analyses.
2. Genetic analysis may not produce accurate information.

D. The Range of Genetic Analyses Potentially Applicable to Genetic Data

Taylor observes that information might be regarded as 'data + interpretation'.[23] It is not the case, however, that all data can only be subject to one interpretation. This is true for genetic data and genetic analysis in relation to the production of socially relevant information. The significance of the applicability of multiple interpretations—multiple genetic analyses—is true for many types of genetic data, but is most prominently true for raw genomic data.

Multiple types of genetic analysis can be applied to any large set of genomic data. The full range of possible analyses might be referred to as the absolute analytical potential of the available data set.[24] The absolute analytical potential of any set of sequenced genomic data is a function of two factors. First, it is a function of the genomic data at hand. Whilst an individual's DNA contains their complete genome, it is not always the case that the complete genome will be available for analysis—for example, if the sequencing process aimed at extracting data from the genome was not intended to sequence the whole genome. Naturally, limitations on the genomic data available places limitations on the analyses possible, and thus limitations on the range of socially relevant information which can be extracted. Second, it is a function of the state of the art in scientific knowledge. The socially significant information which can be extracted from

[21] Antoinette Rouvroy, *Human Genes and Neoliberal Governance: A Foucauldian Critique* (Routledge-Cavendish 2008) 105–7 (hereafter Rouvroy, *Human Genes and Neoliberal Governance*).

[22] Rouvroy, *Human Genes and Neoliberal Governance* (n. 21) 105–7.

[23] Mark Taylor, *Genetic Data and the Law: A Critical Perspective on Privacy Protection* (Cambridge University Press 2012) 42 (hereafter Taylor, *Genetic Data and the Law*).

[24] Taylor, *Genetic Data and the Law* (n. 23) 43–4. Taylor refers to the concept of interpretative potential. As the idea of genetic analysis has already been introduced in this chapter, the term analytical potential is preferred.

sequenced genomic data naturally depends on what is known—in the abstract—about the significance of the data available.

Absolute analytical potential, however, may be further limited by factors specific to the context of processing. The analytical potential in context might be referred to as the contextual analytical potential. The contextual analytical potential is defined by two further factors, supplemental to those defining absolute analytical potential. The first factor is the type of entity processing the genomic data. This will define the aims of processing and the range of analyses likely to be applied. For example, the analysis of genetic data by an insurance company will likely be focused on the risk of disease contraction, whereas the use of genetic data in criminal forensics will likely aim to extract identity information relating to criminal investigations. The second factor is the capabilities and expertise available to the entity conducting the analysis. For example, analytical potential will differ depending on whether the analysing entity in question relies on trained geneticists or on genetic testing kits.

Analytical potential, however, is not static. It is liable to change as shifts occur in key determinative factors. Such shifts may occur in relation to either absolute or contextual analytical potential. In terms of absolute analytical potential, the scope of possible analyses is likely to continually expand because of advances in genetic science. Every day, more information about the function of the genome and its relationship with extra-genomic—both biological and environmental—factors comes to light. It seems highly unlikely that progression in this understanding is likely to slow or stop anytime soon. As analytical potential depends on the state of the art in genetic science, the consequence of this development is that the analytical potential of genetic data will continue to expand over time. For example, not long ago, over 98 per cent of the genome was regarded as junk DNA. Now, it is apparent that this junk DNA has several functions; for example, in genome regulation and expression.[25] As Kellis et al. observe: 'Many human genomic regions previously assumed to be nonfunctional have ... been found to be teeming with ... activity.'[26]

In terms of contextual analytical potential, the context of analysis is liable to change. Change may happen as the context itself undergoes change—for example, if a new business model requiring novel genetic analysis is introduced into a company. Equally, the analytical context itself can shift. Just because genetic data is subject to one sort of genetic analysis in one context today, does not mean it cannot be transferred and analysed in another context tomorrow.

Finally, whilst providing analyses to extract significance from a genome can be complex, this need not necessarily the case. It is true that conducting an extensive analysis of a genome is complicated and expensive. In the first instance, expensive sequencing equipment is required—although this is getting cheaper, as will be discussed in the subsequent chapters. Without this equipment, it will not be possible to turn the raw

[25] Elizabeth Pennisi, 'ENCODE Project Writes Eulogy for Junk DNA' (2012) *Science* 337(6099) 1159, 1159–61.

[26] Manolis Kellis, Barbara Wold, Michael Snyder, et al., 'Defining Functional DNA Elements in the Human Genome' (2014) *Proceedings of the National Academy of Sciences of the United States of America* 111(17) 6131, 6134.

biological data into the computerised data necessary to conduct the analysis capable of produce socially significant information. In turn, extensive analysis of raw sequenced genomic data requires an expert eye and scientific training. However, identifying the presence of certain sequences in a genome, and thereby identifying the likelihood that the individual from whom the genome comes will possess a certain phenotype, need not be so complicated. Indeed, certain limited forms of analyses can be automated.

E. The Accuracy of Information Produced via Genetic Analysis

There may be a considerable breadth of types of socially significant information which may be revealed about an individual via genetic analysis. It is not, however, always the case that this information will be accurate—in the sense of being true—about that individual.

There are indeed certain types of genetic analysis which will reveal accurate information about an individual. These cases constitute, however, the minority. Analysis of identity from genomic data, for example, tends to be accurate. If an individual's genome is sequenced, the raw sequence data revealed tends to be accurate—although sequencing errors are possible. As each individual's genome is unique, the sequenced genomic can then be said to be an accurate biometric identifier. As Faundez-Zanuy suggests: 'the highest possible accuracy is achieved through DNA identification'.[27] Equally, analysis of the genome can accurately reveal certain types of phenotypic information. Certain phenotypes are completely—or at least almost completely—genetically defined. This is the case in relation to hair colour. As Branicki et al., for example, observe: 'a model based on a subset of 13 single or compound genetic markers from 11 genes' can predict red hair at over 90 per cent, and black hair at almost 90 per cent, accuracy.[28]

Accurate claims through genetic analysis are not limited to analysis of the genome, however. For example, observation of certain genetically defined phenotypes, or possession of relevant family history, may also allow accurate claims to be made about underlying architecture. For example, as discussed above, most Down-syndrome sufferers have a distinct physical phenotype from which an accurate assumption as to the presence of an issue in chromosome 21 can be made.[29]

In most cases, the picture of genome and genome expression is, however, less clear and thus genetic analysis may not reveal accurate socially relevant information. Rather, often, analysis will only reveal limited probabilistic information. There are several

[27] Marcos Faundez-Zanuy, 'Privacy Issues on Biometric Systems' (2005) *IEEE Aerospace and Engineering Systems Magazine* February 13, 14. See also: Beau Sperry, Megan Allyse, and Richard Sharp, 'Genetic Fingerprints and National Security' [2017] *American Journal of Bioethics* 17 <https://www.tandfonline.com/doi/full/10.1080/15265161.2017.1316627> accessed 27 November 2019. Sperry et al. discuss the increasing significance of DNA as an identifier for national security.

[28] Wojciech Branicki, Fan Liu, Kate van Duijn, et al., 'Model-Based Prediction of Human Hair Color Using DNA Variants' (2011) *Human Genetics* 129 453, 453. See also: Jonathan Rees, 'Genetics of Hair and Skin Color' (2003) *Annual Review Genetics* 37 67, 68.

[29] Genetics Home Reference, 'Down Syndrome' (n. 17).

reasons genetic analysis may reveal information of limited accuracy. In the first instance, certain phenotypic traits may indeed have some genetic basis, whilst the precise genetic architecture, or the modalities of its expression, are not yet fully known or understood. In relation to such traits, science is simply not yet able to provide an analytical framework capable of producing accurate information. In turn, the accuracy of analysis will depend on the comprehensiveness of available information. For example, many traits emerge as the result of an interplay between genes and the environment. In relation to such traits, genetic analyses of the genome would only reveal part of the puzzle.

Finally, even if the role of genetics is generally well understood in relation to a trait, in individual cases, genetic analysis may still lead to inaccurate conclusions. To produce genetic science, many individuals' genetic codes may be interrogated to extrapolate a general truth about human—or some human group's—genetics. However, there is in fact no archetype human genome. Each individual genome is unique. Even the huge efforts at producing the complete sequence of the human genome relied on biological samples from limited numbers of individuals. For example, the Celera Genomics human genome sequencing effort—discussed in more detail in the next chapter—used samples from only five volunteers.[30] It is thus not the case that general models of human genetics will always apply to specific individuals. For example, a risk factor for a disease may be produced following interrogation of an individual's architecture. Yet, that individual may have a mutation elsewhere on the genome which renders the problematic architecture irrelevant. The risk factor would thus, in that individual's case, be wrong. As Visscher et al. observe in relation to complex traits: 'each individual will carry several [factors] that increase ... and several [factors] that decrease ... trait ... risk.'[31]

The probabilistic nature of much socially relevant information based on genetic analysis often takes on significance concerning claims that a certain phenotype will manifest in future. Such predictive analysis is most often used to find out an individual's propensity towards contracting medical conditions. It is true that there are illnesses whose onset can be predicted with a degree of certainty through genetic analysis—for example, Huntington's Chorea, whose cause is located solely in one known gene.[32] However, the vast majority of illnesses are either polygenic—resulting from the interplay of multiple genes—or multifactorial—resulting from both genetic and environmental factors operating together. In relation to most of these diseases, the full genetic picture is still not known. As Craig observes, for example: 'For the most part, complex diseases are caused by a combination of genetic, environmental, and lifestyle factors, most of which have not yet been identified. The vast majority of diseases fall into this category.'[33] In these cases, a genetic risk factor might be produced via genetic analysis.

[30] J. C. Venter, M. D. Adams, E. W. Myers, et al., 'The Sequence of the Human Genome' (2001) *Science* 291 1304, 1306.

[31] Visscher, Wray, Zhang, et al., '10 Years of GWAS Discovery' (n. 1) 8.

[32] Marcy MacDonald, Christine Ambrose, Mabel Duyao, et al., 'A Novel Gene Containing a Trinucleotide Repeat That Is Expanded and Unstable on Huntington's Disease Chromosomes' (1993) *Cell* 72(6) 971, 971–83.

[33] Johanna Craig, 'Complex Diseases: Research and Applications' (2008) *Nature Education* 1(1) 184, 184.

However, this risk factor may fall far short of either accurately predicting that the person will ever contract the disease, or accurately predicting how seriously the illness will strike, if it is contracted at all.

The previous sections dealt with types of data which might be subject to genetic analysis to produce socially relevant information, and provided an outline of the content and modalities of information which might be produced. This discussion did not yet, however, touch on the relational aspect of genetic data.

F. The Range of Parties Implicated by Genetic Analyses

Genetic data will—for example, in the case of the genome—tend to be originally taken from, or relate to, one specific individual. Genetic analysis can clearly be applied to this data to produce information about this source individual. Yet, an individual's genetic architecture will also be shared by other individuals. Analysis of one individual's genetic architecture may thus also reveal socially relevant information about other individuals.

First, genetic analysis of one individual's genetic data may reveal information about that individual's direct genetic relatives. Human reproduction is a process of biological copying—it would not be called *re*production otherwise—in which genetic architecture is passed down from parents to their offspring. In this regard, knowledge about how specific genes and traits are passed down from parent to offspring can be used to extrapolate socially relevant information about the genetic relatives of an original source individual. It should also be noted that such possibilities do not stop with the living. Genetic analysis might be used to produce information about already dead relatives—such as grandparents—and future progeny. For example, as the National Institutes of Health have observed in relation to Tay-Sachs disease: 'When 2 carriers of an autosomal recessive disease have children, each child has a 1 in 4 chance to have the disease.'[34]

There are traits about genetic relatives which can be accurately predicted via genetic analysis. If a parent has dark skin, for example, relatively accurate predictions can be made relating to the fact that their offspring will have dark skin as well. Nevertheless, in most cases, the accuracy of socially significant information which might be produced about genetic relatives is limited. Multiple limiting factors are evident. Accuracy will be limited by the distance of the familial relationship in question. The more distant a relative from the source individual, the more diluted similarities in genetic architecture are likely to be, and the less accurate relational information will be. Accuracy will be limited by the state of genetic science. In relation to most phenotypes, inheritance patterns tend to be only partially understood and accordingly, genetic analysis may only reveal information of limited representative precision. Accuracy will be limited by the significance of genetics in relation to environmental factors defining trait expression.

[34] Genetic and Rare Diseases Information Center 'Tay-Sachs Disease' (Genetic and Rare Disease Center) <https://rarediseases.info.nih.gov/diseases/7737/tay-sachs-disease/cases/50741> accessed 27 November 2019.

Naturally, genetic analysis of one individual's genetic data cannot take environmental factors unique to another individual into account. Finally, accuracy will be limited by available information. Predictions about offspring based only on one parent's genetic data, for example, will be less accurate than predictions based on both parents' genetic data.

Second, genetic analysis of one individual's genetic data might also reveal information about those with whom they share genetic architecture, albeit without a clear familial genetic connection. Such shared architecture might arise in two different ways. First, aspects of genetic architecture might be shared by those who share distant common genetic heritage—for example, members of ethnic groups may still share aspects of genetic architecture. Second, aspects of genetic architecture might also be shared by those without a common genetic heritage. This may happen, for example, via the presence of a shared mutation common across human populations. For example, two Huntington's Chorea sufferers may come from completely different families with little genetic connection—yet they would share Huntington's Chorea architecture.[35]

Subjecting genetic data about one individual to genetic analysis, in light of their belonging to a specific genetically defined group, may thus also be used to reveal information about others who share the architecture in question. For example, in order to research Huntington's Chorea, a researcher may only use the genomic sequence of one or a limited number, of Huntington's sufferers. Nevertheless, if the researcher were to find something out about their research subjects in relation to their Huntington's Chorea genetic architecture, this finding could be extrapolated to make genetic claims about all Huntington's Chorea sufferers.

G. Conclusion

There is a range of types of data which might be subject to genetic analysis to produce socially relevant information. These genetic data include raw genomic data as well as other types of data—such as phenotype data and inheritance data. Genetic analysis of these types of data is currently capable of producing a wide range of socially relevant information, including information concerning identity, genetic relationships, phenotype, health, and social and behavioural traits.

It is not the case, however, that each type of genetic data can be subject to only one type of genetic analysis to produce only one type of socially relevant information. Rather, each type of genetic data—particularly genomic data—can be subject to multiple types of genetic analysis. Nor is it necessarily the case that genetic analyses produce socially relevant information which is completely accurate. Rather, the degree of accuracy of information will usually depend on multiple factors.

[35] Genetic and Rare Diseases Information Center, 'Huntington Disease' (Genetic and Rare Disease Center) <https://rarediseases.info.nih.gov/diseases/6677/huntington-disease#ref_8727> accessed 27 November 2019.

Genetic analysis of genetic data can produce socially relevant information about the donor individuals from whom genetic data was collected. Owing to the inherited qualities of genetic data, however, genetic analysis can also produce information about those individuals' genetic relatives. Genetic relatives include individuals with whom donor individuals share a genetic familial bond as well as individuals with whom donors simply share aspects of genetic architecture.

3

The Context and State of the Art in European Biobanking

A. Introduction

Building on the introduction to genetic data and socially relevant information in the first chapter, this second chapter now provides an overview of the context and state of the art in European biobanks and biobanking. Specifically, the chapter seeks to provide an overview of the emergence, function, and practice of the current European biobanking landscape.

The chapter begins by looking at the emergence of biobanks and biobanking—specifically considering the Human Genome Project (HGP) (sections B–D). The chapter then provides an overview of genomic research—the activity biobanks support—and considers its social significance and prospects (sections E and F). Against this background, the chapter offers a definition for the concepts of 'biobank' and 'biobanking' (section G). This definition is then used to map the range of types of biobanks, and biobanking activity, identifiable across Europe (sections H–K). Finally, the chapter concludes with a consideration of trends which will define European biobanking in future (section L).

B. The Human Genome Project: Where It All Began

A discussion of the modern biobanking landscape cannot be had without a prior discussion of the HGP—the project which laid the basis for much of the current landscape.

In the late 1980s, discussions began in the United States as to the feasibility of mapping the human genome. These led to the HGP. The project eventually began in 1990.[1] The main burden was carried by US institutes—the National Institutes of Health and the Department of Energy eventually provided over half of the eventual sequence information. US institutes were, however, assisted by other institutes from all over the world—for example, the Sanger Institute, funded by the Wellcome Trust in the UK, and institutes from France, China, and Japan.[2]

[1] Francis Collins, Michael Morgan, and Aristides Patrinos, 'The Human Genome Project: Lessons from Large-Scale Biology' (2003) *Science* 300 286, 286 (hereafter Collins, Morgan, and Patrinos, 'The Human Genome Project').

[2] Collins, Morgan, and Patrinos, 'The Human Genome Project' (n. 1) 288.

Protecting Genetic Privacy in Biobanking through Data Protection Law. Dara Hallinan, Oxford University Press (2021). © Dara Hallinan.
DOI: 10.1093/oso/9780192896476.003.0003

Yet the project was not without competition. In the late 1990s, a private effort to sequence the genome was launched in parallel. This private effort was led by Venter and the biotechnology firm Celera Genomics.[3] They believed they could achieve the same result as the public project but that they could reach this result faster and at a fraction of the cost using an approach known as whole genome shotgun sequencing,[4] Shotgun sequencing had priorly been used to quickly sequence simple organisms' genomes but had been argued to be unsuitable for the complexity of the human genome.[5] The concern that the private effort would lead to the privatisation of results, and thus limit the benefit these could bring to medical research, sparked a push to complete the public effort.[6]

More than a decade after the first feasibility discussions began, the projects began to produce their first results. In 2001, the public project published the first draft of the complete human genome in *Nature*.[7] The project eventually finished in 2003—having lasted over thirteen years. The private effort published its results in *Science* in the same year as the public project.[8] Despite the official conclusion of both projects, analysis of their results continues until the present day and the projects remain a touchstone for modern genetics.

Despite the incredible achievements of both projects, the end results displayed limitations. Two types of limitation are significant. First, as each genome is unique, the project results do not provide archetype human genomes, but only composite genomes. The projects extracted biological material from a limited number of selected individuals—for example, the Celera Genomics effort only used material from five volunteers.[9] The results therefore do not show the range of possible, or even normal, genetic variations in humans. Second, the aim of the projects was to map the genome. The results are thus reference libraries of nucleotide sequences. These libraries alone cannot provide understanding as to the function of sequences, how they relate to each other, to the environment, or to phenotypes.[10]

The substantive results of the HGP are doubtless significant. However, the project also had other significant legacies. Two deserve specific discussion:

1. Organisational legacies
2. Methodological legacies.

[3] Collins, Morgan, and Patrinos, 'The Human Genome Project' (n. 1) 287–9.

[4] Craig Venter, Mark Adams, Granger Sutton, et al., 'Shotgun Sequencing of the Human Genome' (1998) *Science* 280(5369) 1540, 1540–2.

[5] Philip Green, 'Against a Whole-Genome Shotgun' (1997) *Genome Research* 7 410, 410–17.

[6] Maynard Olson, 'The Human Genome Project: A Player's Perspective' (2002) *Journal of Molecular Biology* 319 931, 934–5.

[7] E. S. Lander, L. M. Linton, B. Birren, et al., 'Initial Sequencing and Analysis of the Human Genome' (2001) *Nature* 409 860, 860–921.

[8] J. C. Venter, M. D. Adams, E. W. Myers, et al., 'The Sequence of the Human Genome' (2001) *Science* 291 1304, 1304–51 (hereafter Venter, Adams, Myers, et al., 'The Sequence of the Human Genome').

[9] Venter, Adams, Myers, et al., 'The Sequence of the Human Genome' (n. 8) 1306.

[10] Irun Cohen, Henri Atlan, and Sol Efroni, 'Genetics as Explanation: Limits to the Human Genome Project' [2016] *eLS* <http://onlinelibrary.wiley.com/doi/10.1002/9780470015902.a0005881.pub3/full> accessed 28 November 2019.

C. Organisational Legacies of the Human Genome Project

Several features of the organisational approach of the HGP survived beyond the project and embedded themselves into the practice of genetics research. Three deserve mention.

First, the collaborative approach of the HGP spurred further collaboration in genomic research projects. Prior to the HGP, genetic research tended to be done within single institutions or within limited consortia. The HGP was deliberately organised between a large number of institutions as an international collaborative effort. Kaye argues the international collaboration approach is now an 'increasingly common hallmark of genomic science, where large interdisciplinary consortia led by scientists are continuingly being united'.[11] She points out other large-scale projects, such as the 1000 Genomes Project and the International HapMap Project, as successors to this collaborative model.[12]

Second, the approach of the HGP spurred further collaborative approaches in sharing research data. Prior to the HGP, samples and data sets tended to be guarded by specific institutions. The philosophy of the public HGP was the opposite. The project worked from the philosophy that all data produced should be shared and open. This was based on two underlying assertions. First, the contents of the human genome should be the shared heritage of mankind and should not be monopolised. Second, as the data produced was the result of public funding it would be unfair to restrict its use to specific institutes or scientists.[13] During the HGP, these ideas were concretised in the Bermuda Agreement in 1996—extended and elaborated during the project in 1997 and 1998.[14] This held that genomic sequence information should be made public twenty-four hours after generation.

This first set of sharing policies sparked successor policies. The 2003 Fort Lauderdale Agreement extended the Bermuda principles beyond the HGP and extended open access policies to all 'community resource projects ... whose primary utility will be ... a resource for the ... scientific community'.[15] Finally, the 2008 Amsterdam, and 2009 Toronto, agreements extended concepts still further. They extended principles beyond genomic and proteomic data sets, to include all large data sets with biological relevance and enlarged the range of organisations which subscribed to data sharing principles beyond large sequencing centres.[16]

[11] Jane Kaye, 'Embedding Biobanks in a Changing Context', in Jane Kaye, Susan M. C. Gibbons, Catherine Heeney, Michael Parker, and Andrew Smart (eds.), *Governing Biobanks: Understanding the Interplay between Law and Practice* (Hart 2012) 32 (hereafter Kaye, 'Embedding Biobanks').

[12] NCBI, 'NCBI Retiring HapMap Resource' <http://hapmap.ncbi.nlm.nih.gov/> accessed 28 November 2019; IGSR, 'IGSR and the 1000 Genomes Project' <http://www.1000genomes.org/> accessed 28 November 2019.

[13] Collins, Morgan, and Patrinos, 'The Human Genome Project' (n. 1) 286–8.

[14] Human Genome Organisation, 'Summary of Principles Agreed at the First International Strategy Meeting on Human Genome Sequencing' (1996) <http://www.casimir.org.uk/storyfiles/64.0.summary_of_bermuda_principles.pdf> accessed 28 November 2019.

[15] Wellcome Trust, Sharing Data from Large-Scale Biological Research Projects: A System of Tripartite Responsibility (Report, 2003) (hereafter Wellcome Trust, 'Sharing Data').

[16] Toronto International Data Release Workshop Authors, 'Prepublication Data Sharing' (2009) *Nature* 461(7261) 168, 168–70.

Based on these policies, policies of data sharing by default have been since elaborated by several other influential organisations. For example, the Wellcome Trust—an important United Kingdom funding body—states 'The Wellcome Trust expects all of its funded researchers to maximise the availability of research data with as few restrictions as possible', and the National Institutes of Health—an important United States funding body—states 'Investigators should submit large-scale human genomic data and relevant associated data (e.g., phenotype and exposure data) to an NIH-designated data repository in a timely manner.'[17] Indeed, as Mascalzoni et al. comment: 'many funding bodies, publishers, and professional communities are encouraging—and increasingly requiring—investigators to deposit their data, including individual-level health information, in research repositories.'[18]

Finally, the HGP leaves a technological legacy. In particular, it sparked a rapid improvement in genomic sequencing technologies. Throughout the HGP, technological limitations posed obstacles to speed and efficiency in the sequencing process. Accordingly, considerable effort was put into developing technologies to circumvent these limitations. The original sequencing technology was developed by Fred Sanger in 1977.[19] This technology was eventually used as the gold standard in the HGP. However, even by the end of the project novel approaches had begun to be deployed—the Amersham and ABI capillary sequencing machines, for example.[20] Recognising sequencing speed as a key bottleneck for genetic research, attention has continued to be focused on improving the time and cost of sequencing. 'Next generation' high output low-cost sequencing technologies, such as the Illumina Genome Analyzer 2X, the Applied Biosystems SOLiD Analyser, or the Roche 454FLX are now available on the market and are supposedly up to 1,000 times more efficient than the original Sanger technology.[21] Whilst the original genome was sequenced at the cost of about $2.7 billion, this is now possible for less than $1,000.[22]

D. Methodological Legacies of the Human Genome Project

The knowledge produced by the HGP has proven a valuable reference library of genomic sequences. However, it also spurred, along with subsequent projects, the

[17] Wellcome Trust, Policy on Data Management and Sharing (Policy, 2017); National Institutes of Health, NIH Genomic Data Sharing Policy (Policy, 2014).

[18] Deborah Mascalzoni, Heidi Beate Bentzen, Isabelle Sylvie Budin-Ljøsne, et al., 'Are Requirements to Deposit Data in Research Repositories Compatible with the European Union's General Data Protection Regulation?' (2019) *Annals of Internal Medicine* 170(5) 332, 332.

[19] Piret Kukk and Bärbel Hüsing, 'Privacy, Data Protection and Policy Implications in Whole Genome Sequencing', in Rinie van Est and Dirk Stemerding (eds.), *Making Perfect Life: European Governance Challenges in 21st Century Bio-Engineering* (European Commission 2012) 51 (hereafter Kukk and Hüsing, 'Privacy, Data Protection and Policy Implications').

[20] Collins, Morgan, and Patrinos, 'The Human Genome Project' (n. 1) 286.

[21] Kukk and Hüsing, 'Privacy, Data Protection and Policy Implications' (n. 19) 51–4.

[22] See, for example, National Human Genome Research Institute, DNA Sequencing Costs: Data from the NHGRI Genome Sequencing Program (GSP) (Fact Sheet, 2016) <https://www.genome.gov/sequencingcostsdata/> accessed 29 November 2019; See also: Kukk and Hüsing, 'Privacy, Data Protection and Policy Implications' (n. 19) 56; and Illumina, HiSeq X Ten Specification Sheet (Information Sheet, 2016) <http://www.illumina.com/content/dam/illumina-marketing/documents/products/datasheets/datasheet-hiseq-x-ten.pdf> accessed 28 November 2019 (hereafter Illumina, HiSeq X Ten Specification Sheet).

realisation that human biology is much more complex than previously thought.[23] Traditional methodological approaches to the study of human genetics, known as genetic research, could not deal with this complexity. Accordingly, a new approach was developed: genomic research.

Prior to the HGP, genetic research was reductive. It approached human biology by breaking it down into its simplest functional parts. Research focused on the analysis of individual genetic components with the intention of finding out their specific function—often the effect of single genes or nucleotide strings in relation to one specific illness.[24] However, this approach presumes that specific genes are the main causal elements of disease. Yet, as Sobradillo et al. observe: 'It is becoming more and more evident that biological functions can only rarely be attributed to individual molecules. Contrarily, most biological systems, in health and in disease, arise from complex interactions [involving multiple genes, cellular components and environmental factors].'[25] Thus, to move forward with research into human genetics, multiple factors would need to be studied simultaneously.

To study multiple factors simultaneously, however, a new approach to research was needed. This approach was genomic research. Building on advances in sequencing capability and computing power, genomic research is predicated on a systemic approach. It considers much larger areas of the genome as its primary unit of analysis. The key methodology developed to support genomic research is the Genome Wide Association Survey (GWAS). GWAS functions by comparing large numbers of genomic data sets from individuals affected by a condition, with large numbers of genomic data sets of similar form from non-affected individuals and then identifying key points of difference across data sets.

The data sets involved in GWAS research may themselves vary significantly in form and size. Variation can relate both to the research subjects involved and to the types of data used.

In terms of research subjects involved: GWAS can include anything from a few hundred to multiple hundreds of thousands of research subjects. One of the largest GWAS ever conducted, for example, investigated obesity and included 339,224 research subjects.[26] In turn, the specific set of research subjects chosen to take part in a GWAS will vary depending on study design.

In terms of data used: these may include only single nucleotide polymorphisms (SNPs)—single nucleotide mutations common across populations, sequenced by special SNP array machines. The number of SNPs sequenced in a GWAS may vary from only a handful up to hundreds of thousands or even millions—Visscher et al.

[23] Kaye, 'Embedding Biobanks' (n. 11) 36–42.

[24] Patricia Sobradillo, Francisco Pozo, and Álvar Agustí, 'P4 Medicine: The Future Around the Corner' (2011) *Archivos de Bronconeumologia* 47(1) 35, 35–6 (hereafter Sobradillo, Pozo, and Agustí, 'P4 Medicine').

[25] Sobradillo, Pozo, and Agustí, 'P4 Medicine' (n. 24) 36.

[26] Adam Locke, Bratati Kahali, and Sonja Berndt, 'Genetic Studies of Body Mass Index Yield New Insights for Obesity Biology' (2015) *Nature* 518 197, 197.

observe the ability of normal array machines to quickly and cheaply sequence between 200,000 and 2,000,000 SNPs.[27] They may also include whole genome sequences—the complete genome, sequenced by genome sequencing machines. As whole genome sequencing becomes cheaper, however, this approach is becoming increasingly prevalent.[28] Depending on the focus of the study, data sets may also include health, lifestyle or biographical information, or other types of information relating to research subjects.

However, whilst systemic approaches offer a valuable alternative to reductionist approaches, they are also resource-intensive. In the first instance, in order to conduct genomic research, significant computing power—to deal with the analysis of available sequence information—must be available. In turn, and perhaps even more importantly, in order to produce statistically significant results, each GWAS relies on the availability of biological samples—and potentially associated data—from large numbers of suitable research subjects. As Asslaber et al. observe, the number of research subjects can run into the tens of thousands.[29] The more samples and data which are available, and the more these can be reused, the better for genomic research.

Genomic research is not, however, simply a novel approach to researching human genetics. It is now a key approach. This is largely driven by its perceived social utility and its potential to deliver improvement in human health.

E. The Promises of Genomic Research

There are two ways in which genomic research is perceived as key to the future of research into human genetics and for the future improvement of human health.

1. Genomics allows new research into a great number of significant diseases.
2. Genomics provides the basis for personalised healthcare.

New research: whilst the reductive nature of genetic research was suited largely only for the consideration of monogenic diseases—those caused by single specific genes—the systemic approach supported by genomic research allows the investigation of polygenic diseases—diseases with more than one contributing genetic factor—and multifactorial diseases—those diseases which may have multiple genetic and non-genetic contributing factors.[30]

[27] Peter Visscher, Naomi Wray, Quan Zhang, et al., '10 Years of GWAS Discovery: Biology, Function, and Translation' (2017) *American Journal of Human Genetics* 101(1) 5, 6 (hereafter Visscher, Wray, Zhang, et al., '10 Years of GWAS Discovery').

[28] Visscher, Wray, Zhang, et al., '10 Years of GWAS Discovery' (n. 27) 15.

[29] Martin Asslaber and Kurt Zatloukal, 'Biobanks: Transnational, European and Global Networks' (2007) *Briefings in Functional Genomics and Proteomics* 6(3) 193, 194 (hereafter Asslaber and Zatloukal, 'Biobanks: Transnational, European and Global Networks').

[30] Kaye, 'Embedding Biobanks' (n. 11) 36–8.

Although scientists estimate that there are over 10,000 monogenic diseases, these, in comparison with polygenic and multifactorial diseases, are in fact rather rare. Monogenic diseases are also rarer in incidence compared with polygenic and multifactorial diseases. In this regard, many conditions with high incidence in modern society—for example, cancer, heart disease, and diabetes—are either polygenic or multifactorial.

New approaches to medicine: current approaches to healthcare are predominantly reactive—a problem emerges with an individual and the healthcare system seeks to resolve it.[31] This approach is limited in when and how it addresses disease. In turn, the approach is resource-intensive at a time when there are growing demands on healthcare systems. Personalised medicine, or P4 medicine—personalised, predictive, preventative, and participatory medicine—offers an alternative approach.[32] This approach to healthcare envisions a healthcare system which will engage with the individual both before, during, and after illness based on the ongoing collection and analysis of genetic and health-relevant information.[33] The development and success of any move towards personalised medicine, however, will be based on knowledge about disease aetiology and risk factors. This knowledge will be produced through genomic research.[34] It is genomic research which will support the stratification of populations and the identification of key biomarkers indispensable to the personalised healthcare.[35]

Despite the research and health opportunities seemingly opened by genomics, it should be noted that its success to date, and its prospects for success moving forwards, remain disputed.

F. The Unfulfillable Promises of Genomic Research?

Visscher et al. highlight the huge resource investment in genomics to date.[36] On the one hand, certain commentators are optimists and are certain of the success—both current and future—of genomic research and the value of this investment. On the other hand, other commentators are pessimists and are far less convinced of the success of genomic research and the value of the investment.

Genomic optimists point, in particular, to the amount of data generated through GWAS and its significance for clinical practice and science. Visscher et al., in 2012,

[31] Sobradillo, Pozo, and Agustí, 'P4 Medicine' (n. 24) 35–6.

[32] Expert Group on Dealing with Ethical and Regulatory Challenges of International Biobank Research, Biobanks for Europe: A Challenge for Governance (European Commission Report, 2012) 17–18 (hereafter Expert Group, Biobanks for Europe).

[33] Sobradillo, Pozo, and Agustí, 'P4 Medicine' (n. 24) 35–6.

[34] Robert Hewitt, 'Biobanking: The Foundation of Personalized Medicine' (2011) *Current Opinion in Oncology* 23 112, 112–19.

[35] Peter Visscher, Matthew Brown, Mark McCarthy, et al., 'Five Years of GWAS Discovery' (2012) *American Journal of Human Genetics* 90(1) 7, 9 (hereafter Visscher, Brown, McCarthy, et al., 'Five Years of GWAS Discovery').

[36] Visscher, Brown, McCarthy, et al., 'Five Years of GWAS Discovery' (n. 35) 18.

provided a summary of GWAS supported developments in both these categories. In terms of data generated, they observed, for example, the identification of 2,000 statistically significant loci through GWAS—each of which offers a new lead in understanding disease.[37] In terms of clinical interventions, they observed, for example, treatments such as the Anti-IL-17 therapy for ankylosing spondylitis, whose development rested heavily on GWAS research.[38] Finally, in relation to science generally, they observe insights into human evolution made possible solely on the back of GWAS. For example: 'the discovery of genes affecting genetic recombination and their correlation with natural selection'.[39] Revisiting GWAS progress in 2017, Visscher et al. observed yet further progress has been made in each category and finally concluded: 'There is now much more acceptance of the experimental design because the empirical results have been robust and overwhelming.'[40]

The genomic sceptics, in contrast, point to the lack of clear findings and the relatively small number of clinical interventions emerging from genomic research. In terms of the lack of clear findings, they observe that—despite the number of significant loci identified—the genetic risk factor for common diseases for each locus has generally turned out to be small. In turn, the cumulative genetic risk factor for most diseases has also turned out to be smaller than expected.[41] As a consequence, they question a fundamental assumption behind genomic research and GWAS: that genetic factors play a defining role in the contraction of common diseases. In turn, they go further and observe peculiarities in the results produced through GWAS. For example, they observe that many GWAS results have not been able to be verified.[42] In terms of clinical interventions, they observe that genomic research has produced more limited results than previously expected.[43]

The previous sections provided an overview of the development of the context of modern genomic research practice and its goals. This background sets the scene for a closer look at the organised repositories of biological samples, and associated data which facilitate this research: biobanks.

G. Defining Biobanks: A Loose Definition for a Heterogeneous Class

The first step in a consideration of biobanks is to provide an overview of the concept of a biobank, and its associated concept, biobanking. What superficially seems like a

[37] Visscher, Brown, McCarthy, et al., 'Five Years of GWAS Discovery' (n. 35) 9–10.
[38] Visscher, Brown, McCarthy, et al., 'Five Years of GWAS Discovery' (n. 35) 16.
[39] Visscher, Brown, McCarthy, et al., 'Five Years of GWAS Discovery' (n. 35) 17.
[40] Visscher, Wray, Zhang, et al., '10 Years of GWAS Discovery' (n. 27) 5.
[41] Terry Manilo, Francis Collins, Nancy Cox, et al., 'Finding the Missing Heritability of Complex Diseases' (2009) *Nature* 461 747, 747–8.
[42] Visscher, Brown, McCarthy, et al., 'Five Years of GWAS Discovery' (n. 35) 8.
[43] Visscher, Brown, McCarthy, et al., 'Five Years of GWAS Discovery' (n. 35) 8.

straightforward activity, however, becomes more complex due to the heterogeneity of research collections of biological samples and associated data.

A general outline for the term biobank is easy to provide. The concept has emerged as an umbrella term to describe all collections of biological samples and associated data supporting genomic research. Particularly over the last ten years, the form and purpose of collections of biological samples and associated data for research have changed considerably.[44] As a result of this change, there has been terminological instability. Many terms have been employed to describe such collections. However, as Hewitt et al. observe, the term biobank has now emerged as universally understood common terminology to describe all such collections supporting research.[45]

Under this umbrella term, sub-terminology has also emerged. Special types of biobank may be referred to with special terms—for example, population-wide collections, such as the Estonian Biobank, or UK Biobank, may be referred to as population biobanks whilst biobanks containing only samples of specific disease tissue may be referred to as disease biobanks. Further specific terminology has been developed to refer to infrastructure related to biobanks—for example, biobanks connected through information or material exchange agreements may be referred to as biobank networks, whilst the systems cataloguing and providing search facilities for resources in these networks are referred to as virtual biobanks.

A general outline for the term biobanking is also relatively easy to provide. The term has emerged to describe the set of activities associated with biobanks, and the genomic research they support. In general, biobanking might be said to consist of four types of activity:

1. The collection and storage of biobanking substances (henceforth, the term substances will be used to describe all biological samples and data involved in biobanking).
2. The preparation of substances for use in research—including the sequencing of biological materials within or outside the biobank.
3. The distribution of substances, for use in genomic research, to external researchers.
4. In certain cases, the collection, storage, and further distribution of results of the research process.

[44] There are multiple other purposes for stores of human biological material, each with their own rationale. These include: as tools for social control and order—as in police forensic DNA banks; as repositories of material for later use—as in sperm, egg, or cord blood banks; as repositories of frozen bodies for potential future reanimation—as in cryogenic body banks. In this book, the term biobank only refers to collections of human biological samples and associated data used to support scientific and medical research. See for example, Filipe Santos, Helena Machado, and Susana Silva, 'Forensic DNA Databases in European Countries: Is Size Linked to Performance?' (2013) *Life Sciences, Society and Policy* 9(12) <http://www.lsspjournal.com/content/9/1/12> accessed 28 November 2019; National Health and Medical Research Council, Biobanks Information Paper (Information Paper, 2010) 10 (hereafter National Health and Medical Research Council, Biobanks Information Paper).

[45] Robert Hewitt and Peter Watson, 'Defining Biobank' (2013) *Biopreservation and Biobanking* 11(5) 309, 309.

From these four types of activity, five different types of substances involved in biobanking might also be identified:

1. Biological samples
2. Health, lifestyle, and biographical information[46]
3. Sequenced genomic data
4. Individual research results—results of genomic research relevant to specific individual research subjects
5. Scientific conclusions—abstract conclusions about human genetics resulting from genomic research.

Complexity emerges, however, in trying to pin down exact definitions for what constitutes a biobank and the activity of biobanking. Since the emergence of common terminology, attempts have been made to codify authoritative definitions. Unfortunately, these attempts exhibit significant differences and, as a result, no consensus has been reached. For example, the OECD, in their Guidelines for Human Biobanks 2009, give a broad definition for biobanks as: 'structured resources that can be used for the purpose of genetic research, which include: a) human biological materials and/or information generated from the analysis of the same, and b) extensive associated information'.[47] Other sources have opted for narrower definitions. For example, the Swedish Act on Biobanks 2002, in Section 2, defines biobanks as: 'biological material from one or several human beings collected and stored indefinitely or for a specified time and whose origin can be traced to the human or humans from whom it originates'.[48]

Superficially, these definitional differences appear small. They are, however, significant in delineating different objects as belonging within the biobank class. For example, additional data is specifically mentioned in the OECD Guidelines. Yet, under the Swedish Act, there is no reference to data related to the biological sample as relevant to the definition of biobank. If the Swedish definition were to be taken, all databases of extracted and related information, and all virtual biobanks, would be excluded.

Perhaps the reason there is no definitive codification of the terms biobank and biobanking is that biobanks are highly heterogeneous and the sector highly dynamic. In this regard, Heeney proposes a useful way forward. She observes that producing such a specific typology would be 'in tension with the dynamic nature of the characteristics and associations: between [genetic databases] and with the wider environment'.[49] Consequently, she observes that genetic databases have 'a variety of features and not

[46] The terms health, lifestyle, and biographical information are to be understood broadly. Lifestyle information may include, for example, how often a subject exercises, whether they smoke, how often they go to the pub etc. Biographical information, for example, may include information on occupation, family status, geographical location, ethnicity etc.

[47] OECD, Guidelines on Human Biobanks and Genetic Research Databases (Guidelines, 2009) 22.

[48] Biobanks in Medical Care Act 2002, Sect. 2.

[49] Catherine Heeney, 'Dynamic Networks of Practice', in Jane Kaye, Susan M. C. Gibbons, Catherine Heeney, Michael Parker, and Andrew Smart (eds.), *Governing Biobanks: Understanding the Interplay between Law and Practice* (Hart 2012) 94 (hereafter Heeney, 'Dynamic Networks of Practice').

only many comparable examples of the same features'.[50] She thus suggests that biobanks might be classified: 'within the concept of a 'polythetic class ... a class that is defined by the congruence of multiple characteristics no one of which is essential'.[51] Accordingly, she proposes, rather than relying on an inflexible concrete definition, that a more productive approach might be to rely on a flexible list of typical characteristics.

In this regard, the definition offered by the Australian National Health and Medical Research Council in their 2010 Biobanks Information Paper provides a good example of such a definition. The definition is built around six typical features:

1. Biobanks contain an organised collection of biological samples. These may be linked with additional information about the sample subject ...
2. Biobanks tend to be ongoing projects. The use of materials in research may continue into the future. Certain future uses may be unspecified at the time of collection ...
3. Biobanks may facilitate the use of samples by external researchers.
4. Biobanks tend to apply some form of anonymisation (or pseudonymisation) procedure ...
5. Biobanks tend not to promise direct benefit to subjects ...
6. Biobanks tend to have procedures and governance structures in place—such as consent and ethics review committees.[52]

The utility of this flexible definition has been demonstrated by its use in other significant works on biobanking. For example, a variation on this list appears in the report 'Biobanks for Europe: A Challenge for Governance'.[53]

The fact that a broad set of characteristics provides the best approach to defining the concept of a biobank necessarily indicates the significant variation in the class. Whilst it is beyond the scope of this book to outline the totality of variation, a brief look at the differences defining the European biobanking landscape is warranted. Variations might be loosely grouped into four categories:

1. Scientific approach
2. Organisational structure
3. Substance ownership and intellectual property
4. Approach to research subjects.

H. Variations in European Biobanking: Scientific Approach

European biobanks display key differences in the types of research question they seek to support and the scientific approaches they facilitate. The choices made in relation

[50] Heeney, 'Dynamic Networks of Practice' (n. 49) 95.
[51] Heeney, 'Dynamic Networks of Practice' (n. 49) 95.
[52] National Health and Medical Research Council, Biobanks Information Paper (n. 44) 7.
[53] Expert Group, Biobanks for Europe (n. 32) 13.

to these variables then have knock-on effects on other factors such as size, type of biological samples and data collected, and research subject demographic.

Biobanks are often conceptualised and developed in relation to a specific type of research question.[54] Riegman et al. identify three types of biobanks grouped according to the types of research supported.[55] First, population biobanks: biobanks which consist of vast numbers of samples from healthy research subjects in a population. These are designed to support the identification of specific biomarkers denoting population identity and, over time, to observe the development of disease in the population and support identification of specific biomarkers denoting disease susceptibility. Second, disease-oriented biobanks for epidemiology: these consist of samples collected from healthy research subjects and samples from research subjects with a certain disease. These allow comparisons to be made between the two subject sets allowing detection of disease-specific biomarkers. Third, disease-oriented general biobanks: these are collections of samples from sufferers of a disease throughout the life-cycle of disease progression and treatment. The analysis of disease samples facilitates the detection of biomarkers of disease and disease progression.

Depending in part on their conceptualisation and supporting research question, biobanks may thus differ considerably in size. Certain biobanks may house large collections. Such larger collections may be necessary to support more ambitious population or epidemiological studies. This will particularly be the case in relation to population biobanks. Such larger collections can reach into the multiple hundreds of thousands of subjects. For example, the UK Biobank has 500,000 research subjects.[56] In their 2010 work on mapping biobanking in the EU, Zika et al. observed that 22 per cent of biobanks surveyed had between 10,000 and 50,000 samples, and 13 per cent over 50,000, samples.[57] Other biobanks may house much smaller collections. Disease-specific biobanks—especially rare-disease-specific biobanks—will not always be able to, or have the resources to, collect the number of samples held by population biobanks. Zika et al. observe that, in the EU, 25 per cent of biobanks surveyed held less than 1,000 participant samples whilst 30 per cent held between 1,000 and 10,000 samples.[58]

The concept and research question will also, at least in part, define whether a biobank will collect additional research subject information. On the one hand, biobanks may seek to support research only into the genome. These biobanks will not need to collect any additional information from their research subjects. On the other hand, biobanks may seek to support broader research into, for example, epidemiology or

[54] Although several older biobanks exist which are now used as sources of substances for genomics research which were not established with a specific research approach in mind.

[55] P. H. Riegman, M. M. Morente, F. Betsou, et al., 'Biobanking for Better Healthcare' (2008) *Molecular Oncology* 2 213, 214–15 (hereafter Riegman, Morente, Betsou, et al., 'Biobanking for Better Healthcare').

[56] UK Biobank, About UK Biobank (Information Sheet, 2019) <http://www.ukbiobank.ac.uk/about-biobank-uk/> accessed 28 November 2019 (hereafter UK Biobank, About UK Biobank).

[57] Eleni Zika, Daniele Paci, Tobias Schulte in den Bäumen, et al., Biobanks in Europe: Prospects for Harmonisation and Networking (European Commission 2010) 19 (hereafter Zika, Paci, Schulte in der Bäumen, et al., Biobanks in Europe).

[58] Zika, Paci, Schulte in der Bäumen, et al., Biobanks in Europe (n. 57) 19.

gene-environment interaction. For such approaches, the collection of genomic sequence information alone will be insufficient.

If biobanks do collect additional information, the form of research question they support will play a role in defining which information this will be. Certain epidemiological biobanks may require only supplemental information relating to a research subject's health. This information may be collected directly from the individual or via medical records.[59] Broader forms of research question, however—for example, considering genome-environment interaction—may also require information relating to a research subject's lifestyle or biography.

The design of the biobank will also likely play a role in defining which kinds of biological samples will be collected. It is not the case that all biological samples have the same characteristics or can be used for the same scientific purposes. For example, certain forms of research into the genome and human reproduction can only happen using spermatozoa. In this regard, biobanking collections exist of, for example: DNA; whole blood; serum; blood spots—'Guthrie Cards'; spermatozoa; various types of tissue; and urine. Depending on which type of tissue has been collected, different storage processes will then also be needed. For example, Guthrie Cards can be stored and maintained at room temperature. Other types of sample, however, may require cooling systems: certain samples may be put in cold storage between 5°C and –20°C; others may require ultra-low storage between –70° and –80°C; others may require liquid nitrogen storage at – 190°C—a temperature at which biological activity stops and samples can be stored indefinitely.[60]

Finally, the aim of the biobank will play a role in defining the research subject demographic the biobank will recruit. Certain types of biobank are limited in the moment and location they can collect samples. For example, cord blood banks can only collect substances directly after childbirth. Equally, disease-specific biobanks rely on patients exhibiting the relevant disease before collecting a sample. Other biobanks, however—disease-oriented biobanks for epidemiology, for example—may also collect samples from healthy volunteers. These biobanks may be linked to a clinical context, but they may also have a special collection infrastructure to which prospective research subjects may donate directly.[61]

I. Variations in European Biobanking: Organisational Structure

EU biobanks also display marked differences in organisation. Organisational variation appears, in particular, concerning funding, the external researchers' permitted access, the conditions of access, and collaboration with other biobanks.

[59] Zika, Paci, Schulte in der Bäumen, et al., Biobanks in Europe (n. 57) 21.

[60] Asslaber and Zatloukal, 'Biobanks: Transnational, European and Global Networks' (n. 29) 195–6.

[61] Normally, biobanks will source their substances from the country in which they are located. However, this need not always be the case. See, for example, Shaun Falkingbridge, *The Future of Biobanks: Regulation, Ethics, Investment and the Humanization of Drug Discovery* (Business Insight 2009) 99.

To set-up and operate, different biobanking projects may rely on different sources of supporting capital. There are several funding models. Three might be highlighted. First, biobanks may be publicly funded: under this model, all funding is provided by the government. The Manchester Allergy, Respiratory & Thoracic Surgery Biobank, for example, was established by the local UK National Health Service (NHS) Foundation Trust.[62] Second, biobanks may operate a public–private model:[63] under this model, supporting funding—and subsequent rights and obligations—are divided between public and private bodies. For example, initial funding for the Estonian Biobank was partially provided by the Estonian government and partially by the company EGeen.[64] Third, biobanks may be completely privately funded: this will often be the case for biobanks established by pharmaceutical companies or charitable trusts conducting research. The Swiss pharmaceutical company, Roche, for example, operates an internal research biobank.[65]

Biobanks may then choose to implement broader or narrower access policies for external researchers. In some cases, access is restricted according to affiliation. For example, 20 per cent of respondent biobanks in Zika et al.'s survey permitted only researchers who collected samples access, whilst 10 per cent of respondents permitted only researchers from the host institute access.[66]

In other cases, access is restricted based on geography. For example, 14 per cent of respondent biobanks in Zika et al.'s survey only allow access to researchers from their country, and 17 per cent only allow EU wide access. Only 33 per cent of biobanks allowed access to researchers worldwide.[67] The above types of restrictions, however, are not exhaustive. Access may also be restricted according to the aim of research or commercial affiliations. For example, commercial researchers cannot access the 1958 Birth Cohort Resource.[68] As Goisauf et al. observe, however, collaboration between biobanks and external health industry partners is far from unusual.[69]

When reviewing applications for access, biobanks will tend to have mechanisms in place for ensuring substances are used towards scientifically and ethically sound

[62] NHS, Manchester Allergy, Respiratory and Thoracic Surgery Biobank (Information Sheet, 2019) <https://www.hra.nhs.uk/planning-and-improving-research/application-summaries/research-summaries/manchester-allergy-respiratory-thoracic-surgery-biobank/> accessed 28 November 2019.

[63] Herbert Gottweis and Georg Lauss, 'Biobank Governance: Heterogenous Modes of Ordering and Democratization' (2012) *Journal of Community Genetics* 3(2) 61, 66.

[64] Rain Eensaar, 'Estonia: Ups and Downs of a Biobank Project', in Herbert Gottweis and Alan Petersen (eds.), *Biobanks: Governance in Comparative Perspective* (Routledge 2008) 60–3 (hereafter Eensaar, 'Estonia: Ups and Downs of a Biobank Project').

[65] See: Roche, Roche Position on Human Specimen Resources (Biobanks) (Position Statement, 2017) <https://www.roche.com/dam/jcr:5aa0f3e7-fa20-4153-a8b8-38df4477712f/10_Position%20on%20Human%20Specimen%20Resources%20(Biobanks)_reviewed_4_2017.pdf> accessed 28 November 2019; Cathy Schaeffer, C-A3-04: Project Collaboration, 'The Kaiser Permanente Research Program on Genes, Environment and Health: A Resource for Genetic Epidemiology in Adult Health and Aging' (2011) *Clinical Medicine and Research* 9(3–4) 177, 177–8.

[66] Zika, Paci, Schulte in der Bäumen, et al., Biobanks in Europe (n. 57) 22.

[67] Zika, Paci, Schulte in der Bäumen, et al., Biobanks in Europe (n. 57) 22.

[68] METADAC, How to Apply (Information Sheet, 2015) <https://www.metadac.ac.uk/data-access-through-metadac/> accessed 28 November 2019.

[69] Melanie Goisauf, Gillian Martin, and Heidi Beate Bentzen, 'Data in Question: A Survey of European Biobank Professionals on Ethical, Legal and Societal Challenges of Biobank Research' (2019) *PLOS ONE* 14(9) 11 <https://journals.plos.org/plosone/article/file?id=10.1371/journal.pone.0221496&type=printable> accessed 5 June 2020.

ends.[70] If initial checks are passed and access is granted, however, biobanks display variety in relation to subsequent access conditions. There are key differences in financial conditions. The P3G project observes, for example: 'Most biobanks use a cost-recovery model, while others use a sliding scale depending on the intended use (e.g., industrial vs. academic use).'[71] There are differences in operational requirements. Some biobanks carry out sequencing and analysis on biological samples in in-house labs and only release data—the UK Biobank tends to use this approach—whilst other biobanks may rely on third-party sequencing and analysis.[72] Finally, the rights and obligations attached to access vary. These will tend to be listed in documents such as Material Transfer Agreements (MTAs). Depending on the biobank, these agreements may place a range of obligations on the recipient concerning, for example: sample care; confidentiality; restrictions on re-identification of subjects; and data security.[73]

Finally, there are broad differences evident in relation to biobanks' choices to collaborate with other biobanks. On the one hand, certain European biobanks operate completely detached from other biobanks. Zika et al. observed this to be the largest portion of biobanks in Europe at 68 per cent of respondents.[74] On the other hand, other biobanks have chosen to form relationships with comparable institutions. Zika et al. observed that 20 per cent of respondents had formed a partnership with biobanks in the same geographical location, and 12 per cent had formed partnerships with biobanks abroad.[75] In turn, such collaborative relationships differ in scale. On a large scale, for example, the Biobanking and BioMolecular Resources Research Infrastructure (BBMRI) is a '[pan-] European research infrastructure for biobanking'.[76] On a much smaller scale, for example, the Telethon network consists of only eleven Italian biobanks.[77]

J. Variations in European Biobanking: Substance Ownership and Intellectual Property

In the substances stored in biobanks, there is considerable economic value. Significant differences in European biobanks' approaches to the realisation and distribution of this value have thus emerged.

[70] Most biobanks will have Research Ethics Committees in place to decide on the ethical and scientific validity of research. Zika, Paci, and Schulte in der Bäumen, et al., Biobanks in Europe (n. 57) 22.

[71] Susan Wallace, P3G Sample and Data Access: Core Elements (Position Statement, 2008) 4.

[72] UK Biobank, Access Procedures: Application and Review Procedures for Access to the UK Biobank Resource (Policy, 2011) Article B4.5 <http://www.ukbiobank.ac.uk/wp-content/uploads/2012/09/Access-Procedures-2011.pdf> accessed 28 November 2019 (hereafter UK Biobank, *Access Procedures*).

[73] See, for example, BBMRI-ERIC, Material Transfer Policy and Agreement (Policy, 2012) <http://www.bbmri-eric.eu/wp-content/uploads/Sample-Data-and-Material-Transfer-Agreement.pdf> accessed 28 November 2019.

[74] Zika, Paci, Schulte in der Bäumen, et al., Biobanks in Europe (n. 57) 16.

[75] Zika, Paci, Schulte in der Bäumen, et al., Biobanks in Europe (n. 57) 16.

[76] BBMRI-ERIC, About Us (Information Sheet, 2019) <http://www.bbmri-eric.eu/BBMRI-ERIC/about-us/> accessed 28 November 2019.

[77] Fondazione Telethon, Telethon Network of Genetic Biobanks (Information Sheet, 2019) <http://biobanknetwork.telethon.it/> accessed 28 November 2019.

In the first instance, biobanks have taken different approaches to the question of ownership over substances collected for research. On the one hand, certain biobanks claim ownership over substances themselves. For example, the UK Biobank claim ownership over the biological samples they collect and store.[78] On the other hand, other biobanks do not claim ownership over substances at all and assert they only function as custodians.[79] Here, biobank participants may be recognised as owners of their own substances with biobanks only possessing use rights. When ownership questions have not been resolved from the outset, further claimants may appear. For example, researchers who have initially collected samples have also claimed that they, rather than the biobank or participants, own research substances.[80]

Biobanks have also taken different approaches over how profit might be generated from the use of substances. Certain European biobanks choose to operate as, or in partnership with, commercial entities which obtain exclusive rights over the development of products from research uses of substances. For example, the initial public-private funding model proposed for the Estonian Biobank would have allowed EGeen an exclusive twenty-five-year commercial licence for the use of biobank data.[81] Other European biobanks operate with indifference to external commercial use of substances. The UK Biobank, for example, is permissive of commercial researchers' access to substances and to the further commercialization of products developed through use of substances.[82]

Finally, biobanks may operate a variety of benefit-sharing approaches with research subjects or communities. Benefit sharing can be, for example, in the form of financial remuneration. In Iceland, the agreement with the private company deCode was that 6 per cent of all profit made on the back of biobank operation would be given over to the Icelandic government.[83] Equally, benefit sharing can be in the form of special access to research subjects, or communities, to products or treatments created using their substances.

K. Variations in European Biobanking: Approach to Research Subjects

At several points through the biobanking process, biobanks interact with, or must consider the rights, interests, and needs, of research subjects. There are differences in how biobanks approach these issues.

[78] UK Biobank, Access Procedures (n. 72) 10.

[79] R. Yassin, N. Lockhart, M. González del Riego, et al., 'Custodianship as an Ethical Framework for Biospecimin-Based Research' (2010) Cancer, Epidemiology, Biomarkers and Prevention 19(4) 1012, 1012–15.

[80] Jean Cadigan, '"That's a Good Question": University Researchers' Views on Ownership and Retention of Human Genetic Specimens' (2011) *Genetics in Medicine* 13 569, 569–70.

[81] Eensaar, 'Estonia: Ups and Downs of a Biobank Project' (n. 64) 62.

[82] UK Biobank, UK Biobank Ethics and Governance Framework (Policy, 2007) 18.

[83] Garðar Arnason, Icelandic Biobank: A Report for GenBenefit (Report, 2007) 6.

In terms of the way in which substances are taken into biobanks, differences exist both in relation to whether consent must be obtained, and the form of consent which must be obtained. At one extreme, there are biobanks which do not require research subject consent for the collection of substances. Most biobanks do, however, obtain consent. As Zika et al. state: 'consent for approval of biobank-based research is almost ubiquitously required'.[84] However, forms of consent vary widely. These include, for example: [85] democratic community consent—also known as presumed consent or opt-out—presumes agreement to the use of substances leaving only a right to opt-out; broad consent allows the biobank to use collected substances for a range of future genomic research; sectoral consent allows the use of substances for a specific type of genomic research—for example, cancer research; specific informed consent restricts the use of substances to a specific research project; and, dynamic consent imagines ongoing interaction with research subjects via a 'personalised, digital communication interface'.[86]

Following from differences in granting consent, differences in withdrawing consent are also evident. At one end of the spectrum, 15 per cent of biobanks responding to Zika et al.'s survey stated that withdrawal of consent was not possible at all.[87] The majority of European biobanks do, however, foresee withdrawal possibilities. They foresee, however, different possibilities. For example, the consequences of withdrawal may vary from the removal of identifying information from substances to the complete destruction of substances. For example, the UK Biobank suggests complete withdrawal should be followed by, whenever possible, destruction of the sample.[88] In contrast, the Estonian Biobank suggests withdrawal normally only implies: 'The ... deletion of the code that allows ... identification.'[89]

In terms of the feedback of research information, only certain biobanks recognise an obligation to communicate with participants. In Zika et al.'s survey, several European biobanks suggested they would feed relevant information back to research subjects. Thirty-seven per cent of biobanks indicated that they would refer results back provided the research subject had consented whilst 6 per cent stated that they would refer information back in all cases.[90] The remaining 57 per cent of respondent biobanks, however, claimed they 'would never refer any information back'.[91] Various arguments have been put forward to support this position. These will be discussed in later chapters.[92]

[84] Zika, Paci, Schulte in der Bäumen, et al., Biobanks in Europe (n. 57) 23.

[85] For an overview of types of consent, see: Dara Hallinan and Michael Friedewald, 'Open Consent, Biobanking and Data Protection Law: Can Open Consent be "Informed" under the Forthcoming Data Protection Regulation?' (2015) *Life Sciences, Society and Policy* 11(1) 4–6 <https://lsspjournal.springeropen.com/track/pdf/10.1186/s40504-014-0020-9?site=lsspjournal.springeropen.com> accessed 29 November 2019.

[86] See, for a discussion of dynamic consent: Jane Kaye, Edgar Whitley, David Lund, et al., 'Dynamic Consent: A Patient Interface for Twenty-First Century Research Networks' (2015) *European Journal of Human Genetics* 23(2) 141, 141.

[87] Zika, Paci, Schulte in der Bäumen, et al., Biobanks in Europe (n. 57) 24.

[88] UK Biobank, Withdrawal Protocol (Policy, 2012) 4 <http://www.ukbiobank.ac.uk/wp-content/uploads/2012/04/Withdrawal-protocol-030412.pdf> accessed 29 November 2019.

[89] Estonian Genome Centre, Estonian Genome Centre 2001–2011 (Report, 2011) 6 <https://www.geenivaramu.ee/sites/default/files/geenivaramu/estoniangenomecenter.pdf> 29 November 2019.

[90] Zika, Paci, Schulte in der Bäumen, et al., Biobanks in Europe (n. 57) 25.

[91] Zika, Paci, Schulte in der Bäumen, et al., Biobanks in Europe (n. 57) 25.

[92] See: Kadri Simm, 'Biobanks and Feedback', in Ruth Chadwick, Mairi Levitt, and Darren Shickle (eds.), *The Right to Know and the Right Not to Know: Genetic Privacy and Responsibility* (Cambridge University Press 2014) 55–70.

Biobanks also preserve the privacy of their research subjects through a variety of technical or organisational approaches. One key factor in security is the removal of identifying information from substances. In this regard, biobanks maintain three different kinds of links between collected substances and research subjects. First, linked—here, no effort is made to obscure the identity of the research subject at all: unsurprisingly, the number of biobanks which work with linked substances is low. Zika et al. estimate 6 per cent or less.[93]

Second, pseudonymised—here, efforts are made to obscure the identity of the research subject: most biobanks employ pseudonymisation. Zika et al. estimate that up to 76 per cent of biobanks employ this approach.[94] Biobanks may pseudonymise via a single coding procedure: substances are stripped of personal identifiers and labelled with a code. The link between the code and individual identifiers is retained by the biobank but is never given to researchers. Biobanks may also pseudonymise via a double coding procedure: the coding process is repeated so the first code is given a code, allowing two levels of separation between substances and subject.[95]

Third, completely de-linked—efforts are made to completely sever the link between substances and research subject:[96] the remainder of biobanks work with completely de-linked substances. According to Zika et al.'s survey, the number of biobanks using completely de-linked substances is low, at only 9 per cent.[97] Using this type of substance might be optimal from a security and privacy perspective, but is not an option for most biobanks for operational and scientific reasons. Completely de-linking substances, for example, precludes the possibility of associating substances with further information from research subjects.[98] This significantly limits research value. As Quinn observes: 'data that is truly anonymous may often offer little or no potential in terms of research value'.[99]

The previous sections have provided an overview of the context out of which modern European biobanking emerged, how it works and some of its common variations. I now turn briefly to consider some of the trends which will dictate where European biobanking is heading in the future.

L. Future Trends in European Biobanking

Identifying future trends in European biobanking is difficult—biobanking is a highly dynamic phenomenon and limited empirical data is available. Nevertheless, three

93 Zika, Paci, Schulte in der Bäumen, et al., Biobanks in Europe (n. 57) 26.

94 Zika, Paci, Schulte in der Bäumen, et al., Biobanks in Europe (n. 57) 18.

95 For a more complete breakdown see Bernice Elger and Arthur Caplan, 'Consent and Anonymisation in Research Involving Biobanks: Differing Terms and Norms Present Serious Barriers to an International Framework' (2006) *EMBO reports* 7(7) 661, 661–6.

96 The term completely de-linked has been preferred to anonymised to avoid confusion. The term anonymised appears with a specific meaning in data protection law and will be used in its legal context in subsequent chapters.

97 Zika, Paci, Schulte in der Bäumen, et al., Biobanks in Europe (n. 57) 26.

98 This prevents further subject engagement with substances—no possibilities for feedback or withdrawal. This also prevents research reliant on the ongoing collection of information from the donor. Daniela Budimir, Ozren Polašek, Ana Marušić, et al., 'Ethical Aspects of Human Biobanks: A Systemic Review' (2011) *Croatian Medical Journal* 52(3) 262, 268.

99 Paul Quinn, 'The Anonymisation of Research Data: A Pyric Victory for Privacy that Should Not Be Pushed Too Hard by the EU Data Protection Framework?' (2017) *European Journal of Health Law* 24 1, 15.

broad trends might tentatively be suggested. Each of these is fuelled by the need for biobanking to support increasingly numerous and ambitious genomic research projects:

1. The trend towards growth
2. The trend towards collaboration
3. The trend towards substance optimisation.

The trend towards growth: there is an expansion in both the number and size of individual biobanks. In terms of the growth of numbers of individual biobanks, there has been an explosion in numeric growth continuing since the completion of the HGP. Zika et al., for example, observed that 37 per cent of surveyed European biobanks only started activity after 2000.[100] The recognition there is growth in numbers is supported in scholarship. Arampatzis et al., for example, comment: '[biobanks have] significantly increased in number [up until 2016]'.[101] In terms of the increasing size of biobanks, most biobanks surveyed by Zika et al., for example, indicated no clear point at which they would stop collecting substances and that they had a 'high potential for growth'.[102] The recognition that there is growth in biobanks is also supported in scholarship. Polašek, for example, states: 'Despite numerous uncertainties, it seems ... likely that the biobanks of the future will become bigger in size.'[103]

The trend towards collaboration: there is a trend towards biobank networking and a harmonisation of practices. In relation to networking, there has been considerable growth in biobanking networks around Europe over the past years. [104] For example, the BBMRI network included 225 organisations—mostly biobanks—in 2011 and, now includes over 280. The expansion of the network shows no signs of slowing.[105] In terms of harmonisation, evidence for a trend may be gleaned from a consideration of the number of biobanks joining networks.[106] Networks require harmonisation of

[100] Zika, Paci, Schulte in der Bäumen, et al., Biobanks in Europe (n. 57) 19.

[101] Asterios Arampatzis, Ioanna Papagiouvanni, Doxakis Anestakis, et al., 'A Classification and Comparative Study of European Biobanks: an Analysis of Biobanking Activity and Its Contribution to Scientific Progress' [2016] *Archives of Medicine* 8(3:6) 4 <http://www.archivesofmedicine.com/medicine/a-classification-and-comparative-study-of-european-biobanks-an-analysis-of-biobanking-activity-andits-contribution-to-scientific-p.pdf> accessed 29 November 2019.

[102] Zika, Paci, and Schulte in der Bäumen, et al., Biobanks in Europe (n. 57) 18.

[103] Ozren Polašek, 'Future of Biobanks: Bigger, Longer, and More Dimensional' (2013) *Croatian Medical Journal* 54(5) 496, 498.

[104] Asslaber observes: 'in a genome scan for a genetic polymorphism associated with a certain disease, DNA of about 10,000 diseased individuals should be analysed' and that reaching the relevant critical mass of samples can be significantly expedited 'if biobanks cooperate ... so that cases from different biobanks can be combined'. Asslaber and Zatloukal, 'Biobanks: Transnational, European and Global Networks' (n. 29) 194.

[105] BBMRI-ERIC, Home Page (Home Page, 2019) <http://www.bbmri-eric.eu/> accessed 10 June 2020.

[106] Asslaber and Zatloukal observe obstacles created by differing legal and ethical requirements between jurisdictions. Asslaber and Zatloukal, 'Biobanks: transnational, European and global networks' (n. 29) 196–7. Riegman et al. further observe the significance of variation in data practices: 'For large studies, shared data needs to be comparable and have exactly the same meaning and have been collected following similar coding practices and data controls. If not, the scientific end result might get severely impaired.' To overcome these obstacles, standard operating procedures are required. Riegman, Morente, Betsou, et al., 'Biobanking for Better Healthcare' (n. 55) 217–19.

practice to function.[107] The BBMRI network, for example, has an extensive list of operational obligations network members must fulfil. Evidence may also be gleaned from a consideration of standardisation initiatives and best practice policies and documents. These have proliferated over the last decade. These are now available through international biobanking organisations—for example, the Global Alliance for Genomics and Health—and international organisations—for example, the OECD.[108]

The trend towards the optimisation of substances: there is a trend towards optimisation available substances and towards advances in sequencing technologies. In terms of the optimisation of available substances, there is an ever-increasing ability to subject available samples to novel types of analysis. For example, there are huge quantities of Formalin-Fixed, Paraffin-Embedded (FFPE) samples available across Europe. Previously, useable material extractable from these samples allowed only limited analyses to be conducted—analyses which considered the form of cells present and the presence of proteins in these cells. Asslaber et al., however, observe that, on the back of technological advances, FFPE samples can now be subject to processes which allow the recovery of DNA and even RNA fragments, allowing DNA and RNA analysis.[109] In terms of advances in sequencing technologies, turn of century sequencing technologies were slow and expensive. Now, modern sequencing technologies, based around 'single DNA molecule sequencing' promise the possibility to 'deliver whole human genome sequencing at less than $1,000 per genome'.[110] The Helicos HeliScope was the first platform available on the market. Several others are now available—for example, the Illumina HiSeq X-10.[111] Beyond these, yet more advanced technologies are in development—including technologies such as Nanopore DNA Sequencing and Tunnelling Currents DNA Sequencing.[112] These are touted to offer improvements in sequencing efficiency of orders of magnitude.[113]

M. Conclusion

Biobanks and biobanking emerged, in large part, on the back of the legacies of the Human Genome Project. In particular, the project spurred a change in the way genetic

[107] BBMRI-ERIC, The European Research Infrastructure for BioBanking and Biomolecular Resources Partner Charter (Policy, 2014) <http://www.bbmri-eric.eu/wp-content/uploads/2016/08/Partner-Charter-approved-AoM2.pdf> 29 November 2019.

[108] See, for example: Global Alliance for Genomics and Health, Framework for Responsible Sharing of Genomic and Health-Related Data (Policy, 2014); OECD, Best Practice Guidelines for Biological Resource Centres (Policy, 2007).

[109] Asslaber and Zatloukal, 'Biobanks: Transnational, European and Global Networks' (n. 29) 195.

[110] Kukk and Hüsing, 'Privacy, Data Protection and Policy Implications' (n. 19); See also:

[111] Illumina, HiSeq X Ten Specification Sheet (n. 22).

[112] See for example, Yanxiao Feng, Yuechuan Zhang, Cuifeng Ying, et al., 'Nanopore-Based Fourth-Generation DNA Sequencing Technology' *Genomics Proteomics Bioinformatics* 13(4), 4–16; and Takahito Ohshiro, Makusu Msutsui, Kazuki Matsubara, et al., 'Single-Molecule Tunnel-Current Based Identification of DNA/RNA towards Sequencing by Using Nano-MCBJ' (2012) *16th International Conference on Miniaturized Systems for Chemistry and Life Sciences* 204, 204–6.

[113] See: Thomas Niedringhaus, Denitsa Milanova, Matthew Kerby, et al., 'Landscape of Next-Generation Sequencing Technologies' (2012) *Analytical Chemistry* 83(12) 4327, 4339.

health research was conducted: the move from genetics to genomics. Genomic research holds great promise, both as it permits the holistic investigation of complex and socially prevalent diseases, but also as it is integral to the development of personalised healthcare systems. Genomic research also, however, requires the availability of large quantities of research subject samples and associated data.

Biobanks are the research infrastructure which collects, organises, and makes research subject samples and data available for genomic research. Biobanking is then the range of activities in which biobanks engage. Despite the simplicity of these descriptions, there is a huge range of different types of biobanks in Europe, engaging in a wide range of different types of activities. Variety emerges in relation to scientific approach, organisational structure, substance ownership and intellectual property, and treatment of research subjects.

Biobanking in Europe is also, however, an evolving practice. In this regard, there are several trends identifiable which will define its future development. Three are significant. First, there is a trend towards growth—both of individual biobanks and of the overall number of biobanks. Second, there is a trend towards collaboration—including increasing collaboration between biobanks and a harmonisation of biobanking practices. Finally, there is a trend towards the optimisation of substances—including the optimisation of existing substances and advances in sequencing technologies.

4

Genetic Privacy and Other Interests in Biobanking

Conflict and Confluence

A. Introduction

The previous chapter provided an overview of the context and practice of modern biobanking. The chapter did not, however, do more than briefly touch on the concept of genetic privacy and how this concept unpacks in the biobanking context. This fourth chapter thus moves to fill this gap and to describe the concept of genetic privacy and its relationship with biobanking. This description includes a mapping of the range of relevant genetic privacy rights identifiable in the biobanking context as well as—given genetic privacy rights do not exist in a vacuum—a mapping of the ways in which these rights relate to each other and to other legitimate interests engaged by biobanking.

The chapter starts by elaborating the concepts of privacy and genetic privacy (sections B–C). The chapter then proceeds to map the range of genetic privacy rights engaged by the biobanking process along two axes: the transactional axis—genetic privacy rights held by research subjects; and the relational axis—genetic privacy right held by genetic relatives and genetic groups (sections D–F). Subsequently, the chapter moves to map other types of interests engaged by biobanking—including interests related to the research process and third-party non-research interests in accessing biobank substances (sections G–H). Finally, the chapter offers a rough schematic of the relationships—including conflicts and confluences—between identified rights and interests (sections I–J).

B. Privacy: As a Condition and as a Right

To understand the concept of genetic privacy, it is first necessary to understand the concept of privacy generally. This includes understanding privacy as a condition, how this condition might be valued, and how this valuation might lead to the recognition of privacy rights.

Laurie offers a useful starting point to think about privacy. He begins by describing privacy as a condition: 'a state in which an individual is apart from others, either in a bodily or psychological sense or by reference to the inaccessibility of certain intimate

Protecting Genetic Privacy in Biobanking through Data Protection Law. Dara Hallinan, Oxford University Press (2021). © Dara Hallinan.
DOI: 10.1093/oso/9780192896476.003.0004

adjuncts to their individuality, such as personal information'.[1] In this regard, Laurie observes two different types of subject matter in relation to which such states of separation might be relevant:

1. Aspects of the body or mind: Laurie refers to privacy concerning these subjects as spatial privacy.
2. Personal information and other aspects of personality: Laurie refers to privacy concerning these subjects as information privacy.[2]

In a society, the ability to hold aspects of life in separation may be judged to have value. This may then translate into recognition of privacy rights. Margulis observes that the condition of privacy in western liberal democracies has been consistently regarded to have value in relation to twin goals. He summarises that privacy protection serves the 'ultimate aim of ... enhanc[ing] autonomy and/or minimiz[ing] vulnerability'.[3] Laurie provides clarification using the example of medical information: 'Undoubtedly patients have considerable interests in their own information, not only because it may be used by against them by others with harmful outcomes such as upset, discrimination or prejudice ... but also by virtue of the simple fact that personal information is an intimate adjunct of personality. Respect for personal information is a means to demonstrate respect for the individual.'[4] When privacy is seen to have value, the recognition of a privacy right may follow. On a general level, for example, the European commitment to the value of individuals' ability to maintain certain aspects of life in a state of privacy is visible in Article 8—the right to respect for private and family life—of the European Convention on Human Rights (ECHR).[5]

Modern societies, however, are complicated. Accordingly, privacy rights tend to be contextually variable. In the first instance, societies are comprised of many different actors, relationships, and interactions. The strength of privacy rights will thus vary depending on the aspect of life to which they relate, the type of third party to whom they relate, and the context of interaction to which they relate. For example, an individual's interaction with doctors in a clinic is different from interactions with police on a street and is different from familial interactions at home. In turn, it is not the case that a privacy right in relation to an aspect of life need necessarily always be valuable. For example, privacy rights might be recognised in relation to personal information. A national insurance number is personal information. However, there is little value in the ability to hold a national insurance number separate from tax authorities. Finally, even if a privacy right is identifiable in one context, other competing rights or interests

[1] Graeme Laurie, *Genetic Privacy: A Challenge to Medico-Legal Norms* (Cambridge University Press 2002) 6 (hereafter Laurie, *Genetic Privacy*).

[2] Laurie, *Genetic Privacy* (n. 1) 6.

[3] Stephen Margulis, 'Conceptions of Privacy: Current Status and Next Steps' (1977) *Journal of Social Issues* 33(3) 5, 10.

[4] Laurie, *Genetic Privacy* (n. 1) 64.

[5] Council of Europe Convention for the Protection of Human Rights and Fundamental Freedoms as amended by Protocols No. 11 and No. 14, ETS 005, 1950 (Protocol 11, ETS 155, 1998) (Protocol 14, CETS 194, 2010) Article 8.

may be still valued more. For example, if one person's privacy conflicts with the ability of a society to protect itself, the privacy right may be overridden.

In turn, privacy rights, even when they are contextually relevant, may be subject to negotiation and waiver. In reality, the boundary between the private and non-private must usually be porous. Otherwise social interaction would scarcely be possible. Accordingly, privacy rights also, tendentially, imply a parallel right to their negotiation and waiver.

Thus, rather than simple obstructions on access to aspects of life, privacy rights might usually be better understood, as Laurie observes, as means to facilitate 'control of transactions between persons(s) and other(s)'.[6] For example, spatial privacy in relation to the body is particularly valued. However, important medical research relies on engaging with the bodies of research subjects. Accordingly, without individuals having the ability to waive spatial privacy rights, medical research could not happen.

Naturally, the effect of such negotiation and such waivers depends on what kind of privacy right is in play. In relation to spatial privacy, a waiver might describe permission for one party to engage with an individual's body for a given purpose. The interaction is finite as, when the body is taken out of the context of interaction, no more engagement is possible. In relation to information privacy, however, negotiations can be much more complex. When information is released by an individual, this information can be copied, transferred, used for multiple purposes, and stored indefinitely without ever re-engaging with the source individual.

Negotiations of information privacy may thus involve complicated sets of permissions—who can possess which information, for which purpose, over which duration, etc. Even the right to negotiate and waive privacy rights, however, may not be absolute. In the first instance, there may be special situations in which the individual is not, *prima facie*, in the position to negotiate relevant states of separation. For example, there may be instances in which information subject to a privacy right is produced in a context beyond the individual and without their awareness. Privacy rights may certainly pertain in relation to this information whilst the individual is not in the position to negotiate its use. In turn, the right to negotiate and waive privacy rights may be subject to conditions or prohibitions. These may be put in place, for example by law, based on some overriding need to protect either the individual or some other societal interest.

In all cases, Taylor observes that legitimate privacy rights can be identified where these rights are 'grounded in ... norms'.[7] He observes that norms might be considered as 'a) typical, usual or expected patterns of behaviour or b) a required standard (which is a matter of obligation)'.[8] Thus, in a given context, when some aspect of life—body, mind, or information—can be held in a certain state of separation, and a norm can be identified which suggests that this is a valued state of separation, a legitimate privacy right might be seen to exist.

[6] Laurie, *Genetic Privacy* (n. 1) 21.
[7] Mark Taylor, *Genetic Data and the Law: A Critical Perspective on Privacy Protection* (Cambridge University Press 2012) (hereafter Taylor, *Genetic Data and the Law*) 23.
[8] Taylor, *Genetic Data and the Law* (n. 7) 25.

Far from being a separate unique concept—despite its name—genetic privacy is simply a sub-concept of privacy referring to states of separation and exclusivity arising in relation to the processing of genetic data. Genetic privacy rights, then, are simply a subset of privacy rights relating to the processing of genetic data.

C. Genetic Privacy Rights: A Subset of Privacy Rights

The discussion of genetic privacy rights emerged in the mid-1990s alongside the first proposals to engage in large-scale genome sequencing.[9] This discussion emerged based on the assertion that genetic data—in particular the genome—relates to individuals in a different way to other types of personal data and thus, that genetic data demanded specific consideration in terms of privacy rights. Broadly speaking, three arguments support the claim that genetic data deserve special consideration from a privacy rights perspective.

First, genetic data display novel characteristics in relation to source individuals, which raise novel questions as to how privacy rights concerning the restriction of states of access should be protected. A range of unique characteristics of genetic data has been proposed. In relation to these characteristics, arguments tendentially propose genetic data required a higher degree of protection in comparison to other types of data—for example, health information—and thus, as Rothstein puts it: 'genetic information should be addressed separately from other ... information'.[10]

The list of characteristics with the most weight in European law is that proposed by the Article 29 Working Party.[11] Nevertheless, other legal fora, such as the United Nations Educational, Scientific and Cultural Organization (UNESCO), and other legal scholars, have also composed lists.[12] A composite list might contain nine characteristics:

1. Genetic data is unique and distinguishes individuals from other individuals
2. Genetic data can reveal parentage and family links
3. Genetic data can be predictive
4. Genetic data may carry the potential for stigma
5. Genetic data may reveal information unknown to the source individual
6. Genetic data do not depend on the source individual's will
7. Genetic data are not modifiable
8. Genetic data can be easily obtained from raw material

[9] Ilhan Ilkilic, 'Coming to Grips with Genetic Exceptionalism: Roots and Reach of an Explanatory Model' (2009) *Medicine Studies* 1 131, 131.

[10] Mark Rothstein, 'Genetic Exceptionalism and Legislative Pragmatism' (2007) *Journal of Law, Medicine and Ethics* 2(Suppl.) 59, 59 (hereafter Rothstein, 'Genetic Exceptionalism').

[11] Article 29 Working Party, Working Document on Genetic Data (Working Document, WP 91, 2004) 4–5 (hereafter Article 29 Working Party, Working Document on Genetic Data).

[12] United Nations Educational, Scientific and Cultural Organization International Declaration on Human Genetic Data (16 October 2003) 32 C/Resolutions Article 4; Rothstein, 'Genetic Exceptionalism' (n. 10) 61.

9. Developments in genetic science mean genetic data may be analysed to reveal more information about a source individual in the future.[13]

Whether these characteristics indeed single out genetic data as different from other types of information from a privacy perspective remains the subject of debate. On the one hand, the novelty of these characteristics in relation to other types of data is disputed along with the logic of any special consideration of genetic data. As Wilkinson observes: 'these characteristics are apparent in ... other types of information ... For example, my name, date and time of birth could amount to a "unique identifier" of me. Knowledge of an HIV + status, or infertility may cause me to suffer "serious psychological harm" ' or indeed stigma.[14]

On the other hand, this thinking might be considered somewhat reductionist. It might be pointed out, as Sarata does, that: 'there is little ... personal information that shares *all* of these characteristics with genetic information, and that therefore, genetic information is unique in that way'.[15] It might also be pointed out that certain of these characteristics, whilst present in relation to other types of information, manifest quantitatively differently in relation to genetic data. For example, whilst many types of information may reveal future information about health, only the genome can reveal all future genetic determinants of an individual's health. Finally, it might be pointed out that, whilst attempts to identify specific novel characteristics in genetic data may indeed be flawed, this is not necessarily a reason not to recognise the special privacy significance of genetic data. This is a form of data which, after all, facilitates a novel approach to the interrogation of individuals—engaging with biological essence as opposed to social biography.

Second, the capacity of new information about an individual to be produced via genetic analysis of genetic data raises novel questions in relation to privacy rights relating to the return of novel information. Traditional considerations of privacy rights in information predominantly focused on states of separation between individuals and third parties, in terms of the ability of third parties to access data about individuals—for example, the ability of third parties to access an individual's health records. In this consideration, an underlying presumption is that the individual in question is already aware of the existence and content of the processed information.

Through genetic analysis, however, it is possible to produce novel significant information about an individual, about which that individual has no prior knowledge. For example, as discussed in previous chapters, genetic analysis can be used to produce predictive health information.[16] This raises novel questions about the privacy rights connected to the return of this information to the individual. In particular: when does

[13] There are other characteristics which appear more sporadically, such as the unique public perception of genetic data as observed by Rothstein: 'Genetic Exceptionalism' (n. 10) 61.

[14] Ruth Wilkinson, 'Genetic Information: Important But Not "Exceptional"' (2010) *Identity in the Information Society* 3(3) 457, 460.

[15] Amanda Sarata, Genetic exceptionalism: Genetic information and public policy (Congressional Research Service Report, 2008) 1.

[16] See chapter 2, section C.

the individual have privacy rights to know—to breach states of separation obstructing their own knowledge of information; and when do they have privacy rights right not to know—to have states of separation withholding information from them, whether by choice or otherwise, maintained?[17]

Third, the capacity of genetic analysis to reveal information about multiple parties simultaneously raises novel questions about which parties might hold privacy rights in relation to one set of genetic data. Traditional considerations of privacy rights tended to focus on an individual's ability to retain aspects of their lives in states of separation from others. In this consideration, it was only that individual who was regarded to have a relevant relationship with the aspect of life in question.

In the conduct of genetic analysis, however, it is possible to extract socially relevant information about multiple parties from one set of genetic data.[18] This raises novel questions concerning which privacy rights holders can be identified, alongside the original donor, in a set of genetic data. Two groups, in particular, have been highlighted as candidates. First, privacy concerns have been raised concerning genetic relatives. Annas, for example, in 1995, already highlighted privacy concerns related to the fact that genetic analysis allowed the generation of: 'probabilistic health information about that individual's family, especially parents, siblings, and children.'[19] Second, privacy concerns have been raised in relation to genetic groups. Gostin, for example, also writing in 1995, observed: 'to decide whether to continue to accumulate vast amounts of genomic information, it is necessary to measure the probable effects on the privacy of... groups.'[20]

Considering the novel aspects of privacy rights to be taken into account in relation to the processing of genetic data, Taylor proposes that legitimate underlying genetic privacy rights, in any given context, might be mapped along two axes: the transactional axis and the relational axis:[21]

1. The transactional axis: this axis focuses on the original donor individual. To identify the donor individual's legitimate genetic privacy rights, it is first necessary to consider the range of privacy relevant transactions in a context—all transactions involving transitions of states of separation in relation to aspects of life potentially subject to a genetic privacy claim. In relation to these transactions, reference to underlying norms can then be used to clarify which transactions are subject to genetic privacy rights.
2. The relational axis: this axis then focuses on other possible genetic privacy rights holders. To identify other genetic privacy rights holders, it is first necessary to consider which other parties might also lay claim to the privacy rights identified

[17] Bartha Maria Knoppers, Yann Joly, Jacques Simard, et al., 'The Emergence of an Ethical Duty to Disclose Genetic Research Results: International Perspectives' (2006) *European Journal of Human Genetics* 14 1170, 1170.

[18] See chapter 2, section F.

[19] George Annas, 'Genetic Prophecy and Genetic Privacy: Can We Prevent the Dream from Becoming a Nightmare?' (1995) *American Journal of Public Health* 85(9) 1196, 1197.

[20] Lawrence Gostin, 'Genetic Privacy' (1995) *Journal of Law, Medicine and Ethics* 23 320, 324.

[21] Taylor, *Genetic Data and the Law* (n. 7) 26–9.

along the transactional axis. In relation to these parties, reference to underlying norms can then be used to clarify legitimate rights holders.

Taylor's approach to mapping genetic privacy rights provides an ideal approach to mapping the range of legitimate genetic privacy rights engaged by biobanking. Naturally, there are different degrees of strictness which might be applied to the identification of legitimate privacy rights. This is particularly true in relation to the level of support—for example, legal support—needed to identify an underlying norm qualifying a privacy right. For the purposes of providing an initial overview of underlying genetic privacy rights in biobanking, however, a broad approach should be employed—recall that the recognition of the legitimacy of a privacy right need not mean this right must always be protected in law.

D. Mapping Genetic Privacy Rights Engaged by Biobanking: The Research Subject's Genetic Privacy Rights on the Transactional Axis

In the biobanking context, the research subject is the person from whom substances are collected—the donor individual. The research subject is thus the point of reference for the analysis of privacy rights along the transactional axis. Accordingly, a schematic of potentially genetic privacy relevant transactions along the transactional axis can be provided by considering when of the five types of genetic privacy relevant substances used in biobanking transition through states of access in typical biobanking activities—outlined in the previous chapter. By reference to underlying norms, a number of types of biobanking transactions—exchanges of substances and data—engaging genetic privacy rights might be identified. Broadly speaking, the genetic privacy rights related to these transactions might be clustered into five types of right:[22]

[22] A further two types of privacy are implicated in the biobanking process. Whilst related, these cannot, however, be regarded as aspects of genetic privacy.

First, bodily privacy. Intervention on the human body is necessary to remove samples. This does not qualify as genetic privacy as the intervention itself has no genetic implications. The concept of bodily privacy has played a key role in the development of bioethics and biomedical law in Europe. Annas highlights that 'modern bioethics was born at the Nuremberg Doctors' Trials'. These revolved around the horrific medical experiments which were forcibly conducted on the bodies of research subjects by Nazi doctors. George Annas, 'The Legacy of the Nuremberg Doctors' Trial to American Bioethics and Human Rights' (2009) *Journal of Law, Science and Technology* 10(1) 19, 19.

Second, privacy in detached bodily material. Following sample removal, samples are stored ready for further processing. The use of this material might be seen to engage a specific type of bodily privacy linked to the body itself, as opposed to its genetic make-up. It thus does not constitute a type of genetic privacy. Support for the legitimacy of this type of privacy right can be found in legislation in Europe. For example, the UK's Human Tissue Act, Sect. 1.

The Act was an attempt to balance 'the rights and expectations of individuals [in controlling access to their tissue] … and broader considerations such as research'. UK Parliament, Human Tissue Act 2004 Explanatory Note (Explanatory Note, 2004).

1. An information privacy right to restrict states of access in relation to the biological sample
2. An information privacy right to restrict states of access in relation to associated data—genomic and otherwise
3. An information privacy right to choose to know one's own genetic data produced during research
4. An information privacy right to choose not to know one's own genetic data produced during research
5. A spatial privacy right to not be informed of potentially harmful genetic information produced during research.

The information privacy right to the restriction of states of access in relation to the biological sample: the first stage of the biobanking process involves the collection of a biological sample. These samples may then be transferred to other parties—such as other biobanks or external researchers. Detached biological samples contain genetic data. If information can already be seen to exist in solid samples, then samples are information carriers—like USB sticks.[23] The biological sample, as an information carrier, thus transitions through states of separation moving away from a research subject. This forms the background to the information genetic privacy right to restrict such transitions.

The principled justification for the legitimacy of the right becomes clear via analogy. If biological samples are information carriers, any information privacy rights recognised in the sequenced genome might also be recognised in samples—there is no informational difference. As there are clear legitimate information privacy rights relating to restricting states of access to the sequenced genome—discussed below—the same rights might be recognised in samples.[24]

The legitimacy of the right finds recognition in law. There remains little direct legislative or jurisprudential consideration of information privacy rights in samples. Nevertheless, significant European legal fora do recognise samples as subjects of legitimate information privacy rights. The European Court of Human Rights (ECtHR), for example, in the *Marper* case, states: 'The Court notes that … cellular samples … constitute personal data.'[25] The Court then went on to discuss the significance of biological samples and the information they contain in relation to the information privacy rights of donor individuals.[26] At EU Member State level, the Estonian Human Genes Research Act 2000 specifically recognises that samples should be subjected to the same legal regime as personal data.[27]

[23] Marion Albers, 'Rechtsrahmen und Rechtsprobleme bei Biobanken' (2013) *Medizinrecht* 31(8) 483, 487 (hereafter Albers, 'Rechtsrahmen und Rechtsprobleme bei Biobanken').

[24] Lee Bygrave, 'The Body as Data? Biobank Regulation via the "Back Door" of Data Protection Law' (2010) *Law, Innovation and Technology* 2(1) 1, 1.

[25] *S. and Marper v. United Kingdom*, Apps nos 30562/04 and 30566/04, 2008, 4 December 2008 para. 68 (hereafter *S. and Marper v. United Kingdom*). The argument outlining the logic of viewing samples in terms of the data they contain will be elaborated in detail in chapter 7.

[26] *S. and Marper v. United Kingdom* (n. 25) para. 72.

[27] Human Genes Research Act 2000, Article 7(1). Unofficial English translation <https://www.riigiteataja.ee/en/eli/531102013003/consolide> accessed 4 December 2019.

The information privacy right to restrict states of access in relation to data—genomic data and associated data: following storage, biological samples will be sequenced to produce genomic data. Samples and genomic data may be stored alongside other research subject data—for example, health, lifestyle, and biographical information. This data may then be analysed as part of the biobanking research process—by researchers outside the biobank—and may be used to produce more information. In certain cases, each of these types of data may be further transferred to external third parties not involved in the research process at all—see section H, below. Each of these types of data might be regarded—as discussed in previous chapters—as genetic data.[28] Genetic data in biobanking thus may transition through several states of separation moving away from the research subject. This forms the background to an information genetic privacy right regarding restriction of such transitions.

The principled basis of this right is easy to identify. As proposed above—in section B—privacy rights in data might be argued to exist when data can be regarded as an adjunct of an individual's personality, on the one hand, or a substance which might be used to harm the person on the other. In the case of biobanking data, both justifications are relevant. As discussed previously, much socially significant information can be extracted from genetic data—in particular from the genome.[29] It is easy to see why research subjects have an interest in controlling how this data circulates—for example, information about disease propensity. It is equally easy to see how uses of this information could be harmful to subjects—for example, the use of disease propensity to exclude them from life insurance products.

The legitimacy of the right is confirmed in law. The ECtHR has repeatedly recognised individuals' information privacy rights in relation to third parties' access to information concerning them. A significant body of case law exists concerning health data—which, as will be discussed later in the book, could be argued to encompass all data processed in biobanking. For example, in the case of *L.H. v. Latvia*, the ECtHR stated: 'The Court reiterates that the protection of personal data, not least medical data, is of fundamental importance to a person's enjoyment of the right to respect for his or her private life.'[30] The right also receives specific recognition and protection in EU law. The General Data Protection Regulation (GDPR) sets out specific limitations on when biobanks, external researchers, and third parties may collect and process research subject data. One of the justifications for this is the recognition of individuals' underlying information privacy rights in relation to restricting states of access to their own data. There is also general international legal recognition of the right in relation to medical research. For example, the requirement for a research subject's informed consent to conduct research in Article 32 of the Declaration of Helsinki reflects a recognition of an information privacy right in data.[31]

[28] See chapter 2, section B.

[29] *S. and Marper v. United Kingdom* (n. 25) para. 72.

[30] *L. H. v. Latvia*, App no 52019/07, 29 April 2014, para. 56.

[31] World Medical Association, Declaration of Helsinki: Ethical Principles for Medical Research Involving Human Subjects (Policy, 1964 [updated 2013]).

The information privacy right to choose to know one's own novel genetic information produced during research: it may be the case that, during biobanking research, novel genetic data about an individual research subject may be produced—for example, genomic sequence data or even significant health status information. As discussed, it is possible that the individual is not aware of this information.[32] This provides the background to the recognition of an information privacy right to choose to know this genetic data.

The principled argument supporting the right is straightforward. Legitimate research subject privacy rights have already been recognised in relation to all types of research subject data in biobanking—including novel information produced during research. These rights include the right to negotiate states of separation in relation to this data. There is no reason these rights should not apply if the informational content of data is not known by the research subject. Nor is there reason to think that such control only applies to information flowing outwards from the research subject—as opposed to inwards towards the research subject. Accordingly, there is no reason the basic principle that a research subject should be able to exercise control over access to data produced during research does not extend to a right to choose to know data produced in the course of research.

The legitimacy of the right finds support in law. Direct recognition and protection is available in EU law. The GDPR recognises the right in Article 15. The Article grants the research subject broad access rights to all forms of data about them produced during biobank research. Recognition is also available at EU Member State level. The Estonian Human Genes Research Act, for example, in Article 11, specifically states: 'Gene donors have the right to access ... their data stored in the Gene Bank.' The right has also received international legal recognition. For example, UNESCO's Declaration on the Human Genome and Human Rights expresses, in Article 5, that: 'The right of every individual to decide ... to be informed of the results of genetic examination ... should be respected.'[33]

The information privacy right to choose not to know one's own novel genetic information produced during research: as outlined above, novel data may be produced about a research subject in the biobanking process. It is possible that the individual will not want to know this data. It is easy to see why individuals might prefer not to know their genetic data. Imagine, for example, the anguish potentially resulting from learning of certain disease predispositions. In certain instances, as discussed in the previous chapter, biobanks may even provide this information regardless of research subjects' desires. This provides the background for recognising an information privacy right to choose not to know genetic data.

32 Ruth Chadwick, Mairi Levitt, and Darren Shickle, 'The Right to Know and the Right Not to Know: The Emerging Debate', in Ruth Chadwick, Mairi Levitt, and Darren Shickle (eds.), *The Right to Know and the Right Not to Know: Genetic Privacy and Responsibility* (Cambridge University Press 2014) 13, 13–24.

33 United Nations Educational, Scientific and Cultural Organzation Universal Declaration on the Human Genome and Human Rights (11 November 1997) 29 C/Resolutions + CORR, Article 5.

The principled argument supporting the right builds on that supporting the right to choose to know. The basis of the argument supporting the right to know was that research subjects have a persistent right to negotiate states of separation in data even if this data was produced externally to them and they do not know its informational content. Logically then, research subjects may also be argued to have a right to choose not to know this data. As Andorno puts it: '"autonomy"... provides a theoretical basis for a right not to know one's genetic status'.[34]

The legitimacy of the right is recognised in law. The right has, thus far, received little direct consideration in European jurisprudence. Nevertheless, there are a growing number of Member States in which the right has received protection. For example, Article 11(1) of the Estonian Human Genes Research Act clarifies that: 'Gene donors have the right not to know their genetic data.' The right has also received explicit recognition in certain international legal instruments. For example, Article 10 of UNESCO's International Declaration on Human Genetic Data recognises: 'The right to decide... not to be informed about research results.'

The spatial privacy right to not be informed about potentially harmful genetic information produced during research: during research, genetic analysis might reveal information about susceptibility to a certain genetic illness. In some cases, there may be no cure for the condition in question, no indication of when—or if—the condition will hit and nothing the research subject can do to prepare. The communication of such information has been shown to be capable of causing significant psychological harm. For example, Almqvist et al. found that suicide rates for persons informed they had a genetic predisposition to Huntington disease were ten times above average.[35] Where subjects have not expressed desires to know or not to know such research results, their wishes cannot be followed. In turn, to put them in a position to exercise control, they would need to be informed that there was some information for them to exercise control over. Yet, as Laurie observes, this would, in some cases, be tantamount to informing them there is something to know and may come close to informing them of the harmful information itself.[36] This forms the background to recognising a spatial privacy right not to be informed of potentially harmful information.

This may seem very much like the subject of an information privacy right—it does concern, after all, information relating to disease predispositions. Laurie, however, makes the observation that: 'spatial privacy relates to the sphere of the self—a zone of privateness surrounding the individual that cannot and should not be invaded without due cause'.[37] It is really this aspect of the research subject's privacy—their psychological

[34] Roberto Andorno, 'The Right Not to Know: An Autonomy Based Approach' (2004) *Law, Ethics and Medicine* 30 435, 435.

[35] E. Almqvist, M. Bloch, R. Brinkman, et al., 'A Worldwide Assessment of the Frequency of Suicide, Suicide Attempts, or Psychiatric Hospitalisation After Predictive Testing for Huntington Disease' (1999) *American Journal of Human Genetics* 64(5) 1293, 1298.

[36] Graeme Laurie, 'Privacy and the Right not to Know: A Plea for Conceptual Clarity', in Ruth Chadwick, Mairi Levitt, and Darren Shickle (eds.), *The Right to Know and the Right Not to Know: Genetic Privacy and Responsibility* (Cambridge University Press 2014) 38, 40–1.

[37] Laurie, *Genetic Privacy* (n. 1) 64.

sanctity—in question in this case. In this regard, a principled argument can be put forward for the legitimacy of the right. If information can be identified as harmful, then its communication may violate a subject's zone of self and ought therefore not to happen.

The legitimacy of the right might be justified by reference to law. The right has, thus far, received only limited recognition in law in Europe. Nevertheless, recognition is evident in key legal instruments. For example, Article 10(3) of the Council of Europe's (CoE) Convention on Human Rights and Biomedicine states: 'In exceptional cases, restrictions may be placed by law on ... [feedback] in the interests of the patient.'[38]

The discussion in this section identified five different types of genetic privacy right along the transactional axis in relation to the research subject. This provides a basis to move to consider which genetic privacy rights might be identified along the relational axis.

E. Mapping Genetic Privacy Rights Engaged by Biobanking: Genetic Relatives' and Genetic Groups' Genetic Privacy Rights on the Relational Axis

On the relational axis, two further parties—alongside the research subject—might be argued to have a legitimate claim to the genetic privacy rights outlined in the previous section:

1. Genetic relatives
2. Genetic groups.

Genetic relatives: genetic data is potentially revelatory about both a research subject and their genetic relatives.[39] About whom information is eventually produced or used is a result of the analysis applied to genetic data and the context of use. Accordingly, whenever a research subject's substances are retained in, or transition through, a state of separation, genetic data about their genetic relatives might also be said to be retained in, or transition through, the same state of separation. This forms the background for recognising genetic relatives' genetic privacy rights in biobanking.

The principled argument supporting genetic relatives' rights claims is straightforward. If the genetic data of the original research subject contains information about these genetic relatives, then this data is both an adjunct of personality of these genetic relatives and can be used to harm these relatives. The basic justification behind recognising each research subject's genetic privacy rights thus also sits logically behind recognising genetic relatives' privacy rights.

[38] Council of Europe Convention for the Protection of Human Rights and Dignity of the with regard to the Application of Biology and Medicine: Convention on Human Rights and Biomedicine (opened for signatures 4 April 1997, entered into force 1 December 1999) ETS No. 164 Article 10(3).

[39] See chapter 2, section F.

The legitimacy of genetic relatives' rights finds support in law. There remains little direct consideration of the issue. Nevertheless, there are instances in which rights have been recognised. In EU data protection law, tentative jurisprudential recognition has been offered. The Article 29 Working Party, for example, observe: 'To the extent that genetic data has a family dimension, it can be argued that it is "shared" information.'[40] Certain European states have gone one step further and have directly recognised relatives' rights. For example, in the case of *Ragnhildur Guðmundsdóttir v. The State of Iceland,* a woman was found to have a right to decide whether her dead parent's information became part of the Icelandic Health Sector Database.[41] Equally, Article 6(9) of Portugal's law on genetic information provides that individuals have the right to know if medical files contain genetic information relating to them or their families.[42]

Genetic groups: two forms of data related to genetic groups might be argued to be processed in biobanking. First, the content of research subject genetic data is revelatory about each person with whom the research subject shares relevant genetic architecture.[43] Taken together, these individuals might be regarded to form genetic groups. Thus, one might state that each individual's genetic data is about each of the genetic groups of individuals which share their genetic architecture. In relation to the genetic data collected in biobanking, many genetic groups might be identified. The genetic family is the most obvious genetic group. The genetic family is then nested within several broader sets of genetic groups with shared genetic inheritance.[44] Other genetic groups can be observed which are not formed via shared genetic ancestry at all. For example, specific genetic mutations independent from heritage might be visible across individuals. Second, much of the work in biobanking is based on the production of scientific conclusions about specific human genetic subgroups. Both of these types of data on genetic groups may be maintained in, or transition through, states of separation in biobanking. This forms the background for recognising genetic groups' rights.

At a general level, arguments might be put forward supporting genetic groups privacy rights in biobanking which mirror those supporting research subject's genetic privacy rights.[45] Genetic data, and scientific conclusions, may be argued to be adjuncts of personality of genetic groups and/or as being capable of harming these groups. In terms of the personality and autonomy of genetic groups, Juengst observes: 'even those who envision human groups as simply free associations of atomistic contractors recognize the moral authority of ... groups to make collective decisions about the ... interests of

[40] Article 29 Working Party, Working Document on Genetic Data (n. 11) 8.

[41] *Ragnhildur Guðmundsdóttir v. The State of Iceland* [2003] No. 151/2003.

[42] Law no. 12/2005 of 26 January: Personal Genetic Information and Health Information 2005, Article 6(9). Unofficial English translation <https://www.eshg.org/fileadmin/www.eshg.org/documents/Europe/LegalWS/Portugal_Law-UnofficialEnglishTranslation.pdf> accessed 4 December 2019.

[43] See chapter 2, section F.

[44] A. L. Lowe, A. Urquhart, L. A. Foreman, et al., 'Inferring Ethnic Origin by Means of an STR Profile' (2001) *Forensic Science International* 119 17, 17–22. Even at the level of the human race we might not stop. Humans belong to yet broader species groups—mammals for example.

[45] The discussion of genetic groups in this chapter relies on reworked argumentation from: Dara Hallinan and Paul De Hert, 'Genetic Classes and Genetic Categories: Protecting Genetic Groups Through Data Protection Law', in Linnet Taylor, Luciano Floridi, and Bart van der Sloot (eds.), *Group Privacy* (Springer 2017) 175, 175–96.

their members'.[46] In terms of the idea that harms might come to genetic groups through genetic data, Juengst further observes: 'For some studies ... there are risks analogous to those that individuals ... face ... For example, finding that some particular group carries a relatively greater genetic propensity for alcoholism may [result in] stigmatization of members of that group [and] could ... be used ... to deny them social goods.'[47]

If the proposition of groups' genetic privacy rights holders seems strange, consider that acts of grouping and judging individuals according to perceived biological characteristics has an abhorrent history. The most prominent example is the horrific treatment of those regarded as of inferior biology by the Nazi regime in Germany. However, eugenics programmes existed prior to the Nazi regime and have existed since. Cases touching on eugenics have even recently appeared in front of European courts—such as the ECtHR in *V.C. v. Slovakia* in 2011.[48] Considering the past, should it be surprising that norms of behaviour towards genetic groups exist? If not, then why not norms which can be described in terms of genetic privacy?

The legitimacy of genetic groups' privacy rights claims finds support in law. Groups may constitute rights holders in European law. Article 34 of the ECHR refers to the possibility for the ECtHR to hear complaints from groups. In turn, several fundamental rights—such as Article 9, freedom of religion—would scarcely function without the ability for groups to be recognised as rights holders.[49] There has been, to date, little consideration of whether genetic groups should be regarded as privacy rights holders in Europe. There is, however, a small, but growing, body of legal and jurisprudential recognition they can. At EU level, for example, the Article 29 Working Party, considering the applicability of data protection law to genetic data, state: 'a legally relevant social group can be said to have come into existence—namely, the biological group'.[50] At international level, similar recognition is evident. Article 10 of the UNESCO Universal Declaration on the Human Genome and Human Rights, for example, states: 'No research or research applications concerning the human genome ... should prevail over respect for the human rights ... of groups of people.' The issue has also started to be raised in national legal fora—albeit not yet in Europe. In the *Havasupai* case in the United States, for example, the Havasupai Indian Tribe argued that the group possessed dignitary interests which could be impacted through unconsented uses of members of the group's genetic information.[51]

[46] Eric Juengst, 'Groups as Gatekeepers to Genomic Research: Conceptually Confusing, Morally Hazardous and Practically Useless' (1998) *Kennedy Institute of Ethics Journal* 8 183,185 (hereafter Juengst, 'Groups as Gatekeepers').

[47] Juengst, 'Groups as Gatekeepers' (n. 46) 186.

[48] *V.C. v. Slovakia*, App no 18968/07, 8 November 2011. The case charts a long history of practice.

[49] Several areas of law are completely based around protecting rights held by groups. Examples include international law and the rights of sovereign states and indigenous peoples law. See, for example, International Convention of American States Montevideo Convention on Rights and Duties of States (opened for signature 26 December 1933, entered into force 26 December 1934); United Nations Declaration on the Rights of Indigenous Peoples (adopted 13 September 2007) 61/295.

[50] Article 29 Working Party, Working Document on Genetic Data (n. 11) 9.

[51] Kristof Van Assche, Serge Gutwirth, and Sigrid Sterckx, 'Protecting Dignitary Interests of Biobank Research Participants: Lessons from Havasupai Tribe v. Arizona Board of Regents' (2013) *Law, Innovation and Technology* 5(1) 54, 62.

The above provided a general outline of the justification behind genetic groups having genetic privacy rights. Close consideration shows, however, that the situation is a little more complicated. In fact, from the perspective of privacy rights, not all genetic groups are the same.

F. Genetic Classes and Genetic Categories: Two Different Kinds of Genetic Groups

When perceived through a socio-legal frame, two types of genetic group are identifiable. The differences between these groups are significant both regarding the underlying justification of their privacy rights as well as regarding the specific privacy rights with which they may be attributed. These two groups will be referred to as:

1. Genetic classes
2. Genetic categories.

Genetic classes: these are genetic groups which map to objectively recognisable social groups and have an independent social existence—for example, disease-sufferer groups.[52] These groups will share characteristics with other types of objectively recognisable social group. Members of such classes are likely to be aware of their status as a member of the class. They will be aware of what being a member of the class means to them, and to their lives, and may have desires and goals resulting from class membership. In turn, they are likely to know other members of the class—or at least be able to get in contact with them. Through the communication of class members, a group identity may be established, as may the elaboration of common positions on matters of importance to the class. Such classes may even have found it useful to organise themselves and to establish communal decision-making structures and channels for external communication. Indeed, many such classes have found it useful to seek formal recognition in law—for example, in the case of representative organisations for recognisable ethnic minorities.

The independent social existence of these groups is significant to the justification of their claims to genetic privacy rights: justifications can closely mirror those of research subjects. An individual's identity is tightly tied up with the social groups they are part of. Accordingly, the autonomous existence of such groups is essential for the individual to be able to freely develop his or her personality in association with others. In turn, such groups play important social and political roles—indeed, they are essential for the pluralism at the core of a democratic society.[53] As Raab observes, such genetic classes might be regarded as 'autonomous units' within societies, with unique histories,

[52] For example, Downs syndrome sufferers. Down's Syndrome Association, 'Home Page' (*Down's Syndrome Association* 2019) <http://www.downs-syndrome.org.uk/> accessed 4 December 2019.

[53] See the discussion of groups and pluralism in; *Leyla Şahin v. Turkey*, App no. 44774/98, 10 November 2005, para. 100.

identities, cultures, and intentions extending beyond their temporary membership.[54] Thus they might be recognised to have desires concerning, and be subject to harm via, the processing of genetic data relating to them.

Accordingly, genetic classes might be argued to have a similar set of legitimate genetic privacy rights in biobanking to research subjects.[55] For example, certain genetic classes may have specific origin stories. As McGregor observes, information disproving origin stories may emerge during genetic analysis.[56] This information may cause irreparable harm to the collective identity of the class. The class may thus claim to have a right to restrict external access to their genetic data and have rights connected with choosing to know, or not to know, the results of such an analysis, if it were to take place.

Genetic categories: these are genetic groups which are not objectively recognisable and have no independent social existence—for example, individuals who share architecture associated with disease predisposition with no visible traces. Members of genetic categories may have no idea they possess the architecture placing them in a genetic category. Category members will thus unlikely be aware of other category members. In turn, category members may not have felt any impacts from their possession of the architecture in question and may therefore have no sense of the consequence of their membership of the category. Without the ability to understand one's own category membership and the significance of this membership, and without the ability to share experience with others, a genetic category will lack collective personality, opinion, and decision-making structures.

The justification that such groups can have genetic privacy rights thus cannot follow that used for individuals or genetic classes: if individuals do not know they are members of a category, the key building block in establishing group personality and autonomy—communication between members—is not present. Accordingly, genetic categories are not able to make autonomy claims in relation to privacy rights. Nevertheless, justifications may follow another approach. Each individual member of a genetic category has rights in relation to the effects of genetic data processing on him or her. When genetic data relating to a genetic category is processed, each individual member of that category is thus potentially affected. It is true that this concern could be boiled down to a set of unconnected individual rights in not being harmed based on category membership.[57] Yet, as Floridi observes, this represents a highly 'atomistic' approach, and the phenomena of processing on the level of categories of individuals might not be possible to deal with at the level of the single individual.[58]

[54] Charles Raab, 'Privacy, Social Values and the Public Interest', in Andreas Busch and Jeanette Hofmann (eds.), *Politik und die Regulierung von Information* (Nomos 2012) 129, 140–4

[55] Jason Allen, 'Group Consent and the Nature of Group Belonging: Genomics, Race and Indigenous Rights' (2010) *Journal of Law, Information and Science* 20(2) 28, 31–8.

[56] J. McGregor, 'Racial, Ethnic, and Tribal Classifications in Biomedical Research with Biological and Group Harm' (2010) *American Journal of Bioethics* 10 23, 23–4.

[57] The fear that individual rights could be adversely affected using genetic data related to groups has been reflected in sector-specific genetic non-discrimination legislation. See, for example, Council of Europe Additional Protocol to the Convention on Human Rights and Biomedicine, concerning Biomedical Research (opened for signatures 25 January 2005, entered into force 1 September 2007) CETS No. 195.

[58] Luciano Floridi, 'Open Data, Data Protection and Group Privacy' (2014) *Philosophy and Technology* 27(1) 1, 2.

In this regard, a collective privacy right at the level of the genetic category might be recognised. The members of the category, taken together, can be seen to have collective rights in how data relating to the category is processed and how that category is treated. Whilst a genetic category itself may not be in the position to exercise these privacy rights, privacy rights may still nevertheless be seen to exist and may, in turn, be given life via external bodies reading them in. In this regard, note that it is far from unusual for external bodies to read-in rights on behalf of entities which cannot communicate.[59] As Beyleveld et al. observe, for example, it is unquestionable that *incapax* have privacy rights whilst being incapable of effective communication.[60]

As a result of this justification, genetic categories cannot be argued to have the same range of underlying genetic privacy rights in biobanking as research subjects or genetic classes. The collective rights justification supports the possession of genetic privacy rights related to the restriction of states of access to data concerning them—rights relating to the prevention of activity which might lead to how the category is treated. It is harder to see, however, that genetic categories should have rights related to novel information produced during research—rights which relate predominantly to subject autonomy and self-awareness. How, for example, could a genetic category be seen to have information or spatial privacy rights in relation to knowing or not knowing its genetic data?

The above sections identified a broad range of genetic privacy rights, and rights holders, engaged in the biobanking process. However, biobanking also engages a series of other legitimate interests. As with genetic privacy rights, a broad approach is employed in the identification of these interests—simply as a legitimate interest might be seen to exist, does not mean it will, or should, always be protected in law. Broadly speaking, two types of legitimate interest can be identified:

1. Interests tied up with the conduct and outcome of biobank research
2. Third-party non-research interests in accessing biobank substances.

G. Mapping Other Interests Engaged by Biobanking: Interests Tied Up with the Conduct and Outcome of Biobank Research

The first set of interests relates to the access and use of biobanking substances in the conduct and outcome of research. Three types of interest deserve consideration:

1. Researcher interests
2. Societal interests
3. Private sector interests.

[59] In fact, many legally relevant interests exist on behalf of entities which cannot communicate, or are deemed to be insufficiently capable of communication—children, animals, the environment etc.

[60] Deryck Beyleveld and Roger Brownsword, *Consent in the Law* (Hart 2007) 114–25 (hereafter Beyleveld and Brownsword, *Consent in the Law*).

Researcher interests: researchers have interests in being allowed to conduct biobanking research as freely as possible. The basic interest of researchers is to conduct research. The interest of those involved in biobanking-based research is no different. This interest is best served by researchers being endowed with maximum access capabilities, and being as unencumbered as possible by restrictions, to biobanking substances.

The legitimacy of researcher interests has clear recognition in European law. Generally, Rouillé-Mirza and Wright have suggested that: 'medical research could be regarded as ... a right to freedom of speech for scientists'.[61] More explicit recognition is found in certain EU Member States. For example, Taupitz and Weigel observe, in Germany: 'Researchers at biobanks are guaranteed the freedom of science according to art. 5, para. 3 of the Grundgesetz, regardless of whether they are performing commercial research or research at a [non-commercial institution].'[62] The legitimacy of this interest has received specific legal recognition in the biobanking context.[63] Certain EU Member States, for example, have passed legislation recognising the rights of researchers to access biobanking substances. For example, the Estonian Human Genes Research Act, in Article 16, explicitly endows researchers with the possibility to access and use substances stored in the Estonian Biobank.

Societal interests: society has an interest in genomic research—biobanking may thus be regarded as in the public interest. The public interest in biobanking can be conceived in terms of an interest in the products of research. In the first instance, this interest may be conceived in terms of the provision of better individual and public health on the back of discoveries made through genomic research. In turn, this interest may be conceived in terms of the pure scientific value of genomic research. In both cases, the public interest is best served by optimally efficient conduct of biobanking.[64]

The legitimacy of the public interest in the conduct of research has broad recognition in European law. Recognition is generally evident at European level. The GDPR, for example, recognises research as a public interest. Recognition is also generally evident at EU Member State level. Lattanzi, for example, observes constitutional recognition in Italy. He observes that medical research contributes to the community's interest in detecting the cause of disease and accordingly, ultimately to 'the right to health as a community interest enshrined in Article 32(1) of the Constitution'.[65] He also observes

[61] Ségolène Rouillé-Mirza and Jessica Wright, 'Comparative Study on the Implementation and Effect of Directive 95/46 on Data Protection in Europe: Medical Research', in Deryck Beyleveld, David Townend, Ségolène Rouillé-Mirza, and Jessica Wright (eds.), *The Data Protection Directive and Medical Research Across Europe* (Ashgate 2004) 189, 199.

[62] Jochen Taupitz and Jukka Weigel, 'The Necessity of Broad Consent and Complementary Regulations for the Protection of Personal Data in Biobanks: What Can We Learn from the German Case' (2012) *Public Health Genomics* 15 263, 265 (hereafter Taupitz and Weigel, 'The Necessity of Broad Consent').

[63] Individual researchers' interests may, in future, take other forms. In *Washington University*, a doctor who collected samples sought to move from the organisation he was affiliated with. The doctor then claimed a proprietary interest in the samples. The myriad permutations of biobank organisation, and the dynamic evolution of the sector, means successful cases for researcher ownership cannot be excluded in future. *Washington University v. Catalona* [2007] nos. 06-2286 and 06-2301 (hereafter *Washington University*).

[64] A public interest in biobanking could also be recognised in economic terms. See, for example, OECD, Biological Resource Centres: Underpinning the Future of Life Sciences and Biotechnology (Position Statement, 932001041E1, 2011).

[65] Roberto Lattanzi, 'Processing of Personal Data and Medical/Scientific Research within the Framework of Italy's Legal System', in Deryck Beyleveld, David Townend, Ségolène Rouillé-Mirza, and Jessica Wright (eds.),

the commitment of the Italian constitution to furthering knowledge creation: 'Freedom of science (Article 33(1) of the Constitution), the duty to encourage scientific research, development and progress that is committed by the constitution to the state (as per Article 9(1) and 4(2) of the Constitution, respectively).'[66] The legitimacy of the interest has received specific legal recognition in the biobanking context. Certain EU Member States, for example, have passed biobank legislation aimed at facilitating biobanking and at supporting societal interests in the outcome of biobank-based research. The Finnish Biobank Act 2012, for example, in Article 1, outlines its core aim as: '[supporting] research that utilises human biological samples'.[67]

Private sector interests: private sector actors have an interest in accessing biobanking substances and may have proprietary interests in both research substances and the products of research. The private sector forms an integral part of the chain between basic research, end products, and health care. They thus have two forms of interest in biobanking. First, to develop novel clinical interventions, private sector actors rely on research and development. The private sector thus has an interest in the maximum availability and usability of resources to support these activities—including biobank resources. Second, when private industry engages in research activities, they invest resources, speculating on producing something profitable. For private involvement to makes sense, companies must thus be sure that results cannot be copied, and that investment will not be wasted. Accordingly, at different points in the research process the private sector may have an interest in staking proprietary claims to protect investment.

Legitimation of both types of private sector interest is evident in European law. The commercial interest in accessing and using biobanking research substances finds general legitimation as a special form of researcher, or public interest, in the conduct and outcome of research. In relation to researcher interests, recall Taupitz and Weigel's observation, for example, that, in Germany: 'Researchers ... are guaranteed the freedom of science according to art. 5, para. 3 of the Grundgesetz, regardless of whether they are performing commercial research.'[68] In relation to the public interest in research, the GDPR observes, in Recital 159, that the public interest in research extends to: 'privately funded research'.

Proprietary interests in relation to research are also generally recognised in the EU. The European Patent Convention, for example, is applicable in all EU Member States—and even beyond—and allows patents to be granted in relation to inventions and innovations.[69] Indeed, proprietary interests have received specific recognition in several ways relevant to biobanking. They have been recognised in biological samples

Implementation of the Data Protection Directive in Relation to Medical Research in Europe (Ashgate 2004) 193, 196 (hereafter Lattanzi, 'Processing of Personal Data and Medical/Scientific Research').

[66] Lattanzi, 'Processing of Personal Data and Medical/Scientific Research' (n. 65) 196.

[67] Biobank Act 2012, Article 1. Unofficial English Translation <http://www.finlex.fi/fi/laki/kaannokset/2012/en20120688.pdf> accessed 4 December 2019.

[68] Taupitz and Weigel, 'The Necessity of Broad Consent' (n. 62) 265.

[69] Contracting States Convention on the Grant of European Patents (opened for signature 5 October 1973, entered into force 7 October 1977).

themselves. Albers observes the recognition of samples as property in German law.[70] They have been recognised in collections of substances—both of biological samples and data. For example, the EU Database Rights Directive 1996 protects proprietary rights in 'a collection of... data or other materials arranged in a systematic or methodical way'.[71] They have been recognised in relation to data produced though the analysis of biobank substances. For example, the initial funding model proposed by the Estonian Biobank offered EGeen an exclusive commercial licence for the use of biobank data.[72] Finally, they have been recognised in the end products of research. A variety of types of patents exist concerning research products.[73] For example, patents exist in relation to immortal cell-lines developed from a research subject's genetic material. In the famous *Moore* case, one research subject's cellular material was used to create an immortal cell line, which was then patented and used in product development.[74]

H. Mapping Other Interests Engaged by Biobanking: Third-Party Non-Research Interests in Accessing Biobanking Substances

The second set of interests relates to the access and use of biobanking substances for non-research purposes. Four types of interest deserve discussion:[75]

1. Insurance industry interests
2. Employer interests
3. Law enforcement interests
4. Public administrator interests.

Insurance industry interests: insurance industry interests in accessing substances rest on economic rationale. Insurance works based on categorising individuals into risk groups. The accuracy of risk calculation depends on the quantity, type, and accuracy of information available.[76] In a business model founded on the scope and accuracy of information, it is not hard to see why insurance companies might have an interest in accessing the genetic data in biobanks. On the one hand, genetic data can provide insurance relevant insight into individuals, allowing tailored and accurate individual risks to be calculated and supporting profit generation. On the other hand, the insurance

[70] Albers, 'Rechtsrahmen und Rechtsprobleme bei Biobanken' (n. 23) 486; *Washington University* (n. 63).

[71] Directive 96/9/EC of the European Parliament and of the European Council on the Protection of Databases [1996] OJ L77/20 Article 1.

[72] Rain Eensaar, 'Estonia: Ups and Downs of a Biobank Project', in Herbert Gottweis and Alan Petersen (eds.), *Biobanks: Governance in Comparative Perspective* (Routledge 2008) 56, 60–3.

[73] Kshitij Singh, *Biotechnology and Intellectual Property Rights: Legal and Social Implications* (Springer 2015) 21 (hereafter Singh, *Biotechnology and Intellectual Property Rights*).

[74] *Moore v. Regents of University of California* [1990] 51 Cal.3d 120.

[75] As genetic science develops, more information will be extractable from the genome. Accordingly, new non-research actors with interests in accessing biobank substances are likely to emerge over time.

[76] Janneke Gerards, 'General Issues Concerning Genetic Information', in Janneke Gerards, Aalt Heringa, and Heleen Janssen (eds.), *Genetic Discrimination and Genetic Privacy in a Comparative Perspective* (Intersentia 2005) 5, 14–15 (hereafter Gerards, 'General Issues Concerning Genetic Information').

industry has argued that, should they not have the right to access genetic data, this could have negative effects for the industry. As Gerards observes, a doomsday scenario has even been put forward around the consequence of a lack of access to genetic data: 'Eventually, an imbalance in knowledge about genetic risks and the resulting process of adverse selection may result in liquidation of insurance companies.'[77]

The legitimacy of the insurance industry's claim to need access to genetic data has received certain legal recognition in Europe. In the UK, for example, there is the obligation to divulge to insurers the results of certain—limited—genetic tests for certain insurance premiums of more than £500,000.[78] However, it should be noted that, in relation to biobanking, there is currently no European—EU or Member State—legislation recognising insurers' ability to access biobanks directly.[79] Despite the apparently clear rationale supporting insurance access interests, it should also be noted that, in practice, there has been little call for insurance companies to access biobanks. This is likely as the utility of genetic data for insurance companies is currently low—the accuracy of prediction of health risks and mortality via genetic analysis is generally too poor to be useful in insurance risk calculation. However, this does not mean the possibility of insurance access is irrelevant.[80] Certain genetic information—relating to highly penetrant conditions such as Huntington's Chorea—are already regarded as accurate enough to be used in risk calculation.[81] Equally, as genetic science advances, it is likely that genetic tests for other health risks will reach the requisite accuracy.

Employers' interests: employers' interests in accessing biobanking substances are predominantly economic, but may also be based on social responsibilities. In terms of economics, the optimum distribution of an organisation's resources, and therefore the optimisation of profits, is facilitated with advance knowledge of employees', or prospective employees', genetic conditions.[82] For example, knowing if potential employees have genetic conditions which will impair their ability to work, may directly affect an employer's bottom line. In terms of social responsibility, the employer may have obligations to employees in relation to their health and safety on the job, or to the health and safety of society as a whole, which might be assisted by knowing employees', or prospective employees', genetic conditions. For example, there may be jobs which involve exposure to toxins known to be associated with activating genetic predispositions to health problems. Advance knowledge of such predispositions can aid employers in avoiding placing affected individuals in problematic positions.[83]

[77] Gerards, 'General Issues Concerning Genetic Information' (n. 76) 14–15.

[78] Her Majesty's Government and the Association of British Insurers, Code on Genetic Testing and Insurance (Code of Practice, 2018) 15. Although this obligation does, in fact, not apply to genetic data produced in the course of research.

[79] Some biobanks—including the UK Biobank—explicitly foresee allowing insurance companies access to anonymised or pseudonymised data. UK Biobank, 'FAQs' (UK Biobank, 2019) <https://www.ukbiobank.ac.uk/all-faqs/> accessed 4 December 2019.

[80] See, for example, Ruth Stirton, 'Insurance, Genetic Information and the Future of Industry Self-Regulation in the UK' (2012) *Law, Innovation and Technology* 4(2) 212, 212–37.

[81] Herman Nys, Ingrid Dreezen, Imgard Vinck, et al., Genetic Testing: Patients' rights, Insurance and Employment: A Survey of Regulations in the European Union (European Commission Report, 2002) 74.

[82] Gerards, 'General Issues Concerning Genetic Information' (n. 76) 18.

[83] Gerards, 'General Issues Concerning Genetic Information' (n. 76) 18.

Employers' interests in accessing genetic data have received legal recognition in Europe. For example, Article 2 of the Danish Law on the Use of Health Information on the Labour Market 1996 observes the employer may obtain an employee's health information, including genetic data, when this data is relevant for the individual to perform specific work.[84] In relation to biobanking, however, it should be noted that there is currently no European either EU or Member State—legislation recognising employers' ability to access biobanking substances directly. Similarly to insurance industry interests, it should also be noted there has, practically, been little call by employers pushing their interest in directly accessing biobanking substances in Europe.

Law enforcement interests: these are founded on the strong public interest in the detection and prevention of crime. The successful execution of law enforcement depends on the information available to law enforcement professionals in conducting investigations. Genetic data can be useful indeed for law enforcement authorities. In particular, genetic data can aid law enforcement as an accurate identifier—when genetic material is found at a crime scene, this can be sequenced and used to identify suspects.[85] Genetic data can also allow the analysis of familial links and ethnic heritage. In future, genetic data may even allow reconstruction of suspects' physical features.[86]

The legitimacy of law enforcement authorities' interests in accessing genetic data has broad recognition across Europe. This follows from a recognition that, as Taupitz observes, it is a fundamental obligation of a state to ensure: 'criminals, within the bounds of law, can be pursued, judged and punished'.[87] This obligation manifests in evidentiary seizure laws encompassing samples and genetic data in biobanks. In Germany, for example, such evidentiary seizure rules appear in Articles 81 and 94 of the Strafprozeßordnung.[88] In the UK, Kaye comments on the requirement that biobank substances may be subject to police access for the purposes of criminal investigations under Section 9 of the Police and Criminal Evidence Act 1984.[89] Unlike the previous two non-research interests, law enforcement agencies have already shown willingness to access biobanking substances in European states. For example, in Sweden, police accessed PKU Biobank samples to identify former Foreign Minister Anna Lindh's

[84] Act on the Use of Health Data etc. on the Labour Market 1996, Part II, Article 2.

[85] Nuffield Council of Bioethics, The Forensic Use of Bioinformation: Ethical Issues (Policy Paper, 2007) 8–11.

[86] See, for example, Andrew Pollack, 'Building a Face, and a Case, on DNA' *New York Times* (New York, 23 February 2015) <http://www.nytimes.com/2015/02/24/science/building-face-and-a-case-on-dna.html> accessed 27 November 2019.

[87] Jochen Taupitz and Jukka Weigel, 'Biobanken—das Regelungskonzept des Deutschen Ethikrates' (2012) *Wissenschaftsrecht* 45 35, 48. Author translation of: 'Straftäter im Rahmen der geltenden Gesetze verfolgt, abgeurteilt und einer gerechten Bestrafung zugeführt werden'.

[88] Strafprozeßordnung 1987 Articles 81 and 94.

[89] Jane Kaye, 'Police Collection and Access to DNA Samples' (2006) *Genomics, Society and Policy* 2(1) 16, 23 (hereafter Kaye, 'Police Collection and Access to DNA Samples'); Police and Criminal Evidence Act 1984.

Accordingly, the UK Biobank recognises, in their governance materials: 'Access to the resource by the police or other law enforcement agencies will ... be acceded to ... under court order.' UK Biobank, *Ethics and Governance Framework*, (Policy, 2007) 13 <https://www.ukbiobank.ac.uk/wp-content/uploads/2011/05/EGF20082.pdf> accessed 4 December 2019.

murderer.[90] Nevertheless, the scale of law enforcement access should not be overstated. The number of relevant cases is limited and access has only been called for in relation to serious crimes.[91]

Public administrators' interests: these are justified by reference to the need for more efficient public administration. There are a range of administrative goals which might be achieved using genetic data. For example, genetic testing can establish the legitimacy of immigration claims. Immigration into European states is generally only permitted in specific situations, one of which is the presence of certain types of genetic relative in a state. Whilst the establishment of relationships would ideally be done based on documentary evidence, this may not always be possible. Genetic testing for kinship offers an accurate alternative. Equally, genetic testing can be used to clarify paternity. This can have implications for claims on government benefits. Finally, there have been suggestions that genetic testing could help prove or disprove the legitimacy of social support claims—for example, claims based on conditions with a genetic basis.[92]

This interest is legitimated by appeal to the public interest in administrative efficiency. As Laurie observes: 'Any state or government has a ... [legitimate] interest in ... efficiency.'[93] In turn, there has been certain specific recognition that genetic data may be used in pursuit of the aims of public administration in Europe. For example, the Swedish government relied on genetic testing to prove the paternity of foreign fathers to secure financial support.[94] Equally, the UK Government recognises the utility of DNA testing in relation to public administrative tasks such as testing immigration claims.[95] In relation to biobanking specifically, however, it should be noted that there is, in fact, currently no European—either EU or Member State—legislation explicitly recognising public administrators' ability to access substances. It should also be noted that, as with insurance and employment interests, there do not appear to have been any efforts by public administrators in Europe to access biobanking substances directly.

In the preceding sections, a range of underlying legitimate genetic privacy rights and rights holders, as well as a range of other interests, in the biobanking process were identified. Based on this mapping, a rough schematic of the basic relationships between identified rights and interests might now be drawn up. Relationships can be grouped into two categories.

1. Conflicts
2. Confluences.

[90] Kaye, 'Police Collection and Access to DNA Samples' (n. 89) 17.

[91] See, for example, Vilius Dranseika, Jan Piaseck, and Marcin Waligora, 'Forensic Uses of Research Biobanks: Should Donors Be Informed?' (2016) *Medicine, Health Care and Philosophy* 19 141, 141–6.

[92] Laurie, *Genetic Privacy* (n. 1) 174.

[93] Laurie, *Genetic Privacy* (n. 1) 176.

[94] Laurie, *Genetic Privacy* (n. 1) 177.

[95] UK Government, 'Get a DNA test' (UK Government 2019) <https://www.gov.uk/get-dna-test> accessed 5 December 2019.

I. Mapping the Relationships between Genetic Privacy Rights and Other Interests: Conflicts

Genetic privacy rights and other interests in biobanking exist in the same space. Unsurprisingly, in many cases, they optimally benefit from different conditions of access to substances. In these cases, interest conflicts might be identified. There are three main forms of interest conflict identifiable:

1. Conflicts between different genetic privacy rights and rights holders
2. Conflicts between genetic privacy rights and interests tied up with the conduct and outcome of research
3. Conflicts between genetic privacy rights and third-party non-research interests.

Conflicts between genetic privacy rights and rights holders: three different types of conflict might be identified. First, research subjects', genetic relatives', and genetic groups' information privacy rights in restricting states of third-party access come into conflict. In the first instance, to facilitate each rights holder's right, each rights holder would need to be informed the right was engaged. This would mean potentially breaching a research subject's desired restriction of access to information on biobank participation in relation to genetic relatives and genetic groups. In turn, in terms of the exercise of the rights, if all privacy rights holders' desired states of separation in biobanking did not correspond, certain rights holders' privacy rights to restrict access would need to be overridden to the benefit of other rights holders.

Second, research subjects', genetic relatives', and genetic groups' information privacy rights to choose to know their genetic data conflict with information privacy rights to restrict states of access to genetic data produced during research. If each type of rights holder's right to know were recognised, each would have a right to know the results of sequencing and research. Yet, to give life to each rights holders' right to know would mean overriding other rights holders' rights to maintain research results in specific states of separation.

Finally, there is a conflict between information privacy rights to choose to know genetic data and spatial privacy rights not to know. The information privacy right to know asserts rights holders have the power to choose to know their genetic information, whilst the spatial privacy right not to know requires that a rights holder is kept in the dark about the existence of genetic information.

Conflicts between genetic privacy rights and interests tied up with the conduct of research: three types of interest conflict are evident. First, genetic privacy rights conflict with research interests in the broadest possible use of substances. For example, information privacy rights to restrict states of access to biological samples and associated data presuppose an underlying requirement to request research subjects', and potentially their genetic relatives' and any relevant genetic groups', permission to use substances in research. This is an obvious obstacle to uninhibited use by researchers.

Second, to have any serious concrete existence, genetic privacy rights need to be facilitated by biobanking actors. This requires a diversion of resources away from the research process and is therefore in conflict with the goals of research. Facilitation of genetic privacy rights may, for example, require developing protocols for the execution of rights holders' desires. Equally, facilitation may require organisational and computing systems to ensure obligations are recorded and fulfilled.[96]

Third, genetic privacy rights may conflict with proprietary interests. Proprietary interests aim to facilitate maximum exclusive use or exploitation of resources. The breadth of such interests, however, can be limited by other rights and interests. In this regard, wherever genetic privacy rights exist alongside proprietary interests in biobanking substances, these may be limiting factors to maximum exploitation.[97]

Conflicts between genetic privacy rights and third-party non-research interests: two types of interest conflict are identifiable. First, third-party non-research access interests manifest when substances cannot be secured from an individual. Accordingly, this access will proceed without, or in the absence of, permission from privacy rights holders.[98] Third-party claims thus directly conflict with information privacy rights in restricting and controlling states of access to substances. This conflict is made particularly acute as third-party non research access may produce judgments about rights holders which may be regarded as harmful by those rights holders—for example, the use of genetic information to inform unfavourable insurance premiums.[99]

Second, in certain situations, third-party non-research access and use of substances may be aimed at finding out specific information about individuals. Consequent use of this information would, in many cases, have the likely side effect of the individual learning of the information produced. For example, if genetic information sourced from a biobank was used as the basis of an insurance judgment, this may require informing the insured of the information used. This forced awareness would conflict with information—and perhaps even, in some cases, spatial—privacy rights not to know.

[96] Christian Simon, Jamie L'Heureux, Jeffrey Murray, et al., 'Active Choice But Not Too Active: Public Perspectives on Biobank Consent Models' (2011) *Genetics in Medicine* 13(9) 821, 823.

[97] There may also be interest conflicts between research interests, as well as between research interests and proprietary interests. It is not always the case that individual researchers wish to share substances with others. In this case, the interests of researchers, for example, conflict with societal interests in research outcomes. See, for example, *Washington University* (n. 63). The exclusivity of proprietary interests may function in the same way. For example, Myriad Genetics proprietary claims around the BRCA 1 and 2 breast cancer genes restricted testing for the genes to Myriad's laboratories. Singh, *Biotechnology and Intellectual Property Rights* (n. 73) 154–63.

[98] Kaye, 'Police Collection and Access to DNA Samples' (n. 89) 21–3.

[99] A. Lemke, W. Wolf, J. Hebert-Beirne, et al., 'Public and Biobank Participant Attitudes toward Genetic Research Participation and Data Sharing' (2010) *Public Health Genomics* 13(6) 368, 372.

J. Mapping the Relationships between Genetic Privacy Rights and Other Interests: Confluences

It is not always the case, however, that genetic privacy rights and other interests will be in conflict. A subtle consideration of rights and interests also shows points of confluence. Two such types of confluence are worthy of note:

1. Confluence between genetic privacy rights
2. Confluence between genetic privacy rights and interests tied up with the research process.

Confluence between genetic privacy rights: two types of confluence between genetic privacy rights are identifiable. First, information genetic privacy rights may converge when each relevant rights holder holds the same opinion as to desired states of separation of biobank substances—for example, if a research subject and their genetic relatives each desired to allow a biobank to have access to relevant substances.

Second, each genetic privacy rights holder might generally be assumed to want to prevent third-party access to substances. Owing to the communal nature of genetic data, third parties may use biobank substances to make judgments about all genetic privacy rights holders and to harm those rights holders. For example, access to one family member's biological sample and information by law enforcement would allow familial searching and therefore also have an impact on genetic relatives.[100]

Confluence between genetic privacy rights and interests tied up with the research process: two types of confluence are identifiable. First, genetic privacy rights may be aligned with the conduct of research. In relation to information privacy rights, for example, a genetic privacy rights holder may wish to waive their privacy to allow a biobank to collect, store, and use substances for research.[101] The exercise of the right would thus align with researcher interests in being allowed to use substances.

Second, the success of research depends on recognition and respect for privacy rights. In the first instance, research subjects are the source of biobanking substances. Equally, biobanking and genomic research rely on public support—for example, for funding and access to health care data.[102] The public consists of the same individuals which are, either currently, or prospectively, research subjects with privacy rights in biobanking research. Subjects and potential subjects are only likely to be supportive to research if their desires and expectations are met. Accordingly, to maximise research potential, those with interests in the research process should ensure that privacy rights are taken into account where possible.[103] In this regard, as Laurie observes: 'privacy

[100] See also: Elly Lynch, Rebecca Doherty, Clara Gaff, et al., 'Cancer in the Family and Genetic Testing: Implications for Life insurance' (2003) *Medical Journal of Australia* 179 480, 480.

[101] Beyleveld and Brownsword, *Consent in the Law* (n. 60) 4–5.

[102] Susan Wallace and Bartha Knoppers, 'The Role of P3G in Encouraging Public Trust in Biobanks', in Peter Dabrock, Jochen Taupitz, and Jens Ried (eds.), *Trust in Biobanking* (Springer 2012) 189, 189–90.

[103] Taylor, *Genetic Data and the Law* (n. 7) 34–6.

protection ... has a role that serves the dual purpose of promoting both research and the interests of research subjects'.[104]

It might finally, generally, be noted that the nature of biobanking research mitigates the brisance of conflicts between privacy and research interests. The research process generally has no intention of using substances in relation to specific privacy rights holders, and no intention of using substances to make socially consequential judgments about rights holders. This mitigates the chance of direct harms, or disadvantages, to rights holders which might emerge from biobank research. For example, no one person will have a higher insurance premium flowing directly from the research process.[105]

K. Conclusion

Privacy might be regarded as a condition where an aspect of life is held in some state of separation from others. In relation to information, this might be referred to as information privacy. In relation to the body and mind, this might be referred to as spatial privacy. In certain cases, these states of separation might be perceived to have value in a society and be perceived to be worthy of protection. In these cases, a privacy right might be recognised. Genetic privacy rights are simply a subset of privacy rights related to the processing of biological samples and genetic data.

In the biobanking context, a range of genetic privacy rights are engaged. In relation to the research subject, five different types of genetic privacy rights are identifiable. These include rights to hold biological samples and associated data in states of separation from third parties, rights to know and not know genetic data produced in the course of research, and a right not to be informed of potentially harmful genetic information produced in the course of research. Each of these rights can also be considered to be held by two further types of genetic privacy rights holders: genetic relatives and genetic groups.

Naturally, genetic privacy rights do not exist in a vacuum in biobanking. Rather, they share the space with a series of other legitimate interests. A first set of legitimate interests can be identified connected with the conduct and outcome of research—for instance, the interests of researchers in conducting research. A second set of legitimate interests can be identified connected with third-party, non-research, access to biobanking substances—for instance, the interests of insurance companies and law enforcement authorities.

Unsurprisingly, a broad and complicated set of potential conflicts between genetic privacy rights and legitimate interests is identifiable. Conflicts are identifiable between different types, and different holders, of genetic privacy rights, as well as between genetic privacy rights and legitimate interests. There are also, however, confluences between rights and interests identifiable. Of particular significance is the fact there is broad confluence between genetic privacy rights and interests connected with the conduct and outcome of research.

[104] Laurie, *Genetic Privacy* (n. 1) 167.

[105] Harms may still, of course, result from research. See, for example, D. Beyleveld and E. Histed, 'Betrayal of Confidence in the Court of Appeal' (2000) *Medical Law International* 4(3&4) 277, 277–311.

5

The Protection of Genetic Privacy in Biobanking at International Level

Establishing a Baseline Standard for Genetic Privacy Protection in Biobanking

A. Introduction

The previous chapter mapped the range of genetic privacy rights identifiable in the biobanking context and the other legitimate interests which exist alongside them, and showed how these rights and interest relate. The chapter did not yet, however, touch on how the law might provide a scheme for balancing conflicts between these rights and interests. In this regard, this chapter sketches how genetic privacy rights are protected in biobanking and how they are balanced against other interests, in the international framework. The analysis of the international framework constitutes the analysis and identification of top-level, generally accepted, principles. The analysis of the international framework thus provides principles which may be considered as a baseline standard of protection, against which all other legal systems—including European data protection law under the General Data Protection Regulation (GDPR)—can be evaluated.

The chapter begins by charting the structure of the international framework—identifying relevant instruments and discussing their providence and legal force in EU Member States (section B). Next, the chapter outlines the protection offered to genetic privacy rights identifiable in biobanking—along both transactional and relational axes. This analysis includes an identification of both common international principles and emerging international principles—the former constituting principles identifiable in a majority of all instruments and the latter constituting principles identifiable only in a majority of newer, biobank-specific, instruments (sections C–F). Finally, the chapter offers a critical analysis of the protection offered under the international framework—including a critique of structure, the range of genetic privacy rights protected, and the standard of protection offered (sections G–J). This critique does not aim to undermine the legitimacy of identified international principles as offering a baseline level of protection. Rather, it merely aims to highlight that the protection provided has flaws, and thus should not be regarded as definitive, or perfect.

Protecting Genetic Privacy in Biobanking through Data Protection Law. Dara Hallinan, Oxford University Press (2021). © Dara Hallinan.
DOI: 10.1093/oso/9780192896476.003.0005

B. The Structure of the International Framework

A consideration of the structure of the international framework provides the basis for a substantive analysis of the protection offered. This structure can be considered from three perspectives:

1. The range of relevant international instruments
2. The provenance of relevant international instruments—where they came from and what they were designed to do
3. The legal force of relevant instruments in European states.

1. Relevant International Instruments

A search for international instruments reveals a vibrant international landscape.[1] Nine key international instruments, with clear applicability to biobanking and genomic research, and with clear hortatory significance, are identifiable:[2]

1. Council of Europe (CoE), 1997: Convention for the Protection of Human Rights and Dignity of the Human Being with regard to the Application of Biology and Medicine: Convention on Human Rights and Biomedicine
2. United Nations Educational, Scientific and Cultural Organization (UNESCO), 1997: Universal Declaration on the Human Genome and Human Rights
3. UNESCO, 2003: International Declaration on Human Genetic Data

[1] Two searches were conducted. The first was a search of the HumGen database. See: HumGen International, 'GenBiblio: Database of Laws and Policies' (HumGen International, 2019) <http://www.humgen.org/> accessed 5 December 2019.

The second was a review of relevant literature regarding the international regulation of biobanking. The most relevant studies are: Adrian Thorogood and Ma'n Zawati, 'International Guidelines for Privacy in Genomic Biobanking (or the Unexpected Virtue of Pluralism)' (2015) *Journal of Law, Medicine and Ethics* 43(4) 690, 690–702 (hereafter Thorogood and Zawati, 'International Guidelines for Privacy in Genomic Biobanking'); Ciara Staunton, Santa Slokenberga, and Deborah Mascalzoni, 'The GDPR and the Research Exemption: Considerations on the Necessary Safeguards for Research Biobanks' (2019) *European Journal of Human Genetics* 27 1159, 1162–3 (hereafter Staunton, Slokenberga, and Mascalzoni, 'The GDPR and the Research Exemption'). Other literature included considerations of specific aspects of regulation relevant to genetic privacy at international level. See, for example; Roberto Andorno, 'Global Bioethics at UNESCO: In Defence of the Universal Declaration on Bioethics and Human Rights' (2007) *Journal of Medical Ethics* 33(3) 150, 150–4 (hereafter Andorno, 'Global Bioethics at UNESCO').

[2] Documents deemed irrelevant for analysis fell into two groups. First, certain documents proved thematically irrelevant—with either too broad or too narrow a scope. Second, certain instruments, whilst thematically relevant, had been drafted by organisations whose norm-setting capacity was uncertain. The Global Alliance for Genomics and Health is an example. The Global Alliance has a wide membership and has produced several best practice guidelines of high quality. For example, Global Alliance for Genomics and Health, Framework for Responsible Sharing of Genomic and Health-Related Data (Policy, 2014); Patricia Kosseim, Edward Dove, and Carmen Baggaley, 'Building a Data Sharing Model for Global Genomic Research' (2014) *Genome Biology* 15(430) <https://genomebiology.biomedcentral.com/track/pdf/10.1186/s13059-014-0430-2?site=genomebiology.biomedcentral.com≥ accessed 5 December 2019. However, the organisation is relatively new—founded in 2013—and there is little empirical evidence to show how its instruments have been adopted by members, or non-members.

4. CoE, 2005: Additional Protocol to the Convention on Human Rights and Biomedicine, concerning Biomedical Research.[3]
5. UNESCO, 2005: Universal Declaration on Bioethics and Human Rights[4]
6. Organization for Economic Co-operation and Development (OECD), 2009: Guidelines on Human Biobanks and Genetic Research Databases
7. The World Medical Association (WMA), 2013: Declaration of Helsinki—Ethical Principles for Medical Research Involving Human Subjects
8. CoE, 2016: Recommendation CM/Rec(2016)6 of the Committee of Ministers to member States on research on biological materials of human origin[5]
9. WMA, 2016: Declaration of Taipei on Ethical Considerations regarding Health Databases and Biobanks.[6]

2. Provenance of Instruments

In terms of providence, four groups of instruments are evident. The first group was designed to provide general principles for the protection of human rights in bioscience and biotechnology. This group includes UNESCO's Universal Declaration on Bioethics and the CoE's Convention. As observed in the Explanatory Memorandum to the Convention, for example, the drafting process aimed to provide: 'common general standards for the protection of the human person in the context of the development of the biomedical sciences'.[7] The second group was designed to provide principles for biomedical research. This group includes the CoE's Additional Protocol and the WMA's Declaration of Helsinki. As Williams observes regarding the Declaration of

[3] There are questions around the applicability of the CoE Additional Protocol to biobanking. Article 1 of this Protocol clarifies its application to: 'research ... involving interventions on human beings'. Interventions are defined as 'physical'. The Explanatory Memorandum, however, clarifies the Protocol applies to 'the full range of research activities in the health field involving interventions on human beings. This includes all aspects of the research project from start to finish, including selection and recruitment of the participants [and] ... research interventions designed to procure biological materials or data are covered under this Protocol'. Thus, the Protocol is intended to apply to biobanking activity in which samples and substances are collected with the intention to use these in research. The Explanatory Memorandum also states, however, that: 'The Protocol does not address established medical interventions independent of a research project, even if they result in biological materials or personal data that might later be used in biomedical research.' The Protocol thus may not technically apply to biobanking activity involving samples and data collected in the clinical context—provided these were not collected with the intention to be used in research. Even in these cases, however, the Protocol can still be regarded as a significant instrument. The Protocol constitutes a key authoritative source clarifying the position of the CoE on human rights and biomedical research and thus should not be ignored. Council of Europe, Explanatory Report to the Additional Protocol to the Convention on Human Rights and Biomedicine, concerning Biomedical Research (Explanatory Memorandum, 2005) 3–4.

[4] United Nations Educational, Scientific and Cultural Organization Universal Declaration on Bioethics and Human Rights (21 October 2005) 33 C/Resolutions + CORR. + CORR.2 + CORR.3 + CORR.4 + CORR.5.

[5] Council of Europe Recommendation of the Committee of Ministers to member States on research on biological materials of human origin (11 May 2016) CM/Rec(2016)6.

[6] World Medical Association, Declaration of Taipei on Ethical Considerations regarding health databases and biobanks (Policy, 2002 [updated 2016]).

[7] Council of Europe, Explanatory Report to the Convention for the protection of Human Rights and Dignity of the Human Being with regard to the Application of Biology and Medicine: Convention on Human Rights and Biomedicine (Explanatory Report, 1997) 2. See also: Roberto Andorno, 'The Oviedo Convention: A European Legal Framework at the Intersection of Human Rights and Health Law' (2005) *Journal of International Biotechnology Law* 2 133, 133 (hereafter Andorno, 'The Oviedo Convention').

Helsinki: 'Its purpose was to provide guidance to physicians engaged in clinical research and its ... focus was the responsibilities of researchers.'[8] The third group was designed to provide principles relevant to the processing of biological samples and genetic data. This group includes UNESCO's Universal Declaration on The Human Genome and UNESCO's International Declaration on Human Genetic Data. The final group was designed specifically for biobanking. Significantly, this group includes three of the four instruments drafted in the last decade: the OECD's Guidelines, the CoE's Recommendation, and finally, the WMA's Declaration of Taipei.

3. Legal Force of Instruments in European States

Three groups of instruments are identifiable. The first group consists of instruments which elaborate principles with advisory power. This category includes the WMA Declarations of Helsinki and Taipei. This category also includes the OECD Guidelines. These guidelines take the form of an OECD Recommendation and are thus not legally binding on OECD Members.[9] The second category constitutes instruments whose principles are expressions of intent with a view to becoming law, but which do not themselves constitute legislation. This category includes the three UNESCO Declarations. As Andorno observes: '[a] UNESCO document makes up part of the so-called soft law instruments—instruments ... not intended to oblige states to enact enforceable rules ... but to encourage them to do so'.[10] The category also includes the CoE's Recommendation.[11] The third category consists of instruments which are, in principle, intended to have legal effect in European States. This category includes only the CoE's Convention and the CoE's Additional Protocol. A CoE Convention constitutes an international treaty. In this regard, Andorno considers the Convention as: 'the first multilateral binding instrument entirely devoted to biomedical law'.[12]

The mapping of the structure of the international framework provides the basis for the analysis of the substantive protection offered by the framework. In this regard, however, the framework consists of different instruments which do not necessarily correspond in the protection they offer. Accordingly, only where a principle has the support of a critical mass of instruments, can it be argued to be an international principle. I propose the threshold for such critical mass might be considered in two ways. First, the threshold can be argued to be met when a principle is present in a clear majority of international instruments: a common international principle. The following two

[8] John Williams, 'The Declaration of Helsinki and Public Health' (2008) *Bulletin of the World Health Organisation* 86(8) <http://www.scielosp.org/scielo.php?pid=S0042-96862008000800022&script=sci_arttext> accessed 5 December 2019.

[9] '*Recommendations* are not legally binding.' OECD, 'OECD Legal Instruments' (*OECD*) <http://www.oecd.org/legal/legal-instruments.htm> accessed 5 December 2019.

[10] Andorno, 'Global Bioethics at UNESCO' (n. 1) 151.

[11] As the CoE puts it: '[a Recommendation] is not binding ... it provides a policy framework ... governments can implement' Council of Europe, 'The Recommendation' (Council of Europe, 2020) <http://www.coe.int/en/web/enter/the-recommendation> accessed 5 December 2019.

[12] Andorno, 'The Oviedo Convention' (n. 7) 134.

sections thus elaborate common international principles for the protection of genetic privacy in biobanking against this threshold. The sections discuss, in turn, common international principles which:

1. Protect research subjects' genetic privacy along the transactional axis[13]
2. Protect genetic relatives' and genetic groups' genetic privacy along the relational axis.

C. Common International Principles Regarding Research Subjects' Genetic Privacy on the Transactional Axis

Common international principles identifiable along the transactional axis are discussed within a framework consisting of a typology of privacy provisions.[14] The framework is not only useful to structure the discussion in this chapter, but also to provide a standardised framework, which will be used throughout the book to analyse and compare protection provided across legal systems. The framework consists of eight types of provision:

1. Oversight
2. Legitimation of the collection and use of substances
3. Rights retained by the research subject in collected substances
4. Obligations on biobanking actors in relation to collected substances
5. Transfers of substances between jurisdictions
6. Transfers of substances to external researchers
7. Transfers of substances to non-research actors
8. Sanctions for infringements.[15]

Common international principles are identifiable in seven of the eight categories. Interestingly, there is no common principle identifiable concerning transfers between biobanks and external researchers.

1. Oversight

A common principle is identifiable that all biobanking activity must submit to advance supervision. This is a universal requirement. Most instruments—eight of

[13] Recall the five types of genetic privacy rights as identified in chapter 4, section D.
[14] This is not a typology built with normative significance but rather a useful analytical tool.
[15] The typology was constructed via a cluster analysis of provisions in legislation identified in the previous step and in international data protection legislation. In relation to the latter, see, in particular OECD, Guidelines Governing the Protection of Privacy and Transborder Flows of Personal Data (Policy, 1980); Council of Europe Convention for the Protection of Individuals with regard to Automatic Processing of Personal Data (opened for signature 28 January 1981, entered into force 1 October 1985) ETS 108. Also referred to as Convention 108.

nine—addressed the requirement directly. For example, the UNESCO Universal Declaration on Bioethics and Human Rights requires, in Article 19(a), that independent ethics committees should 'assess the relevant ethical, legal, scientific and social issues related to research projects'. Equally, the CoE's Convention on Bioethics and Human Rights and its Additional Protocol, in Articles 16(i) and 9(i) respectively, require that research only proceed following advance review by an ethics committee. In turn, the WMA's Declaration of Helsinki, requires, in Articles 17, 22, and 23 that each research project have a protocol charting possible risks involved as well as submit to evaluation by an independent ethics committee.[16]

2. Legitimation of Collection and Use of Substances

A common principle is identifiable that a research subject, in principle, must have given informed consent for biobanking to proceed. Consent principles, as commented on by Staunton et al., are omnipresent across instruments.[17] Thorogood and Zawati additionally recognise that: '[i]nternational research ... guidelines describe a participant's right to control the collection, use, and disclosure [of substances]'.[18] For example, the UNESCO Declaration on the Human Genome, states, in Article 5(b): 'In all cases, the prior, free and informed consent of the person concerned shall be obtained'. Equally, the OECD Guidelines, in Article 4.B, observe: 'informed consent should be obtained from each participant'.

Beneath the surface, however, differences are identifiable between instruments. Two differences are significant. First, there is no concurrence concerning the absolute nature of the principle. Whilst certain instruments are strict in requiring consent, others foresee exceptions. For example, Article 32 of the Declaration of Helsinki states: 'where consent would be impossible or impracticable to obtain ... the research may be done ... after consideration and approval of a research ethics committee'. Second, there is no consensus as to the scope of consent permitted: certain instruments are not clear on the scope of consent they permit, certain instruments required project-specific consent, and a final set of instruments permit broad consent. Compare, for example, the project-specific consent permitted under Article 13 of the CoE Additional Protocol—where consent may be given to 'a research project'—with Article 12 of the Declaration of Taipei—which permits consent for: 'multiple ... uses'.

[16] The UNESCO International Declaration was the exception. It recognised the need for oversight, however, indirectly. In Article 6(b), the Declaration refers to the relevant provisions on advance oversight outlined in the UNESCO Declaration on the Human Genome.

[17] Staunton, Slokenberga, and Mascalzoni, 'The GDPR and the Research Exemption' (n. 1) 1162. In their article, Staunton et al. do recognise that one instrument they analyse does not outline consent conditions. The instrument in question—the OECD Principles and Guidelines for Access to Research Data from Public Funding 2007—is not, however, a subject of analysis in this chapter. OECD, Principles and Guidelines for Access to Research Data from Public Funding (Policy, 2007).

[18] Thorogood and Zawati, 'International Guidelines for Privacy in Genomic Biobanking' (n. 1) 693. See also: Eleni Kosta, *Consent in European Data Protection Law* (Martinus Nijhoff 2013) 112.

3. Rights Retained by the Research Subject in Collected Substances

A common principle is identifiable that the research subject must retain the right to withdraw consent. This is unsurprising. Melham et al., for example, observe the right developed alongside consent as 'a central tenet of medical research ethics'.[19] This principle is explicitly referenced, in similar terms, in eight of nine instruments. For example, the WMA Declaration of Helsinki clarifies, in Article 26, that the research subject has the 'right to ... withdraw consent ... at any time' whilst the UNESCO International Declaration elaborates, in Article 9(a), that 'consent may be withdrawn by the person concerned unless such data are irretrievably unlinked'.[20]

Behind superficial concurrence, however, no common principle is identifiable as to the consequences of exercise of the right. Certain instruments are silent on the issue, others mandate specific consequences—such as anonymisation or destruction—whilst a final group leaves the choice to the research subject. Compare, for example, the CoE Recommendation, which, in Article 13(1), requires either anonymisation or destruction, with the UNESCO International Declaration, which, in Article 6(c), permits the research subject to choose what happens.

4. Obligations on Biobanking Actors in Relation to Collected Substances

A common principle is identifiable that actors must store substances securely and confidentially. The obligation is explicitly mentioned in all instruments. For example, the WMA Declaration of Taipei states, in Article 10, that '[c]onfidentiality is essential for maintaining trust and integrity in Health Databases and Biobanks' and in Article 21, that '[g]overnance measures must include ... security measures to prevent unauthorized access or inappropriate sharing'. Equally, the OECD Guidelines elaborate, in Article 1.D that: 'the operators and users of the HBGRD should ... secure the protection of participants' privacy and the confidentiality of data and information'.

[19] Karen Melham, Linda Briceno Moraia, Colin Mitchell, et al., 'The Evolution of Withdrawal: Negotiating Research Relationships in Biobanking' (2014) *Life Sciences, Society and Policy* 10(16) 1 <https://lsspjournal.springeropen.com/track/pdf/10.1186/s40504-014-0016-5?site=lsspjournal.springeropen.com> accessed 5 December 2019 (hereafter Melham, Briceno Moraia, Mitchell, et al, 'The Evolution of Withdrawal'); 'War Crimes Tribunal at Nuremberg, The Nuremberg Code (1947)' (1996) *British Medical Journal* 313 1448, 1448.

[20] The exception is the UNESCO Universal Declaration on the Human Genome. Here, however, it may be argued the right is implied. Article 5(b) refers to the obligation to obtain informed consent. The concept of informed consent arguably presupposes the possibility to withdraw. See: Melham, Briceno Moraia, Mitchell, et al, 'The Evolution of Withdrawal' (n. 19) 1.

5. Transfers of Substances between Jurisdictions

A common principle is identifiable that transfers to jurisdictions where standards cannot be upheld are prohibited. This principle is evident in all instruments. There are two approaches to its expression. First, most instruments elaborate explicit prohibitions. For example, the CoE Additional Protocol states, in Article 29: 'Sponsors or researchers ... that plan to undertake ... research ... in a State not party to this Protocol shall ensure that, without prejudice to the provisions applicable in that State, the research project complies with the principles on which the provisions of this Protocol are based.' Second, the remainder of instruments contains indirect prohibitions. These take the form of general prohibitions on activities which reduce research subject protection—including transfers of substances to jurisdictions with inadequate protection. For example, the OECD Guidelines, in Articles 7.B and 7.C, state, with relevance for transfers, that these should only take place if principles are upheld.

6. Transfers to Non-Research Actors

A common principle is identifiable that substances should not be transferred to non-research actors. This principle is universally recognised. There were two approaches to its elaboration. First, certain instruments subsume the principle under sweeping confidentiality provisions. This was the approach adopted by both WMA instruments. Article 24 of the Declaration of Helsinki, for example, clearly states: 'Every precaution must be taken to protect the privacy of research subjects and the confidentiality of their personal information.' Second, other instruments outlined express prohibitions. For example, Article 14(b) of UNESCO's International Declaration states: 'Human genetic data, human proteomic data and biological samples linked to an identifiable person should not be ... made accessible to third parties.'

Behind superficial concurrence, however, there is no consensus as to how far exceptions are permissible. Certain instruments—such as the two WMA Declarations—foresee no exceptions. Other instruments foresee exceptions for a variety of public interest reasons. For example, the second clause of Article 14(b) of the UNESCO International Declaration qualifies the general prohibition for: 'an important public interest reason in cases restrictively provided for by domestic law consistent with the international law of human rights or where the prior, free, informed and express consent of the person concerned has been obtained'.

7. Sanctions for Infringements

A common principle is identifiable that infringements of privacy should be subject to sanctions. A decisive majority of instruments—six of nine—outline provisions related to sanctions. Certain instruments outline specific sanctions. The CoE's Convention and its Additional Protocol, for example, outline three specific forms of sanctions—in Chapter VIII and Chapter X: first, that states should 'provide appropriate judicial protection to prevent or ... stop ... unlawful infringement of ... rights'; second, that an individual 'who has suffered damage as a result of participation ... shall be entitled to fair compensation'; and finally, that states 'shall provide ... appropriate sanctions to be applied in the event of infringement'. The remainder of the six do not address sanctions directly but require that states take measures to ensure provisions are effective—including adopting sanctions. For example, Article 22 of both the UNESCO Universal Declaration on the Human Genome and the Universal Declaration on Bioethics require states to take 'appropriate measures' to give effect to the principles outlined. Only the OECD Guidelines on Human Biobanks and the Declaration of Taipei are silent on the issue of sanctions—in the case of the OECD Guidelines, the silence is accounted for as the guidelines are intended to provide a set of best-practice principles addressed to biobanks rather than a system which requires sanctions.

D. Common International Principles Regarding Genetic Relatives' and Groups' Genetic Privacy on the Relational Axis

Superficially, it appears international instruments extend a range of types of protection to genetic relatives and genetic groups. Closer investigation, however, reveals no identifiable common principles.

1. Protection of Genetic Relatives

There is a common recognition across instruments that genetic relatives should be protected. However, approaches to protection are disparate and eventually, no common principle is identifiable. Three approaches are evident. First, four instruments—the CoE's Convention, its Additional Protocol and UNESCO's Declarations on the Human Genome and on Bioethics fail to recognise genetic relatives' genetic privacy rights at all. Second, one instrument recognises the legitimacy of rights without extending concrete protection. The CoE's Recommendation, in Article 4, simply observes that: 'The risks for the [research subject] ... and, where appropriate, for their family ... in particular ... risks to private life, should be minimised.' Finally, four instruments recognise genetic relatives' rights through the extension of concrete protection. The types of protection offered, however, differ across instruments. For example, only the OECD Guidelines, in Article 2.5 recognise the need for family members to be engaged in consultations regarding biobanking. Only the two WMA Declarations recognise the possibility for genetic relatives to be engaged in the consent process.[21] Only the UNESCO International Declaration, in Article 10, recognises: 'Where appropriate, the right not to be informed should be extended to identified relatives.'

2. Protection of Genetic Groups

There is a common recognition across instruments that genetic groups should be protected. However, approaches to protection are disparate and, eventually no common principle is identifiable. Three approaches are evident. First, three instruments—the CoE's Convention, its Additional Protocol and its Recommendation—avoid recognising genetic groups' rights altogether. Second, UNESCO's Universal Declaration on the Human Genome recognises the legitimacy of genetic groups' genetic privacy rights without specifying how these should be protected. Article 10 simply states: 'No research or research applications ... should prevail over respect for the human rights, fundamental freedoms and human dignity ... of groups of people.' Finally, the remaining five instruments extend specific protection to genetic groups. The types of protection extended, however, differ. The OECD Guidelines on Human Biobanks propose, in Article 2.5, that identifiable genetic groups may need to be involved in consultation processes prior to setting up a biobank. The UNESCO International Declaration considers, in Article 14, that: 'States should endeavour to protect the privacy ... and the confidentiality of human genetic data linked to an identifiable ... where appropriate, group.' The UNESCO Universal Declaration on Bioethics and Human Rights recognises, in Article 6(3), that: 'In appropriate cases of research, additional agreement of the legal representatives of the group or community concerned may be sought.' Finally, the WMA's Declaration of Helsinki, in Article 25, recognises that: '[there are instances in which] it may be appropriate to consult family members or community leaders' as part of biobanking consent.

A broad range of common international principles for the protection of genetic privacy in biobanking is thus identifiable. There is a problem, however, with the concept of a common international principle. The concept treats all instruments as equally relevant to the regulation of biobanking. This is not the case. Biobanking is a unique phenomenon in research. As Karlsen et al. observe: 'With the emergence of ... biobanking ... basic and applied biomedical ... research undergoes a qualitative change.'[22] Accordingly, special weight might be given to principles outlined in instruments specifically designed to apply to biobanking. To address this problem, a second

[21] The WMA's Declaration of Taipei fails to directly refer to genetic relatives' genetic privacy interests. Nevertheless, this Declaration does clarify its principles are to be understood as additional to those outlined in the Declaration of Helsinki.

[22] Jan Reinert Karlsen, Jan Helge Solbakk, and Søren Holm, 'Ethical Endgames: Broad Consent for Narrow Interests; Open Consent for Closed Minds' (2011) *Cambridge Quarterly of Healthcare Ethics* 20 572, 573.

method for identifying international principles is necessary. This approach recognises the threshold for identifying an international principle has been met when an approach to protection is evident only in a majority of biobank-specific instruments: an emerging international principle. The following two sections thus discuss identifiable emerging international principles. The sections address, in turn, emerging international principles which:

1. Protect research subjects' genetic privacy along the transactional axis
2. Protect genetic relatives' and genetic groups' genetic privacy along the relational axis.

E. Emerging International Principles Regarding Research Subjects' Genetic Privacy on the Transactional Axis

For consistency, the range of emerging international principles identifiable along the transactional axis is also discussed within the framework of general types of privacy provisions outlined in section C.

A consideration of only the three biobank-specific instruments—the OECD Guidelines, the WMA Declaration of Taipei, and the CoE Recommendation—reveals emerging principles for the protection of research subjects' genetic privacy in four categories of privacy provision.

1. Oversight

An emerging principle is identifiable that all research activity must be subject to a process of ongoing oversight. The obligation for oversight is evident in all three biobank-specific instruments. The WMA Declaration of Taipei states, in Article 19: 'the ethics committee must . . . have the right to monitor on-going activities'. The OECD Guidelines state, in Article 3.6 states: 'The operators of the HBGRD should anticipate that over its lifespan there will be a need to review and modify its policies, protocols and procedures. A process should be in place for undertaking such review and modification.' Finally, the CoE Recommendation, in Article 20(2), states that: 'Each collection should be subject to independent oversight.'

2. Legitimation of collection and use of substances

Two emerging principles are identifiable, both of which serve to clarify the conditions of consent. First, there is an emerging principle present in all instruments, which clarifies that exceptions are permissible to the general rule that consent must be obtained.

There are, however, differences in the conditions of exceptions. The strictest set of conditions is outlined in the Declaration of Taipei, Article 16 of which recognises: 'In the event of a clearly identified, serious and immediate threat where anonymous data will not suffice, the requirements for consent may be waived to protect the health of the population.' Slightly softer is the approach of the CoE Recommendation, which permits uses of substances without consent, in Article 21, provided the participant cannot be contacted, an important scientific goal is pursued, and there is no evidence that the participant would object. Finally, the OECD Guidelines provide the most permissive approach. Use of substances in biobanking without consent is permissible, under Article 4.B, provided consent cannot be obtained, that exceptions are possible under national law, and the project has ethics approval.

Second, there is an emerging principle, identifiable in all instruments, endorsing the legitimacy of broad consent. The relevance of this emerging principle must be given specific consideration given the idea of non-project-specific consent did not emerge as a theme of discussion until a few years after the turn of the millennium, and could thus not have been considered in non-specific instruments which preceded this period. As Cambon-Thomsen et al. observed in 2007: 'Recently, the possibility of a somewhat broader consent for long-term projects ... is emerging.'[23] In this regard, Article 12 of the WMA Declaration of Taipei permits: 'data or biological material [to be] collected ... for multiple and indefinite uses'. Article 4.6 of the OECD Guidelines suggests biobank operators may obtain consent 'used to address unforeseen research questions'. Article 11 of the CoE's Recommendation suggests consent need only be 'as precise as possible with regard to the envisaged research use'.

3. Obligations on Biobanking Actors in Relation to Collected Substances

An emerging principle is identifiable that biobanking actors are obliged to track the distribution and use of substances. All three biobank-specific instruments clarify the need for tracking systems to ensure genetic privacy conditions attached to substances are upheld. The Declaration of Taipei states, in Article 21: '[substances must be] documented and traceable in accordance with the consent of the concerned persons'. The CoE Recommendation states, in Article 16(4): 'Each sample of biological material in the collection should be appropriately documented and traceable, including information on the scope of any consent or authorisation.' The OECD Guidelines, in Article 1.F, simply states: 'operators ... should develop and maintain clearly documented operating procedures and policies for the procurement, collection, labelling, registration,

[23] Anne Cambon-Thomsen, Emmanuelle Rial-Sebbag, and Bartha Knoppers, 'Trends in Ethical and Legal Frameworks for the Use of Human Biobanks' (2007) *European Respiratory Journal* 30 373, 376.

processing, storage, tracking, retrieval, transfer, use and destruction of ... materials, data and/or information'.

4. Transfers of Substances to External Researchers

Two emerging principles are identifiable in relation to transfers between biobanks and external researchers. First, biobanks must conduct a review of the scientific and ethical legitimacy of an application prior to transfer—particularly concerning whether the scope of consent permits transfer. The obligation is evident in two of the three biobank-specific instruments. The WMA Declaration of Taipei, in Article 19, requires: 'the ethics committee ... approve use of data and biological material'. The OECD Guidelines state, in Articles 7.3 and 7.4 that: 'operators ... should have in place mechanisms to review applications for access to human biological materials and/or data' and 'to review the envisaged uses of ... biological materials and/or data for consistency with the types of research ... agreed to by a participant'.

Second, biobanks are required to make transfer policies public. This principle is also evident in two of the three biobank-specific instruments. The CoE Recommendation states, in Article 18(3): 'Transparent access policies should be developed and published.' The OECD Guidelines state, in Article 7.1: 'operators ... should make publicly available ... access policies and procedures'.

F. Emerging International Principles Regarding Genetic Relatives' and Groups' Genetic Privacy on the Relational Axis

Superficially, it appears biobank-specific instruments take both genetic relatives' and genetic groups' privacy into account. Closer observation, however, shows no emerging principles can be identified.

1. Protection of Genetic Relatives

A common recognition that genetic relatives should be protected is evident in biobank-specific instruments. However, approaches to protection are disparate and give rise to no emerging principle. As discussed above, the CoE's Recommendation recognises relatives' genetic privacy rights without extending any concrete protection. The remaining two instruments extend concrete protection, but the protection extended does not correlate. The OECD Guidelines, in Article 2.5, recognise the need for family members to be engaged in consultations regarding biobanking. The WMA Declaration, in Article 11, however, recognises the possibility for genetic relatives to be engaged in the consent process.

2. Protection of Genetic Groups

A common recognition that genetic groups should be protected is evident in biobank-specific instruments. However, approaches to protection are disparate and give rise to no emerging principle. The WMA Declaration of Taipei and the CoE Recommendation recognise the need to protect genetic groups without extending specific protection. The WMA Declaration, for example, in Article 17, states: 'The interests and rights of the communities concerned, in particular when vulnerable, must be protected.' Only the OECD Guidelines go further and outline specific concrete principles relating to genetic groups. Specifically, the Guidelines propose, in Article 2.5, that relevant genetic groups may need to be involved in consultation processes prior to setting up a biobank.

The previous sections provided an overview of the common and emerging principles constituting the international framework—on both transactional and relational axes—for the protection of genetic privacy in biobanking (summarised in Table 5.1). This overview now provides the basis for a critical analysis of the protection provided by the international framework.[24] This analysis is structured around four questions:

1. Is the international framework suitably structured to provide optimal protection—is the framework internally coherent and can its principles actually protect rights holders?
2. Does the international framework provide protection for the full range of research subjects' genetic privacy rights along the transactional axis?
3. Does the international framework provide protection for the full range of genetic relatives' and genetic groups' genetic privacy rights along the relational axis?
4. Does the international framework, where it provides substantive protection, provide adequate protection?

When the international framework is examined in relation to these questions, several flaws emerge. Thus, whilst the international framework might certainly be regarded as providing a baseline standard of protection for genetic privacy in biobanking, it should not be viewed as providing a complete, or flawless, standard of protection.

G. Problems of Structure: The International Framework Is Not Hard Law

In terms of structure, an efficacy problem is identifiable. The description of the structure of the international framework above reveals a system out of which largely only

[24] A critique of the procedural legitimacy of the international framework would also be worthwhile. See: E.-B Van Veen, P. H. Riegman, W. N. Dinjens, et al., 'TuBaFrost 3: Regulatory and ethical issues on the exchange of residual tissue for Research across Europe' (2006) *European Journal of Cancer* 42 2914, 2915–6.

Table 5.1: Overview of international principles protecting research subjects, genetic relatives, and genetic groups

Gaps in Member State Approaches without Data Protection			Genetic Privacy Rights Holder (Protected Subjects Marked with Dot)		
			Research Subject	Genetic Relatives	Genetic Groups
Principles of International Law	Common Principles	Principle 1: Biobanking actors must submit to advance oversight	•		
		Principle 2: Collection and use of substances should, in principle, only proceed with research subject consent	•		
		Principle 3: The research subject should have the right to withdraw consent	•		
		Principle 4: Biobanking actors must retain substances securely and confidentially	•		
		Principle 5: Substances should not be transferred to jurisdictions which do not ensure adequate protection for genetic privacy	•		
		Principle 6: Substances should not, in principle, be transferred to non-research actors	•		
		Principle 7: Penalties should be imposed for infringements of genetic privacy	•		
	Emerging Principles	Principle 1: Biobanking actors should be subject to ongoing oversight	•		
		Principle 2: The principle that consent must be obtained to collect and use materials may be subject to exceptions	•		
		Principle 3: The scope of consent may include broader, non-project-specific consent	•		
		Principle 4: Biobanking actors are obliged to ensre that the conditions for tracking substances are in place	•		
		Principle 5: Biobanking actors are obliged to engage in ethicaal review of external researchers' access requests	•		
		Principle 6: Biobanking actors must make access policies public and accessible	•		

guiding principles can emerge. Accordingly, the international framework can scarcely be directly relied upon as a system for the protection of genetic privacy in biobanking in European states.

Most relevant instruments were never designed to be instruments of hard law—they only ever aimed to outline non-binding principles. Seven of nine instruments can be categorised as guidelines or statements of intent. These instruments arguably play a significant role in establishing templates for modes of behaviour in biobanking. Dove observes generally that '[t]he normative, hortatory force of these instruments is demonstrable'.[25] Andorno specifically highlights the utility of UNESCO Declarations as: '[presenting] the advantage of permitting ... countries to gradually become familiar with the proposed standards before they are confronted with the adoption of enforceable rules'.[26] Much as these observations may be true, however, they do not change the fact that these instruments will never be hard law and thus cannot be relied upon by rights holders seeking protection.

In turn, even the instruments designed to be hard law have received limited recognition in European states. The CoE's Convention and its Additional Protocol were indeed designed to be hard law. Close inspection of these instruments, however, reveal caveats to their legal force. To constitute binding law in a European state, CoE Conventions require signature and ratification. Several significant European states, including Germany and the UK, are still to ratify the Convention.[27] The Additional Protocol has received yet fewer ratifications. Indeed, in 2020, the number of ratifications sat at a meagre twelve—of forty-seven CoE member states.[28] In turn, there remains little evidence as to whether, and how, states which have ratified the Convention and Protocol, have actually implemented the relevant provisions into national law.[29]

H. Problems Along the Transactional Axis: The International Framework Does Not Provide Protection for the Full Range of Research Subjects' Genetic Privacy Rights

The set of identified common and emerging principles certainly aim to provide protection for information genetic privacy rights relating to the restriction of states of access to biological samples and associated data. The principles, however, provide no

[25] Edward Dove, 'Biobanks, Data Sharing, and the Drive for a Global Privacy Governance Framework' (2015) *Journal of Law, Medicine and Ethics* 43(4) 675, 675.

[26] Andorno, 'Global Bioethics at UNESCO' (n. 1) 151.

[27] See for full list: Council of Europe, 'Chart of Signatures and Ratifications of Treaty 164' (Council of Europe 2020) <https://www.coe.int/en/web/conventions/full-list/-/conventions/treaty/164/signatures?p_auth=fUdbBxOL> accessed 5 December 2019.

[28] See for full list: Council of Europe, 'Chart of signatures and ratifications of Treaty 195' (*Council of Europe* 2020) <https://www.coe.int/en/web/conventions/full-list/-/conventions/treaty/195/signatures?p_auth=fUdbBxOL> accessed 5 December 2019.

[29] There is a general lack of evidence as to how international instruments have impacted on the national legislation of EU Member States. This is a subject worthy of future research.

protection for the remaining three types of genetic privacy right. Yet, in each case, the absolute lack of protection lacks clear justification.

First, the framework does not protect the information privacy right to choose to know one's own genetic data. Although protection is not completely absent from instruments, protection is not sufficiently present to give rise to either a common or emerging principle.[30] There are arguments justifying such a lack of protection. Two arguments deserve discussion. First, it has been observed that recognising the right might come at a—potentially significant—cost to interests tied up with research. It might thus be argued that these costs are too high to warrant protecting the right. Murphy et al., for example, recognise: 'the enormous financial, logistic, and time burdens that responsible return of results would incur'.[31] Second, it has been argued that the right may not always serve research subjects in terms of providing them with useful information. Knoppers et al., for example, highlight: 'genetic association studies imperfectly predict the development and severity of a condition . . . and could mislead [research] participants to overestimate the significance of the results'.[32]

These arguments, whilst legitimate, do not, however, justify a complete lack of protection. Rather, they justify limitations on protection. In relation to the first argument, there may indeed be instances in which the cost to the research mission is too high to warrant protection. But this will be contextually variable. There are instances in which the impact on research interests will not be so high, or the research subject's right to choose to know may simply be greater. Knoppers et al. observe, for example, several factors relevant in considering a proportionate approach: 'Resolution of the question of whether there is a duty to return . . . genetic research results depends on the type of study, the clinical significance and reliability of the information, and whether the study involves patients, genetically "at-risk" families for a tested predisposition or healthy volunteers'.[33] In relation to the second argument, the consequences of the provision of imperfect information to research subjects might be ameliorated by subtle protection. For example, issues of uncertainty surrounding results could be mitigated through obligations for supplementary communication with research subjects to explain uncertainties.

Second, the framework does not protect the information privacy right to choose not to know one's own genetic data. Although protection is not completely absent from instruments, protection is not sufficiently present to give rise to either a common or emerging principle.[34] Unlike the other two omitted rights, it is hard to find arguments

[30] For example, the UNESCO Universal Declaration on the Human Genome, in Article 5(c).
[31] Juli Murphy, Joan Scott, David Kaufman, et al., 'Public Expectations for Return of Results from Large-Cohort Genetic Research' (2009) *American Journal of Bioethics* 8(11) 36, 37.
[32] Bartha Knoppers, Yann Joly, Jacques Simard, et al., 'The Emergence of an Ethical Duty to Disclose Genetic Research Results: International Perspectives' (2006) *European Journal of Human Genetics* 14 1170, 1170 (hereafter Knoppers, Joly, Simard, et al., 'Public Expectations of an Ethical Duty to Disclose Genetic Research Results').
[33] Knoppers, Joly, Simard, et al., 'Public Expectations of an Ethical Duty to Disclose Genetic Research Results' (n. 32) 1176.
[34] For example, the UNESCO International Declaration on Human Genetic Data in Article 10.

which legitimate the exclusion of protection for the information privacy right not to know. The only argument which might be put forward is that protection may require administrative resources to be allocated to facilitate research subject choice. Such an allocation of resources would naturally involve a diversion of resources from research and would impact on research interests.

This argument, however, can scarcely be relied upon as a justification for a complete lack of protection. In the first instance, the right is only relevant in certain, limited, circumstances: when the research subject is known, when this subject is in the position to make a choice about feedback and when there is an enforced feedback procedure in place—otherwise the research subject would remain uninformed as a matter of course. Given these circumstances, it is not clear that the resources allocated to permit a choice not to know would be more excessive than those required for an obligatory feedback system.[35] Even if—for whatever reason—obligatory feedback systems did need to be in place, simple *ex ante* information obligations could be operationalised, ensuring some protection for the right. For example, obligations could be in place ensuring that research subjects are informed of the obligatory feedback policy prior to substance collection—during a consent procedure, for example. This would allow research subjects to decline to participate if they did not wish to receive information.

Finally, the framework does not protect the spatial privacy right not to be informed of potentially harmful genetic information. Indeed, the right was only protected in one instrument: in Article 10 of the CoE Convention. There are arguments which can be put forward which justify the lack of protection for the right. Two arguments deserve discussion. First, from a fundamental perspective, the value of the right is contested. In this regard, the right has been argued, as Andorno puts it: '[to] represent a return to a paternalistic attitude as it puts people in a state of ignorance, depriving them of choice ... [and is therefore] opposed to autonomy'.[36] If autonomy is seen as a key foundational element a system of research subject protection, then the right may be regarded as an aberration. Second, there is a practical argument which doubts whether biobanking personnel are best placed to make choices on behalf of research subjects as to what they should not know. The right choice as to whether to withhold significant information will be contextually variable. The choice will depend on the content of information at hand—its medical validity, its accuracy etc. The choice will also depend on the research subject—their tendency to be harmed by such information, their family history etc. In this regard, biobanking personnel are not always doctors. Indeed, they need not even have medical training. It may thus be argued they may not be best placed to evaluate the information in question. Nor will they necessarily have the requisite knowledge of, or relationship with, the research subject.

[35] An empirical study would be worthwhile.

[36] Roberto Andorno, 'The Right Not to Know: An Autonomy Based Approach' (2004) *Law, Ethics and Medicine* 30 435, 436.

Whilst these are legitimate arguments, they do not justify a complete lack of protection. In terms of the first argument, whenever a research subject has not expressed an opinion on the feedback of harmful information, they may not be able to exercise autonomy in relation to potentially harmful information. Accordingly, some form of paternalism is unavoidable. At any rate, as Laurie observes, paternalism is not necessarily always a bad thing: 'Paternalism has become a dirty word... but it is disingenuous at the same time to deny the presence of paternalism and, at times, the value of certain forms of it.'[37] In terms of the second argument, it is true biobanking personnel may not always be best placed to make a choice. However, this does not mean they will never be capable of making any choices at all. Significantly, certain information has less contextual variability than other information. Recall, for example, Almqvist et al.'s finding that suicide rates for persons informed of a genetic predisposition to Huntington disease were ten times above average.[38] Such evidence removes some of contextual uncertainty around harms. In turn, certain biobanking personnel may be both doctors and have personal relationships with research subjects. In such cases, the relevant type of relationship will be present. Such subtleties could be considered in designing a schema of protection to include the right.

I. Problems Along the Relational Axis: The International Framework Does Not Provide Protection for the Full Range of Genetic Privacy Rights Holders

The international framework does not provide any concrete protection for either genetic relatives or genetic groups. Yet, in each case, the complete lack of protection lacks clear justification.

Regarding genetic relatives, whilst most instruments recognise the legitimacy of genetic relatives' rights, there is no concrete common, or emerging, principle relating to the protection of these rights. There are arguments which might be put forward advocating caution in extending protection to genetic relatives. In particular, an argument may be put forward that including genetic relatives as subjects of protection would constitute a threat to the primacy of the research subject as the focus of protection. In this regard, the inclusion of genetic relatives as subjects of protection would mean the inclusion of multiple subjects of protection. Extending protection to these subjects may thus mean a dilution of protection offered to research subjects.

Yet there are strong arguments that the research subject's genetic privacy rights are stronger than those of their relatives and that such a dilution is undesirable. Technically, the strength of a privacy claim can be seen as a function of the form and content of connection between an individual and their genetic substances. In terms of the form of

[37] Graeme Laurie, 'A Response to Andorno' (2004) *Law, Ethics and Medicine* 30 439, 440.

[38] E. Almqvist, M. Bloch, R. Brinkman, et al., 'A Worldwide Assessment of the Frequency of Suicide, Suicide Attempts, or Psychiatric Hospitalisation After Predictive Testing for Huntington Disease' (1999) *American Journal of Human Genetics* 64(5) 1293, 1298.

connection: the genome acts as a unique biometric identifier only for research subjects. Whilst a research subject's genome can be used to identify genetic relatives, the process is much more complex and imprecise. For example, familial DNA searching in law enforcement databases is subject to several potential inaccuracies. As Kim et al. observe, the approach may falsely identify unrelated individuals in the database.[39] In terms of the content of connection: as discussed previously, a great deal of information can be extracted about a research subject from their genome.[40] Whilst it is true that information about genetic relatives can also be extracted from a research subject's genome, the quantity and accuracy of this information is not comparable.[41] As Laurie observes concerning disease predisposition: 'the risk of ... relatives being affected by a ... condition is reduced because of the different ... influences to which they have been subjected compared with the proband'.[42]

This argument, whilst strong, does not, however, serve to completely exclude the possibility to extend certain protection to genetic relatives. The argument is legitimate in relation to actionable rights in biobanking substances—for example, research subject rights related to decisions as to whether substances are used in the biobanking process or not. The idea of granting the possibility to consent to participate in research to genetic relatives, for example, would genuinely be akin to regarding research subject and genetic relatives' rights as equal. This would indeed constitute a direct threat to the primacy of the research subject in a scheme of protection. Such arguments are not, however, valid for all types of principles. There are several principles which could be extended to both research subjects and genetic relatives with little, if any, impact on research subjects' rights. One clear example is the confidentiality principle outlined in Article 14 of the UNESCO International Declaration. It would be unproblematic to require that data on both research subjects and genetic relatives be held confidentially.

Regarding genetic groups, whilst most instruments recognise the legitimacy of genetic groups' rights, there is no concrete common, or emerging principle, identifiable relating to the protection of these rights. There are arguments which justify caution when considering the extension of protection to genetic groups. Two arguments deserve discussion. First, there is an argument that including genetic groups as subjects of protection would function to the detriment of the protection of the research subject. This is certainly a troubling proposition. The research subject's rights certainly trump those of genetic groups. The previous chapter did outline the justification for genetic groups'

[39] Joyce Kim, Danny Mammo, Marni Siegel, et al., 'Policy Implications for Familial Searching' (2011) *Investigative Genetics* 2(22) 3 <https://www.ncbi.nlm.nih.gov/pmc/articles/PMC3253037/pdf/2041-2223-2-22.pdf> accessed 5 December 2019. See also: Rori Rohlfs, Erin Murphy, Yun Song, et al., 'The Influence of Relatives on the Efficiency and Error Rate of Familial Searching' (2013) *PLOS One* 9(1) 1 <https://journals.plos.org/plosone/article?id=10.1371/journal.pone.0070495> accessed 5 December 2019; Sonia Suter, 'All in the Family: Privacy and DNA familial searching' (2010) *Harvard Journal of Law & Technology* 23(2) 309, 319.

[40] See chapter 2, section C.

[41] See chapter 2, section F.

[42] Graeme Laurie, 'Challenging Medical-Legal Norms: The Role of Autonomy, Confidentiality and Privacy in Protecting Individual and Familial Group Rights in Genetic Information' (2001) *Journal of Legal Medicine* 22 1, 12.

Table 5.2: Overview of deficits in the international protection of genetic privacy rights and rights holders

Gaps in Member State Approaches without Data Protection		**Types of Genetic Privacy Rights Holder (Gaps in Protection Marked with a Dot)**		
		Research Subjects	Genetic Relatives	Genetic Groups
Types of Genetic Privacy Engaged by Biobanking	Information privacy right to restrict states of access to biological samples		•	•
	Information privacy right to restrict states of access to associated data		•	•
	Information privacy right to know one's own genetic data	•	•	•
	Information privacy right to choose not to know one's own genetic data	•	•	•
	Spatial privacy right not to be informed of harmful genetic information	•	•	•

rights in biobanking. Yet, this justification remains highly theoretical—there remains no European jurisprudence explicitly recognising the privacy rights of genetic groups.[43] Second, the inclusion of genetic groups as a subject of protection could come at a high cost to other interests tied up with the research process. Specifically, any need to protect genetic groups would mean recognising the need to implement protections in relation to scientific conclusions. Such protection could thus form obstacles to the production and dissemination of scientific research.

Whilst these arguments provide strong justifications against a heavy-handed extension of protection to genetic groups, they are not justifications for a complete absence of protection. The first argument functions as a strong justification for the exclusion of genetic groups from actionable rights in substances. Yet, as discussed

[43] As I have observed elsewhere, 'the tyranny of the genetic group is an ominous possibility and ... a problem to avoid'. Dara Hallinan and Paul De Hert, 'Genetic Classes and Genetic Categories: Protecting Genetic Groups Through Data Protection Law', in Linnet Taylor, Luciano Floridi, and Bart van der Sloot (eds.), *Group Privacy* (Springer 2017) 175, 190.

above in relation to genetic relatives, not all principles relate to actionable rights. The second argument is a reason to exercise caution in extending duties which restrict the scientific use of genetic group data. Yet, not all principles need be based on restrictions of use. Bearing these caveats in mind, there is no reason that a comprehensive scheme of protection could not include principles capable of protecting genetic groups. There is no reason, for example, that data relating to genetic groups should not be required to be held accurately. Significantly, as any principles which can fulfil the limitations of the above caveats cannot relate to rights to know and not know the results of research, they will be suitable for protecting both genetic classes and genetic categories.

J. Problems with the Standard of Protection: The International Framework Provides Incomprehensive Protection

Even when the international framework provides protection for a type of genetic privacy, held by a type of genetic privacy rights holder, the protection provided is unjustifiably limited. That protection is unjustifiably limited is shown by considering principles evident in international instruments which appear too sporadically to constitute either common or emerging principles.

There are several principles which appear in instruments too sporadically to be either common or emerging principles. These appear in five categories of genetic privacy provision. *Oversight:* the OECD Guidelines suggests privacy be overseen by a supplementary, specially designated, body. *Research subject rights*: first, three instruments—including the CoE's Additional Protocol—offer the right to genetic counselling alongside feedback; second, the WMA Declaration of Taipei gives subjects the right to access and correct incorrect information. *Obligations on biobanking actors:* first, two instruments—including the UNESCO International Declaration—require biobanking actors to restrict the identifiability of substances wherever possible; second, the OECD Guidelines require contact be maintained with research subjects throughout the biobanking process. *Transfers between jurisdictions:* first, two instruments—including the UNESCO Universal Declaration on Bioethics and Human Rights—require an ethical review of research activity in sending and receiving states; second, two instruments—including the CoE Recommendation—require a recipient to provide specific privacy guarantees; and finally, the CoE Recommendation mandates transfers be done in conditions securing confidentiality. *Transfers to external researchers:* the OECD Guidelines require that transfer conditions be documented in transfer agreements.

Yet, in relation to certain of these principles, there is no legitimate reason for their absence from a comprehensive scheme of protection. It is true that objections may be posed to the inclusion of several provisions discussed in the above paragraph in a scheme of protection. Certain principles might be objected to based on a lack of necessity. For example, the OECD requirement that a separate oversight body be integrated into biobanking processes to deal with privacy issues might be argued to be superfluous—given international principles already require such oversight to be conducted by other bodies. Certain other mechanisms might be objected to based on disproportionate cost. For example, Bledsoe et al. observe that there would be financial and organisational costs to 'the need to ensure access to appropriate counselling'. They argue these might be a factor in making certain biobanking projects untenable.[44]

Such objections, however, do not apply to all principles. For example, the obligation to restrict identifiability of substances as much as possible is, generally speaking, neither superfluous nor particularly onerous. There may be situations where coding or anonymisation is not possible or would indeed be disproportionately difficult or expensive. Here, however, exceptions could be foreseen. Indeed, many of the principles which appear in instruments too sporadically to be either common or emerging principles already constitute best-practice approaches in biobanking. For example, as Hirtzlin et al. observed, as early as 2003, it is already common practice to restrict the identifiability of substances as far as possible.[45] Equally, it is already common practice to require that documented agreements regarding privacy are made with transferees.

K. Conclusion

An impressive range of international instruments outlining principles relevant for the protection of genetic privacy in biobanking is identifiable. In total, nine key instruments with significant hortatory power, drafted by four different international organisations—including the OECD, the CoE, the WMA, and UNESCO—are identifiable. Most of these outline general principles—concerning, for example, the collection and processing of biological samples and genomic data, and the conduct of biomedical research—relevant to biobanking. Certain newer instruments, however, outline principles specific to biobanking.

A comparison of principles evident across instruments also reveals an impressive set of common and emerging principles relevant for the protection of the research subject's genetic privacy rights engaged by biobanking—including, for example, the obligation for biobanks to obtain a research subject's consent to legitimate activities. Despite the range of principles identifiable relating to the protection of the research subject, however, no concrete principles are identifiable providing protection to genetic relatives' or genetic groups' genetic privacy rights.

Although the international framework initially appears vibrant and extensive, a critical analysis shows it to be far from perfect. In terms of structure, the framework

[44] Marianna Bledsoe, Ellen Wright, and Amy McGuire, 'Return of Research Results from Genomic Biobanks: Cost Matters' (2013) *Genetic Medicine* 15(2) 103, 105.

[45] Isabelle Hirtzlin, Christine Dubreuil, Nathalie Préaubert, et al., 'An Empirical Survey on Biobanking of Human Genetic Material and Data in Six EU Countries' (2003) *European Journal of Human Genetics* 11 475, 478.

scarcely comprises of instruments of hard law. In terms of the range of genetic privacy rights protected, the framework fails to provide protection for several types of research subject genetic privacy rights, whilst completely failing to protect genetic relatives' and genetic groups' privacy rights. Even where genetic privacy rights are protected, the standard of protection offered is often inadequate.

6

Do We Need Data Protection at All?

Evaluating Protection for Genetic Privacy in Biobanking in Europe *Excluding* Data Protection

A. Introduction

The previous chapter provided an analysis of protection for genetic privacy in international instruments. This analysis established a baseline standard of protection against which other legal approaches might be measured. The analysis in the previous chapter went a long way towards setting the scene for an analysis of the standard of protection offered by European data protection law under the General Data Protection Regulation (GDPR). There is one question, however, which must be addressed before such an analysis can be undertaken: is there any need to consider European data protection law as a framework for the protection of genetic privacy in biobanking in Europe at all? To answer the question, this chapter conducts a thought experiment and considers what the standard of protection in Europe would look like if one were to *exclude* data protection law from consideration. This is merely a thought experiment, as data protection already plays, and will continue to play, a significant role in the protection of genetic privacy in biobanking in Europe. The exercise is enlightening, however, in showing the extent of flaws in protection in European legal systems stripped of data protection.

The chapter begins with a brief discussion of the choice of European legal systems analysed—the EU system, the Estonian system, the German system, and the UK system (section B). The chapter then proceeds by mapping the approach to the protection of genetic privacy in biobanking, *excluding* data protection, along the transactional and relational axes, in relation to each system (sections C–F). Next, the chapter moves to provide a critical analysis of the protection offered by these systems *excluding* data protection—including in terms of the adequacy of their structure, the range of genetic privacy rights they protect, the standard of protection they offer the genetic privacy rights they do protect, and the degree to which systems are compatible with one another (sections G–K). Finally, the chapter highlights—considering the problems found with systems *excluding* data protection—why it makes clear sense to look to EU data protection law as a source of solutions (section L).

Protecting Genetic Privacy in Biobanking through Data Protection Law. Dara Hallinan, Oxford University Press (2021). © Dara Hallinan.
DOI: 10.1093/oso/9780192896476.003.0006

B. Selection of European Legal Systems to Analyse

To form an impression of the legal situation in Europe *excluding* data protection law, it is necessary to consider EU law. Article 4(3) of the Treaty of the Functioning of the European Union (TFEU) grants the EU shared competence in relation to research: 'In the areas of research ... the Union shall have competence to carry out activities.'[1] However, EU law is not the only relevant legal system.

The second clause of Article 4(3) states: 'the exercise of [EU] competence shall not result in Member States being prevented from exercising theirs'. EU Member State law is thus also relevant. To gain an overview of the complete situation at state level, an analysis of all Member States would be necessary. This would be a colossal task and beyond the scope of this book. Accordingly, three European states have been chosen as exemplars to bridge the gap.[2]

These three states were chosen to provide a panorama of the situation in Europe. Accordingly, the choice of states aimed to reflect two types of relevant differences between European legal systems: first, differences between common law systems and civil law systems;[3] and second, differences in approaches to the regulation of biobanking. In relation to the second form of difference, as Rial-Sebbag et al. observe: 'There are two positions taking shape in EU countries.'[4] The first position is that: 'specific legislation has been adopted'.[5] The second position is that, as the Expert Group on International Biobank Research observe: 'provisions about biobanks or bio-collections are integrated into broader administrative and legislative instruments [pre existing in a state's legal framework]'.[6] In light of these differences, the following states were selected for analysis:

[1] Consolidated Version of the Treaty on the Functioning of the European Union [2012] OJ C326/01, Article 4(3).

[2] There are limitations with the selection of only three states for analysis. Descriptively, it may be that approaches adopted in these states are not representative. Normatively, there may be state legal systems not analysed which offer strengths not evident in analysed systems.

[3] Monateri, for example, refers to: 'the classical Common law/Civil law distinction'. Pier Giuseppe Monateri, 'Methods in Comparative Law: An Intellectual Overview', in Pier Giuseppe Monateri (ed.), *Methods of Comparative Law* (Elgar 2012) 18. Further subdivisions have been offered. Here, the dual classification will be relied upon to avoid placing too much emphasis on these taxonomies, which have been the subject of criticism. See, for example, Jaakko Husa, 'Classification of Legal Families Today: Is It Time for a Memorial Hymn?', (2004) *Revue Internationale de Droit Comparé* 1 11, 13.

[4] Emmanuelle Rial-Sebbag, 'The Emergence of Biobanks in the Legal Landscape: Towards a New Model of Governance' (2012) *Journal of Law and Society* 39(1) 113, 121 (hereafter Rial-Sebbag, 'The Emergence of Biobanks').

[5] Rial-Sebbag, 'The Emergence of Biobanks' (n. 4) 121.

[6] Expert Group on Dealing with Ethical and Regulatory Challenges of International Biobank Research, Biobanks for Europe: A Challenge for Governance (European Commission Report, 2012) 39 (hereafter Expert Group, Biobanks for Europe). The tailored law approach is the position taken in, for example, Estonia, Hungary, and Finland. The non-specific approach has been taken in, for example, Germany and France. See also: Katharina Beier and Christian Lenk, 'Biobanking Strategies and Regulative Approaches in the EU: Recent Perspectives' (2015) *Journal of Biorepository Science for Applied Medicine* 3 69, 77 (hereafter Beier and Lenk, 'Biobanking Strategies and Regulative Approaches in the EU').

1. Estonia[7]
2. Germany[8]
3. UK.[9]

The selection of systems thus provides a background for a discussion of the substantive protection offered by each system *excluding* data protection. Systems are discussed in the following order: EU, Estonia, Germany, and finally, the UK. The discussion of each system follows a standard pattern, equivalent to that used to discuss the international framework in the previous chapter. First, the structure of the system is discussed—including a discussion of relevant instruments within a system, their provenance, and their scope of applicability to biobanking. Second, the substantive protection provided to the research subject's genetic privacy rights along the transactional axis is discussed.[10] For consistency, and to ease comparison, discussion of protection along the transactional axis is structured within the same general framework consisting of a typology of privacy provisions used in the previous chapter.[11] Finally, the substantive protection provided to genetic relatives and genetic groups along the relational axis is discussed.

C. EU Law *Excluding* Data Protection

1. The Structure of EU law

a) Relevant Law

Surprisingly, *excluding* data protection, there is no relevant EU law for the protection of genetic privacy in biobanking. Superficially, this does not seem to be the case. An initial search reveals a raft of apparently relevant law. Two types of law seem particularly relevant. First, EU clinical trials legislation—elaborated through Regulation 536/2014.[12] Prominent authorities on the topic such as the Expert Group on International Biobank Research have specifically observed the relevance of clinical trials law for biobanking: 'The principles [in clinical trials law] have also been applied to biobanking.'[13] Second, there are laws relating to the collection and use of specific types

[7] Estonia belongs to the civil law tradition and offers an example of an EU Member State which has adopted biobank-specific legislation.

[8] Germany belongs to the civil law tradition and offers an example of a state which has chosen not to regulate biobanking through biobank-specific legislation.

[9] The UK belongs to the common law tradition and provides an example of a state which has chosen not to regulate biobanking through biobank-specific legislation.

Over the course of writing this book, the UK left the EU. It seems likely, however, that the UK and the EU will retain strong links in the research sector and, accordingly, that UK law will remain relevant for biobanking in the EU. In turn, the long history of UK involvement in the EU, as well as the fact that the UK remains part of other European supranational organisations—including the Council of Europe (CoE)—means its system remains a relevant point of comparison for EU approaches.

[10] Seechapter 4, section D.

[11] See chapter 4, sections E–F.

[12] Regulation (EU) No 536/2014 of the European Parliament and of the Council of 16 April 2014 on clinical trials on medicinal products for human use, and repealing Directive 2001/20/EC [2014] OJ L158/1.

[13] Expert Group, Biobanks for Europe (n. 6) 36.

of biological material. Most important among these laws is Directive 2004/23/EC—the Tissues and Cells Directive.[14] Academic commentators have also highlighted the relevance of these laws to biobanking. Townend, for example, considers: '[this an] area of legislation that has a direct bearing on ... biobanking ... to the tissues themselves that are kept in the databases and biobanks'.[15]

Yet, a closer look at the scope of applicability of these instruments reveals their limited relevance. In relation to clinical trials laws: Article 1 of the Clinical Trials Regulation clearly states: '[the law does] not apply to non-interventional studies'. It cannot therefore apply to the computer-based genomics research undertaken in biobanking. In relation to tissue and cells laws: Article 2 of the Tissue and Cells Directive clearly states it applies only to: 'the donation, procurement, testing, processing, preservation, storage and distribution of human tissues and cells intended for human applications and of manufactured products derived from human tissues and cells intended for human applications'. Accordingly, the law does apply to the research activities engaged in by biobanking actors. Indeed, as even Townend concedes: 'the scope of this Directive is much more in the clinical use of the tissues and cells, rather than the research uses of a biobank or genomic database'.[16]

Given the lack of relevant EU law, there is no need to proceed to map further aspects of structure or content.

D. Estonian Law *Excluding* Data Protection

1. The Structure of Estonian Law

a) Relevant Law

A search for relevant Estonian legislation reveals two generally relevant sets of legislation. First, the centrepiece of Estonian biobanking law is the Human Genes Research Act 2000. The Act entered into force in August 2001 and has since been amended twice—in 2007 and in 2010.[17] Whilst there is little secondary law providing further clarification of the Act's provisions, there are certain Ministerial Ordinances detailing procedures foreseen in the Human Genome Research Act.[18] A certain interpretative

[14] Directive 2004/23/EC of the European Parliament and of the Council of 31 March 2004 on setting standards of quality and safety for the donation, procurement, testing, processing, preservation, storage and distribution of human tissues and cells [2004] OJ L102/48.

[15] David Townend, 'EU Laws on Privacy in Genomic Databases and Biobanking' (2016) *Journal of Law, Medicine & Ethics* 44(4, part. 1) 128, 131 (hereafter Townend, 'EU Laws on Privacy in Genomic Databases').

[16] Townend, 'EU Laws on Privacy in Genomic Databases' (n. 15) 131.

[17] Human Genes Research Act 2000 list of amendments unofficial English translation <https://www.riigiteataja.ee/en/eli/531102013003/consolide> accessed 11 December 2019.

[18] These include: Requirements for Processor of Gene Bank 2019; Procedure for Issuing Tissue Samples, Descriptions of DNA and Descriptions of Health Condition of Gene Donors 2019 (hereafter Procedure For Issuing Tissue Samples 2019); Terms and Conditions for Storage of Pseudonymised Tissue Samples, Descriptions of DNA and Descriptions of Health Condition of Gene Donors 2019 (hereafter Terms and Conditions 2019); Procedure for destroying the gene donor's tissue sample, description of DNA, description of health condition and data which enables de-pseudonymisation 2019 (hereafter Procedure for destroying 2019). Ministerial Ordinances 2019. Unofficial English translations of all documents <https://genomics.ut.ee/en/access-biobank/legislation> accessed 23 April 2020.

weight may also be given—owing to its central position in Estonian biobanking—to the operating policies of the Estonian Biobank.

Second, provisions contained in the Estonian criminal code are also relevant.[19] Five Articles are particularly important: Article 138 relating to consent in research; Articles 138[1] and 140 relating to forced tissue donation; and Articles 157 and 157[1] concerning the confidentiality of information. Article 138[1], for example, states: 'Placing a person in a situation where organs, tissue or cells are removed from him or her, if such act is performed through deprivation of liberty, violence, deceit, threatening to cause damage, by taking advantage of dependence on another person, helpless situation or vulnerable situation of the person ... is punishable by up to five years' imprisonment.'

b) Provenance of Law

There are two strands evident in the development of identifiable relevant law in relation to biobanking. First, the Human Genes Research Act. The Act was specifically designed for one Estonian biobank. In the late 1990s, as Metspalu recalls 'a small group of Estonian scientists, physicians, entrepreneurs, and politicians incorporated into a non-profit foundation: "Estonian Genome Foundation"'.[20] This foundation was created with the aim of establishing a population biobank drawing on research subject samples and healthcare records. The Estonian government felt that the size and scope of the project warranted a clear legal basis.[21] The Human Genes Research Act was the response providing the legal footing for the project.[22] The Act remains the legislative basis for all the Estonian Biobank's activities.

Second, relevant provisions of the criminal code. These were not designed specifically with the Estonian Biobank in mind. In certain cases, the development of provisions may possibly have some connection to the creation and activity of the biobank—for example, Articles 138[1] and 140 relating to forced tissue donation. In other cases, however, the development of provisions rests on different justifications—for example, professional confidentiality duties in Article 157 and 157.[1]

c) Applicability of Law

The applicability of relevant Estonian law can be broken down along the same lines as its provenance. First, the Estonian Human Genes Research Act. The Act applies, almost without exception, to all activities of the Estonian Biobank. This breadth of applicability

[19] Estonian Penal Code 2001. Unofficial English translation <https://www.riigiteataja.ee/en/eli/522012015002/consolide> accessed 11 December 2019. The University of Tartu Act is also important in establishing the institutional context in which the Human Genes Research Act operates. University of Tartu Act 1995. Unofficial English translation <https://www.riigiteataja.ee/en/eli/ee/Riigikogu/act/522082014009/consolide> accessed 11 December 2019.

[20] Andres Metspalu, 'The Estonian Genome Project' (2004) *Drug Development Research* 62 97, 97.

[21] Liis Leitsalu, Toomas Haller, and Tõnu Esko, 'Cohort Profile: Estonian Biobank of the Estonian Genome Center, University of Tartu' (2015) *International Journal of Epidemiology* 44(4) 1137, 1138.

[22] The Estonian Biobank remains the epicentre of Estonian genome research. In a country with a population of around one million, the Biobank boasts a cohort of 200,000 gene donors. University of Tartu Institute of Genomics, 'Estonian Genome Centre' (University of Tartu Institute of Genomics) <https://genomics.ut.ee/en/about-us/estonian-genome-centre> accessed 16 June 2020.

is outlined in Article 1(1): 'The objectives of this Act are to regulate the establishment and maintenance of the Gene Bank, to organise the genetic research necessary therefore, to ensure the voluntary nature of gene donation and the confidentiality of the identity of gene research subjects, and to protect persons from misuse of genetic data and from discrimination based on interpretation of the structure of their DNA and the genetic risks are rising therefrom.'

Second, relevant provisions of the criminal code. These apply both to the Estonian Biobank and to other biobanking activity. Despite their broad applicability, these provisions still display limiting criteria. Articles 138^1 and 140 concern the voluntary donation of biological samples. They therefore do not apply to research subject data. Articles 157 and 157^1 concern specific confidentiality obligations owed, respectively, in professional relationships and in relation to sensitive data. They therefore do not apply when no professional duty exists or where non-sensitive data is processed. Article 138 outlines a general obligation to obtain consent to conduct research on human subjects. The article will therefore only apply when biobanking is connected to research on human subjects.

2. Principles in Estonian Law Protecting Research Subjects' Genetic Privacy on the Transactional Axis

a) Oversight

Estonian law only foresees a supervision system in relation to the activities of the Estonian Biobank. Oversight is only specifically addressed in the Human Genes Research Act. The Act outlines, in Article 29, that ordinary supervision of the biobank concerning the provisions of the Act is undertaken by a special Ethics Committee.[23] As Sándor and Bárd observe: 'in relation to the ... legal domain ... ethical supervision ... in Estonia is conducted by a separate ethics committee that deals only with the Estonian [Biobank]'.[24] According to Article 29, The Ethics Committee is tasked with responsibility for assessing 'the processing procedures of the ... bank'.

It should, however, also be noted that the Act places limitations on the oversight powers of the Committee. Two limitations are significant. First, in Article 29(1), the Act clarifies that, under normal circumstances, the 'assessment of the Ethics Committee is not binding'. Second, the Act refrains from granting the Committee power to engage in ongoing oversight over external projects using biobank substances.[25]

[23] The system includes other supervisory bodies. Most importantly, under Article 53 of the University of Tartu Act, the Ministry of Education and Research oversees the 'legality of the activities of universities'. However, these seem to play little role in day to day supervision.

[24] Judit Sándor and Petra Bárd, The Legal Regulation of Biobanks: National Report: Estonia (CELAB Paper Series, No. 5, 2009) 19 (hereafter Sándor and Bárd, The Legal Regulation of Biobanks).

[25] There are, however, practical indications suggesting ongoing review may be the norm in practice. For example, external applicants are obliged to sign forms outlining conditions concerning ongoing oversight. Research Ethics Committee of the University of Tartu, Continuous Review Document Requirements (Policy, 2009) <http://www.ut.ee/sites/default/files/ut_files/CONTINUOUS%20REVIEW%20DOCUMENT%20REQUIREMENTS%20of%20UT%20REC%202012.pdf> accessed 11 December 2019.

b) Legitimation of the Collection and Use of Substances

Estonian law requires research subject consent be obtained by the biobanking actor in two instances. From these instances, Leitsalu et al. suggest that Estonia is among EU Member States which, '[require] all participants [to] have signed an informed consent form to ensure voluntary and informed participation.'[26] First, in relation to the Estonian Biobank, the obligation is explicitly, without exception, outlined in Article 9(1) of the Human Genes Research Act: 'It is prohibited to take a . . . sample and prepare a description of state of health or genealogy without the specific . . . voluntary consent of the person.'

Second, with more general applicability, the criminal code, in Articles 138, 138^1, and 140 place broad restrictions on scientific research conducted on biological samples collected from individuals without consent.

The scope of consent which may be sought under the Human Genes Research Act is broad. This is clarified in Article 12, which, as Kaye et al. put it, legitimates a 'broad description of the purpose' of collection and use for all future research.[27] There is, however, no guidance as to the scope of consent as required under Articles 138, 138^1, and 140 of the criminal code.

c) Rights Retained by the Research Subject in Collected Substances

Estonian law provides research subjects with rights in their substances only in relation to the Estonian Biobank. Three types of rights are identifiable. First, Article 12(7) of the Human Genes Research Act explicitly elaborates that participants have 'the right to withdraw . . . consent at any time.'[28] Article 12(7) is, however, not clear on what withdrawal means. Certain commentators, such as William et al., suggest this implies a strict approach: 'In Estonia, there seems little room for negotiation, as donors have the right to have their data deleted from the database.'[29] However, I would argue that Article 12(7), read in conjunction with Article 10—which outlines the conditions for the complete destruction of substances—implies that withdrawal of consent only requires the biobank to destroy all information allowing the research subject to be identified.[30] The correctness of this position is supported by recent Ministerial Ordinance.[31]

[26] Liis Leitsalu, Helene Alavere, Mari-Liis Tammesoo, et al., 'Linking a Population Biobank with National Health Registries: The Estonian Experience' (2015) *Journal of Personalized Medicine* 5(2) 96, 98 (hereafter Leitsalu, Alavere, and Tammesoo, 'Linking a Population Biobank with National Health Registries').

[27] Jane Kaye, Hördur Helgason, Ants Nõmper, et al. 'Population Genetic Databases: A Comparative Analysis of the Law in Iceland, Sweden, Estonia and the UK' (2004) *TRAMES: A Journal of the Humanities and Social Sciences* 8(1/2) 15, 22 (hereafter Kaye, Helgason, and Nõmper, 'Population Genetic Databases: A Comparative Analysis').

[28] Interestingly, this conflicts with the consent form on the Estonian Genome Centre website, which, in Article 10, suggests withdrawal is permitted until coding has occurred—i.e. directly after collection. University of Tartu Institute of Genomics, Annex 1 to the Ministry of Social Affairs Decree No 36 (Policy, 2007) <http://www.geenivaramu.ee/sites/default/files/gene_donor_consent_form.pdf> accessed 11 December 2019.

[29] R. William G. Watson, E. W. Kaye, and D. Smith, 'Integrating Biobanks: Addressing the Practical and Ethical Issues to Deliver a Valuable Tool for Cancer Research' (2010) *Nature Reviews Cancer* 10 646, 650.

[30] Complete destruction of samples and data—outlined in Article 10(2)—may only follow when the identity of the donor has been unlawfully disclosed.

[31] See: Procedure for Destroying 2019 (n. 18), Article 3. The Procedure also outlines detailed requirements and procedures for the destruction of substances.

Second, Article 11 of the Act provides the research subject with, as Bovenberg et al. put it: 'the right to access personally their data stored ... [and] with the choice as to whether they want information fed back or not'.[32] The question of the research subject's rights to choose to know and not to know their genetic data is, according to Article 12, to be discussed with the participant in the consent procedure. In this regard, Article 11(1) recognises that the default position is that feedback will not occur. Article 11(2), then recognises that, following written notice from the research subject, they may 'access personally their data stored in the Gene Bank'. The Article 11(2) right encompasses almost all research subject data held by the Estonian Biobank, including genomic data; associated health, lifestyle and biographical data; and individual research results—the only exception is genealogy information. When research subjects exercise the right to know, Article 11(4) of the Act provides them with the supplemental 'right to genetic counselling'.

Finally, Article 11 provides research subjects with a series of rights concerning the ongoing control of data stored by the biobank. Article 11(2) allows research subjects to access and to check information about them stored in the biobank, and Article 11(5) allows research subjects to submit additional relevant information.

d) Obligations on Biobanking Actors in Relation to Collected Substances

Estonian law foresees two different kinds of obligations on biobanking actors in relation to collected substances. First, there is the obligation to hold substances confidentially. This obligation emerges in relation to the Estonian Biobank under Article 8 of the Human Genes Research Act.[33] To ensure confidentiality is maintained, Article 23 requires that all substances are allocated a code—pseudonymised. The obligation emerges for biobanks beyond the Estonian Biobank under Articles 157 and 157^1 of the criminal code. These Articles require confidentiality in relation to, respectively, doctors and other professionals with a legal duty of confidentiality and in relation to sensitive data.

Second, Article 22(5) of the Human Genes Research Act requires the Estonian Biobank to hold all substances accurately: 'In order to verify the authenticity of data to be entered into the Gene Bank before coding, the chief processor and authorised processor are permitted to compare such data with data stored in other databases and to correct the data if necessary.'

e) Transfers of Substances between Jurisdictions

Estonian law only specifically regulates international transfers in relation to the Estonian Biobank. The Human Genes Research Act places no specific restriction on the ability of foreign researchers to apply for access to research subject data—genomic or otherwise. There are tighter restrictions in place, however, around the

[32] J. Bovenberg, T. Meulenkamp, E. Smets, et al., 'Your Biobank, Your Doctor? The Right to Full Disclosure of Population Biobank Findings' (2009) *Genomics, Society and Policy* 5(1) 55, 65.

[33] Detailed elaboration of certain conditions for the secure and confidential storage of Estonian Biobank substances are also found in Ministerial Ordinances. See: Terms and Conditions 2019 (n. 18).

transfer of biological samples. Article 18(4) of the Human Genes Research Act requires, as Sándor and Bárd observe, that: 'All tissue samples shall be stored on the territory of the Republic of Estonia.'[34] Here, however, exceptions are available permitting certain transfers abroad. Article 18(4) outlines conditions for exceptions to be applicable. In particular: special permission must be granted by the government; the Estonian Biobank must always retain effective control over any samples transferred abroad; and finally, all uses of samples must be commensurate with Estonian law.

Beyond the Estonian Biobank, identified law places no specific restrictions on transfers. Transfers are thus permissible provided they fulfil all generally applicable rules—for example, regarding the scope of consent.

f) Transfers of Substances to External Researchers

Estonian law only regulates transfers to external researchers in relation to the activity of the Estonian Biobank. Article 16(1) of the Human Genes Act outlines the principle that: 'The Gene Bank may be used ... for scientific research, research into ... illnesses of gene donors, public health research and statistical purposes.' The Act also, however, clarifies that transfers may only happen provided certain conditions are fulfilled: an external researcher's proposal must first have been authorised by the Ethics Review Committee on Human Research of the University of Tartu;[35] the recipient's storage facilities must be in line with certain minimum standards—including standards concerning security and confidentiality; when an external researcher's application has been approved, a contract must be signed outlining the conditions of the researcher's use of substances;[36] and finally, under normal circumstances, only coded substances may be transferred.

Beyond the Estonian Biobank, transfers are not subject to specific regulation. Transfers are thus permissible provided they fulfil all other generally applicable rules—for example, regarding the scope of consent.

g) Transfers of Substances to Non-Research Actors

Transfers of substances from biobanking actors to non-research actors are only specifically regulated in relation to the operation of the Estonian Biobank. Almost all non-research access to substances in the Estonian Biobank is prohibited. Article 16(1) of the Human Genes Research Act is clear: 'Use of the Gene Bank for other purposes [not

[34] Sándor and Bárd, The Legal Regulation of Biobanks (n. 24) 17.

[35] The Estonian Genome Centre requires that: 'Data and/or biological samples can only be requested to be issued if the Estonian Committee on Bioethics and Human Research ... has positively assessed the research.' University of Tartu Institute of Genomics, 'Issuing of Data and/or Biological Samples' (University of Tartu Institute of Genomics) <http://www.geenivaramu.ee/en/biobank.ee/data-access> accessed 11 December 2019 (hereafter University of Tartu Institute of Genomics, 'Issuing of Data').

[36] The Estonian Genome Centre requires that: 'The Biobank and the person requesting the data and/or biological samples shall enter into a contract.' University of Tartu Institute of Genomics, 'Issuing of Data' (n. 35). The obligation is also elaborated in Ministerial Ordinances. See: Procedure for Issuing Tissue Samples 2019, Article 5 (n. 18).

research], especially to collect evidence in civil or criminal proceedings or for surveillance, is prohibited.'[37] As Keis clarifies: 'Providing any information to insurance companies or employers is prohibited. The information and biological materials collected in the biobank also may not be used in forensic investigations or in court.'[38] There are, however, exceptions outlined in the Act. In particular—as the biobank is part of the Estonian healthcare infrastructure—Article 16(2) permits: 'The doctor of a gene donor... to obtain the decoded description of the state of health of the gene donor... to treat the gene donor.' Under Article 24(2)(7), even these medical transfers are, however, limited. They may only occur in relation to a participant's description of health with the patient's consent.

Beyond the Estonian Biobank, the lack of specific regulation means there is no explicit prohibition on third-party transfers. Such transfers are thus permissible provided they are legitimate under otherwise applicable rules—for example, regarding the scope of consent.

h) Sanctions for Infringements

Estonian law foresees criminal sanctions for infringements of certain substantive genetic privacy provisions. Criminal sanctions outlined in the criminal code are relevant in relation to all types of biobanking activity—to Estonian Biobank activity and beyond. The following five criminal code provisions are most significant. Article 138 criminalises scientific research on human subjects without consent. Articles 138^1 and 140 criminalise forcing individuals to donate samples to research. Finally, Articles 157 and 157^1 criminalise breaches of confidentiality relating to, respectively, professional confidentiality and sensitive data. Violation of these Articles—with the exception of Article 157 relating to breaches of professional confidentiality of non-sensitive data, which only carries a fine—are punishable with non-trivial custodial sentences.

3. Principles in Estonian Law Protecting Genetic Relatives' and Groups' Genetic Privacy on the Relational Axis

a) Protection of Genetic Relatives

Estonian law provides only a vanishingly small extension of protection to genetic relatives. Genetic relatives' rights are only protected in relation to genealogy information in the Estonian Biobank. Genealogy information may allow sensitive information about a participant's genetic relatives to be revealed—for example, unknown familial relationships. Thus, the Act places limitations on the circulation of genealogy information. Two limitations are noteworthy. First, Article 11(2) of the Act excludes genealogy information from the set of information to which research subjects may request access.

[37] In fact, Estonian law goes further than to prohibit access by non-research third parties. Articles 27 and 28 even prohibit employers and insurers from asking for genetic data fed back to participants.

[38] Aime Keis, 'Biobanking in Estonia' (2016) *Journal of Law, Medicine & Ethics* 44(4, pt 1) 20, 22 (hereafter Keis, 'Biobanking in Estonia').

Second. Article 17(1) places restrictions on the purposes for which genealogies may be used: 'Genealogies may be used only within the Gene Bank for structuring tissue samples, descriptions of DNA and descriptions of state of health based on blood relationships.'

b) Protection of Genetic Groups

The protection of genetic groups is non-existent under identified Estonian legislation. As Kaye puts it, Estonian law is underpinned by the 'dominant principle ... of individual rights'.[39] It is thus unsurprising that there is no reference to genetic groups as subjects of protection.

E. German Law *Excluding* Data Protection

1. The Structure of German Law

a) Relevant Law

A search for relevant German legislation reveals many relevant instruments and areas of law.[40] The most significant area of law is property law as outlined in the Bürgerliches Gesetzbuch (BGB)—the German Civil Code. As Albers observes: 'the overwhelming interpretation of the civil law norms is that biological samples constitute a "thing" in the sense of Article 90 of the German Civil Code'.[41] Therefore property law must apply. Property law is supplemented by a range of sector-specific law. The most significant of these for the purposes of this chapter are: the Musterberufsordnung für Ärzte 2015—the Code of Conduct for Doctors; confidentiality duties in Article 203 of the Strafgesetzbuch (StGB)—the Criminal Code; confidentiality duties in Article 35 of the Sozialgesetzbuch I (SGB I)—book 1 of the Social Code; the court-developed concept of Persönlichkeitsrechte—personality rights; the Gendiagnostikgesetz 2009—the Gene

[39] Kaye, Helgason, and Nõmper, 'Population Genetic Databases: A Comparative Analysis' (n. 27) 28.

[40] The quantity of relevant law is apparent with a glance at the tables of legislation provided in Haier's three-part work on biobanking law in Germany. Jörg Haier, 'Gegenwärtige rechtliche Rahmenbedingungen für den Betrieb und die Nutzung von Biobanken. Teil 1: Rechtsgrundlage' (2013) *Der Chirurg* 84(9) 785, 785 (hereafter Haier, 'Gegenwärtige rechtliche Rahmenbedingungen für den Betrieb und die Nutzung von Biobanken. Teil 1'); Jörg Haier, 'Gegenwärtige rechtliche Rahmenbedingungen für den Betrieb und die Nutzung von Biobanken. Teil 2: Datenschutz und Informierte Einwiligung' (2013) *Der Chirurg* 84(10) 892, 892 (hereafter Haier, 'Gegenwärtige rechtliche Rahmenbedingungen für den Betrieb und die Nutzung von Biobanken. Teil 2'); Jörg Haier, 'Gegenwärtige rechtliche Rahmenbedingungen für den Betrieb und die Nutzung von Biobanken. Teil 3: Eigentum und Nutzungsrechte' (2013) *Der Chirurg* 85(10) 918, 918 (hereafter Haier, 'Gegenwärtige rechtliche Rahmenbedingungen für den Betrieb und die Nutzung von Biobanken. Teil 3').

Germany is a federal republic consisting of sixteen states. Each of these states also has certain competence to rule on issues relating to biobanking. A consideration of the various approaches in state laws would be fascinating and worthwhile. This task is, however, beyond the scope of this chapter, which focuses on the federal level.

[41] Bürgerliches Gesetzbuch 2002, Article 90; Marion Albers, 'Rechtsrahmen und Rechtsprobleme bei Biobanken' (2013) *Medizinrecht* 31(8) 483, 486 (hereafter Albers, 'Rechtsrahmen und Rechtsprobleme bei Biobanken'). Translation by the author of: 'Nach der Ausgestaltung und der inzwischen ganz überwiegenden Interpretation der zivilrechtlichen Normen wird ein Körperteil aber mit der Trennung vom Körper eine Sache i. S. des Article 90 BGB'.

Diagnosis Law; and the evidentiary access conditions in Articles 81(a), (c), (e)–(h) and 94 of the Strafprozeßordnung (StPO)—criminal procedural code.[42]

b) Provenance of Law

The development of the relationship between relevant instruments and biobanking shows no overarching intent. As Hoppe observes: 'Despite lengthy discussions about the enactment of a *sui generis* Biobank Act (Biobankengesetz) in Germany, there is currently no dedicated legal framework for this type of research infrastructure.'[43] Rather, German law is comprised of instruments which were never specifically designed for biobanking.

In terms of the development of their relationship to biobanking, instruments can be broken into two groups. First, Hoppe identifies a group of 'abstract norms [adapted to apply] ... to the procurement, storage, and use of human tissues and cells (and associated data)'.[44] This group of instruments have been interpreted to be applicable to biobanking through use, custom and consensus. The group includes, for example, property law under Article 90 of the BGB.

Second, there is legislation which applies to biobanking by virtue of its scope intentionally covering an aspect of biobank activity, without the instrument having been deliberately designed to deal with biobanking activity. This group includes, for example, the Musterberufsordnung für Ärtzte, which was designed to apply to German physicians whenever they conduct research.

c) Applicability of Law

Not one instrument, or area of law, applies comprehensively across the biobanking process. Three different types of limitation are identifiable. First, limitations relating to substances: these impact property rights under Article 90 of the BGB and confidentiality obligations under Article 35 of SGB I. Property rights only apply to biological samples but not to sequenced genomic data or associated health, lifestyle, or biographical data. Indeed, Haier recognises property law may not even apply to copies of a sample: 'more difficult is the question of applicability [of property law] to altered samples, as here, changes to the original content of a sample occurs with the result that a thing with new qualities appears'.[45] Confidentiality duties in Article 35 of SGB I only apply to 'social

[42] Bundesärztekammer, *Musterberufsordnung für die in Deutschland tätigen Ärztinnen und Ärzte* (Policy, 1997 [updated 2018]); Strafgesetzbuch 1998; Sozialgesetzbuch 1975 (updated 2017); Gendiagnostikgesetz 2009.

The Musterberufsordnung is not legislation, but a professional code of conduct. Nevertheless, its significance in regulating the conduct of doctors in Germany conveys a quasi-legal status. Accordingly, it is considered a significant instrument in the German legal framework.

[43] Nils Hoppe, 'Privacy Laws and Biobanking in Germany' (2016) *Journal of Law, Medicine & Ethics* 44(4) 35, 37 (hereafter Hoppe, 'Privacy Laws and Biobanking in Germany'). See also: Jochen Taupitz and Marie Schreiber, 'Biobanken—zwischen Forschungs- und Spenderinteressen' (2016) *Bundesgesundheitsblatt - Gesundheitsforschung - Gesundheitsschutz* 59 304, 304.

[44] Hoppe, 'Privacy Laws and Biobanking in Germany' (n. 43) 37.

[45] Jörg Haier, 'Gegenwärtige rechtliche Rahmenbedingungen für den Betrieb und die Nutzung von Biobanken. Teil 3' (n. 40) 919. Translation by the author of: 'Schwieriger ist die Einordnung von verarbeiteten Biomaterialien, da hier eine Wandlung des Hauptgehaltes der Probe erfolgt ist und neue wesentliche Eigenschaften der Sache ... hinzutreten'.

data'. These are data which are, as Hoppe states, 'processed for the purposes of providing health and social care'.[46]

Second, limitations relating to biobanking actors: these are evident in relation to the Musterberufsordnung für Ärzte and confidentiality obligations in Article 203 of the StGB. As the Preamble to the Musterberufsordnung states: 'physicians in Germany provide themselves with the following Professional Code'.[47] Accordingly, the Ordnung will only apply to biobanks when their activities involve physicians. Confidentiality duties under Article 203 of the StGB only apply to the professions and roles listed in the Article—which may not cover all biobank actors in all situations.

Finally, limitations relating to types of biobanking activities: these impact the Gendiagnostikgesetz, personality rights, and Articles 81(a), (c), (e)–(h) and 94 of the StPO. The Gendiagnostikgesetz clarifies, in Article 2(2) that it does not apply to the use of biological samples or any associated data 'for the purposes of research'. Accordingly, as Albers recognises: 'the Gendiagnostikgesetz is only of peripheral applicability'.[48] Personality rights are likely only to become relevant in relation to specific biobanking activities which negatively impact the personality of a research subject—for example, in relation to morally problematic uses of a biological sample. Finally, Articles 81(a), (c), (e)–(h), and 94 of the StPO will only be relevant in relation to law enforcement uses of substances.

2. Principles in German Law Protecting Research Subjects' Genetic Privacy on the Transactional Axis

a) Oversight

German law requires biobanking actors to submit to oversight only when a physician is engaged in the process. The Musterberufsordnung für Ärzte is the only instrument which outlines oversight requirements. In Article 15, it requires: 'Physicians participating in a research project using human bodily materials or data … linked to a specific individual, must make sure that advice on issues of professional ethics and conduct associated with the project is obtained from an Ethics Committee … before beginning research.'[49] Even where the obligation applies, however, limitations are evident. Specifically, the obligation only applies to identifiable biological substances and associated data and oversight is then only obligatory prior to research activity going ahead—there is apparently no general obligation for ongoing oversight.

[46] Hoppe, 'Privacy Laws and Biobanking in Germany' (n. 43) 42.

[47] Translation by the author of: 'Dafür geben sich die in Deutschland tätigen Ärztinnen und Ärzte die nachstehende Berufsordnung'.

[48] Albers, 'Rechtsrahmen und Rechtsprobleme bei Biobanken' (n. 41) 489. Translation by the author of: 'so dass es bei Biobanken lediglich in Rand- und Sonderkonstellationen greift'.

[49] Translation by the author of: 'Ärztinnen und Ärzte, die sich an einem Forschungsvorhaben beteiligen, bei dem in die Körpermaterialien oder Daten verwendet werden, die sich einem bestimmten Menschen zuordnen lassen, müssen sicherstellen, dass vor der Durchführung des Forschungsvorhabens eine Beratung erfolgt, die auf die mit ihm verbundenen berufsethischen und berufsrechtlichen Fragen zielt und die von einer bei der zuständigen … Ethik-Kommission … durchgeführt wird.'

Authors such as Beier and Lenk observe the significance of biobank registration in Germany. With regard to the German Biobank Registry, they observe: '[Germany is one of] several European countries [which] have established national biobank registries to keep track of existing biobanks'.[50] However, a close look at the function of this registry reveals it plays no legal role in biobank oversight. The registry is not linked to oversight apparatus, and there is no legal obligation on biobanks to register.

b) Legitimation of the Collection and Use of Substances

German law mandates the research subject's consent be obtained to collect, and further use, their biological sample. The consequence of defining biological samples as 'things' under Article 90 of the BGB is that the research subject gains sole right of disposal under Article 903 BGB: 'The owner of a thing may ... deal with the thing at his discretion.' This means a biobanking actor requires research subject consent to collect and use a sample. Albers observes that this obligation is strict. Indeed, she even observes that: 'the research subject does not ... give up their property rights ... by ... leaving their biological sample without comment following a procedure'.[51] Significantly, in no relevant German law is there a parallel consent obligation in relation to research subject data.

The scope of consent permissible under Article 90 remains unclear. Specifically, there remains uncertainty as to the validity of broader forms of consent. The door to broader consent formats is not explicitly closed. However, as the German Ethics Council observes: 'ethics commissions on this aspect vary ... Some require that the donor knows the specific research project for which his sample and data material is to be used.'[52]

c) Rights Retained by the Research Subject in Collected Substances

German law foresees that the research subject retains the right to withdraw consent to the use of their biological sample. It is settled law in Germany that, for consent to be legitimate, it must come with the parallel right to withdraw. As Haier states: 'To ensure that consent is freely given, according to the Bundesgerichtshof, [the right to withdraw consent at any time is a] fundamental principle [and] must be observed.'[53]

It should be noted, however, that the meaning and consequences of withdrawal of consent are unclear. As Kersten observes: 'nobody knows the precise situation at the moment ... what consequence ... withdrawal ... has for the biological samples'.[54] It is

[50] Beier and Lenk, 'Biobanking Strategies and Regulative Approaches in the EU' (n. 6) 76.

[51] Albers, 'Rechtsrahmen und Rechtsprobleme bei Biobanken' (n. 41) 486. Translation by the author of: 'Der Betroffene gibt sein Eigentumsrecht auch keineswegs allein dadurch auf, dass er das Körpermaterial nach einer Invasion oder Untersuchung kommentarlos zurücklässt.'

[52] German Ethics Council, Human Biobanks for Research: Opinion (Opinion, 2010) 18 (hereafter German Ethics Council, Human Biobanks for Research).

[53] Haier, 'Gegenwärtige rechtliche Rahmenbedingungen für den Betrieb und die Nutzung von Biobanken. Teil 2' (n. 40) 897. Translation by the author of: 'Zur Gewährleistung der notwendigen Freiwilligkeit bei der Einwilligung müssen laut BGH folgende Grundsätze beachtet werden ... jederzeitige Widerrufbarkeit.'

[54] Jens Kersten, 'Biobanken sind zu wichtig, um nicht geregelt zu sein' (LMU Medizinrecht Blog Interview, 13 April 2015) <https://www.uni-muenchen.de/forschung/news/2015/kersten_interview_biobanken.html> accessed 11 December 2019. Translation by the author of: 'Aktuell weiß niemand so genau ...welche Wirkung der Widerruf der Einwilligung der Spenderinnen und Spender für die Verwendung ihres Materials und ihrer Daten ... entfaltet' See also: Albers, 'Rechtsrahmen und Rechtsprobleme bei Biobanken' (n. 41) 490–1.

unclear, for example, whether anonymisation of samples would constitute a legitimate response to a withdrawal, or whether destruction would be necessary.

d) Obligations on Biobanking Actors in Relation to Collected Substances

German law clarifies a limited set of biobanking activities are bound by confidentiality obligations. Obligations arise from three sources. First, in the case that a doctor treating a patient is also engaged in research using that patient's substances, Article 9 of the Musterberufsordnung für Ärzte binds the physician to strict professional confidentiality.

Second, civil law, through Article 35 SGB I, places confidentiality duties on the use of 'social data'. As Hoppe recalls: 'Additional norms for the protection of ... "social data" ... are [provided] by a ... statutory duty of confidentiality (Article 35 SGB I).'[55] Accordingly, whenever biobanking actors use of this form of data, they will also be subject to confidentiality obligations.

Finally, criminal law, under Article 203 StGB, outlines a series of professional and official confidentiality obligations.[56] For example, as Hoppe highlights, under Article 203: '[publicly funded biobanking] staff are ... bound by the duty to keep personal secrets confidential'.[57]

e) Transfers of Substances between Jurisdictions

German law places no specific limitations on international transfers of biobanking substances. Provided the transfer proceeds within the scope of a research subject's consent and all other relevant obligations are upheld, there are no specific genetic privacy relevant conditions applicable to transfers outside the country.

f) Transfers of Substances to External Researchers

German law recognises no specific limitations on transfers of substances to external researchers. Provided the transfer is for a purpose covered by the scope of a research subject's consent and to a researcher who will fulfil all other relevant obligations, no further genetic privacy relevant obligations are elaborated.

g) Transfers of Substances to Non-Research Actors

German law appears to foresee the possibility for law enforcement authorities to force access to biobanking substances. The prevailing opinion is that law enforcement actors may force access to substances. Goers, for example, in considering Article 81(a), (c) and (e)–(h) of the StPO—concerning bodily testing and genetic testing and law enforcement—points to the relevance of generally applicable evidentiary seizure conditions under Article 94 in relation to biobanks.[58] The German Ethics Council support

[55] Hoppe, 'Privacy Laws and Biobanking in Germany' (n. 43) 42.

[56] Johannes Drepper, 'Data Protection in Biobanks from a Practical Point of View: What Must Be Taken into Account During Set-up and Operation?' (2019) *Journal of Laboratory Medicine* 43(6) 301, 302.

[57] Hoppe, 'Privacy Laws and Biobanking in Germany' (n. 43) 42.

[58] Matthias Goers, 'StPO § 81e Molekulargenetische Untersuchung', in Jürgen-Peter Graf (ed.), *Beck'scher Online-Kommentar StPO mit RiStBV und MiStra* (29th Edition, Beck 2018) rn. 6 <https://beck-online.beck.de/?vpath=bibdata/komm/beckok_29_BandStPO/cont/beckok.StPO%2Ehtm> accessed 11 December 2019.

this position in observing: 'In Germany... it is in principle possible for... security services to access biobank samples and data.'[59]

Other non-research actors—such as insurance companies or employers—under identified law, cannot force access to biobanking substances. However, in no law is there a strict prohibition concerning their potential to access biobanking substances. Transfers to non-research actors might thus go ahead provided these fulfil all other generally applicable legal requirements—for example, if they are explicitly permitted in a consent protocol.[60]

h) Sanctions for Infringements

German law provides a range of sanctions for breaches of principles protecting research subject privacy. Two types of sanctions are identifiable. First, sanctions relate to the misuse of biological samples. In this regard, Haier observes that research subjects may pursue civil sanctions for a missing, flawed, or ignored consent agreement under compensation provisions in Articles 253 or 823 of the BGB.[61] Further, he observes that if the sample is misappropriated, criminal sanctions under Article 246 of the StGB may also be available.[62]

Second, sanctions relate to misuses of research subject data. Civil sanctions are available for breaches of duties of confidentiality under, for example, Article 35 SGB I. Criminal sanctions may also be available for certain more serious breaches of confidentiality under either the Musterberufsordnung für Ärtzte or Article 203 of the StGB.

3. Principles in German Law Protecting Genetic Relatives' and Groups' Genetic Privacy on the Relational Axis

a) Protection of Genetic Relatives

Genetic relatives do not constitute a subject of protection in any relevant identified German law. There are instances in which genetic relatives' rights in a research subject's genomic information are recognised in German law. Most importantly, Article 10 of the Gendiagnostikgesetz recognises that results emerging from genetic testing may be significant for genetic relatives—although the highly limited relevance of this law for biobanking should be borne in mind. The legal response, however, is simply to recommend to the test subject that they inform relatives to seek genetic counselling. Accordingly, even when relatives' rights are recognised, rather than offering them direct protection, the position is restated that all protection is reserved for the research subject.

[59] German Ethics Council, Human Biobanks for Research (n. 52) 14.

[60] It should also be noted that, should a biobank feed information back to a donor, the donor may be required to divulge this information to third parties. For example, Article 19 of the Gendiagnostikgesetz elaborates an obligation to divulge insurance relevant information for certain insurances when contracts worth over a certain amount are being concluded.

[61] Jörg Haier, 'Gegenwärtige rechtliche Rahmenbedingungen für den Betrieb und die Nutzung von Biobanken. Teil 3' (n. 40) 924.

[62] Haier, 'Gegenwärtige rechtliche Rahmenbedingungen für den Betrieb und die Nutzung von Biobanken. Teil 1' (n. 40) 791.

b) Protection of Genetic Groups

Genetic groups do not constitute a subject of protection in any relevant identified German law. As opposed to genetic relatives, the rights of genetic groups have received no consideration in German law at all.

F. UK Law *Excluding* Data Protection

1. The Structure of UK Law

a) Relevant Law

A search for UK legislation reveals a startling number of relevant instruments and areas of law. The key piece of legislation is the Human Tissue Act 2004—which regulates the removal, storage, and use of human tissue, including for research. The Act is further clarified by authoritative guidance from the Human Tissue Authority. Alongside the Human Tissue Act, a range other statutory instruments also play a role—either in augmenting and clarifying the Act, or in providing specific rules relevant to specific biobanking activities. In this regard, Kaye et al. highlight the following as significant:[63] The National Health Service Act 2006; the Regulatory Enforcement and Sanctions Act 2008; the Health and Social Care Act 2012; and the Care Act 2014.[64] The Police and Criminal Evidence Act 1984 and the Health Service (Control of Patient Information) Regulations 2002 are also relevant.[65] Alongside statutory legislation, jurisprudence and common law doctrine also play a role. On the one hand, Kaye et al. observe the lack of specific case law relating to biobanking: 'As yet, there have been no reported cases that have related specifically to biobanking.'[66] On the other hand, however, they observe the relevance of existing jurisprudential principles: 'in many areas relevant to biobanking ... crucial issues are decided by case law'.[67] In this regard, the common law doctrine of confidentiality is particularly important.

b) Provenance of Law

No instrument in UK law was designed to deal with biobanking. Rather, applicable law has emerged ad hoc. As Kaye et al. observe, relevant statutory law developed unconnected to the specifics of biobanking but rather has: 'come about in a reactionary, ad hoc way, in

[63] Jane Kaye, Jessica Bell, Linda Briceno, et al., 'Biobank Report: United Kingdom' (2016) *Journal of Law, Medicine & Ethics* 44(4, pt 2) 96, 98 (hereafter Kaye, Bell, Briceno, et al., 'Biobank Report: United Kingdom'). Kaye et al. also highlight other instruments which play a more minor role. For example, the Computer Misuse Act 1990, and the Human Fertilisation and Embryology Act 2008.

[64] National Health Service Act 2006; Regulatory Enforcement and Sanctions Act 2008; Health and Social Care Act 2012; Care Act 2014.

[65] Health Service (Control of Patient Information) Regulations 2002.

[66] Kaye, Bell, Briceno, et al., 'Biobank Report: United Kingdom' (n. 63) 98.

[67] Kaye, Bell, Briceno, et al., 'Biobank Report: United Kingdom' (n. 63) 98. See also, for an example of the significance of case law concerning confidentiality: Ian Brown, Lindsey Brown, and Douwe Korff, 'Using NHS Patient Data for Research Without Consent' (2010) *Law Innovation and Technology* 2(2) 219, 234–7; Onora O'Neil and Charles Manson, *Rethinking Informed Consent in Bioethics* (Cambridge University Press 2007) 26–68.

response to public health scandals.'[68] This is true, for example, in relation to the Human Tissue Act. The Act was passed as a response to a series of tissue retention scandals in UK hospitals. As Price comments: 'The Act is principally a response to the furore generated by responses to the retention and use of human tissue in the Bristol Royal Infirmary... and Alder Hey Children's Hospital ... Inquiry Reports ... [which] catalogued local practices resulting in relatives... of dead children, lacking appreciation of... tissue retention and use for research.'[69]

Relevant jurisprudence and common law doctrine have also developed ad hoc. Unlike the development of statutory instruments, however, relevant common law doctrine has been developed predominantly in reaction to cases concerning clinical medicine. For example, the latest relevant case concerning the confidentiality doctrine—*ABC v. St George's Healthcare NHS Trust & Others*—deals with relatives' access to genetic information in the clinical setting.[70]

c) Applicability of Law

There is no single identified UK instrument or area of law which applies across the biobanking process.[71] Broadly speaking, in terms of applicability, two groups of law emerge. The first group consists of law applicable to the collection and use of samples. The Human Tissue Act has the broadest applicability here. The scope of the Act encompasses the extraction and use of biological samples for research and the extraction and use of genetic data from samples. In the biobanking context, however, there are notable limitations to its applicability. In particular, the Act only applies to 'relevant material'. This concept does not encompass, as Gibbons observes: '[a]cellular, subcellular and genetic materials— such as extracted DNA'. [72] Nor does it include biological samples manufactured outside the body—such as immortal cell lines.

The second group consists of law predominantly applicable to research subject data. In terms of statutory instruments, the Health Service (Control of Patient Information) Regulations, the National Health Service Act, the Health and Social Care Act, and the Care Act all apply only to research subject data. They do not, however, apply to all types of biobanking data. Rather, they only apply to NHS patient data. In terms of common

[68] Kaye, Bell, Briceno, et al., 'Biobank Report: United Kingdom' (n. 63) 97.

[69] David Price, 'The Human Tissue Act 2004' (2005) *Modern Law Review* 68(5) 798, 798.

[70] *ABC v. St George's Healthcare NHS Trust & Others* [2020] EWHC 455 (QB) (hereafter *ABC v. St George's Healthcare NHS Trust & Others*).

[71] Due to the constitutional make-up of the UK—the UK consists of England, Scotland, Wales, and Northern Ireland—there are certain regional differences in applicable law. For example, the Human Tissue Act actually only applies in England, Wales, and Northern Ireland whilst Scotland has bespoke legislation. Nevertheless, it is customary to speak of UK law. A consideration of regional specificities would be interesting and worthwhile but outside the scope of the chapter. See, for example, Kaye, Bell, Briceno, et al., 'Biobank Report: United Kingdom' (n. 63) 96–105.

[72] Susan Gibbons, 'Mapping the Regulatory Space', in Jane Kaye, Susan M. C. Gibbons, Catherine Heeney, Michael Parker, and Andrew Smart (eds.), *Governing Biobanks: Understanding the Interplay between Law and Practice* (Hart Publishing 2012) 51, 71 (hereafter Gibbons, 'Mapping the Regulatory Space'); Human Tissue Authority, *Guidance on Relevant Material* (Policy, 2014) <https://www.hta.gov.uk/policies/relevant-material-under-human-tissue-act-2004> accessed 12 December 2019.

law doctrine, confidentiality can only apply to research subject data. This doctrine, however, also employs supplemental applicability criteria restricting its applicability to types of biobanking data. In the first instance, the doctrine only applies to identifiable data. The *Source Informatics* judgment clarifies that, as soon as data have been anonymised or pseudonymised, the doctrine ceases to apply.[73] As Grubb observed in his commentary on the case: 'disclosure of anonymised information can *never* be a breach of confidence'.[74] In turn, in relation to identifiable information, the doctrine will only certainly be engaged in biobanking if certain types of professional relationship are in play—for example, doctor–patient relationships. Apart from these, as Nicholas observes, applicability will be dependent on 'the circumstances in which [information] is disclosed [and the expectations of the parties involved]'.[75]

2. Principles in UK Law Protecting Research Subjects' Genetic Privacy on the Transactional Axis

a) Oversight

UK law outlines a multilayered system of oversight relevant for biobanking actors. This system consists of two key bodies. First, in Part 2 and Schedule 2 of the Human Tissue Act, the Human Tissue Authority is made responsible for oversight of the provisions of the Act.[76] Articles 15 and 16 outline the obligation for biobanking actors using 'relevant material', to consult with, and receive approval from, the Authority in advance of research. The Authority clarifies that, in certain cases, biobanks can request broad advance approval: 'The HTA [permits] generic ... approval for a research tissue bank's arrangements for collection, storage and release of tissue.'[77] Such broad approval can also extend to the activities of external researchers using a biobank's substances. Following advance approval, according to Article 48 and Schedule 5 of the Act, the Human Tissue Authority has the power to conduct ongoing oversight of biobanking actors. This oversight may include inspections which check for ongoing compliance with the Act and conditions imposed on advance approval.

Second, Research Ethics Committees also play a significant role. There is no general obligation to obtain Research Ethics Committee approval in UK law. Research Ethics Committee approval is, however, relevant in a range of cases concerning biobanking.

[73] *R v. Department of Health ex parte Source Informatics Limited* [1999] All ER (D) 1491.

[74] Andrew Grubb, 'Breach of Confidence: Anonymised Information' (2000) *Medical Law Review* 8(1) 115, 118.

[75] Nick Nicholas, 'Risk Management: Confidentiality, Disclosure and Access to Medical Records' (2007) *The Obstetrician and Gynaecologist* 9 257, 258 (hereafter Nicholas, 'Risk Management').

Other legislation applies in specific cases. For example, the Police and Criminal Evidence Act 1984 applies only concerning police access to biobanking substances.

[76] See also: Andelka M. Phillips and Tamara K. Hervey, 'Brexit and Biobanking: GDPR Perspectives', in Santa Slokenberga, Olga Tzortzatou, and Jane Reichel (eds.), *GDPR and Biobanking: Individual Rights, Public Interest and Research Regulation across Europe* (Springer 2021) 145, 150–151.

[77] Human Tissue Authority, Code of Practice E: Research (Policy, 2017) 24 (hereafter Human Tissue Authority, Code of Practice E)

Two are particularly significant.[78] First, approval will be required when the Human Tissue Act applies and, according to Section 1 of the Act, no consent for processing has been obtained from the research subject for use of their substances. Significantly, Human Tissue Authority guidance recognises that certain Research Ethics Committees are also entitled to grant broad ethical approval to biobanks: 'The HTA and the HRA's Research Ethics Service (HRA RES) have agreed a position whereby its RECs can give generic ethical approval.'[79] As with approval from the Human Tissue Authority, generic approval extends beyond the biobank itself to cover external researchers using a biobank's substances. Second, approval will be required according to Section 117 of the Care Act when NHS patient information is involved and no consent from the subject is available.

b) Legitimation of the Collection and Use of Substances

UK law generally requires consent be obtained from a research subject to collect, store, and use biological samples and genomic data. The general requirement under the Human Tissue Act is that consent is obtained from a subject to use biological samples and conduct genomic analysis. The explanatory note to the Act clarifies: '[The Act] will make consent the fundamental principle underpinning the lawful storage and use of human bodies ... and tissue.'[80] Section 1 elaborates this obligation for biological samples. Section 45 then elaborates the requirement for the analysis, and results of analysis, of DNA. The general principle that consent should be obtained is, however, not absolute. The Human Tissue Act foresees two significant exceptions: first, where samples were collected before 2006; and second, where tissue comes from a living person but the researcher involved has no way of identifying this person and where the biobank, or project, in question has been approved in advance by a Research Ethics Committee.[81]

Significantly, there is no general rule evident in identified UK law relating to the need to obtain consent to collect non-genetic research subject data—for example, health, lifestyle, and biography information. However, whenever a duty of confidentiality applies, then consent will generally be needed before data can be used in research. The only exception to this rule is when specific conditions outlined in the Health Service (Control of Patient Information) Regulations, the National Health Service Act, and the Care Act are fulfilled—including that Research Ethics Committee approval, and Health Research Authority approval, is granted.[82]

The question of the scope of consent has received no direct statutory consideration in UK law. However, the Human Tissue Authority has provided guidance stating that

[78] See: Health and Social Care, NHS Research Scotland, Health and Care Research Wales, NHS Health Research Authority, Governance arrangements for research ethics committees: 2020 edition (Policy, 2020) 30–2.

[79] Human Tissue Authority, Code of Practice E (n. 77) 25. Gibbons also argues that Research Ethics Committees play, *de facto*, a significant role in biobank oversight: 'because the Department of Health, NHS, GMC, professional associations and all leading research funding bodies ... typically insist upon prior ethical approval'. Gibbons, 'Mapping the Regulatory Space' (n. 72) 77–8.

[80] UK Parliament, Human Tissue Act 2004 Explanatory Note (Policy, 2004).

[81] Human Tissue Authority, Code of Practice E (n. 77) 16–17.

[82] NHS Health Research Authority, 'The Health Service (Control of Patient Information) Regulations 2002: regulation 5 decision procedure for research applications' (NHS Health Research Authority, 2017) <https://

'generic consent' may be sought by biobanking actors.[83] With the concept of generic consent, they appear to refer to broad—non-project specific—consent.[84]

c) Rights Retained by the Research Subject in Collected Substances

Relevant UK law foresees that research subjects retain the right to withdraw consent to the use of their samples and genomic data. The Human Tissue Act provides the research subject with the right to withdraw consent to the legitimate use of their biological sample or genomic data. According to the Human Tissue Authority, a withdrawal of consent can take place at any time and means that samples can no longer be stored or used for the purpose for which consent was given.[85] A withdrawal of consent is normally followed by the destruction of a sample, according to the Human Tissue Authority.[86]

Despite the apparently extensive scope of the right, there are limitations. In particular, the right will not extend to the destruction or removal of samples or genomic data stored in relation to completed, or ongoing, research projects. As the Human Tissue Authority explicitly clarify: 'Withdrawal of consent cannot be acted upon where tissue has already been used . . . In addition, if someone withdraws consent for samples to be used in . . . future projects, this does not mean . . . information and research data should be withdrawn from . . . existing projects.'[87]

d) Obligations on Biobanking Actors in Relation to Collected Substances

Relevant UK law foresees two obligations on biobanking actors in relation to collected substances. First, governance and quality control obligations. In relation to biological samples and genomic data, the Human Tissue Authority clarifies that: 'Establishments [processing samples and genomic data must] . . . be able to demonstrate that they have a suitable governance framework, underpinned by clear and controlled documentation, effective audit, staff training . . . an effective system of risk management and suitable systems to deal with adverse events.'[88]

Second, security and confidentiality obligations. These emerge from two sources. In the first instance, the Human Tissue Act requires biobanking actors to ensure the security of samples and genomic data. As the Human Tissue Authority state: 'Establishments meeting . . . Standards will be able to demonstrate . . . their premises . . . are appropriate for their licensed activities and are safe [and] secure.'[89] In turn,

www.hra.nhs.uk/about-us/committees-and-services/confidentiality-advisory-group/guidance-confidentiality-advisory-group-applicants/health-service-control-patient-information-regulations-2002-regulation-5-decision-procedure-research-applications/> accessed 16 June 2020.

[83] Human Tissue Authority, Code of Practice A: Guiding principles and the fundamental principle of consent (Policy, 2017) 11 (hereafter Human Tissue Authority, Code of Practice A).

[84] This is the form of consent used by the UK Biobank. UK Biobank, Consent Form: UK Biobank (Policy, 2011) 1 <http://www.ukbiobank.ac.uk/wp-content/uploads/2011/06/Consent_form.pdf> accessed 11 December 2019.

[85] Human Tissue Authority, Code of Practice A (n. 83) 13.

[86] Human Tissue Authority, Code of Practice 5: Disposal of human tissue (Policy, 2014) 19.

[87] Human Tissue Authority, Code of Practice A (n. 83) 13.

[88] Human Tissue Authority, Code of Practice E (n. 77) 32.

[89] Human Tissue Authority, Code of Practice E (n. 77) 33.

in relation to both genomic data and associated health, lifestyle, and biography information, obligations emerge from the common law duty of confidentiality. When confidentiality might be expected from a biobanking actor, the doctrine requires the actor to take all relevant steps to prevent illegitimate access to information—including adequate security precautions.

e) Transfers of Substances between Jurisdictions

UK law only foresees limitations on the international transfers of substances in relation to biological samples. In relation to the Human Tissue Act, the Human Tissue Authority clarifies that: 'material should be procured, used, handled, stored, transported and disposed, in accordance with the consent which has been given, with due regard for safety considerations and with the dignity and respect accorded to human bodies, body parts and tissue.'[90] Thus, in order to legitimate transfers, the Authority requires UK law is adhered to as samples are transferred.

The lack of provisions in identified law relating to research subject data means transfers of such data abroad may proceed provided they meet otherwise applicable conditions—such as relevant consent conditions.

f) Transfers of Substances to External Researchers

UK law is permissive to the transfer of substances between biobanks and external researchers. Provided the transfer is for a purpose covered by the scope of a subject's consent—or another legitimate purpose—and to a researcher who fulfils all otherwise relevant obligations, no specific limitations are apparent.

g) Transfers of Substances to Non-Research Actors

UK law foresees the possibility for law enforcement access to biobanking substances. Kaye observes that under Sections 8 and 9 of the Police and Criminal Evidence Act: 'In order to gain access to medical information and DNA information in [biobanks], police could approach the custodian directly or apply for an access order through the courts.'[91] The decision to comply or refuse an access order would lie with the biobanking actor—subject to their understanding of confidentiality. Any refusal may then result in a court appearance. In court, a biobanking actor may then be forced to grant access.[92]

Other non-research actors, however, have no legal ability to force access to biobanking substances. Nevertheless, there is no outright prohibition on such actors' accessing biobank substances in identified UK law either. Accordingly, such third parties may legitimately gain access if this fulfils otherwise applicable criteria—for

[90] See Human Tissue Authority, Code of Practice 8: Import and export of human bodies, body parts and tissue (Policy, 2014) 10.

[91] Jane Kaye, 'Police Collection and Access to DNA Samples' (2006) *Genomics, Society and Policy* 2(1) 16, 23.

[92] The UK Biobank confirm the possibility for police access: 'we [will not] allow access to the police ... unless forced ... by the courts'. UK Biobank, Information Leaflet (Information Leaflet, 2011) 9 <http://www.ukbiobank.ac.uk/wp-content/uploads/2011/06/Participant_information_leaflet.pdf?phpMyAdmin=trmKQlYdjjnQIgJ%2CfAzikMhEnx6> accessed 11 December 2019.

example, if a non-research use of a biological sample was included within the scope of consent.[93]

h) Sanctions for Infringements

In certain instances when substantive provisions are violated, UK law foresees sanctions. Sanctions emerge from two sources. First, the Human Tissue Act: the Act outlines several criminal sanctions relating to infringements. In particular, the Act clarifies that the illegitimate distribution and use of biological samples and the illegitimate analysis of DNA—in Sections 5 and 45 respectively—are criminal offences carrying custodial sentences. As an alternative to criminal sanctions—where these are available under the Act—the Regulatory Enforcement and Sanctions Act grants the Human Tissue Authority a range of alternative powers. These include the ability to issue stop notices, issue compliance obligations, or issue restoration requirements.[94] Where criminal sanctions are not available for infringements of provisions under the Act, Section 3 also grants the Human Tissue Authority a range of softer powers. In particular, the Authority has the power to withdraw or suspend a biobanking actor's approval to engage in the collection, storage, or use of biological samples or genomic data.

Second, civil law: civil sanctions might be brought by a research subject following a breach of confidentiality principles. These include, as Nicholas observes, 'injunction[s] ... declaration[s] ... damages ... [and/or] restitutionary damages'.[95]

3. Principles in UK Law Protecting Genetic Relatives' and Groups' Genetic Privacy on the Relational Axis

a) Protection of Genetic Relatives

Relevant identified UK law offers little explicit recognition of genetic relatives' genetic privacy rights. Genetic relatives do appear as topics of legal consideration in UK law directly relevant to biobanking. Family members, for example, are mentioned in the Human Tissue Act and in Human Tissue Authority guidance—for example, in Section 26 of the Human Tissue Act and in the Human Tissue Authority's guidance on post-mortem examination.[96] In none of these cases, however, is there a clear recognition

[93] In relation to insurance, a Code of Practice has been agreed between the UK government and the Association of British Insurers that certain types of genetic information may be used to evaluate certain insurance claims. The Code currently, however, only allows test for 'Huntington's disease, for life insurance coverage totalling above £500,000 per individual' to be used and suggests 'that insurers will not ask customers to provide results of tests obtained exclusively in the context of scientific research'. In relation to employment, the Equality Act 2010—in particular Article 60 of the Act—permits employers to ask for genetic information in two cases: first, when the information is relevant in terms of a potential employee's ability to carry out a job; and second, when the information is relevant in terms of modifications the employer might need to make to the workspace. Equality Act 2010, Article 60.

[94] See: Gibbons, 'Mapping the Regulatory Space' (n. 72) 72–3.

[95] Nicholas, 'Risk Management' (n. 75) 261.

[96] Human Tissue Authority, Code of Practice B: Post-Mortem Examination (Policy, 2017) 5.

of the need to protect relatives' genetic privacy rights. In the two examples given, for example, family members only appear as relevant stakeholders in decisions concerning the use of a deceased relative's remains.

b) Protection of Genetic Groups

Identified UK law offers little recognition of genetic groups' genetic privacy rights. Certain types of group—religious and cultural groups—which may correspond to certain genetic classes are subjects of consideration in UK law. They are considered in both the Human Tissue Act and Human Tissue Authority guidance. In its guidance on consent, for example, the Human Tissue Authority observes: 'Attitudes towards the use of tissue ... may vary widely among cultures and religions.'[97] References to such groups, however, do not extend to providing them with any clear protection.

The previous sections provided a descriptive analysis of the approach to the protection of genetic privacy in biobanking under EU, Estonian, German, and UK law *excluding* through data protection. This descriptive analysis provides the basis for a critique of the efficacy of the protection provided by these systems. Naturally, only if protection can be found to be deficient is there any need to consider European data protection law at all. This critique is structured around five questions:

1. Are systems, *excluding* data protection, suitably structured to provide optimal protection for genetic privacy in biobanking? Specifically, are systems comprehensively applicable and internally coherent?
2. Do systems, *excluding* data protection, provide protection for the full range of genetic privacy rights engaged by biobanking in relation to the research subject along the transactional axis?[98]
3. Do systems, *excluding* data protection, provide protection for the full range of genetic privacy rights engaged by biobanking in relation to genetic relatives and genetic groups along the relational axis?
4. Do systems, *excluding* data protection, where they provide protection for genetic privacy rights, provide adequate protection?
5. Given biobanking is an increasingly international endeavour, do systems, *excluding* data protection, provide harmonised, or compatible, approaches?

Considering analysed legal systems through the prism of these questions reveals numerous problems with each system.

[97] Human Tissue Authority, Code of Practice A (n. 83) 15.
[98] See chapter 4, section D.

G. Problems of Structure: No System—*Excluding* Data Protection—Is Optimally Structured to Protect Genetic Privacy in Biobanking

Excluding data protection, not one state's system is optimally structured for the protection of genetic privacy in biobanking. Not one state's system is either comprehensive or cogent.

Excluding data protection, Estonian law is only comprehensive and cogent in relation to the Estonian Biobank. The core of the Estonian system is the Human Genes Research Act. As the purpose of the Act is to provide a legal basis for the Estonian Biobank, the Act is relatively comprehensive and cogent as far as this biobank is concerned. The significance of this should not be underestimated. The Estonian Biobank constitutes the centre of mass of Estonian biobanking. As Leitsalu et al. observe: 'the Estonian Genome Center ... cohort [is] the largest epidemiological cohort not just in Estonia but in the whole Baltic region'.[99]

However, Keis recognises that there may be a 'great amount of non-official collection of tissue samples' done outside the confines of the Estonian Biobank.[100] It is true that certain identifiable law applies beyond the Estonian Biobank. Recall that provisions of the criminal code have broad applicability. This law is, however, far from cogent. Provisions of the criminal code remain vague in relation to biobanking. For example, recall that, whilst there is a requirement to obtain consent to conduct research on samples extracted from a research subject, there is no clarification as to what scope of consent would be regarded as legitimate. In turn, the relationship between these provisions and the Human Genes Research Act is unclear. For example, the Human Genes Research Act recognises the legitimacy of broad consent. Yet, it is unclear whether this recognition can serve as a guiding principle beyond the confines of the Estonian Biobank.

Excluding data protection, German law exhibits clear problems in relation to both comprehensiveness and cogency. Regarding comprehensiveness, there are large gaps in the applicability of identified German law to research subject data—genetic and otherwise—both collected and generated in biobanking. The only protection for genetic privacy rights in research subject data comes through confidentiality law. Unfortunately, each piece of German confidentiality legislation only appears to apply in limited cases of biobanking. Recall, as discussed in section 5: the Musterberufsordnung für Ärzte applies only to the doctor–patient relationship;

[99] Leitsalu, Alavere, and Tammesoo, 'Linking a Population Biobank with National Health Registries' (n. 26) 97.
[100] Keis, 'Biobanking in Estonia' (n. 38) 23.

Article 35 SGB I only applies to biobanks using health records and even then, only to those health records; and Article 203 StGB only applies to the professions and roles explicitly listed in the Article.

Regarding cogency, the applicability of several principles outlined in identified law is uncertain. Uncertainty exists concerning both the scope and content of identified law. In relation to scope, for example, recall Haier's observation regarding the uncertain applicability of property law to copies of samples and Albers' observation that the limits of personality rights in samples remain speculative. [101] In relation to content, for example, recall the lack of clarity in relation to the scope and consequences of withdrawal of consent.

Excluding data protection, UK law exhibits clear problems in relation to comprehensiveness and cogency. Regarding comprehensiveness, gaps exist in relation to the applicability of identified law to both biological samples and associated data. Concerning biological samples, the Human Tissue Act has broad applicability, yet does not apply to acellular samples or copies of samples—despite these containing a copy of a subject's complete genome. Indeed, As Kaur and Dufour observe, copies might be used for exactly this reason: 'Immortal cell lines are often used in research ... as they ... bypass ... concerns associated with the use of ... human tissue.'[102] Concerning research subject data, gaps in protection are even larger. The key statutory instruments only relate to NHS patient data. The common law doctrine of confidentiality can, in principle, apply to all genetic privacy relevant data about a research subject. However, the doctrine only becomes relevant when confidentiality can be presumed to exist in a relationship and the data in question have not been pseudonymised or anonymised. There is no guarantee these criteria will be fulfilled in biobanking.

Regarding cogency, two problems are identifiable. First, the number and diversity of relevant instruments and areas of law applicable make the UK system difficult to navigate. Indeed, navigation has even proven difficult for legal scholars. Gibbons, for example, observes 'a frankly bewildering array of [law]'.[103] Second, in many instances—particularly, but not solely, in relation to common law doctrine—the applicability of principles remains vague. Recall, for example, that, whilst it is clear the doctrine of confidentiality can apply to biobanking, it is far less clear when it will apply. Outside specific professional relationships—namely doctor–patient relationships—there is little elaboration of criteria clarifying when parties might have legitimate expectations that such a duty of exists.

[101] Jörg Haier, 'Gegenwärtige rechtliche Rahmenbedingungen für den Betrieb und die Nutzung von Biobanken. Teil 3' (n. 40) 919; Albers, 'Rechtsrahmen und Rechtsprobleme bei Biobanken' (n. 41) 486.

[102] Gurvinder Kaur and Jannette Dufour, 'Cell Lines: Valuable Tools or Useless Artefacts' (2012) *Spermatogenesis* 2(1) 1, 1.

[103] Gibbons, 'Mapping the Regulatory Space' (n. 72) 53.

H. Problems with the Protection of Research Subjects' Genetic Privacy: *Excluding* Data Protection, Only Estonia Protects the Full Range of Genetic Privacy Rights

Excluding data protection, only one state's system offers protection for the full range of research subject genetic privacy rights in biobanking. In the two other instances, protection for certain types of genetic privacy rights is absent without justification.

Excluding data protection, the Estonian framework provides protection for each research subject's genetic privacy right on the transactional axis. The only right not explicitly referenced in Estonian law is the spatial privacy right not to be informed of harmful information relating to one's genome. It is the case that relevant harmful genetic information could be produced during research in Estonia and that this could, under current law, be transmitted to the research subject. The right thus appears to be relevant but not protected. Recall, however, that this right only becomes relevant where biobank researchers need to decide whether to feed information back or not. In a system in which research subjects are already granted the right to choose to know and not know their genetic information and are informed of this right during the consent procedure, the spatial privacy right is not at issue.

Excluding data protection, German law provides protection for neither information privacy rights to choose to know and not to know one's own genetic data nor the spatial privacy right not to be informed of harmful genetic information. There are academic arguments about the recognition of these rights in German law. Haier, for example, proposes that such rights might be conceived out of a broad reading of fundamental personality rights: 'In the framework of ... personality rights, the research subject should have the rights to know and not know ... important results in so far as they impact ... personal interests.'[104] Indeed, the information privacy rights to know and not know, at least, have received explicit legal recognition in relation to genetic data in the Gendiagnostikgesetz. Article 11 recognises the right of a subject of genetic analysis to request feedback of results from genetic tests.

Such arguments, however, cannot be accepted. Academic arguments remain disputed and lack clear legislative or jurisprudential support. Hummel and Krawczak, for example, suggest that the current German legal situation rather leaves the rights unprotected.[105] In turn, the Gendiagnostikgesetz does not apply directly to research activity.

The lack of protection would not be an issue if clear justifications, specific to the German context, were evident. This does not appear to be the case. It seems likely that the lack of protection for these rights emerges—rather than from deliberate intent—from a lack of legislative or jurisprudential consideration. Perhaps this should

[104] Haier, 'Gegenwärtige rechtliche Rahmenbedingungen für den Betrieb und die Nutzung von Biobanken. Teil 2' (n. 40) 898. Translation by the author of: 'im Rahmen des Schutzes seiner Persönlichkeit [sollte der Spender] auch das Recht auf Wissen und Nichtwissen [haben] ... Der Spender sollte über Ergebnisse der Forschung informiert werden, sofern die gewonnene Information von entscheidendem persönlichem Interesse für ihn ist'.

[105] Michael Hummel and Michael Krawczak, 'Biobanken im Spannungsfeld zwischen Forschung und Gesellschaft' (2007) *Information Technology* 49(6) 335, 336.

be no surprise, given the legal framework consists of law which is neither specific to biobanking, nor to the genetic privacy issues the activity raises.

Excluding data protection, UK law ignores the information privacy rights to choose to know and not to know one's own genetic data and the spatial privacy right not to be informed of harmful genetic information. It is not the case that rights in relation to information produced during research have completely avoided discussion in UK legal thinking. Johnston and Kaye, for example, recognise that, under the doctrine of negligence, if a research reveals a subject is suffering from a 'serious treatable condition', biobanks could be under a 'duty of care to provide feedback to those . . . affected'.[106] From here, it is only a short step to make an argument supporting the spatial privacy right not to know: if a biobank has an obligation to avoid harm in relation to genetic information produced in research, then surely a biobank could also be argued to be obliged to avoid providing information which could cause harm?

Unfortunately, such arguments stop short of confirming either information or spatial privacy rights to know or not know in biobanking. In relation to information privacy rights, it is notable that, in these arguments, research subject choice plays no role. Rather, the biobank is under an obligation to communicate irrespective of research subject wishes—the obligation would in fact serve to override this form of privacy. In relation to the spatial privacy right, the supporting argument does not, unfortunately, enjoy legal support. UK law currently weighs heavily against the recognition of obligations related to withholding genetic information from a relevant party. The question has been most consistently considered in relation to information in the clinical context—where the decision to withhold information would usually be better informed than the biobanking context. In this context, Brownsword observes of the current legal position: 'healthcare professionals must restrain any paternalistic impulses that they might have'.[107] Given this seems to be the dominant position in the clinical context, it is hard to see how the spatial privacy right not to know could be recognised in the biobanking context.

The lack of protection would not be an issue if clear justifications, specific to the UK context, were evident. This does not appear to be the case. In relation to the information privacy rights to know and not know, it seems likely the lack of protection eventuates, rather than from deliberate intent, from a lack of legislative or jurisprudential consideration. In relation to the spatial privacy right not to know, the argument referring to the primacy of the right to be informed in the UK might be put forward as a country-specific justification for lack of protection. The argument, however, does not justify an absolute lack of protection. There is UK jurisprudence recognising the fact that exceptions to the general principle of informing the patient in the clinical context are conceivable. As the UK Supreme Court observed in *Montgomery v. Lanarkshire*, exceptions to the principle may exist when revelations would be: 'seriously detrimental to

[106] Carolyn Johnston and Jane Kaye, 'Does the UK Biobank Have a Legal Obligation to Feedback Individual Findings to Participants?' (2004) *Medical Law Review* 12(3) 239, 261. See also: Heather Widdows and Sean Cordell, 'The Ethics of Biobanking: Key Issues and Controversies' (2011) *Health Care Analysis* 19 207, 215.

[107] Roger Brownsword and Jeff Wale, 'The Right to Know and the Right Not to Know Revisited: Part One' (2017) *Asian Bioethics Review* 9 3, 9.

the patient's health'.[108] This exception, however, cannot be used to justify a recognition for the spatial privacy right in biobanking. In the first instance, it does not relate to the biobanking context. Equally, as Cave observes: 'few cases refer to [this exception,] even fewer apply it and none have accepted it as a defence'.[109] Nevertheless, it serves as a recognition there are no monolithic obstacles to protecting the right in UK law.

I. Problems with the Protection of Genetic Relatives' and Genetic Groups' Genetic Privacy: No System—*Excluding* Data Protection—Protects Genetic Relatives or Groups

Excluding data protection, no state's system provides protection for either genetic relatives or genetic groups. Not only is protection absent, but in each case, it is absent without justification.

Excluding data protection, the Estonian system fails to provide protection for either genetic relatives or genetic groups—except the vanishingly small recognition of relatives' rights in genealogy information. There is reason, in the Estonian context, to consider whether this lack of protection may indeed be legitimate. The previous chapter outlined policy arguments potentially justifying limitations on the protection offered to genetic relatives and genetic groups in biobanking. In relation to these arguments, it might be suggested that the more concrete a biobanking context, the more legitimate such arguments may become. Given the core instrument in the Estonian system was designed to apply to one biobanking project, perhaps these arguments have traction?

On closer inspection, however, such arguments cannot be accepted as justifying a lack of protection. In the first instance, there seems to be nothing about the operation of the Estonian Biobank which makes it a special case in this regard. Nor is there another clear justification as to why protection was not granted. Even if a lack of protection in relation to the Estonian Biobank were legitimate, this would still not justify a lack of protection in relation to all other biobanking activity.

Excluding data protection, the German system fails to provide any protection for either genetic relatives or genetic groups. There are academic arguments which can be put forward in the Germany context which support the extension of certain rights to genetic relatives under identified law. In particular, arguments can be put forward in support of genetic relatives' rights to know and not know. Specifically, if information about genetic relatives can be generated from a research subject's genome, then, if the research subject can be argued to have the right to know information relevant to their personality, on the basis of personality rights, produced in the course of research, then surely genetic relatives could also be argued to have the same right in relation to information produced in research relevant to their personalities.

[108] *Montgomery v. Lanarkshire Health Board*, [2015] UKSC 11, para. 88.

[109] Emma Cave, 'The Ill-Informed: Consent to Medical Treatment and the Therapeutic Exception' (2017) *Common Law World Review* 46(2) 140, 143.

Unfortunately, however, such arguments fail on the same grounds as those arguments supporting the research subject's genetic privacy rights to know and to not know: they build on peripheral academic arguments without clear support in either legal thinking or jurisprudence.[110]

The lack of protection would not be an issue if clear justifications, specific to the German context, were evident. This does not appear to be the case. It seems there has been little political or jurisprudential deliberation on the matter. Accordingly, rather than assume that protection has been deliberately withheld from relatives or groups, it seems more likely protection is absent due to a lack of consideration. To take an example from the previous chapter, there seems no reason that confidentiality obligations, for example, could not also be owed in relation to genetic relatives in Germany.

Excluding data protection, the UK system fails to protect the rights of both genetic relatives and genetic groups. The issue of genetic relatives' rights in genetic information has been given some consideration in UK jurisprudence. This is particularly the case in relation to relatives' rights to be informed of relevant novel genetic information. Indeed, in the recent case of *ABC v. St George's Healthcare NHS Trust & Others* the High Court recognised, for the first time, that relatives may have a right to be informed by doctors about genetic findings which may significantly impact them.[111]

The decision, however, cannot be directly read to imply that genetic relatives' privacy rights are now recognised and protected in biobanking. In the first instance, the degree to which the decision is applicable to biobanking remains unclear: the decision remains a novel and unique precedent concerning a highly specific factual situation dealing with genetic data produced in the clinical context. In turn, the decision deals only with relatives' rights to be provided with useful information by doctors, rather than with genetic privacy rights. In this regard, Dove et al. more accurately conceptualise the rights involved in the case as 'relatives' [rights] in disclosure'.[112]

The lack of protection would not be an issue if clear justifications for the lack of protection, specific to the UK context, were evident. This does not appear to be the case. The lack of protection for relatives' and groups' rights appears to result, rather than from any directed logic, from a lack of legislative and jurisprudential consideration. The lack of protection for information and spatial privacy rights concerning data produced in the course of research might be asserted as justified based on arguments as to the primacy of research subject confidentiality in the UK at the expense of relatives' and

[110] Even if such arguments could be accepted in principle, there would still be obstacles to overcome. In particular, in all cases in which a confidentiality obligation exists in relation to the research subject, this would constitute an obstacle to the right of a relative to receive information. Confidentiality obligations can be broken for the benefit of a third party such as a genetic relative. Cierniak and Niehaus, however, recognise that this is generally only the case in relation to medically relevant information where there is a clear danger to the third party and the subject of the confidentiality obligation cannot be convinced to treat the information in relation to the third party in a reasonable manner. Jürgen Cierniak and Holger Niehaus, 'StGB § 203 Verletzung von Privatgeheimnisse', in Wolfgang Joecks and Klaus Miebach (eds.), *Münchener Kommentar zur Strafprozessordnung* (3rd edn, Beck 2012) Rn. 90 <https://beck-online.beck.de/?vpath=bibdata/komm/MuekoStGB/cont/MuekoStGB%2Ehtm> accessed 11 December 2019.

[111] *ABC v. St George's Healthcare NHS Trust & Others* (n. 70) para. 188.

[112] Edward Dove, Vicky Chico, Michael Fay, et al., 'Familial Genetic Risks: How Can We Better Navigate Patient Confidentiality and Appropriate Risk Disclosure to Relatives?' (2019) *Journal of Medical Ethics* 45 504, 506.

groups' rights. Yet, these arguments do not serve to justify an absolute lack of protection. In this regard, it is notable that, in UK law, there are exceptions foreseen to the right to confidentiality. As Lucassen and Parker observe, in UK law, there is a general principle that confidence can be breached for the benefit of third parties when: 'breaching ... has the potential to protect ... other individuals from serious harms'.[113] Ngwena and Chadwick recognise this principle has jurisprudential support—for example, in the case of *R. v. Crozier* 'where the Court of Appeal ... upheld the decision to allow a doctor to override the duty of confidence owed to a patient ... to protect ... third parties'.[114] In fact, the relevance of such exceptions to genetic information and genetic relatives has even been confirmed in *ABC v. St George's Healthcare NHS Trust & Others*.[115]

J. Problems with the Adequacy of Protection: No System—*Excluding* Data Protection—Provides Comprehensive Protection

The previous chapter identified a baseline level of protection for genetic privacy in biobanking, which should be met by all legal systems, via an analysis of the international framework—including seven common international principles and six emerging international principles.[116] Accordingly, if states' approaches, *excluding* data protection, fail to incorporate these principles, they may be regarded as providing inadequate protection. *Excluding* data protection, not one analysed state's system meets the minimum standard. Indeed, all systems show multiple deficiencies (see Table 6.2 for a summary).

Excluding data protection, Estonian law is substantially deficient in five categories of genetic privacy provision. *Oversight:* in relation to the Estonian Biobank, there is no obligation for external projects to submit to ongoing oversight. In relation to other biobanking activity, there is no obligation to engage in oversight at all. *Research subject rights:* the Human Genes Research Act gives participants the right to withdraw consent from the Estonian Biobank. In relation to other biobanking activity, however, no such right is identifiable. *Obligations on biobanking actors:* the Human Genes Research Act fulfils all relevant criteria in relation to the Estonian Biobank. In relation to other biobanking activity, however, relevant law does not require that systems be in place to monitor tracking, distribution, and use of substances. *Transfers across jurisdictions:* the Human Genes Research Act outlines prohibitions concerning the transfer of biological samples from the Estonian Biobank outside Estonia. The Act does not, however, place

113 Anneke Lucassen and Michael Parker, 'Confidentiality and Serious Harm in Genetics: Preserving the Confidentiality of One Patient and Preventing Harm to Relatives' (2004) *European Journal of Human Genetics* 12 93, 93.

114 Charles Ngwena and Ruth Chadwick, 'Genetic Diagnostic Information and the Duty of Confidentiality: Ethics and Law' (1993) *Medical Law International* 1 73, 80; *R v. Crozier* [1990] 8 BMLR 128. There is even professional guidance, for example from the Joint Committee on Medical Genetics, which specifically recognises the legitimacy of breaches of confidence for the benefit of genetic relatives. Joint Committee on Medical Genetics, Consent and confidentiality in clinical genetic practice: Guidance on genetic testing and sharing genetic information (Policy, 2nd edn, 2011) viii.

115 *ABC v. St George's Healthcare NHS Trust & Others* (n. 70).

116 See chapter 5, sections C–F.

Table 6.1: Overview of deficits in states' approaches—*excluding* data protection law—concerning types of genetic privacy rights protected and types of genetic privacy rights holders protected

Gaps in Member State Approaches without Data Protection			**EU Member State Approaches Excluding Data Protection Law (Gaps in Protection Marked with a Dot)**		
			UK	Germany	Estonia
Types of Genetic Privacy Engaged by Biobanking	Types of Genetic Privacy Engaged by Biobanking in Relation to the Research Subject	Information privacy right to restrict states of access to biological samples			
		Information privacy right to restrict states of access to associated data			
		Information privacy right to know one's own genetic data	•	•	
		Information privacy right to choose not to know one's own genetic data	•	•	
		Spatial privacy right not to be informed of harmful genetic information	•	•	
	Other Genetic Privacy Rights Holders	Protection for genetic relatives	•	•	•
		Protection for genetic groups	•	•	•

comparable limitations on transfers of genetic privacy relevant data. In turn, transfers of substances from other biobanking actors appear not to be regulated at all. *Transfers to external researchers:* the Human Genes Research Act fails to outline an obligation to make access policies public for the Estonian Biobank. In relation to other biobanking activity, there are no obligations on biobanks to engage in advance ethical review of external applicants or to make access policies transparent.

Excluding data protection, German law is substantially deficient in relation to at least five categories of genetic privacy provision. *Oversight:* the German framework provides no general obligation for biobanking actors to submit to either advance, or ongoing, oversight. The Musterberufsordnung für Ärzte outlines an obligation for advance ethics committee oversight of biobanking activity, but this only applies to biobanks involving physicians. *Legitimation of processing:* there is no general obligation to obtain research subject consent prior to using genetic privacy relevant data. Whilst there is a general obligation under property law to obtain consent prior to the use of a biological sample, this does not extend to data. *Obligations on biobanking actors:* there is no general obligation to retain substances in a secure and confidential manner. Whilst such an obligation does arise when confidentiality obligations are applicable, these are limited in scope and do not apply to biological samples. Nor is there an obligation requiring biobanks to have systems in place to track the distribution and use of substances. *Transfers to other jurisdictions:* identified law places no general prohibition on the transfer of substances to jurisdictions which do not uphold a minimum of protection. *Transfers to external researchers:* identified law provides no provisions obliging biobanks to engage in ethical review of applicant researchers' projects. Nor does law require access conditions to be made public.

Excluding data protection, UK law is substantially deficient in relation to at least four categories of genetic privacy provisions. *Oversight:* under the UK framework, the possibility for biobanks to obtain general permissions from oversight bodies means that biobanks, rather than independent bodies, will be responsible for advance oversight of external research projects. *Obligations on biobanking actors:* there is no general obligation relating to the need to track substances. Whilst the Human Tissue Act outlines a general obligation on biobanking actors to provide tracking systems for biological samples, there is no corresponding obligation regarding associated data. *Transfers across jurisdictions:* there is no general obligation to prevent transfers to jurisdictions not providing adequate privacy protection. Whilst there are limited protections afforded to biological samples under the Human Tissue Act, there is no comparable protection relating to genetic privacy relevant data. *Transfers to external researchers:* relevant UK law foresees no obligation to make biobank access policies transparent.

K. Problems of Harmony: Systems—*Excluding* Data Protection—Are Neither Harmonised, Nor Necessarily Compatible

Ideally, legal systems operating together in relation to biobanking would offer harmonised, or at least compatible, protection for genetic privacy rights. If both harmony and

Table 6.2: Overview of deficits in states' approaches—*excluding* data protection law—compared with baseline international principles

Gaps in Member State Approaches without Data Protection			EU Member State Approaches Excluding Data Protection Law (Gaps in Protection Marked with a Dot)		
			UK	Germany	Estonia
Principles of International Law (Defined in the previous chapter)	Common Principles	Principle 1: Biobanking actors must submit to advance oversight	•	•	•
		Principle 2: Collection and use of substances should, in principle, only proceed with research subject consent		•	
		Principle 3: The research subject should have the right to withdraw consent			•
		Principle 4: Biobanking actors must retain substances securely and cofidentially		•	
		Principle 5: Substances should not be transferred to jurisdictions which do not ensure adequate protection for genetic privacy	•	•	•
		Principle 6: Substances should not, in principle, be transferred to non-research actors		•	
		Principle 7: Penalties should be imposed for infringements of genetic privacy			
	Emerging Principles	Principle 1: Biobanking actors should be subject to ongoing oversight		•	•
		Principle 2: The principle that consent must be obtained to collect and use materials may be subject to exceptions			
		Principle 3: The scope of consent may include broader, non-project specific consent			
		Principle 4: Biobanking actors are obliged to ensre that the conditions for tracking substances are in place	•	•	•
		Principle 5: Biobanking actors are obliged to engage in ethical review of external researchers' access requests		•	•
		Principle 6: Biobanking actors must make access policies public and accessible	•	•	•

compatibility are absent, researchers will be left uncertain as to how to discharge responsibilities in cross-border research and genetic privacy rights holders will be left unsure of the protection to which they are entitled. Unfortunately, *excluding* data protection, the systems considered in this chapter are neither harmonised, nor clearly compatible.

Excluding data protection, there is no relevant EU level law. Not only is there no relevant EU law, there is no EU level legislative process underway to address the issue. There is thus, apparently, no legal impetus towards harmonisation. Kaye observes the significance of the lack of directed harmonisation approach: 'Ultimately, the lack of a uniform regulatory system may have implications for the viability and long-term competitiveness of collaborative European research.'[117] It should be highlighted, however, that this lack of law does not result from a lack of EU competence to legislate. As discussed above, Article 4(3) of the TFEU grants the EU special shared competence to regulate in relation to research. It has been suggested in certain academic commentaries on the matter, for example, by Chassang, that Article 4 TFEU implies: 'an absence of... competency to the EU to harmonise legislations in the field of health and scientific research, the EU having only a support competency in these fields remaining principally regulated by national laws.'[118] This would seem to be an overstatement of the position. The existence of Clinical Trials Regulation demonstrates that the EU both has the power to legislate on medical research and has been willing to use this power.

Excluding data protection, systems also fail to be compatible. Incompatibility is evident at fundamental and technical levels. At a fundamental level, several contradictions between approaches are evident. There are, for example, marked differences in how biobanking substances are categorised by Member State systems. In Germany, for example, research subject data cannot be regarded as property.[119] Yet, in Estonia, Article 35(1) of the Human Genes Research Act specifically recognises the possibility for research subject data to qualify as property—the Article asserts: '[t]he right of ownership of descriptions of state of health, other personal data and genealogies.' This is a clear contradiction between the two systems. It further remains unclear as to how to navigate this incompatibility. What happens when biobanking substances are transferred between Germany and Estonia? Does German biobanking data become capable of being property as it moves over the border?

At a technical level, several contradictions are also evident. There are, for example, evident differences in legal systems' elaboration of the conditions of consent. For example, in the UK, consent relating to a biological sample under the Human Tissue Act can be broad and may cover uncertain future research uses. In Germany, however, the situation is not as clear. There is doubt, for example, that broad consent is legitimate in relation to

[117] Jane Kaye, 'Do We Need a Uniform Regulatory System for Biobanks across Europe?' (2006) *European Journal of Human Genetics* 14 245, 245.

[118] Gauthier Chassang, 'The Impact of the EU General Data Protection Regulation on Scientific Research' [2017] *Ecancermedicalscience* 11(709) <https://www.ncbi.nlm.nih.gov/pmc/articles/PMC5243137/> accessed 11 December 2019.

[119] Albers, 'Rechtsrahmen und Rechtsprobleme bei Biobanken' (n. 41) 487.

biological samples under Article 90 BGB. It is further unclear as to how to navigate this incompatibility. What happens if a German biobank wishes to use a biological sample, collected with a broad consent, from the UK? Does the broad consent remain legitimate by virtue of it being obtained in a state which permits broad consent? Or is use potentially problematic by virtue of the doubtful legitimacy of broad consent in German law?

The previous five sections have highlighted that—based on the analysis of EU, and three states' laws—when data protection is *excluded* from consideration, protection for genetic privacy in biobanking in Europe is decidedly inadequate. This recognition lays the groundwork for looking at European data protection law under the GDPR as a source of solutions. This recognition alone, however, still leaves a significant question unanswered: why, specifically, should the GDPR be considered as an alternative?

L. Looking to Data Protection and the GDPR

In the first instance, considering data protection law under the GDPR as a framework for the protection of genetic privacy in biobanking is not a left-field proposition. In fact, the opposite is true. This chapter engaged in an artificial exercise in *excluding* data protection from analysis of European law on biobanking. Any full investigation of the situation immediately encounters data protection as an area of law with unquestioned relevance. This is certainly true in the three states analysed in this chapter. In Estonia, Article 7(1) of the Human Genes Research Act discusses the relevance of: 'The ... Personal Data Protection Act which regulate[s] the processing of personal data, together with the specifications provided for in this Act.' In Germany, Hoppe discusses data protection as the key area of law relevant to the protection of privacy in data in biobanking.[120] In the UK, Laurie observes the centrality of: 'data protection ... [in] govern[ing] data sharing and linkage'.[121]

The GDPR is the most modern manifestation of data protection law. It replaced Directive 95/46 as the key piece of EU data protection legislation on 25 May 2018.[122] Accordingly, consideration of the function of the GDPR in the protection of genetic privacy in biobanking is, in fact, essential to understanding how genetic privacy protection in biobanking law in Europe actually looks. Fortunately, not only is the GDPR definitive of the legal landscape, even a superficial look at its aims, structure, and content shows a framework highly suited to provide resolutions to each problem identified with states' alternative approaches considered in this chapter.

Regarding the structural problems within European states' systems outlined in section G, the GDPR appears to offer a framework potentially broadly applicable across

[120] Hoppe, 'Privacy Laws and Biobanking in Germany' (n. 43) 37.

[121] Graeme Laurie and Shawn Harmon, Through the Thicket and Across the Divide: Successfully Navigating the Regulatory Landscape in Life Sciences Research (Edinburgh School of Law Research Paper, No. 2013/30, 2013) 4–5.

[122] Directive 95/46/EC of the European Parliament and of the Council of 24 October 1995 on the protection of individuals with regard to the processing of personal data and on the free movement of such data [1995] OJ L281/31.

biobanking activity. Data protection under the GDPR applies to the processing of all personal data. This is a concept with a broad scope, which has been argued to be capable of covering both data and samples processed in biobanking. It thus seems to have the potential to apply to all biobanking substances. With such broad applicability, it looks suited to address issues of comprehensiveness and cogency within states' systems. The applicability of the GDPR to research subject data is beyond doubt. The applicability of the GDPR to biological samples is somewhat more propositional. Nevertheless, the proposition has quite some support. As the Expert Group on Dealing with Ethical and Regulatory Challenges of International Biobank Research observe: 'it should be highlighted that ... data protection ... must be applied not only to the processing of personal data, but also ... to the biological samples used for research purposes'.[123] Indeed, the approach is even already in use in some Member States. This is the approach, for example, which has been adopted in Estonia—Article 7(1) of the Human Genes Research Act explicitly recognises data protection principles should apply to biological samples.

Regarding the substantive problems outlined in sections H–J, the GDPR appears to provide a well-rounded framework for the protection of rights engaged by the processing of information. This appears to be true at both conceptual and substantive levels. Thus, it seems a logical place to look as a source of solutions in relation to substantive inadequacies in other legal approaches. At a conceptual level, the GDPR's aim to provide protection for rights engaged by data processing is clearly highlighted in Article 1: 'This Regulation lays down rules relating to the protection of natural persons with regard to the processing of personal data.' At a substantive level, in the past few decades, European data protection law has developed to comprise an extensive range of protection for rights engaged by the processing of personal data. This development has specifically led scholars to observe its potential utility in providing effective protection for rights engaged by biobanking. Bygrave, for example, comments: 'it is tempting to turn to the framework of data protection law as a possible panacea. That framework appears relatively systematic and comprehensive, with well-established organs for monitoring and enforcement'.[124]

Finally, regarding the lack of harmony and compatibility between systems identified in section K, the GDPR is directly applicable EU law. The GDPR is a Regulation and is thus EU law comprising of a legal instrument which is directly applicable in all EU Member States. In this regard—unless a Member State has made use of an opening clause—principles set out by the GDPR will immediately supersede contradictory provisions in EU Member State law. Whenever the GDPR applies, it will thus exercise a harmonising force across European states. It thus seems suited as a framework to address issues of disharmony and incompatibility between European legal systems. Indeed, harmony between European states' legal systems is an express goal of the GDPR, as clearly stated in Article 1(3): 'The free movement of personal data within the

[123] Expert Group, Biobanks for Europe (n. 6) 38.
[124] Lee Bygrave, 'The Body as Data? Biobank Regulation via the "Back Door" of Data Protection Law' (2010) *Law, Innovation and Technology* 2(1) 1, 22.

Union shall be neither restricted nor prohibited for reasons connected with the protection of natural persons with regard to the processing of personal data.' This has led scholars such as Penasa et al. to observe: 'effective implementation of the EU GDPR will represent a decisive catalyst for adaptive harmonization of biobanks regulation in the European framework'.[125]

M. Conclusion

When data protection law is *excluded* from consideration, no EU law for the protection of genetic privacy in biobanking is identifiable. There is, however, a range of different national approaches identifiable in different European states. For example, Estonia relies on *sui generis* biobanking law, Germany relies on a combination of property law in relation to biological samples and an assortment of confidentiality laws in relation to associated data, and the UK relies on a combination of *sui generis* human tissue law in relation to biological samples and common law doctrine in relation to associated data.

Critically considering the protection offered by national approaches *excluding* data protection law, however, reveals significant flaws: systems are structurally unsuited for the biobanking context—each leaves gaps where no law is applicable, and each fails to provide cogent approaches to protection; systems ignore certain research subject genetic privacy rights; systems ignore genetic relatives' and genetic groups' genetic privacy rights; systems do not provide comprehensive protection for those genetic privacy rights they do protect; and finally, when looked at together—as an ecosystem of legal systems—systems demonstrate neither harmony nor even compatibility.

The fact there are significant flaws in the protection for genetic privacy in biobanking in Europe *excluding* data protection law, opens the door to consider European data protection law under the GDPR as an alternative approach. In the first instance, far from being an alternative left-field approach, data protection law is already recognised as playing a significant role in the protection of genetic privacy in biobanking in Europe. The GDPR will thus be a key piece of legislation which will define the shape of genetic privacy protection in EU biobanking in future. In turn, even a glance at the structure and content of the GDPR reveals an instrument apparently suitably adapted to address issues identified with other approaches.

[125] Simone Penasa, Iñigo de Miguel Beriain, Carla Barbosa, et al., 'The EU General Data Protection Regulation: How Will It Impact the Regulation of Research Biobanks? Setting the Legal Frame in the Mediterranean and Eastern European Area' (2018) *Medical Law International* 18(4) 241, 241.

7

Testing the GDPR in Relation to Biobanking

When Does the GDPR Apply to Biobanking?

A. Introduction

The previous chapter clarified the case for looking to data protection law under the General Data Protection Regulation (GDPR) as a framework for the protection of genetic privacy in biobanking in Europe. Building on this case, the book now moves to begin a more in-depth consideration of data protection law under the GDPR and its relationship with genetic privacy in biobanking. This in-depth consideration begins, in this chapter, with a look at when the GDPR applies, *rationae materiae*, to biobanking—only when the law applies to biobanking, can it be expected to provide any protection for genetic privacy rights in biobanking at all.

The chapter begins with a descriptive elaboration of the GDPR's general applicability criteria and their relevance for biobanking (section B). The chapter then moves to consider the applicability of the concept of 'personal data'—the most significant and involved, yet most complex and confusing, criterion—to biobanking. The chapter begins this exploration by providing an overview of the concept (section C). The chapter then seeks to clarify which biobanking substances, in which contexts, will qualify as personal data—devoting particular attention to the key questions of the status of biological samples and when substances should be regarded as 'identifiable' (sections D–H).

B. The GDPR's General Applicability Principles: Article 2 and Biobanking

Article 2 elaborates the GDPR's general principles of applicability. The Article reads:

> 2(1) This Regulation applies to the processing of personal data wholly or partly by automated means and to the processing other than by automated means of personal data which form part of a filing system or are intended to form part of a filing system.
>
> 2(2) This Regulation does not apply to the processing of personal data: (a) in the course of an activity which falls outside the scope of Union law; (b) by the Member States when carrying out activities which fall within the scope of Chapter 2 of Title V of the TEU; (c) by a natural person in the course of a purely personal or household

Protecting Genetic Privacy in Biobanking through Data Protection Law. Dara Hallinan, Oxford University Press (2021). © Dara Hallinan.
DOI: 10.1093/oso/9780192896476.003.0007

activity; (d) by competent authorities for the purposes of the prevention, investigation, detection or prosecution of criminal offences or the execution of criminal penalties, including the safeguarding against and the prevention of threats to public security.

2(3) For the processing of personal data by the Union institutions, bodies, offices and agencies, Regulation (EC) No 45/2001 applies. Regulation (EC) No 45/2001 and other Union legal acts applicable to such processing of personal data shall be adapted to the principles and rules of this Regulation in accordance with Article 98.

2(4) This Regulation shall be without prejudice to the application of Directive 2000/31/EC, in particular of the liability rules of intermediary service providers in Articles 12 to 15 of that Directive.

The provisions in the Article can be considered in terms of two categories.

1. Provisions placing limitations on the processing activities—processing sectors—to which the GDPR applies. This group includes Articles 2(2), 2(3), and 2(4).
2. Provisions placing limitations on the mechanics of data processing to which the GDPR applies. This group consists of Article 2(1).

In terms of provisions relating to the sectors to which the Regulation applies, only Article 2(2)(d) is relevant to biobanking.[1] This Article serves to exclude the applicability of the Regulation to law enforcement processing. Article 2(2)(d) excludes applicability regardless of in terms of the type of law enforcement authority engaging in processing or in terms of the type of law enforcement processing in question. Recall, as observed in previous chapters, law enforcement authorities are one of the key non-research

[1] Articles 2(2)(a)–(c) are largely irrelevant to biobanking. Article 2(2)(a) is irrelevant as research constitutes an activity which falls within the scope of EU law as clarified by Part 1, Title 1, Article 4(3) of the Treaty on the Functioning of the European Union. In the future, however, it is possible that activities which fall outside the scope of Union law may be supported by the access and use of biobanking substances. For example, Member States generally retain competence over certain national citizenship claims. See Hanneke Van Eijken, 'European Citizenship and the Competence of Member States to Grant and to Withdraw the Nationality of their Nationals' (2010) *Utrecht Journal of International and European Law* 27(72) 65, 66. As discussed in chapter 4, section H, Member States may be able to use genetic materials to support or refute such claims. Article 2(2)(b) refers to activities concerning European Union Common Foreign and Security Policy and is accordingly highly unlikely to be relevant to biobanks. Consolidated Version of the Treaty on European Union [2012] OJ C326/13 Title V, Chapter 2. Finally, Article 2(2)(c) concerns individuals' private domestic use of information as opposed to large-scale processing by biobanks.

Articles 2(3) and 2(4) are also irrelevant to biobanking. These Articles describe processing sectors in which the rules of the GDPR are superseded or replaced by rules in other EU law. Article 2(3) refers only to legislation relevant for European Union bodies and does not concern biobanking. Article 2(4) refers to Regulation 2000/31/EC concerning information society services. These are services which are: 'normally provided for remuneration, at a distance, by electronic means'. This definition does not describe biobanking. Directive 2000/31/EC of the European Parliament and of The Council of 8 June 2000 on certain legal aspects of information society services, in particular electronic commerce, in the Internal Market (Directive on electronic commerce) [2000] OJ L178/1. Definition provided in: Directive 98/34/EC of the European Parliament and of the Council of 22 June 1998 laying down a procedure for the provision of information in the field of technical standards and regulations [1998] OJ L204/37 Article 1; and Directive 98/34/EC of the European Parliament and of the Council of 22 June 1998 laying down a procedure for the provision of information in the field of technical standards and regulations and of rules on Information Society services [1998] OJ L217/18 Article 2.

third parties with an interest in accessing biobanking substances.[2] As Kaye observes, biobanks may 'be attractive to the police, because they will be an easy entry into a comprehensive and useful body of information'.[3] The use of genetic materials in law enforcement has an already lengthy history, and the willingness of law enforcement to access biobanks has already been demonstrated. Recall the use of biobank substances by law enforcement in the Anna Lindh case.[4]

In terms of criteria associated with the mechanics of processing, Article 2(1) is highly relevant to biobanking. The Article can be broken down into two separate, cumulative, applicability criteria. First, the mechanics of processing must correspond to the Article's definition of processing. In Article 4(2), 'processing' is defined as: 'any operation or set of operations which is performed on personal data or on sets of personal data, whether or not by automated means, such as collection, recording, organisation, structuring, storage, adaptation or alteration, retrieval, consultation, use, disclosure by transmission, dissemination or otherwise making available, alignment or combination, restriction, erasure or destruction'. Eventually, the concept is so broad as to provide virtually no limitation on the scope of the GDPR in relation to biobanking at all. Accordingly, every type of biobanking processing will qualify as processing.

Second, processing must be done on a certain type of substance: personal data. Accordingly, given that biobank processing—excluding law enforcement processing—qualifies as 'processing' under the GDPR, whenever biobanking involves personal data, the GDPR will apply. The precise scope of applicability of this criterion, however, is harder to clarify. Superficially, the term seems straightforward. In fact, there are few concepts in EU data protection law which have caused such confusion. Accordingly, to clarify when biobanking involves personal data, in-depth consideration is required.

Given the complexity of the concept, such a consideration must begin with an elaboration of the concept of personal data and its constituent criteria.

C. Personal Data and Its Constituent Criteria

In Article 4(1), the GDPR provides a brief definition of the concept: 'personal data means any information relating to an identified or identifiable natural person "data subject"'.[5] With regard to this definition, the concept of personal data can usefully be looked at as describing two aspects of a processing operation.

[2] See chapter 4, section H.

[3] Jane Kaye, 'Police Collection and Access to DNA Samples' (2006) *Genomics, Society and Policy* 2(1) 16, 23.

[4] Flavio D'Abramo, 'Biobank Research, Informed Consent and Society: Towards a New Alliance?' (2015) *Journal of Epidemiology and Community Health*, 69(11) Online First: doi:10.1136/jech-2014-205215 1, 2.

[5] The concept outlined in Article 4(1) is substantively the same as the definition for personal data used in Article 2(a) of Directive 95/46: 'personal data shall mean any information relating to an identified or identifiable natural person ("data subject")'. Accordingly, jurisprudence on concept in the Directive, retains validity in relation to the Regulation.

1. The type of substance being processed
2. The type of link between a substance and an individual.

Concerning the type of substance being processed: based on the definition in the GDPR, the Article 29 Working Party suggest a substance must fulfil three cumulative criteria in order to qualify as personal data:[6]

a. Information
b. Relating to
c. Natural person.

Information: the GDPR does not offer a definition for the term information.[7] However, the Article 29 Working Party provide clarification as to its meaning from three perspectives.[8] With regard to the nature of information, it suggests that the concept 'includes any sort of statements about a person', both subjective and objective.[9] For example, both the following statements would constitute information: 'John is five years old' and 'we have reason to believe that John might be five years old at the moment'. With regard to the content of information, they observe that the concept is broad and must extend to any sort of information.[10] Finally, the Working Party is clear that the medium in which information is stored and transferred is irrelevant. They state: 'the concept . . . includes information available in whatever form, be it alphabetical, numerical, graphical, photographical or acoustic, for example. It includes information kept on paper, and information stored in a computer memory by means of binary code . . . for instance'.[11]

Relating to: the GDPR also provides no further clarification of the concept of relating to. However, the Article 29 Working Party suggest a simple test can be used to consider whether the criterion is fulfilled: 'In general terms, information can be considered to "relate" to an individual when it is about that individual.'[12] They propose three forms of connection which qualify information as being 'about' an individual: 'In

[6] Article 29 Working Party, Opinion 4/2007 on the concept of personal data (Policy, 01248/07/EN WP 136, 2007) 6 (hereafter Article 29 Working Party, Opinion 4/2007).

[7] The concept of information has largely escaped consideration as a subject of investigation in data protection law. Yet, how the concept is understood and the different roles it occupies in data protection law are a valuable point of further study. See: Dara Hallinan and Raphaël Gellert, 'The Concept of "Information": An Invisible Problem in the GDPR' (2020) *Scripted* 17(2) 269, 269–319 (hereafter Hallinan and Gellert, 'The Concept of "Information" ').

[8] Article 29 Working Party, Opinion 4/2007 (n. 6) 6–9.

[9] 'It covers "objective" information, such as the presence of a certain substance in one's blood. It also includes "subjective" information, opinions or assessments.' They also observe that: 'for information to be personal data, it is not necessary that it be true or proven'. Article 29 Working Party, Opinion 4/2007 (n. 6) 6. The position has been confirmed in the CJEU case of *Nowak*. In the case, the Court stated: 'all kinds of information . . . also subjective, in the form of opinions and assessments [are personal data]'. *Peter Nowak v. Data Protection Commissioner* [2017] ECLI:EU:C:2017:994, para. 34. See also: Dara Hallinan and Frederik Zuiderveen Borgesius, 'Opinions Can Be Incorrect (In Our Opinion)! On Data Protection Law's Accuracy Principle' (2019) *International Data Privacy Law* 10(1) 1, 5.

[10] This includes 'information touching the individual's private and family life "stricto sensu", but also information regarding whatever type of activity is undertaken by the individual, like that concerning working relations or the economic or social behaviour of the individual'. Article 29 Working Party, Opinion 4/2007 (n. 6) 6.

[11] Article 29 Working Party, Opinion 4/2007 (n. 6) 7.

[12] Article 29 Working Party, Opinion 4/2007 (n. 6) 9.

order to consider that the data "relate" to an individual, a "content" element OR a "purpose" element OR a "result" element should be present.' The content element 'is present ... where—corresponding to the most obvious and common understanding ... of the word "relate"—information is given about a particular person'. For example, the statement 'John is five years old' contains information which clearly relates to John, the specific single individual. A purpose element is present 'when the data are used or are likely to be used ... to evaluate, treat in a certain way or influence the status or behaviour of an individual'. For example, if the statement 'the occupants of number 24 East Terrace Drive are lazy and do not want to work' were used to judge a tenant's social support application, this would constitute information whose purpose would be to evaluate the tenant and would thus relate to the tenant. Finally, a result element is present when data use is 'likely to ... impact on a certain person's rights and interests'.[13]

Natural person: the concept of the natural person is an old legal concept referring to a living human being. As Harbinja observes, the concept is 'understood generally as a person having legal capacity, starting with the birth and ending with her death'.[14] This follows the line of previous Article 29 Working Party guidance: 'The protection afforded by [data protection] applies to natural persons, that is, to human beings.'[15] The limits of the term are elaborated in Recitals 14 and 27 of the GDPR, which explicitly clarify, respectively, that the Regulation does not apply to deceased persons or legal persons.

Concerning the type of link between a substance and an individual: the Regulation requires that, in order to be personal data, a substance relates to—has a certain link to—a specific individual. The Regulation uses the criterion of 'identified or identifiable' to establish the presence of this link. The general concept of identified or identifiable is clarified in Article 4(1): 'an identifiable person is one who can be identified, directly or indirectly, in particular by reference to an identifier such as a name, an identification number, location data, online identifier or to one or more factors specific to the physical, physiological, genetic, mental, economic, cultural or social identity of that person'.[16]

The Article 29 Working Party then provide further elaboration of the terms 'direct' and 'indirect'. They clarify that direct identifiability relates to the presence of information which is unique to an individual—information which allows an individual to be singled out without requiring any further data. They clarify that indirect identifiability relates to the phenomenon of 'unique combinations'—combinations of otherwise unidentifiable information used to construct a profile unique to one single person.[17]

[13] Article 29 Working Party, Opinion 4/2007 (n. 6) 10–12.

[14] Edina Harbinja, 'Does the EU Data Protection Regime Protect Post-Mortem Privacy and What Could Be the Potential Alternatives?' (2013) *Scripted* 10(1) 19, 27.

[15] Article 29 Working Party, Opinion 4/2007 (n. 6) 21.

[16] The Article 29 Working Party provide further clarity as to the meaning of the terms 'identified' and 'identifiable': 'a natural person can be considered as "identified" when, within a group of persons, he or she is "distinguished" from all other members of the group. Accordingly, the natural person is "identifiable" when, although the person has not been identified yet, it is possible to do it'. Article 29 Working Party, Opinion 4/2007 (n. 6) 12.

[17] They state: 'In cases where prima facie the extent of the identifiers available does not allow anyone to single out a particular person, that person might still be "identifiable" because that information combined with other pieces of information (whether the latter is retained by the data controller or not) will allow the individual to be distinguished from others.' Article 29 Working Party, Opinion 4/2007 (n. 6) 12–13.

The types of factors which should be taken into account in defining an identified or identifiable link in any specific processing context are clarified in Recital 26 of the Regulation: 'account should be taken of all the means reasonably likely to be used . . . by the controller or by another person to identify the natural person directly or indirectly. To ascertain whether means are reasonably likely to be used to identify the natural person, account should be taken of all objective factors, such as the costs of and the amount of time required for identification, taking into consideration the available technology at the time of the processing and technological developments.'

Whilst the Recital is somewhat vague, the Article 29 Working Party provide two significant points of further clarification. First, they clarify that the key concept 'means reasonably likely to be used' indicates that not all theoretically identifiable data will necessarily qualify as identifiable. However, they also clarify that the standard for identifiability is 'very high'.[18] In fact, for data to be regarded as unidentifiable—anonymous—they observe that identification must be '"reasonably" impossible'.[19] As Quinn observes: 'Whilst the use of the word "reasonably" may seem to connote a low standard for anonymisation, the working party has made it clear, in particular with its juxtaposition to the word "impossible", that the standard is actually very high.'[20] The strictness of the standard has been highlighted by the Court of Justice of the European Union (CJEU) in the *Breyer* judgment. In this case, the Court came to the conclusion that even 'a dynamic IP address registered by an online media services provider . . . constitutes personal data'.[21] In the case, even though the defendant did not store any identifying information, the fact that identifying information was held by a third party was enough to qualify the IP address as personal data.

Second, the Article 29 Working Party observe that, if data will foreseeably be identifiable at any point in the lifespan of processing, these data must be regarded as 'identifiable' throughout the lifespan of processing. They state in this regard that, for data to be anonymous: 'identification may not be anticipated to be possible during the "lifetime" of the information'.[22]

This section clarified that the concept of personal data can be considered in terms of the substance being processed and the presence of an identified or identifiable link between the substance and a specific individual. Accordingly, to clarify when personal data is processed in biobanking, two questions might be asked:

1. Which biobanking substances could potentially be personal data?
2. Which types of biobanking link qualify as identified or identifiable?

[18] Article 29 Working Party, Opinion 05/2014 on Anonymisation Techniques (Policy, 0829/14/EN WP 216, 2014) 6 (hereafter Article 29 Working Party, Opinion 05/2014).

[19] Article 29 Working Party, Opinion 05/2014 (n. 18) 8.

[20] Paul Quinn, 'The Anonymisation of Research Data: A Pyric Victory for Privacy that Should Not Be Pushed Too Hard by the EU Data Protection Framework?' (2017) *European Journal of Health Law* 24 1, 18.

[21] *Patrick Breyer v. Bundesrepublik Deutschland* [2016] ECLI:EU:C:2016:779, para. 49. See also: *Scarlet Extended SA v. Société belge des auteurs, compositeurs et éditeurs SCRL (SABAM)* [2011] ECLI:EU:C:2011:771, para. 51.

[22] Article 29 Working Party, Opinion 05/2014 (n. 18) 15.

D. Which Biobanking Substances Could Potentially Be Personal Data?

In chapter 3, the biobanking process was broken down into a list of five commonly processed substances.[23] This list constitutes a useful reference point for the current analysis:

1. Biological samples
2. Health, lifestyle, and biographical information
3. Sequenced genomic data
4. Individual research results
5. Scientific conclusions.

In relation to four out of five substances, the answer to the question of potential qualification as personal data is clear. Health, lifestyle, and biographical information, sequenced genomic data, and individual research results can fulfil all three criteria and can be personal data.[24] It is equally clear that scientific conclusions cannot fulfil the criteria to be personal data—as these cannot relate to natural persons.[25] There is less clarity, however, in relation to biological samples. The Regulation and other primary sources of data protection law are silent on the issue. There is a range of relevant jurisprudence on the topic. A look through the opinions of the legal fora which have dealt with the status of biological samples, however, reveals, as Bentzen and Høstmælinge put it: 'myriad interpretations ... some interpreted "personal data" to include human biological samples ... whereas others did not'.[26]

[23] See chapter 3, section G.

[24] Health, lifestyle, and biographical information consists of objective or subjective facts. They thus qualify as information. In turn, information is collected about a single individual's heath, lifestyle or biography. It thus relates to a single natural person. Recital 36 is explicit that the concept of personal data encompasses this information: 'all data pertaining to the health status of a data subject which reveal information relating to the past, current or future physical or mental health status of the data subject'.

Sequenced genomic data relate to single natural persons—they are sequenced from one individual's sample and can be analysed to produce information about that individual. There is a question as to whether they can constitute information as the concept has been used in the Regulation. Sequenced genomic data are not subjective or objective 'facts' and therefore do not qualify as information as the concept is outlined by the Article 29 Working Party. Article 4(13) of the Regulation is, however, conclusive that they can. It clarifies that genetic data are a particular type of personal data: '"genetic data" means personal data relating to the inherited or acquired genetic characteristics of a natural person which give unique information about the physiology or the health of that natural person and which result, in particular, from an analysis of a biological sample from the natural person in question'. Sequenced genomic data result from an 'analysis of a biological sample' and relate to 'inherited or acquired genetic characteristics' of the donor and thus fall under the definition. Individual research results are simply normal pieces of information about a research subject, the genesis of which happens to be genomic research. Recital 39 and Article 4(13) explicitly recognise that information derived from the testing or examination of a body part or bodily substance is personal data.

[25] Scientific conclusions are generalised truths about the human genome. They are not facts about any one person's genome. Thus, they have no relationship with a single individual and cannot be personal data.

[26] Heidi Beate Bentzen and Njål Høstmælinge, 'Balancing Protection and Free Movement of Personal Data: The New European Union General Data Protection Regulation' (2019) *Annals of Internal Medicine* 170(5) 335, 335.

Interpretations supporting the treatment of biological samples as personal data are found at European and state level. In terms of European fora, the European Court of Human Rights (ECtHR) directly addressed the issue in the *Marper* case.[27] The Court stated: 'cellular samples, constitute personal data'.[28] The Court then reinforced its position in the more recent cases of *Gaughran* and *Trajkovski and Chipovski*.[29] In terms of European states, the position has been taken in various states' conceptualisations of the concept of personal data.[30] Article 7 of the Estonian Human Genes Research Act 2000, for example, states: 'The provisions of the Personal Data Protection Act . . . apply to the taking of tissue samples.'

Interpretations refuting the treatment of biological samples as personal data, however, are also found at European and state level. At EU level, this position has been taken by the Article 29 Working Party. They state: 'Human tissue samples (like a blood sample) are . . . sources out of which biometric data are extracted, but they are not biometric data themselves (as for instance a pattern for fingerprints is biometric data, but the finger itself is not). Therefore the extraction of information from the samples is collection of personal data . . . [whilst the] collection, storage and use of tissue samples themselves may be subject to separate sets of rules.'[31] At state level, the position has been adopted in several national conceptualisations of the concept of personal data. This is the position taken, for example, in Germany, Belgium, the UK, and Spain.[32] Dammann, for example, observes, regarding German law: 'extracts of teeth, fingers and hair, as such, will not be personal data'.[33]

As no clear answer is forthcoming as to whether biological samples should be regarded as personal data in an analysis of the positions of relevant legal fora, a deeper substantive consideration is warranted. Surprisingly, despite the existence of the debate for several years, such deeper considerations have rarely been performed.[34] I would

[27] *S. and Marper v. United Kingdom*, App nos 30562/04 and 30566/04, 4 December 2008 (hereafter *Marper v. United Kingdom*).

[28] *Marper v. United Kingdom* (n. 27) para. 68

[29] *Gaughran v. United Kingdom*, App no 45245/15, 13 February 2020, para. 63; *Trajkovski and Chipovski v. North Macedonia*, App nos 53205/13 and 63320/13, [2020], 13 February 2020, para. 43. See also: Hallinan and Gellert, 'The Concept of "Information"' (n. 7) 287–91.

[30] See, for example, Sylvia Tomova, 'Implementation of Directive 95/46/EC in Relation to Medical Research in Bulgaria' in Deryck Beyleveld, David Townend, Ségolène Rouillé-Mirza, and Jessica Wright (eds.), *Implementation of the Data Protection Directive in Relation to Medical Research in Europe* (Ashgate, 2004) 43, 46; Liana Ples, 'The Implementation in Domestic Law of Directive 95/46/EC in Romania', in Deryck Beyleveld, David Townend, Ségolène Rouillé-Mirza, and Jessica Wright (eds.), *Implementation of the Data Protection Directive in Relation to Medical Research in Europe* (Ashgate, 2004) 341, 346.

[31] Article 29 Working Party, Opinion 4/2007 (n. 6) 9.

[32] See, for example, Herman Nys, 'Report on the Implementation of Directive 95/46/EC in Belgian Law', in Deryck Beyleveld, David Townend, Ségolène Rouillé-Mirza, and Jessica Wright (eds.), *Implementation of the Data Protection Directive in Relation to Medical Research in Europe* (Ashgate, 2004) 29, 41 (hereafter Nys, 'Report on the Implementation of Directive 95/46/EC in Belgian Law'); Deryck Beyleveld, Andrew Grubb, David Townend, et al., 'The UK's Implementation of Directive 95/46/EC', in Deryck Beyleveld, David Townend, Ségolène Rouillé-Mirza, and Jessica Wright (eds.), *Implementation of the Data Protection Directive in Relation to Medical Research in Europe* (Ashgate 2004) 403, 428; C. M. Romeo Casabona and Pilar Nicolás, 'The Implementation of Directive 95/46/EC in Spain', in Deryck Beyleveld, David Townend, Ségolène Rouillé-Mirza, and Jessica Wright (eds.), *Implementation of the Data Protection Directive in Relation to Medical Research in Europe* (Ashgate 2004) 357, 379.

[33] Ulrich Dammann, 'Artikel 3', in Spiros Simitis (ed.), *Bundesdatenschutzgesetz* (Nomos 2014) 315, 321. Translation by the author of: 'Zähne, Finger, Haare und Narben sind als solche keine personenbezogen Daten.'

[34] One such effort is that of Hallinan and De Hert. The discussion of biological samples in this chapter relies on reworked argumentation from this piece. Dara Hallinan and Paul De Hert, 'Many Have It Wrong—Samples Do Contain Personal Data: The Data Protection Regulation as a Superior Framework to Protect Donor Interests in

argue that such an analysis illuminates, at least for the biobanking context, strong justifications for considering biological samples in terms of personal data.[35] Three separate arguments might be put forward supporting this position:

1. There are significant practical parallels between biological samples and sequenced genomic data.
2. Biological samples can be considered in terms of information.
3. Biological samples can be considered in terms of information as the term is used in the Regulation.

E. Biological Samples as Personal Data? Practical Parallels Between Biological Samples and Sequenced Genomic Data

The first argument asserts there is a strong normative basis for considering biological samples as personal data due to the practical parallels between the collection and use of samples and the collection and use of sequenced genomic data. This argument rests on three assertions.

First, all processing of biological samples is done for the purpose of collecting sequenced genomic data and therefore engages the same set of genetic privacy rights as the processing of genomic data. In previous chapters, it was observed that, in biobanking, samples are only processed for the sequenced genomic data which may be extracted from them—after all, the biological sample is the substance which contains the research subject's genome.[36] Practically then, it may be asserted that the collection or exchange of the sample is equivalent to the collection and exchange of sequenced genomic data: biological samples and genomic data move together.

It must thus be recognised that the processing of the sample engages the same set of genetic privacy rights as the processing of genomic sequence data.[37] As Bygrave observes: 'it is increasingly difficult, in practice, to distinguish between data/information and their biological carriers ... there is frequently an intimate link between biological samples and the information they generate'.[38] This was the line of argumentation taken by the ECtHR in its *Marper* judgment when it stated: 'In addition to the highly personal

Biobanking and Genomic Research', in Brent Mittelstadt and Luciano Floridi (eds.), *The Ethics of Biomedical Big Data* (Springer, 2016) 119, 119–37 (hereafter Hallinan and De Hert, 'Many Have It Wrong').

[35] It should be noted that biological samples may be collected in a variety of contexts. The argumentation here is logical in considering the potential applicability of the Regulation to the collection and use of biological samples in biobanking. It is possible to imagine other contexts, however, in which the Regulation would not necessarily apply. For example, the removal and disposal of bodily material during surgery would arguably not count as processing in the meaning of Article 4(2).

[36] See chapter 3, section G.

[37] See also: chapter 4, section D.

[38] Lee Bygrave, 'The Body as Data? Biobank Regulation via the "Back Door" of Data Protection Law' (2010) *Law, Innovation and Technology* 2(1) 1, 20 (hereafter Bygrave, 'The Body as Data').

nature of cellular samples, the Court notes that they contain much sensitive information about an individual, including information about his or her health.'[39]

Second, if biological samples and genomic data essentially move together—are collected for the same purpose and engage the same genetic privacy rights—they should be afforded the same treatment in law. As Bygrave observes in this regard: 'All of this demonstrates the need to subject both samples and information to a baseline of essentially similar, harmonised sets of rules.'[40] To do so would serve twin aims. In the first instance, it would ensure the same standard of protection for privacy rights applicable to all genetic privacy relevant substances. In turn, it would ensure that unnecessary distinctions between legal regimes could be avoided. Earlier in this chapter, it was established that sequenced genomic data qualify as personal data. It would thus make practical sense for data protection rules to be able to be applied to biological samples as well.

Finally, treating biological samples as a subject of data protection law is possible with a principled interpretation of the concept of personal data. The intention behind the GDPR is to provide protection for rights engaged by the processing of personal data. To continue to provide this protection in light of constant changes in information processing, the concepts and definitions of the law have been designed to be flexible. This flexibility also relates to the concept of personal data. This was explicitly clarified by the Commission when discussing the concept of personal data in the legislative process leading up to Directive 95/46: 'the definition of "personal data" should be as general as possible, so as to include all information concerning an identifiable individual'.[41] Accordingly, as the practical logic of treating the biological sample and genomic data is the same, this provides the practical justification for extending the concept of personal data to biological samples.

This practical argument, whilst strong, still fails to engage with legal technicalities—it does not actually assert that biological samples can fulfil the three criteria necessary to be a substance capable of qualifying as personal data. There is no question that biological samples can fulfil two of the three criteria: relate to; and natural person. The third criterion—information—however, is more problematic. In this regard, the second argument asserts that, in principle, biological samples can be regarded as information.

F. Biological Samples as Personal Data? Biological Samples Can Be Considered in Terms of Information

Several authoritative sources which deny biological samples can be personal data rely on the objection that biological samples must be regarded in terms of solid matter, and

[39] *Marper v. United Kingdom* (n. 27) para. 72.
[40] Bygrave, 'The Body as Data' (n. 38) 20.
[41] Commission of the European Communities, Amended proposal for a Council Directive on the protection of individuals with regard to the processing of personal data and on the free movement of such data (Policy, COM (92) 422 final—SYN 287, OJ C311/03, 1992) 9.

therefore cannot be information. The Government of Australia, for example, when considering the application of information privacy principles to biological samples, state: 'privacy principles are designed to regulate the collection, use and disclosure of personal information, not the source of that information [samples]'.[42] Nys puts the same sentiment differently: 'data are representations of reality, whereas human biological materials are real themselves'.[43] The key protagonist of this position in terms of European data protection law, however, is the Article 29 Working Party. They make the clear statement: 'Human tissue samples (like a blood sample) ... are not ... data themselves'.[44] Yet, when one considers biological samples in more detail, the logical fallacies of these arguments are revealed.

In the first instance, discussing the biological sample in terms of solid matter is the wrong focus of consideration. Of course, it makes no sense to claim a solid object is purely information—there is no utility in considering a table as purely informational. There is a legitimate distinction to be made between the corporeal and incorporeal. From this perspective, the sample is solid matter and not information. Yet, even if solid objects are not themselves information, they can still be considered as containers for information. In relation to the concept of personal data, whether an object can be conceptualised as solid matter is not relevant. The only relevant question is whether the object in question can be seen to contain information. For example, USB sticks and computer hard drives are solid. Yet both may be considered in terms of information if they contain information. The consideration of biological samples should be no different.[45] The question which must be answered is thus: do biological samples contain information? A focal point for the consideration of this question must be the key part of the biological sample regarding information storage. DNA.

It is without doubt possible to think of DNA as information. This is certainly how DNA is perceived in popular consciousness. There are numerous common popular informational metaphors for DNA. Indeed, such metaphors are the most dominant—even perhaps the only—descriptors of DNA in popular understandings of the genome. Consider the following examples: the genetic code; the genome as the book of life; the genome as a blueprint for life. Indeed, on the occasion of the completion of the Human Genome Project, for example, then US President Bill Clinton described DNA as: 'the language in which God created life'.[46]

However, the idea of DNA as information is not just a popular metaphor. The idea is also a functional concept in genetic science. For decades, the genetic sciences have relied on information theory and metaphors to understand DNA's structure and

42 Government of Australia, Full Australian Government Response to ALRC Report 96 (Policy, 2005) 6.

43 Nys, 'Report on the Implementation of Directive 95/46/EC in Belgian Law' (n. 32) 41.

44 Article 29 Working Party, Opinion 4/2007 (n. 6) 9.

45 Marion Albers, 'Rechtsrahmen und Rechtsprobleme bei Biobanken' (2013) *Medizinrecht* 31(8) 483, 486–7.

46 Office of the Press Secretary, Remarks Made by the President, Prime Minister Tony Blair of England (via satellite), Dr Francis Collins, Director of the National Human Genome Research Institute, and Dr Craig Venter, President and Chief Scientific Officer, Celera Genomics Corporation, on the Completion of the First Survey of the Entire Human Genome Project (Press Conference Report, 2000).

function.[47] Over this period, as Cobb observes: 'information as a metaphor, with genetic information having an instructional nature, has survived and flourished'.[48] Using information theory, geneticists have moved from understanding DNA as a physical molecule to understanding DNA as a medium for information storage and transfer. In this understanding, DNA has been described by Manson as biological 'communicative information'.[49] Indeed, evolutionary biologist Williams proposes it to be more logical to conceive of genes as information rather than as corporeal entities.[50]

A deeper exploration of the information metaphor for DNA reveals how significant and apt it really is. As I have observed elsewhere, this is shown via the various ways in which the structure and function of DNA can be described in informational terms.[51] The language of biological information is built around four symbols—nucleotides A, C, T, and G. The grammar is provided by the arrangement of nucleotides along the 3.2 billion molecule nucleotide chain. The content of information relates to phenotype construction. The senders and recipients of information are parents and their progeny, respectively.[52] In fact, DNA has even been proposed as offering an alternative to digital storage media. Church, for example, has gone as far as to encode a book in DNA.[53] Church et al. observe: 'as digital information continues to accumulate, higher density and longer-term storage solutions are necessary. DNA has many potential advantages as a medium for ... storage needs.'[54]

The fact that biological samples can be considered in terms of information goes a long way to concluding that samples can fulfil the information criterion of the concept of personal data in the GDPR. It is not, however, conclusive. That biological samples can be understood as information in some regards, does not necessarily mean they can be understood as the concept is used in the GDPR.[55] In this regard, scholars such as Bygrave have raised the suggestion that the concept of information in data protection law may have been taken from informatics, and that this discipline-specific concept

[47] Paul Griffiths and Karola Stotz, *Genetics and Philosophy: An Introduction* (Cambridge University Press 2013) 143–53.

[48] Matthew Cobb, '1953: When Genes Became "Information"' (2013) *Cell* 153(1) 503, 505.

[49] Neil Manson, 'The Medium and the Message: Tissue Samples, Genetic Information and Data Protection Legislation', in Heather Widdows and Caroline Mullen (eds.), *The Governance of Genetic Information: Who Decides* (Cambridge University Press 2009) 15, 24.

[50] George Williams, *Natural Selection: Domains, Levels and Challenges* (Oxford University Press 1992) 10–13.

[51] Hallinan and De Hert, 'Many Have It Wrong' (n. 34) 132.

[52] John Maynard Smith, 'The Concept of Information in Biology' (2000) *Philosophy of Science* 67(2) 177, 190.

[53] Sebastian Anthony, 'Harvard Cracks DNA Storage, Crams 700 Terabytes of Data into a Single Gram' *Extremetech* (17 August 2012) <http://www.extremetech.com/extreme/134672-harvard-cracks-dna-storage-crams-700-terabytes-of-data-into-a-single-gram> accessed 11 December 2019.

[54] George Church, Yuan Gao, and Sriram Kosuri, 'Next Generation Digital Information Storage in DNA' (2012) *Science* 337(6102) 1628, 1628.

[55] Shabani and Borry offer an interesting variant on this argument. They suggest that, as the concept of genetic data is defined in the Regulation but does not cover biological samples—see also the next chapter—an interpretation of the concept of personal data as covering samples may be awkward. I would suggest, however, that the scope of the definition of genetic data—as only one form of personal data—need not be taken as definitive of the scope of personal data as a whole. This is particularly the case in relation to the status of biological samples, given the legislator did not appear to have had the issue in mind when designing the Regulation. Mahsa Shabani and Pascal Borry, 'Rules for Processing Genetic Data for Research Purposes in View of the New EU General Data Protection Regulation'(2018) *European Journal of Human Genetics* 26 149, 151 (hereafter Shabani and Borry, 'Rules for Processing Genetic Data').

may not be broad enough to subsume biological samples.[56] The third argument thus addresses this objection and highlights that there are no objections to biological samples qualifying as information as the term is used in the GDPR.

G. Biological Samples as Personal Data? Biological Samples Can Be Considered as Information as the Term Is Used in the GDPR

As Bygrave, the author who as has dealt most extensively with the proposition, puts it: '[those refuting the idea that biological samples can be personal data] seem often to do so for conceptual reasons, applying a view of "data" and "information" in line with the ... conceptual framework common in informatics and computer science'.[57] However, as one considers the assertions the position rests on, it becomes clear the argument is a flimsy obstacle to recognising samples as information under the GDPR. Three assertions are problematic.

First, the objection relies on the assertion that the concept of information in the Regulation builds on a concept drawn from informatics. Yet, the evidence does not support the position. Two evidentiary problems are identifiable. In the first instance, there is no documentary evidence supporting the position. There is no indication, in any preparatory work or authoritative policy paper on EU data protection law—relating either to the GDPR or the Directive—that informatics provided the disciplinary inspiration for the concept of information. As Bygrave further observes in this respect: 'we often cannot be sure whether the architects of data protection law have applied such an understanding of data and information'.[58] In turn, there is significant divergence between the relevant terminology in data protection law and informatics. Should informatics have provided the template for concepts of information in data protection law, it seems highly unlikely that such divergence would have emerged. One prominent example revolves around the terms data and information.[59] In informatics, there is a clear and important distinction drawn between the two terms. In data protection law, however, the terms are often used as equivalents.

Second, the argument rests on the assumption that there are clearly defined concepts for data and information in informatics—if data protection law really relies on a concept of information drawn from informatics, then there must be a clear concept on which to rely. In fact, such a clear concept is not apparent. Rather, a multitude of different definitions is found for the terms in informatics. In Zins' work on the issue, for example, forty-five informatics scholars proposed widely divergent definitions of

[56] Bygrave, 'The Body as Data' (n. 38) 14–16.
[57] Bygrave, 'The Body as Data' (n. 38) 16.
[58] Bygrave, 'The Body as Data' (n. 38) 14.
[59] Chaim Zins, 'Conceptual Approaches for Defining Data, Information and Knowledge' (2007) *Journal of the Association for Information Science and Technology* 58(4) 479, 479 (hereafter Zins, 'Conceptual Approaches for Defining Data, Information and Knowledge').

the terms data and information.[60] Compare, for example, the following two proposed definitions for the concept of information: 'Information is resources useful or relevant or functional for information seekers' and '[i]nformation is a relationship between an inner arrangement . . . of a system and its present embodiment in reality (explicate order) including mediating memory processes . . . releasing the meaning'.[61] These definitions differ in multiple ways. For example, the first definition paints information as a subjective entity, relevant only to an observing agent, whilst the second definition paints information as an inherent quality of a system.

Finally, the argument rests on the assertion that concepts of information in informatics are defined by criteria which rule out DNA from qualifying. In fact, this is not necessarily the case. In Zins' work, some scholars proposed definitions for the concepts of data and information which could include DNA.[62] For example: 'Data are perceptible or perceived—if and when the signal can be interpreted by the "user"—attributes of physical, biological, social or conceptual entities' or '[data] are a representation of facts or ideas in a formalized manner, and hence capable of being communicated or manipulated by some process'.[63] Indeed, DNA can even qualify as information according to leading informatics definitions of the term. For example, DNA can fall within the definition provided in ISO 2382-1—Information technology—Vocabulary—Part 1: Fundamental terms.[64] Here, the ISO offer the following definition for the concept of data: 'A reinterpretable representation of information in a formalized manner suitable for communication, interpretation, or processing . . . Data can be processed by humans or by automatic means.' As I have observed elsewhere, DNA can fulfil each of the constituent criteria of this definition. DNA is reinterpretable—otherwise it would be biologically useless. DNA is a representation of information—concerning phenotypic specificity. DNA presents in a formalised manner—set arrangements of nucleotides along the genome. Finally, DNA can be processed both by humans as well as automatically.[65]

The previous four sections dealt with the first question concerning the qualification of personal data in the biobanking context: which biobanking substances could potentially be personal data? The conclusion was that biological samples, health, lifestyle, and biographical information, sequenced genomic data, and individual research results will each fulfil all relevant criteria. Building on these conclusions, I now move to consider the second question: which biobanking links qualify as identified or identifiable?

[60] Zins, 'Conceptual Approaches for Defining Data, Information and Knowledge' (n. 59) 487–9.

[61] Zins, 'Conceptual Approaches for Defining Data, Information and Knowledge' (n. 59) 483 and 484–5.

[62] Definitions which excluded DNA tended to focus on: the need for machine involvement in creation or storage of data or information; conscious human involvement in collection of data or information; or on the need for representation in alphabetic or numeric form of data or information. Zins, 'Conceptual Approaches for Defining Data, Information and Knowledge'(n. 59) 484.

[63] Zins, 'Conceptual Approaches for Defining Data, Information and Knowledge' (n. 59) 485 and 486.

[64] International Standards Organisation, Information Technology—Vocabulary—Part 1: Fundamental Terms (Policy, ISO 2382-1, 1993 [Revised by ISO/IEC 2382-1, 2015]).

[65] Hallinan and De Hert, 'Many Have It Wrong' (n. 34) 134.

H. Which Biobanking Links Qualify as Identified or Identifiable?

Chapter 3 provided a list of three common types of link maintained between substances and research subjects in biobanking. This list constitutes a useful reference point for the current analysis:[66]

1. Linked
2. Pseudonymous
3. Completely de-linked.

It is immediately evident that two out of three types of link will qualify as identified or identifiable. The Regulation is explicit that any substance processed in either a linked or pseudonymous state—in Article 4(1) and Recital 26 respectively—will qualify as identifiable.[67] The status of completely de-linked data, however, is less obvious. This seems counter-intuitive. Surely substances processed in a completely de-linked state cannot qualify as identifiable? It is true that certain substances processed in biobanking, which can be personal data, taken alone, will not be identified or identifiable in a completely de-linked state. Remove identifying information from discrete items of health, lifestyle, and biographical information, for example, and they may not be identifiable. This is, however, not the case for genomic data—whether in the form of biological samples or sequenced genomic data. Even when genomic data are processed in a completely de-linked state, they remain identifiable.[68] In this regard, genetic data in the biobanking

[66] See chapter 3, section K.

[67] Linked substances: as there is a clear connection maintained with a donor, there is no doubt that the identified or identifiable criteria will be fulfilled. As Article 4(1) states: 'an identifiable person is one who can be identified ... in particular by reference to an identifier such as a name, an identification number'.

Pseudonymous substances: Recital 26 of the Regulation clarifies that pseudonymous substances will qualify as identifiable: 'Data which has undergone pseudonymisation, which could be attributed to a natural person by the use of additional information, should be considered as information on an identifiable natural person.' Whilst the Regulation is the first EU data protection instrument to explicitly address the identifiability of pseudonymous substances, it merely codifies a position previously stated in data protection jurisprudence. The Article 29 Working Party, for example, in relation to the Directive, clarified that pseudonymous data qualify as identifiable: 'Retraceably pseudonymised data may be considered as information on individuals which are indirectly identifiable.' Article 29 Working Party, Opinion 4/2007 (n. 6) 18.

Mourby et al. offer an interesting take on the status of pseudonmyised data under the Regulation. Namely: 'anonymisation processes under the GDPR do not necessarily exclude pseudonymisation in the conventional sense, such as key-coding, as long as other environmental controls are in place to prevent the "data situation" yielding identifiable data'. Miranda Mourby, Elaine Mackey, Mark Elliot, et al., 'Are "Pseudonymised" Data Always Personal Data? Implications of the GDPR for Administrative Data Research in the UK' (2018) *Computer Law and Security Review* 34 222, 232. The authors basically propose a more contextual understanding of pseudonymisation. This approach has not yet received clear recognition in European jurisprudence or, to my knowledge, among EU DPAs. Equally, despite the subtle argumentation in the paper, the text of Recital 26 seems clear in classifying pseudonymised data as identifiable. As Shabani and Borry observe: 'In Recital 26, the Regulation asserts that pseudonymized data should be considered personal data.' Shabani and Borry, 'Rules for Processing Genetic Data' (n. 55) 151. Nevertheless, the argumentation is interesting and, subject to jurisprudential developments, its time may come.

[68] It is true that, if sequence data consist only of a small number of SNPs, it may not be possible to identify an individual. As Ziętkiewicz et al. observe: 'to achieve the level of discrimination ... [necessary only] ... 50–100 ... [SNPs] need to be genotyped'. Ewa Ziętkiewicz, Magdalena Witt, Patrycja Daca, et al., 'Current Genetic Methodologies in the Identification of Disaster Victims and in Forensic Analysis' (2012) *Journal of Applied*

context should be regarded as, as Morrison et al. put it: 'inherently identifying'.[69] Given that the central goal in collecting and processing all non-genomic data in biobanking is to process this data alongside genomic data, all substances stored or processed alongside either a biological sample or sequenced genomic data will thus always be identifiable by association. Two arguments support the position that genomic data remain identifiable even when processed in a completely de-linked state.

First, the genome alone contains sufficient information that re-identification of a research subject is a possibility. The basic position of the GDPR, as outlined above, is that a substance will classify as identifiable unless identification of an individual from the substance is 'reasonably impossible'.[70] This is not the case in relation to genomic data. There are means available to re-identify individuals in practical use.

Technically, several means of re-identification exist. Of these—as discussed previously—DNA fingerprinting and DNA profile creation are particularly significant.[71] *DNA fingerprinting*: the arrangement of nucleotides on an individual's genome is unique. As a result, a genome is a unique identifier for one single person.[72] Accordingly, the content of the genome always contains the raw data allowing a connection with an individual to be established. This connection can be established by cross-matching an unidentified biological sample or genomic data set with an identified sample or data set from another context. *DNA profile creation*: a genome stores vast quantities of information about an individual. Accordingly, through genome analysis, information can be revealed about an individual's physical appearance, ethnic background, or health status. Through the extraction of such information, a profile capable of identifying a single individual can be assembled. This can happen through the interrogation of the genome to reconstruct identifying physical features. This is the aim of forensic DNA phenotyping, which aims to reconstruct facial features for criminal investigations from DNA.[73] This can also happen through the combination of the results of DNA analysis with other public information. For example, Gymrek et al. have shown it is possible to re-identify supposedly anonymous genomes by matching inherited DNA markers with publicly available genealogy and surname records.[74]

Practically, both methods have already been used in contexts which require the identification of unknown individuals from a biological sample. DNA fingerprinting has proven particularly useful for police investigations and is in daily use. The method even

Genetics 54 41, 46. Sequenced data supporting GWAS, however, will usually consist of more than the required number of SNPs.

[69] Michael Morrison, Jessica Bell, Carol George, et al., 'The European General Data Protection Regulation: Challenges and Considerations for iPSC Researchers and Biobanks' (2017) *Regenerative Medicine* 12(6) 693, 697.

[70] Article 29 Working Party, Opinion 05/2014 (n. 18) 8.

[71] See chapter 2, section C.

[72] Harald Schmidt and Shawneequa Callier, 'How Anonymous Is "Anonymous"? Some Suggestions towards a Coherent Universal Coding System for Genetic Samples' (2012) *Journal of Medical Ethics* 38(5) 304, 304–9.

[73] Bert-Jaap Koops and Maurice Schellekens, 'Forensic DNA Phenotyping: Regulatory Issues' (2008) *Columbia Science and Technology Law Review* 9 158, 161–5.

[74] Melissa Gymrek, Amy McGuire, David Golan, et al., 'Identifying Personal Genomes by Surname Interface' (2013) *Science* 339 321, 321–4.

has clear relevance in relation to biobanking. As O'Doherty et al. observe: 'Situations can … arise in which the investigative opportunities afforded by databases [of biological samples] are of great interest for forensic and related purposes.'[75] The previously mentioned, use by police in Sweden of DNA fingerprinting on biobank samples in the investigation of the murder of Anna Lindh is one example of such use.[76] The approach has also been useful in other contexts. For example, Swedish biobank legislation was altered in 2004 to permit the use of biobank samples in DNA fingerprinting to identify victims of the tsunami in Thailand.[77] Forensic DNA phenotyping has also been used in law enforcement. The approach is newer than DNA fingerprinting and has been much less frequently used. There are, however, reports of use. As Pollack reports in the *New York Times*: 'the police in Columbia, S.C. … released a sketch of a possible suspect. Rather than an artist's rendering based on witness descriptions, the face was generated by a computer relying solely on DNA found at the scene of the crime.'[78]

Second, even if effective initial anonymisation of genomic data were possible, genomic data cannot foreseeably remain anonymous. Recall that, under the Regulation, a substance must foreseeably remain anonymous over the lifespan of processing to avoid qualifying as identifiable. As the Article 29 Working Party observe, one of the key factors to take into account regarding this foreseeability is the: '[possibility] for [technological] development [during processing relevant to identifiability]'.[79] In the case of genomic data, the unpredictability of advances in genetic science relevant to identifiability mean ongoing anonymity cannot be foreseeable. In this regard, Shabani and Marelli highlight the varying types of technologies which may be involved in processing genetic data as a reason that: 'de-identification of genetic data … for any given dataset … cannot be achieved once and for all'.[80] Two aspects of technological advance are significant in terms of identifiability.

The first type of technological advance concerns genome analysis. The state of the art in genetic science defines the type and quantity of information about an individual extractable from their genome. Accordingly, it defines how feasible it is to identify an individual from their genome. It also defines how valuable re-identification will be—the more, and the more accurate, the information extractable from a genome, the more valuable it will be to identify the genome's source. These factors, functioning together, will be significant in defining which third parties might seek to engage in re-identification attempts and thus how likely re-identification is to occur. It is virtually certain that genomic research will yield further insights into the function of the

[75] Kieran O'Doherty, Emily Christofides, Jeffrey Yen, et al., 'If You Build It, They Will Come: Unintended Future Uses of Organised Health Data Collections' (2016) *BMC Medical Ethics* 17(54) 6 <https://www.ncbi.nlm.nih.gov/pmc/articles/PMC5011895/pdf/12910_2016_Article_137.pdf> accessed 11 December 2019.

[76] Kieron O'Hara and Nigel Shadbolt, *The Spy in the Coffee Machine: The End of Privacy as We Know it* (Oneworld 2008) 107 (hereafter O'Hara and Shadbolt, *The Spy in the Coffee Machine*).

[77] O'Hara and Shadbolt, *The Spy in the Coffee Machine* (n. 76) 107.

[78] Andrew Pollack, 'Building a Face, and a Case, on DNA' *New York Times* (New York, 23 February 2015) <http://www.nytimes.com/2015/02/24/science/building-face-and-a-case-on-dna.html> accessed 11 December 2019.

[79] Article 29 Working Party, Opinion 4/2007 (n. 6) 15.

[80] Mahsa Shabani and Luca Marelli, 'Re-identifiability of Genomic Data and the GDPR: Assessing the Re-identifiability of Genomic Data in Light of the EU General Data Protection Regulation' (2019) *EMBO Reports* 20 4 <https://www.embopress.org/doi/epdf/10.15252/embr.201948316> accessed 1 June 2020.

genome.[81] Yet the genome remains a subject of great mystery. For example, the function of vast swathes of nucleotides remains unclear. Equally, even when there is clear information regarding correlation between genotype and phenotype, the causation between the two remains little clarified.[82] Given how little understood of the genome, it is impossible—unforeseeable—to say when scientific breakthroughs in genome function will occur or what shape they will have, including those related to identifiability.

The second type of technological advance concerns genome sequencing technology. The state of this technology defines how fast, cost-effectively, and conveniently, sequenced genomic data can be produced from biological samples. Accordingly, it defines the contexts in which sequenced genomic data can be usefully collected and used. As a result, it defines the range of contexts in which genomic information will be available to re-identify a research subject—the more genomic information available, the more likely re-identification can be attempted and will occur. For example, biological samples are a highly accurate and readily available biometric identifier. However, they cannot currently be effectively used as tokens in most biometric identification systems. As Jain et al. observe: 'technology for DNA matching requires cumbersome chemical methods (wet processes) involving an expert's skills'.[83] The technology is thus unsuitable as a biometric identifier outside forensic profiling. Yet, as discussed in previous chapters, sequencing technology is improving all the time and work is ongoing to alleviate these issues.[84] For example, in relation to the cumbersome nature of sequencing, Oxford Nanopore Technologies' product MinION, now allows: 'Portable, real-time biological [genome] analyses'.[85] However, it is hard to predict—unforeseeable—the precise form or speed of improvements in sequencing technologies, or to predict how far technologies will eventually improve.

I. Conclusion

The GDPR's applicability criteria are outlined in Article 2. Criteria concern both the types of processing activity covered by the GDPR and the mechanics of processing covered by the GDPR. In terms of the types of biobanking processing activity covered,

[81] Chris Tyler-Smith, Huanming Yang, Laura Landweber, et al., 'Where Next for Genetics and Genomics?' (2015) *PLOS Biology* 13(7) <http://journals.plos.org/plosbiology/article/asset?id=10.1371%2Fjournal.pbio.1002216.PDF> accessed 11 December 2019.

[82] Peter Visscher, Matthew Brown, Mark McCarthy, et al., 'Five Years of GWAS Discovery' (2012) *American Journal of Human Genetics* 90(1) 7, 8.

[83] Anil Jain, Arun Ross, and Salil Prabhakar, 'An Introduction to Biometric Recognition' (2004) *IEEE Transactions on Circuits and Systems for Video Technology* 14(1) 4, 8.

[84] Consider the difference in the last decade in speed and cost: the first full genome was sequenced by the Human Genome Project in 2001. The process took ten years, a $3bn investment, and the collaborative efforts of 200 scientists. By 2014, technology was available which allowed the sequencing of forty-nine genomes per day at only $1,000 each. See: E. S. Lander, L. M. Linton, B. Birren, et al., 'Initial Sequencing and Analysis of the Human Genome' (2001) *Nature* 409 860, 860–1; Illumina, *HiSeq X Ten Specification Sheet* (Information Sheet, 2016). <http://www.illumina.com/content/dam/illumina-marketing/documents/products/datasheets/datasheet-hiseq-x-ten.pdf> accessed 11 December 2019.

[85] Oxford Nanopore Technologies, 'MinION' (Oxford Nanopore Technologies, 2019) <https://nanoporetech.com/products/minion> accessed 11 December 2019.

the situation is clear. Only law enforcement processing of biobanking substances is excluded. All other biobanking processing falls squarely within the scope of the GDPR. In relation to the mechanics of biobank processing, the situation is, however, less clear. The key question which emerges is which types of biobanking substances can qualify as personal data?

The concept of personal data can be usefully broken down into two aspects of any processing operation. First, the substance being processed: to qualify as personal data, a substance must be able to fulfil three criteria. A substance must be 'information', it must 'relate to' a specific person, and that person must be a 'natural person'. In the biobanking context, health, lifestyle, and biographical information, sequenced genomic data, and individual research results certainly fulfil these criteria. Scientific research results certainly do not fulfil these criteria. In the case of biological samples, however, there is, superficially at least, some doubt. The doubt emerges, in particular, in relation to whether samples can fulfil the information criterion. An in-depth investigation, however, assuages these doubts and reveals strong practical and legal-technical arguments for recognising biological samples in terms of information and thus in terms of personal data.

Second, the link between the substance and a specific individual: to qualify as personal data, a substance must relate to an individual who is 'identified or identifiable'. All biobanking substances processed in either linked or pseudonymised form will certainly qualify as 'identified or identifiable'. The only doubt appears in relation to whether substances processed in completely de-linked form qualify as 'identified or identifiable'. An in-depth investigation of the question, however, results in a positive answer. The genome is a unique biometric identifier and accordingly, all biological samples, sequenced genomes, and all associated information will always qualify as identifiable.

8

Testing the GDPR in Relation to Biobanking

How Does the GDPR Classify the Biobanking Process?

A. Introduction

The previous chapter began the in-depth analysis of the General Data Protection Regulation (GDPR) by providing an analysis of its applicability, *rationae materiae*, to biobanking. This chapter continues the in-depth analysis considering how the biobanking process—in the instances in which it falls within the scope of the GDPR—is classified under the GDPR's classification systems. These classification systems do not, themselves, constitute substantive provisions—they do not consist of rights or obligations. They are, however, key in determining the types of actors to whom substantive provisions apply and the way in which substantive provisions apply.

The chapter begins with a detailed elaboration of the GDPR's two key classification systems: the actor classification system; and the personal data classification system (section B). The chapter then proceeds to describe how the actor classification system applies to actors involved in the biobanking process—considering, in particular, the applicability of the concepts of 'data subject', 'data controller', and 'data processor' (section C). Finally, the chapter describes how the personal data classification system applies to personal data processed in biobanking—considering, in particular, the applicability of the concepts of 'genetic data' and 'data concerning health' (section D).

B. Two Classifications Systems: The Actor Classification System and the Personal Data Classification System

The Regulation operates two key classification systems:

1. The first provides a classification of actors. This classification is used to allocate substantive rights and responsibilities.
2. The second provides a classification of types of personal data. This classification system differentiates, as clarified in Recital 51, types of personal data according to the risk their processing poses to fundamental rights. Personal data whose processing poses a particular risk are then subjected to a stricter regime of protection.

In order to clarify how these classification systems apply to biobanking, an in-depth look at their content is warranted.

Protecting Genetic Privacy in Biobanking through Data Protection Law. Dara Hallinan, Oxford University Press (2021). © Dara Hallinan.
DOI: 10.1093/oso/9780192896476.003.0008

The actor classification system: the system consists of three key classifications:

1. The data subject
2. The data controller
3. The data processor.

The concept of data subject serves to define the subject of protection—the parties whose fundamental rights may be affected by processing. The concept is defined in Article 4(1): 'personal data means any information relating to an identified or identifiable natural person ("data subject"); an identifiable natural person is one who can be identified, directly or indirectly'. The definition can logically be broken down into three cumulative criteria:

a. An actor must be a natural person.
b. The natural person must be identified or identifiable from the personal data.
c. The personal data in question must be somehow 'about' this natural person.

The concept of data controller is the primary classification for those whose processing of personal data may impact data subjects' rights. The concept is clarified in two places. First, in the GDPR: Article 4(7) clarifies a data controller as: 'the natural or legal person, public authority, agency or other body which ... determines the purposes and means of the processing'. Second, in jurisprudence: the Court of Justice of the European Union (CJEU), in the *Google Spain* decision, clarifies how the concept should be interpreted. The Court observes the concept should be given 'a broad definition [to ensure] protection of data subjects'.[1] In light of these clarifications, the Article 29 Working Party propose two cumulative criteria defining data controllers:

a. An actor must be 'a natural or legal person, public authority, agency or other body'.
b. An actor must determine the purposes and means of processing.[2]

The concept of data processor is a secondary classification for those whose processing may impact on data subjects' fundamental rights. The concept is defined in Article 4(8) of the Regulation as 'a natural or legal person, public authority, agency or other body which processes personal data on behalf of the controller'. In light of this definition, the Article 29 Working Party propose two cumulative criteria definitive of data processors:[3]

a. An actor must be a legally separate entity from a data controller.
b. This actor must only process data on behalf of, and under the instruction of, a data controller.

[1] *Google Spain SL, Google Inc. v. Agencia Española de Protección de Datos (AEPD), Mario Costeja González* [2014] ECLI:EU:C:2014:317, para. 34.
[2] Article 29 Working Party, Opinion 1/2010 on the Concepts of 'Controller' and 'Processor' (Policy, 00264/10/EN WP 169, 2010) 7 (hereafter Article 29 Working Party, Opinion 1/2010).
[3] Article 29 Working Party, Opinion 1/2010 (n. 2) 25.

The personal data classification system: the Regulation provides a two-tier classification system for personal data:

1. The default classification is normal.
2. A limited set of personal data are classified as sensitive. The types of data belonging in this set are exhaustively listed in Article 9(1) and include: 'data revealing racial or ethnic origin, political opinions, religious or philosophical beliefs, or trade union membership ... genetic data, biometric data for the purpose of uniquely identifying a natural person, data concerning health or data concerning a natural person's sex life or sexual orientation'.

It is immediately apparent that five of the seven types of sensitive data will be of limited relevance in biobanking.[4] The classifications of genetic data and data concerning health, however, deserve further consideration.

Genetic data is defined in two provisions in the Regulation. Article 4(13) provides a primary definition: 'personal data relating to the inherited or acquired genetic characteristics of a natural person which give unique information about the physiology or the health of that natural person and which result, in particular, from an analysis of a biological sample from the natural person in question'. This definition is then elaborated in Recital 34: 'Genetic data should be defined as personal data relating to the inherited or acquired genetic characteristics of a natural person which result from the analysis of a biological sample from the natural person in question, in particular chromosomal, deoxyribonucleic acid (DNA) or ribonucleic acid (RNA) analysis, or from the analysis of another element enabling equivalent information to be obtained.' Read together, these provisions outline two cumulative criteria for personal data to be genetic data, relating, respectively, to the content and genesis of the data:

[4] Through the collection of the genome, biobanks collect data which is a biometric identifier. However, for biometric data to constitute sensitive data, it must be used to 'uniquely [identify] a natural person'. This is not the case in biobanking. To collect data relating to racial or ethnic origin, political opinions, religious or philosophical beliefs, trade union membership, and concerning sex life or sexual orientation, a biobank would likely need to make a direct request to an individual. Such a request will only be made if this type of data is relevant to the research supported. This will seldom be the case. Even when a biobank does request this information, the sensitive classification would only apply to that data point.

Data revealing racial or ethnic origin may be scientifically argued to be collected indirectly through the collection of the genome. As Duster observes: 'there is substantial evidence that developments in several fields of inquiry and practice related to molecular genetics (pharmacogenomics, pharmacotoxicology, clinical genetics, personalized medicine and forensic science) have actually served to re-inscribe race as a biological category'. T. Duster, 'A Post-Genomic Surprise: The Molecular Re-Inscription of Race in Science, Law and Medicine' (2015) *British Journal of Sociology* 66(1) 1, 1. Yet, as Collins further observes: 'It must be emphasized ... that the connection [between race and genetics] is generally quite blurry because of multiple other non-genetic connotations of race, the lack of defined boundaries between populations and the fact that many individuals have ancestors from multiple regions of the world.' Francis Collins, 'What We Do and Don't Know About "Race", "Ethnicity", Genetics and Health at the Dawn of the Genome Era' (2004) *Nature Genetics* 36 513, 513. In turn, Recital 51 in the Regulation seems to disavow the idea of race: 'the use of the term "racial origin" in this Regulation does not imply an acceptance by the Union of theories which attempt to determine the existence of separate human races'. Given this direct disavowal, it is questionable whether the genome can constitute data revealing racial or ethnic origin under the Regulation.

a. Personal data must contain information relating to the 'inherited or acquired genetic characteristics' of an individual.
b. Personal data must be generated through the analysis of a biological sample.[5]

The concept of data concerning health is clarified in the Regulation and in jurisprudence. The Regulation defines the concept in two provisions. Article 4(15) provides a primary definition: 'personal data related to the physical or mental health of a natural person ... which reveal information about his or her health status'. This definition is then elaborated in Recital 35, which states that data concerning health: 'include all data ... which reveal information relating to the past, current or future ... health status of the data subject [and] information derived from the testing or examination of a body part or bodily substance, including from genetic data and biological samples; and any information on, for example, a disease, disability, disease risk, medical history, clinical treatment or ... physiological or biomedical state'.

Jurisprudence provides two further, significant, clarifications. First, jurisprudence clarifies that, in the case of doubt, the concept should be interpreted broadly. The CJEU, in the *Lindqvist* case, observes: 'the expression "data concerning health" ... must be given a wide interpretation'.[6] Second, jurisprudence clarifies that the context of processing is important in determining the presence of health data. The Article 29 Working Party observe that ostensibly non-health-related personal data may become data concerning health when used 'in combination with other data to draw a conclusion about the actual health status or health risk of a person'—i.e. when subject to a health-oriented analysis.[7]

Considering the clarification of the concept in the Regulation and associated jurisprudence, the concept of data concerning health can be considered to encompass three

[5] Objections as to the limited nature of this definition might be put forward. As Taylor observes 'a definition that only recognises genetic data that is the result of analysis may be considered to be too narrow'. Mark Taylor, 'Genetic Discrimination and the Draft European Union General Data Protection Regulation', in Gerard Quinn, Aisling de Paor, and Peter Blanck (eds.), *Genetic Discrimination: Transatlantic Perspectives on the Case for a European-Level Legal Response* (Routledge 2015) 211, 222. These objections are outside the scope of the book and will thus be only briefly discussed. Two are particularly significant.

First, the definition of 'genetic data' provided in the Regulation includes only data generated through the analysis of a biological sample. As discussed in previous chapters—see chapter 2, section A—genomic sequence information can be gathered without analysis of a biological sample. If there were a functional difference which resulted from the way genetic information was generated, this exclusion would be legitimate. There is not. In terms of the significance to an individual and the risks implicit in processing, the means of information generation is irrelevant.

Second, with its focus on the analysis of the genetic sample, the definition also excludes all data which is not directly connected with the genome. Yet, as discussed in previous chapters—see chapter 2—modern understandings of genome expression recognise the significance of environmental factors. For example, the fact that an individual has a poor diet is not genetic information—it is unconnected with the individual's genome. However, if the fact that an individual has a poor diet is analysed in light of their genome, the information will allow new conclusions to be drawn as to the how an underlying genetic propensity towards diabetes is likely to develop. See, for example, Frank Hu, 'Globalization of Diabetes' (2011) *Diabetes Care* 34 1249, 1253. The processing of genomic data is classified as sensitive because it can be used to produce information as to an individual's biologically defined phenotype. Where other information can be used to produce information about biologically defined phenotypes, it would be logical that this information, too, should be classified as genetic data.

[6] *Lindqvist v. Sweden* [2003] ECLI:EU:C:2003:596, para. 50. The broad interpretation approach has also been championed by the Article 29 Working Party. See: Article 29 Working Party, 'Health Data in Apps and Devices', Annex to Communication between the Article 29 Working Party and DG Connect (Policy, 2015) 2 (hereafter Article 29 Working Party, 'Health Data in Apps and Devices').

[7] Article 29 Working Party, 'Health Data in Apps and Devices' (n. 6) 5.

types of personal data, differentiated by their proximity of semantic link with the data subject's health:

a. Personal data which directly relate to, or describe, an individual's health status—'personal data related to the physical or mental health of a natural person'
b. Personal data which can be analysed to reveal information related to health status—'all data ... which reveal information relating to the past, current or future ... health status of the data subject' and 'any information on disease risk, medical history, clinical treatment or the physiological or biomedical state of the data subject'
c. Ostensibly non-health-related data used in a health-oriented analysis—personal data which become data concerning health by virtue of the context of processing.

On the back of these clarifications, I now move to consider how the two classification systems apply to biobanking.

C. The Applicability of the Actor Classification System to Biobanking

In order to clarify how the actor classification system applies to biobanking, each of the three classifications might be considered in light of the actors identified as important in the biobanking process in chapters 3 and 4. From this analysis, it is clear that the classifications of data subject and data controller are highly relevant. The classification of data processor, however, is likely to be less relevant.

Concerning the classification of the data subject, only three biobanking actors come into question as candidates. The classification describes actors whose fundamental rights are impacted by a processing operation. As discussed in chapter 4, there are three key actors whose fundamental rights are engaged by biobanking:

1. The research subject
2. The research subject's genetic relatives
3. The genetic groups to which the research subject belongs.

Of these three actors, only research subjects and genetic relatives fulfil all three criteria to qualify as data subjects. The idea that research subjects will qualify as data subjects is uncontroversial. Research subjects unproblematically fulfil all three relevant criteria. First, research subjects will invariably be natural persons. Second, as the previous chapter explained, research subjects will always qualify as identifiable from personal data processed in biobanking. Indeed, as Wjst comments: 'genetic data [and therefore all associated data] are intrinsically self-identifying'.[8] Finally, as previously discussed,

[8] Matthias Wjst, 'Caught You: Threats to Confidentiality Due to the Public Release of Large-Scale Genetic Data Sets' (2010) *BMC Medical Ethics* 11(21) <http://bmcmedethics.biomedcentral.com/articles/10.1186/1472-6939-11-21> accessed 11 December 2019.

both genomic and associated data can be subjected to a range of genetic analyses to reveal facts 'about' an individual.[9]

Genetic relatives can also fulfil all three relevant criteria. First, living genetic relatives will be 'natural persons'. Second, previous chapters have already explained how biological samples and associated data can be used to draw links to a research subject's genetic relatives such that they too are identifiable.[10] As Gabel observes: '[an] individual functions as a genetic beacon who may point the way to ... a family member'.[11] Finally, a research subject's genomic, and associated, data can be used to reveal information about relatives. Provided a phenotype has known inheritance patterns, a research subject's genome can be used to make probabilistic predictions about the presence of that phenotype in their genetic relatives.[12] The question of whether genetic relatives can be data subjects has been seldom directly considered in data protection jurisprudence. Nevertheless, certain jurisprudence is identifiable which supports the analysis above. The Article 29 Working Party, for example, observe: 'family members might also be considered as "data subjects"'.[13] The position also has support in legal scholarship. Taylor, for example, observes: 'the [concept of] personal data may ... be compatible with genetic data being the personal data of secondary data subjects [genetic relatives]'.[14]

Genetic groups—of all types—cannot be data subjects, as they fail to fulfil the first criterion of being natural persons. The previous chapter provided an overview of the concept of natural person in the GDPR—recall Harbinja's observation that the concept is 'understood generally as a person having legal capacity, starting with the birth and ending with her death'.[15] Genetic groups are not living persons. They therefore cannot qualify as natural persons and cannot be data subjects.

Concerning the classification of the data controller, only two biobanking actors come into question as candidates. The concept of data controller relates to actors who engage in data processing. In relation to normal biobanking activity, this limits the potential applicability of the concept to two actors, outlined in chapter 3:

1. Biobanks
2. External researchers.

[9] See chapter 2, section C.
[10] See chapter 2, section F.
[11] Jessica Gabel, 'Probable Cause from Probable Bonds: A Genetic Tattle Tale Based on Familial DNA' (2010) *Hasting's Women's Law Journal* 21(1) 3, 18.
[12] For example, if it is known that a research subject suffers from Canavan's disease, it is possible to assume their parents are carriers of the causal gene. See: Canavan Foundation, 'How Canavan Disease Is Inherited' (Canavan Foundation, 2019) <http://www.canavanfoundation.org/how_canavan_disease_is_inherited> accessed 11 December 2019.
[13] Article 29 Working Party, 'Working Document on Genetic Data' (Policy, 12178/03/EN WP 91, 2004) 8.
[14] Mark Taylor, *Genetic Data and the Law: A Critical Perspective on Privacy Protection* (Cambridge University Press 2012) 107.
[15] Edina Harbinja, 'Does the EU Data Protection Regime Protect Post-Mortem Privacy and What Could Be the Potential Alternatives?' (2013) *Scripted* 10(1) 19, 27.

Despite the narrow selection of potential candidates, both candidates will fulfil both criteria to be data controllers. Defining biobanks as data controllers is straightforward. Concerning the first criterion, biobanks will invariably be legal persons. Concerning the second criterion, biobanks play a key role in the determination of the purposes and means of processing. They determine how and why samples and data are collected and stored. They then determine which third parties—including external researchers—will receive access to substances. For example, Sudlow et al. observe that all applications to use the UK Biobank will be 'assessed and either approved or rejected (with right of appeal) by an independent Access Subcommittee'.[16] Indeed, biobanks even play a role in determining how substances might be used following access. As Yuille observes, biobanks will often require external recipients 'to accept terms and conditions' of use prior to being granted access to substances.[17]

The classification of external researchers as data controllers is less straightforward. The first criterion is unproblematic. External researchers will be natural persons and will work for organisations which will be legal persons. Concerning the second criterion, however, a question mark appears. External researchers will not usually exercise complete control over biobanking substances. As discussed in the previous paragraph, biobanks may refuse external researchers' access to substances altogether or place significant limits on the scope and manner of their use. For example, Sudlow et al. observe that the UK Biobank requires external researchers, in advance, to agree 'not to attempt to identify any participant, to keep the data secure, and to use it only for the purposes of the approved research'.[18] The question thus arises: if limits are placed on external researchers' use of substances by biobanks, do external researchers determine 'the purposes and means of processing'?

The answer is yes. In the first instance, it is possible to have more than one controller in relation to a processing operation. Article 26(1) states: 'Where two or more controllers jointly determine the purposes and means of processing, they shall be joint controllers.' In turn, in considering the concept 'determine the purposes and means of processing', the Article 29 Working Party clarify that absolute control is not required.[19] Instead, they propose two questions determinative of whether a sufficient level of control has been reached. First, 'why is the processing taking place'? Second, 'who initiated it?'[20] In light of the CJEU's clarification that the concept of data controller is to be given

[16] Cathie Sudlow, John Gallacher, Naomi Allen, et al., 'UK Biobank: An Open Access Resource for Identifying the Causes of a Wide Range of Complex Diseases of Middle and Old Age' (2015) *PLoS Med* 12(3) 4 <http://journals.plos.org/plosmedicine/article/file?id=10.1371/journal.pmed.1001779&type=printable> accessed 11 December 2019 (hereafter Sudlow, Gallacher, Allen, et al., 'UK Biobank: An Open Access Resource').

[17] Martin Yuille, Catherine Dixon, Andrew Platt, et al., 'The UK DNA Banking Network: A "Fair Access" Biobank' (2010) *Cell Tissue Bank* 11 241, 247. See also, for example, a Material Transfer Agreement explicitly limiting the scope of use of substances: Newcastle Brain Tissue Resource, Material Transfer Agreement for the Provision of Human-Tissue for (Non-Commercial) Academic Research (Material Transfer Agreement, 2014) <https://nbtr.ncl.ac.uk/uploads/MTA%20-%20NBTR%20standard.pdf> accessed 11 December 2019.

[18] Sudlow, Gallacher, Allen, et al., 'UK Biobank: An Open Access Resource' (n. 16) 4.

[19] Article 29 Working Party, Opinion 1/2010 (n. 2) 12–14.

[20] Article 29 Working Party, Opinion 1/2010 (n. 2) 8. See also the CJEU *Wirtschaftsakademie* case, in which the CJEU recognised the possibility for the administrator of a Facebook page to be considered, alongside Facebook, as a controller, despite not even necessarily processing any personal data themselves. *Unabhängiges Landeszentrum für Datenschutz Schleswig-Holstein v. Wirtschaftsakademie Schleswig-Holstein GmbH*, [2018] ECLI:EU:C:2018:388, paras 29–44.

a broad interpretation, external researchers can certainly qualify as data controllers. External researchers engage in processing solely for their own purposes—the pursuit of their scientific research. They tend to do so following contact with biobanks initiated by them.[21]

Concerning the classification of the data processor, whilst two actors superficially seem relevant, in fact, no actors are candidates. The concept of data processor refers to actors directly involved in a data processing operation. This narrows down the possible list of candidates to the same set of candidates which qualify as data controllers—biobanks and external researchers. This time, however, neither actor can qualify.[22] As the Article 29 Working Party criteria defining data processors highlight, classifications of data controller and data processor are mutually exclusive. This has been confirmed by the CJEU in the *Probst* case: '[a] processor acts only on the controller's instructions'.[23] Accordingly, an actor is either processing on behalf of a data controller and is a data processor, or will be sufficiently in control of the purposes and means of processing to qualify as a data controller. As it has been established that both biobanks and external researchers will qualify as data controllers, neither can qualify as data processors.

D. The Applicability of the Personal Data Classification System to Biobanking

In order to clarify how the personal data classification system applies to biobanking, each of the types of sensitive data relevant to biobanking—genetic data and data concerning health—might be considered in relation to each of the four types of personal data processed in biobanking identified in the previous chapter:

1. The biological sample
2. Health, lifestyle, and biographical information
3. Sequenced genomic data
4. Individual research results.

In this regard, the two concepts of sensitive data apply conclusively to all types of personal data processed in biobanking. Accordingly, all personal data processed in biobanking will qualify as sensitive personal data.

[21] Article 26(1), as Kuner observes, 'requires [joint controllers] to conclude an "arrangement" allocating data protection responsibility between them'. Christopher Kuner, 'The European Commission's Proposed Data Protection Regulation: A Copernican Revolution in European Data Protection Law' (2012) *Bloomberg BNA Privacy and Security Law Report* February 6 1, 7. Despite this discretion, the Article 29 Working Party clarified that the factual realities of a processing operation must be taken into account. Article 29 Working Party, Opinion 1/2010 (n. 2) 25.

[22] This is not to say the concept cannot, or will never, apply to biobanking. For example, it may apply to actors which play a supporting role in the process—for example, external labs or sequencing facilities to which a biobank has outsourced the production of genomic data. Such actors will be legal entities apart from the biobank, yet will only process on the orders of the biobank.

[23] *Josef Probst v. mr.nexnet GmbH* [2012] ECLI:EU:C:2012:748, para. 25.

Concerning the classification of genetic data, two of the four types of personal data processed in biobanking will qualify: sequenced genomic data; and individual research results. Sequenced genomic data qualify, without doubt, as genetic data. With regard to the first criterion, sequenced genomic data relate to an individual's 'inherited or acquired genetic characteristics'. They are translations of the nucleotide sequence in DNA into electronic—even alphanumeric—form. Indeed, a sequenced genome is a complete record of an individual's 'inherited or acquired genetic characteristics'. With regard to the second criterion, the production of sequenced genomic data directly follows the subjection of a biological sample to the analysis of the genomic sequencing process.

Individual research results also unquestionably qualify as genetic data. These are claims about an individual made following an interrogation of an individual's sequenced genomic data. Accordingly, they fulfil the first criterion as they relate to an individual's 'inherited or acquired genetic characteristics'. In turn, individual research results are the—often intentional—end-product of a genetic analysis process beginning with the sequencing of a biological sample. Accordingly, they fulfil the second criterion as 'resulting' from the analysis of a biological sample.

Biological samples, surprisingly, cannot qualify as genetic data. The first criterion defining genetic data is unproblematic. Biological samples certainly contain data which relates to the 'inherited or acquired genetic characteristics' of an individual. As observed in the previous chapter, DNA contained in a sample can be regarded as genetic data in its own right. Recall the observation that 'there is a "genetic code" and that this is contained in DNA is now virtually unchallenged'—even within the genetic sciences.[24] The problem, however, appears with the second criterion. Biological samples do not result from an analysis of biological samples—they are biological samples.

Health, lifestyle, and biographical information fail to qualify as genetic data for a similar reason. With regard to the first criterion, these types of information may qualify as being related to 'inherited or acquired genetic characteristics'. This will, of course, depend on their informational content. For example, medical data may reveal genetic characteristics, whereas exercise information may not. The problem, however, again appears with the second criterion. These types of information will be collected from the research subject or from another source—such as a hospital or a healthcare provider. Accordingly, they will not result from the analysis of a biological sample.

Concerning the classification of data concerning health, all types of personal data processed in biobanking will fall under one, or more, of the three qualifying categories. The biological sample does not directly describe an individual's health and accordingly, will not qualify under category a. However, the sample will qualify under category b. The sample contains the complete genome. As discussed previously, there is no doubt

[24] Dara Hallinan and Paul De Hert, 'Many Have It Wrong—Samples Do Contain Personal Data: The Data Protection Regulation as a Superior Framework to Protect Donor Interests in Biobanking and Genomic Research', in Brent Mittelstadt and Luciano Floridi (eds.), *The Ethics of Biomedical Big Data* (Springer 2016) 119, 132.

that the genome can be analysed to reveal information about the research subject's health. Indeed, the Article 29 Working Party have specifically clarified that 'information about a person's ... genetic predisposition'—including the genome—constitute data on 'disease risk'.[25]

Health, lifestyle, and biographical information may fall under categories a and b. Health data will certainly fall within category a. Lifestyle and biographical information may either directly concern an individual's health and fall under category a, or may be subject to analysis to reveal information about an individual's health and thus fall under category b. All health, lifestyle, and biographical information processed in biobanking, however, will always fall within category c. The Article 29 Working Party explicitly observed that 'medical research using big data'—such as genome-wide association study (GWAS) in biobanking—constitutes a health-oriented analysis.[26] Accordingly, all health, lifestyle, and biographical information in biobanking fall under category c by default.

The status of sequenced genomic data is similar to the biological sample. The data does not directly relate to health and accordingly does not fall within category a. However, it is data which can be analysed to provide information concerning an individual's health and accordingly, will qualify under category b.[27] Indeed, Recital 35 explicitly recognises sequenced genomic data as data concerning health as 'information derived from the testing or examination of a body part or bodily substance, including from ... biological samples'.[28] The Article 29 Working Party make further clear that the 'results of such a test qualify as data concerning health irrespective of whether ... results are ... "healthy" '.[29]

Individual research results may constitute personal data concerning health under category a if they are directly related to a data subject's health.[30] If they do not directly relate to health status, they will nevertheless constitute data concerning health under category b. In the GDPR, Recital 35 specifically clarifies that the concept of data concerning health includes: '[all] information derived from the testing of ... genetic data and biological samples'.

E. Conclusion

There are two key classification systems relevant to the biobanking process in the GDPR: the actor classification system—consisting of the key classifications of data

[25] Article 29 Working Party, 'Health Data in Apps and Devices' (n. 6) 2–3.
[26] Article 29 Working Party, 'Health Data in Apps and Devices' (n. 6) 3.
[27] There may be exceptions for very small quantities of single nucleotide polymorphism (SNP) data. Even here, however, SNPs will tend to be selected for their relevance to disease.
[28] The Article 29 Working Party have also stated: 'genetic data are doubtlessly "personal data on health" '. Article 29 Working Party, Working Document on the Processing of Personal Data Relating to Health in Electronic Health Records (EHR) (Policy, 00323/07/EN WP 131, 2007) 7.
[29] Article 29 Working Party, 'Health Data in Apps and Devices' (n. 6) 2.
[30] There is a lack of clarity as to how the definition of genetic data exists independently from the definition of data concerning health. Article 4(13) and Recital 34 clarify that genetic data are data which result from the analysis of a biological sample. Recital 35 explains that the concept of data concerning health subsumes all information which results from the analysis of a biological sample.

subject, data controller, and data processor; and the personal data classification system—consisting of the key classifications of normal data and sensitive data. In principle, neither of these classification systems serve to outline substantive obligations to which biobanking actors are subject. Each system, however, plays a role in determining how the GDPR's substantive provisions apply to biobanking.

In terms of the actor classification system, research subjects and genetic relatives can qualify as data subjects—although genetic groups will not. Biobanks and external researchers will then qualify as data controllers. Significantly, no significant actors in the biobanking process will qualify as data processors. Superficially, biobanks and external researchers seem possible candidates to be data processors. Their qualification as data controllers, however, precludes their qualification as data processors.

In terms of the personal data classification system, all substances processed in the biobanking process which fall under the scope of applicability of the GDPR will qualify as sensitive personal data. The GDPR elaborates several types of sensitive data. Of these, the concepts of genetic data and data concerning health are most relevant to biobanking. The concept of genetic data is applicable to sequenced genomic data and individual research results—although not to biological samples or to health, lifestyle, and biographical information. The concept of data concerning health is applicable to all types of biobanking substances which qualify as personal data.

9

Testing the GDPR in Relation to Biobanking

How Do the GDPR's Substantive Provisions Apply to Biobanking?

A. Introduction

The previous two chapters clarified when the General Data Protection Regulation (GDPR) applies, *rationae materiae*, to biobanking and how biobanking is classified under the GDPR's classification systems. This chapter now completes the in-depth analysis of the applicability of the GDPR to biobanking by elaborating how the GDPR's substantive provisions apply to biobanking.

The chapter breaks down the relevant substantive provisions in the GDPR into seven groups. The applicability of each group of provisions to biobanking is then dealt with in turn: oversight (section B); legitimate processing (section C); data subject rights (section D); obligations on data controllers (section E); transfers to third countries (section F); sanctions (section G); and derogations (section H).

B. Biobanking and Oversight under the GDPR

The oversight process relevant to biobanking in the GDPR consists of four phases of oversight:[1]

1. *Ex ante* assessment
2. Prior notification and approval
3. Ongoing oversight
4. General oversight.

Ex ante assessment is outlined in Article 35 and involves the conduct of a Data Protection Impact Assessment (DPIA) prior to the start of processing. A DPIA is not always obligatory. However, Article 35(3)(b) specifies that, whenever 'processing on a large scale of special categories of data' is planned, a DPIA is necessary. As van Veen puts it: 'It should be assumed ... a DPIA is necessary for every major research project

[1] See, for an extended discussion of the four oversight mechanisms: Dara Hallinan, 'Biobank Oversight and Sanctions Under the General Data Protection Regulation', in Santa Slokenberga, Olga Tzortzatou, and Jane Reichel (eds.), *GDPR and Biobanking: Individual Rights, Public Interest and Research Regulation across Europe* (Springer 2021) 121, 123–131 (hereafter Hallinan, 'Biobank Oversight and Sanctions').

Protecting Genetic Privacy in Biobanking through Data Protection Law. Dara Hallinan, Oxford University Press (2021). © Dara Hallinan.
DOI: 10.1093/oso/9780192896476.003.0009

with health data.'[2] Given biobanking involves the processing of large amounts of sensitive data, a DPIA will thus invariably be required. The aim of a DPIA, as van Dijk et al. observe, 'is to [assess] ... risks to privacy and [devise] solutions to mitigate such risks' whilst processing is being planned.[3]

Each aspect of a biobanking controller's processing must be covered by a DPIA. Whilst the scope of a DPIA is not precisely defined, Article 35(1) permits that a DPIA may 'address a set of similar processing operations that present similar ... risks'. Accordingly, the Regulation permits multiple biobanking operations involving multiple controllers, to be addressed by one DPIA. As the Article 29 Working Party put it: 'DPIAs aim at systematically studying new situations that could lead to high risks on the rights and freedoms of natural persons, and there is no need to carry out a DPIA in cases (i.e. processing operations performed in a specific context and for a specific purpose) that have already been studied.'[4]

When conducting a DPIA, biobanking controllers must follow certain methodological steps resulting in a DPIA report. These steps are outlined in Articles 35(7)(a)–(d): describe the proposed processing operation, the purpose of processing and the justification for processing; provide an assessment of necessity and proportionality; assess the risks to data subjects; and finally, describe the measures taken to mitigate risks. Article 35(7) is further supplemented by Article 35(9), which requires 'the views of data subjects' to be considered.[5] Although the DPIA is an *ex ante* instrument, should a substantial change in processing occur, Article 35(11) requires a biobanking controller to review processing to ensure compatibility with the original DPIA.

Prior notification and approval is outlined in Article 36 and requires that, in certain cases, biobanking controllers may need to seek Data Protection Authority (DPA) approval prior to engaging in processing.[6] If a DPIA, according to Article 36(1), 'indicates that the processing would result in a high risk in the absence of measures taken by the controller to mitigate the risk', a biobanking controller is obliged to notify the DPA prior to beginning processing. Significantly, De Hert and Papakonstantinou observe that Article 36(1) leaves the decision as to whether the

[2] Evert-Ben van Veen, 'Observational Health Research in Europe: Understanding the General Data Protection Regulation and Underlying Debate' (2018) *European Journal of Cancer* 104 70, 74.

[3] Niels Van Dijk, Raphaël Gellert, and Kjetil Rommetveit, 'A Risk to a Right? Beyond Data Protection Risk Assessments' (2016) *Computer Law and Security Review* 32(2) 286, 289.

[4] Article 29 Working Party, Guidelines on Data Protection Impact Assessment (DPIA) and determining whether processing is 'likely to result in a high risk' for the purposes of Regulation 2016/679 (Policy, 17/EN WP 248, 2017) 7 (hereafter Article 29 Working Party, Guidelines on Data Protection Impact Assessment).

[5] The Article 29 Working Party provide some, albeit limited, guidance on each of these steps. See: Article 29 Working Party, Guidelines on Data Protection Impact Assessment (n. 4) 14–18.

[6] DPAs are public authorities. Article 51(1) clarifies that each State must 'provide for one or more independent public [oversight] authorities'. See also the CJEU's clarification of the scope of the concept of independence in: *Commission v. Hungary* [2014] ECLI:EU:C:2014:237, para. 51.

When biobanks collaborate in European networks, more than one DPA will become relevant. Here, the Regulation elaborates a system of collaboration between DPAs. Central to this system is the designation of a 'lead supervisory authority' under Article 56(1). See: Article 29 Working Party, Guidelines for Identifying a Controller or Processor's Lead Supervisory Authority (Policy, 16/EN WP 244, 2016).

requisite conditions for consultation with the DPA are fulfilled, to the controller themselves.[7]

If a prior consultation is necessary, the biobanking controller is obliged to put the DPA in a position to evaluate processing. To do this, the biobanking controller must provide the DPA with the information outlined in Articles 36(3)(a)–(f), including: the distribution of data protection obligations amongst relevant controllers and processors; the aim and means of processing; any safeguards in place; the DPIA report; and other information requested. If the DPA finds processing compatible with the Regulation, they will permit processing to proceed in accordance with the DPIA. If the DPA concludes that the proposed processing is not compatible, they may, under Article 58(2), allow processing to go ahead only under certain conditions, or simply prohibit processing.

Ongoing oversight is outlined in Articles 39, 57, and 58. Two bodies are involved in ongoing oversight: the DPA; and the Data Protection Officer (DPO).[8] DPAs have no obligation to monitor all biobanking activity. However, they have a mandate, under Article 57(1)(a), to investigate any processing activity engaged in by biobanking controllers in their jurisdiction. In an investigation, the DPA has a range of investigatory powers. These include the power, under Article 58(1)(a), to order the biobanking controller 'to provide any information [the DPA] requires for the performance of its tasks'. If problems are found with processing, the DPA may then call upon a series of corrective powers outlined in Article 58(2). These include powers to warn or reprimand the controller under Article 58(2)(a) and (b) and the power to impose temporary or permanent limitations, or a ban, on processing under 58(2)(f). They may also call upon administrative sanctioning powers—these will be discussed in section G.

The DPO has two key oversight tasks concerning the ongoing oversight of biobanking controllers. These are laid out in Article 39(1). First, the DPO must act as an internal advisory body 'informing and advising' the biobanking controller as to whether its processing is Regulation compliant. Second, the DPO must engage in ongoing oversight to ensure ongoing compliance.

General oversight is outlined in Articles 57 and 70 and involves oversight of the biobanking landscape generally—as opposed to of specific actors. Two oversight bodies engage in general oversight: the DPA; and the European Data Protection Board (EDPB).[9] DPAs have a mandate to engage in general oversight under Article 57. Article 57(1)(i) gives DPAs the task to 'monitor relevant developments, insofar as they have an

[7] Paul De Hert and Vagelis Papakonstantinou, 'The New General Data Protection Regulation: Still a Sound System for the Protection of Individuals?' (2016) *Computer Law and Security Review* 32(2) 179, 192 (hereafter De Hert and Papakonstantinou, 'The New General Data Protection Regulation').

[8] Article 37 clarifies that DPOs are employees of a processing entity. Article 38(3) clarifies they must still operate with independence. DPOs are obligatory, according to Article 37(1)(c), where: 'the core activities of the controller … consist of processing on a large scale of special categories of data'. Article 37(2) permits '[a] group of undertakings [to] appoint a single data protection officer'. The Article 29 Working Party provide some examples of processing which is large scale and processing which is not. Typical biobanking activities map to the former. See: Article 29 Working Party, Guidelines on Data Protection Officers ('DPOs') (Policy, 16/EN WP 243 rev.01, 2016 [revised 2017]) 8.

[9] The EDPB is the successor to the Article 29 Working Party. It is a Union body comprising, according to Article 68(3), of 'the head of one supervisory authority of each Member State and of the European Data Protection Supervisor, or their respective representatives'.

impact on the protection of personal data, in particular the development of information and communication technologies'. Accordingly, a DPA may choose to engage in oversight of the biobanking sector, or in oversight of developments related to data protection relevant to biobanking, as they see fit.

The EDPB is granted similar oversight powers to DPAs. Whereas DPAs function at Member State level, however, the EDPB functions at EU level. Article 70(1)(e) mandates the EDPB with '[examining], on its own initiative, on request of one of its members, or ... the Commission, any question covering the application of [the] Regulation'. The consequence, under Article 70(1)(e), will be the: 'issue [of] guidelines, recommendations and best practices ... to encourage consistent application of [the] Regulation'. These guidelines are, technically, non-binding. However, De Hert and Papakonstantinou consider they will be—at the very least—difficult to ignore: '[the Regulation foresees a] strong and standalone Board ... that is capable of deciding on ... and enforcing ... opinions'.[10]

C. Biobanking and Legitimate Processing under the GDPR

Article 9(1) outlines a general prohibition on the processing of all sensitive data. Article 9(2), however, provides an exhaustive list of ten exceptions to this prohibition.[11] Biobanking controllers must thus be able to point to the relevance of one of these exceptions to justify processing. A glance across these exceptions reveals eight are, from a legal perspective, likely to be, at best, marginally relevant to biobanking.[12] In this

[10] De Hert and Papakonstantinou, 'The New General Data Protection Regulation' (n. 7) 193.

[11] A legitimation must also be found under Article 6. However, if a legitimation for biobanking can be found under Article 9, then a legitimation will also exist under Article 6: for consent under Article 9(2)(a), Article 6(1)(a) will be relevant; for processing necessary for scientific research under Article 9(2)(j), Article 6(1)(f) will be relevant. See, for a brief discussion: European Data Protection Board, Opinion 3/2019 concerning the Questions and Answers on the interplay between the Clinical Trials Regulation (CTR) and the General Data Protection regulation (GDPR) (art. 70.1.b)) (Policy, 2019) 4–9 (hereafter European Data Protection Board, Opinion on Clinical Trials); Dara Hallinan, 'Broad Consent under the GDPR: An Optimistic Perspective on a Bright Future' (2020) *Life Sciences, Society and Policy* 16(1) 4 <https://lsspjournal.biomedcentral.com/track/pdf/10.1186/s40504-019-0096-3> accessed 19 June 2020 (hereafter Hallinan, 'Broad Consent').

[12] These include: processing necessary for employment and social security and social protection; processing necessary 'to protect the vital interests of the data subject' or another person where the data subject cannot consent; processing of members' data by a 'foundation, association or any other not-for-profit body with a political, philosophical, religious or trade union aim'; processing of personal data 'which are manifestly made public by the data subject'; processing necessary for legal claims or procedures before court; processing 'for reasons of substantial public interest'; processing necessary for certain medical or social care purposes; processing for reasons of public health—like protecting against 'serious cross-border threats to health or ensuring high standards of quality and safety of health care'.

In certain instances, biobanking may be legitimated by three of these other exceptions. Their applicability will, however, be limited. First, there is a nascent trend towards individuals self-publishing their genomes. See, for example, openSNP, 'Welcome to openSNP' (openSNP 2019) <https://opensnp.org/> accessed 11 December 2019. It is possible to imagine a biobank relying on data which have been manifestly made public according to Article 9(2)(e). Second, it is possible to imagine biobanking research which meets the Article 9(2)(g) standards of 'processing ... necessary for reasons of substantial public interest'. However, from a legal perspective, there is reason to think this will be rare, owing to the prospective nature of the research ordinarily supported in biobanking. The concept of a substantial public interest might be compared to that of an 'important public interest'. This latter concept is to be distinguished from a mere normal public interest. The Article 29 Working Party have observed, in relation to international transfers, that the concept of 'important public interest' must be 'given a restrictive

regard, I consider, in line with scholars such as Molnár-Gábor, that there are only two exceptions which will have broad applicability:[13]

1. Article 9(2)(a) permits processing when 'the data subject has given explicit consent'.
2. Article 9(2)(j) permits processing when it is 'necessary for ... scientific ... research purposes'.

In order to rely on the consent exception under Article 9(2)(a), a biobanking controller must make sure consent fulfils the conditions outlined in Article 4(11). Article 4(11) states: '"consent" ... means any freely given, specific, informed and unambiguous indication of the data subject's wishes'.[14] This formulation can be broken down into four cumulative criteria:[15]

a. Freely given
b. Specific
c. Informed
d. Unambiguous.

The requirement that consent is 'freely given' relates to the autonomy of the data subject in accepting or rejecting processing. As Kosta observes: 'Consent should be an autonomous act of the data subject, free from ... manipulations.'[16] Recital 43 further clarifies that: 'consent should not provide a valid legal ground ... where there is a clear imbalance between the data subject and the controller'. The Article 29 Working Party also highlight that consent can only be freely given where there is no 'risk of deception,

interpretation' and refers to processing which was 'necessary and ... identified as [an important public interest] by ... national legislation'. Article 29 Working Party, Working document on a common interpretation of Article 26(1) of Directive 95/46/EC of 24 October 1995 (Policy, 2093/05/EN WP 114, 2005) 15. In turn, commentators such as Ploem et al. recognise that, as 'the potential of a research project to yield exceptionally important findings is hard to predict' biobanking will usually unlikely qualify as an 'important ... public interest'. M. Ploem, M. L. Essink-Bot, and K. Stronks, 'Proposed EU Data Protection Regulation Is a Threat to Medical Research: A Suggested Amendment Would Make Most Epidemiological and Health Research Impossible' (2013) *British Medical Journal* 346 1, 1. Third, there is the possibility of biobank work falling within the Article 9(2)(i) justification of processing necessary 'for reasons of public interest in the area of public health, such as protecting against serious cross-border threats to health'. Certain biobanks may be able to rely on this exception concerning work relating to emergency health situations—such as the COVID-19 pandemic. This has been confirmed by the European Data Protection Board. See: European Data Protection Board, Guidelines 03/2020 on the processing of data concerning health for the purpose of scientific research in the context of the COVID-19 outbreak (Policy, 2020) 7–8 (hereafter European Data Protection Board, Guidelines on processing data concerning health for scientific research in the context of COVID-19).

13 Fruzsina Molnár-Gábor, 'Germany: A Fair Balance between Scientific Freedom and Data Subjects' Rights?' (2018) *Human Genetics* 137 618, 620–1.

14 A series of other Articles are also relevant in defining the concept of consent. Article 7, for example, elaborates certain procedural details.

15 See, for an extended clarification of the modalities of each of these criteria: Article 29 Working Party, Opinion 15/2011 on the definition of consent (Policy, 01197/11/EN WP187, 2011) (hereafter Article 29 Working Party, Opinion 15/2011 on the definition of consent); European Data Protection Board, Guidelines 05/2020 on consent under Regulation 2016/679 (Policy, 2020) (hereafter European Data Protection Board, Guidelines on consent).

16 Eleni Kosta, *Consent in European Data Protection Law* (Martinus Nijhoff 2013) 169.

intimidation, coercion or significant negative consequences if he/she [the data subject] does not consent'.[17] Zuiderveen Borgesius et al. suggest the requirement might be interpreted strictly. They even suggest that consent may not be freely given, for example: 'If there is a clear imbalance between a large company and a data subject.'[18] In the biobanking context, the requirement might be taken to mean consent may only be relied upon if it is not granted under duress and is not a prerequisite for access to return services.[19]

The requirement that consent be specific relates to the scope of activity which might be justified by consent. The concept of specificity of purpose has generally been interpreted narrowly in data protection law. For example, the Article 29 Working Party observed that '[v]ague or general purposes such as "improving users' experience", "marketing", "IT-security" ... will—without more detail—usually not meet the criteria of being "specific" '.[20] The GDPR, however, provides special enunciation of the condition relating to research—and therefore to biobanking. Recital 33 clarifies: 'It is often not possible to fully identify the purpose of personal data processing for scientific research purposes at the time of data collection. Therefore, data subjects should be allowed to give their consent to certain areas of scientific research when in keeping with recognized ethical standards for scientific research.'

Accordingly, in biobanking, one consent may permit multiple research purposes.[21] The EDPB, however, offer some further tentative clarification of the scope and conditions of the use of Recital 33. In the first instance, they suggest that the Recital only

[17] Article 29 Working Party, Opinion 15/2011 on the definition of consent (n. 15) 12. See also: European Data Protection Board, Opinion on Clinical Trials (n. 11) 6.

[18] Frederik Zuiderveen Borgesius, Sanne Kruikemeier, Sophie Boerman, et al., 'Tracking Walls, Take-It-Or-Leave-It Choices, the GDPR, and the ePrivacy Regulation' (2017) *European Data Protection Law Review* 3 353, 364.

[19] Arguments have been put forward in certain EU Member States that consent may be difficult to rely on in relation to research conducted by public authorities. See, for example, NHS Health Research Authority, 'Consent in Research' (NHS Health Research Authority, 2018) <https://www.hra.nhs.uk/planning-and-improving-research/policies-standards-legislation/data-protection-and-information-governance/gdpr-guidance/what-law-says/consent-research/> accessed 19 June 2020. This position seems to be based, in part, on a reading of Recital 43 and its observation that power imbalances may exist in relation to public sector processing. As I have observed elsewhere, however, this position seems to be based on a misreading of Recital 43: 'Recital 43 also states, however, that any consideration of power imbalance and dependence must be taken in relation to "a specific case". The Recital thus does not outline a general prohibition on the use of consent under the GDPR by public bodies—or indeed any specific type of entity. In terms of specifics, it is hard to think of any modern European genomic research infrastructure, or project, which would fulfil the criteria of Recital 43—these are characterized, as far as they do rely on consent, by their voluntary nature and the fact that participation is unrelated to reciprocity in the provision of current, or future, goods or health-care'. Hallinan, 'Broad Consent' (n. 11) 5. This position has been confirmed by the EDPB. In relation to the legitimation of the example of a non-interventional study, they state: 'In the view of the EDPB, the [processing] is not considered a case of "clear imbalance of power" as mentioned in Recital 43 and the data subject should be able to give the consent to the researchers. In the example, the data subjects are not in a situation of whatsoever dependency with the researchers that could inappropriately influence the exercise of their free will and it is also clear that it will have no adverse consequences if they refuse to give their consent'. European Data Protection Board, Guidelines on processing data concerning health for scientific research in the context of COVID-19 (n. 12) 7.

[20] Article 29 Working Party, Opinion 03/2013 on purpose limitation (Policy, 00569/13/EN WP 203, 2013) 15 (hereafter Article 29 Working Party, Opinion 03/2013 on purpose limitation).

[21] The scope of purpose will also define the parties to whom the personal data can be given. The Article 29 Working Party commented that personal data may be given to undefined third parties in future, based on consent, provided 'the information provided to the data subject ... [indicated] the purpose(s), the goods and services ... for which those parties' would use the personal data. Article 29 Working Party, Opinion 5/2004 on unsolicited communications for marketing purposes under Article 13 of Directive 2002/58/EC, 11601/EN WP 90, 2004) 5.

becomes applicable when: 'data processing within a scientific research project cannot be specified at the outset'.[22] Under this guidance, biobanks set up intending to support specific research projects may be excluded from relying on Recital 33. Biobanks set up with the intention to operate prospectively, however, are free to rely on the exception. In turn, the Board suggest that whenever the Recital is relied upon, the controller should make sure that they: 'seek other ways to ensure the essence of the consent requirements are served best'.[23] Whilst the Board do not clarify precisely what the term 'essence of consent' means, they suggest that certain measures might be of assistance in making sure the threshold is met, including: allowing the research subject to consent to subsequent steps in the project as these become clear; employing further technical or organisational safeguards; and ensuring further transparency provisions are in place such that the research subject retains an overview of the state of affairs 'as the research project progresses so that, over time, the consent will be as specific as possible'.[24]

The requirement that consent be informed relates to the need to provide the research subject with the information necessary to ensure they understand, as the Article 29 Working Party put it, the 'scope and the consequences of the data processing'.[25] The Regulation does not provide further specific clarification of the contents of the concept. However, Article 13 provides a list of types of information to be given to the data subject in all situations data is collected from the subject. Beyleveld logically argues—in relation to equivalent provisions in Directive 95/46—that Article 13 may be seen as an elaboration of the information which must be provided to ensure the data subject is informed.[26] Accordingly, if biobanking controllers fulfil the obligations outlined in Article 13, they may be seen to fulfil their obligations to inform data subjects under Articles 9(2)(a) and 4(11)—as Article 13 is a data subject transparency right, it will be discussed in detail, in section D, on data subject rights, below.

The requirement for consent to be unambiguous relates to the form of signal to be given by the data subject to indicate their wish to consent. As Custers et al. summarise: 'unambiguous consent means ... the procedure to seek and give consent must leave no doubt as to the data subject's intention'.[27] Recital 32 clarifies the general meaning

[22] European Data Protection Board, Guidelines on consent (n. 15) 30.

Peloquin et al. perceive this guidance as being highly restrictive to broader forms of consent. Indeed, they see it as: 'essentially eviscerating any ability to obtain broad research consent from human sources of personal data and biospecimens'. David Peloquin, Michael DiMaio, Barbara Bierer, et al., 'Disruptive and Avoidable: GDPR Challenges to Secondary Research Uses of Data' (2020) *European Journal of Human Genetics* 28 697, 700 (hereafter Peloquin, DiMaio, Bierer, et al, 'Disruptive and Avoidable'). I appreciate their concerns and have commented elsewhere on the restrictive tone the guidance seems to take. Hallinan, 'Broad Consent' (n. 11) 4–10. A deeper look at the text, however, does not reveal a stance as prohibitive to broader forms of consent as they seem to suggest.

[23] European Data Protection Board, Guidelines on consent (n. 15) 31.

[24] European Data Protection Board, Guidelines on consent (n. 15) 31–2.

[25] Article 29 Working Party, Opinion 15/2011 on the definition of consent (n. 15) 17.

[26] Deryck Beyleveld, 'The Duty to Provide Information to the Data Subject: Articles 10 and 11 of Directive 95/46/EC', in Deryck Beyleveld, David Townend, Ségolène Rouillé-Mirza, and Jessica Wright (eds.), *The Data Protection Directive and Medical Research across Europe* (Ashgate 2004) 68, 70–1. The EDPB suggests that, in some cases, not all information outlined in Article 13 will be necessary to secure consent. However, they are not clear on when or how deviations should be permitted. They also suggest, in general terms: 'In practice, compliance with the information duties [in Article 13] and compliance with the requirement of informed consent may lead to an integrated approach in many cases'. European Data Protection Board, Guidelines on consent (n. 15) 17.

[27] Bart Custers, Simone van der Hof, Bart Schermer, et al., 'Informed Consent in Social Media Use: The Gap between User Expectations and EU Personal Data Protection Law' (2013) *scripted* 10(4) 435, 445.

of the concept: 'Consent should be given by a clear affirmative act establishing ... [an] unambiguous indication of the data subject's agreement ... such as by a written statement, including by electronic means, or an oral statement.'[28] Article 9(2)(a) provides the supplemental clarification that unambiguous consent in relation to sensitive data requires 'explicit' consent. This means, as the EDPB observes: 'the data subject must give an express statement of consent'.[29] In practice, biobanking controllers must secure a clear indication of a data subject's wish to give consent. Both a traditional written consent and clearly intended electronic consent suffice in this regard.[30]

In order to rely on the scientific research exception in Article 9(2)(j), a biobanking controller must make sure a set of conditions, also outlined in Article 9(2)(j), are fulfilled. Two cumulative conditions are evident:

a. The biobanking controller must act in accordance with Article 89(1).[31]
b. The biobanking controller must act based on a Union or Member State law.

Article 89(1) generally requires that biobanking controllers make sure processing is: 'subject to appropriate safeguards, in accordance with this Regulation, for the rights and freedoms of the data subject'. Whilst the Article provides certain specifications of these requirements, these specifications constitute obligations generally relevant for all biobanking controllers under other Articles anyway—these will be further elaborated, in section E, on data controller obligations.[32]

Regarding the second condition, it is not the case that any vaguely relevant Member State law will suffice. Rather, Article 9(2)(j) requires that the law meet three conditions: the law must be 'proportionate to the aim pursued'; the law must respect the essence of data protection; and finally, the law must provide for 'suitable and specific measures to safeguard the fundamental rights and interests of the data subject'. There is no clear data protection jurisprudence establishing objective principles clarifying these conditions in relation to research. Thus, whether a law fulfils the criteria must be considered case by case.[33]

[28] See also, for confirmation that implied consent is not permissible: *Bundesverband der Verbraucherzentralen und Verbraucherverbände—Verbraucherzentrale Bundesverband eV v. Planet49 GmbH* (2019) ECLI:EU:C:2019:801, paras 61–3.

[29] European Data Protection Board, Guidelines on consent (n. 15) 20.

[30] European Data Protection Board, Guidelines on consent (n. 15) 20–2.

[31] Article 9(2)(j) could also be considered as a derogation possibility. Its relevance in legitimating processing, however, makes a consideration of the Article in this section expedient.

[32] The Article states: 'safeguards shall ensure that technical and organisational measures are in place in particular in order to ensure respect for the principle of data minimisation. Those measures may include pseudonymisation provided that those purposes can be fulfilled in that manner. Where those purposes can be fulfilled by further processing which does not permit or no longer permits the identification of data subjects, those purposes shall be fulfilled in that manner.'

[33] There are a number of national laws which elaborate the 9(2)(j) exception which do little in the way of clarifying suitable and specific measures. Whilst there is little jurisprudence on the issue, at least from a legal perspective, question marks appear about whether these laws fulfil the requisite criteria. See, for example, the UK's data protection law: Data Protection Act 2018 (UK).

Most European states have already adopted legislation legitimating processing for scientific research under Article 9(2)(j).[34] It seems this may not be true, however, for all states. The Commission observes, for example, that, at the time of writing in mid-2020, Slovenia still has not adopted new law, or amended its old data protection law, subsequent to the Regulation.[35] Equally, the European Data Protection Supervisor (EDPS), observed, in early 2020, that: 'Article 9(2)(j) ... provides for processing of special categories of data for scientific research ... on the basis of EU or Member State law. However, such laws have yet to be adopted'.[36]

When consent cannot be obtained, only the Article 9(2)(j) research exception will be relevant. Where consent can be obtained, however, both exceptions may appear relevant. The GDPR provides no specific indication a hierarchy of exceptions was intended. In relation to the same lack of specification of hierarchy in Directive 95/46, commentators such as Zanfir thus concluded no hierarchy existed: 'When read carefully ... [this construction] reveals itself as allowing the processing of personal data on ... any ground'.[37] Under this interpretation, the biobanking controller would be free to decide which Article 9(2) exception to rely on. This position currently appears to be the dominant scholarly interpretation of the issue of the hierarchy of legitimations concerning scientific research involving sensitive data. Closer investigation, however, reveals this interpretation to be problematic. I would argue that a more logical position is that the 9(2)(a) consent exception has primacy over the 9(2)(j) research exception. Thus, as Taylor and Whitton suggest: 'if the research can be done with consent, then it should be done with consent'.[38] Three legal arguments can be put forward in support of this position.

First, there is jurisprudence related to the processing of sensitive data under the Directive which indicates that consent for data processing should be given precedence

[34] It is beyond the scope of this book to consider each of the relevant national laws in detail. See, for a more in depth discussion of national law: Santa Slokenberga, Olga Tzortzatou, and Jane Reichel (eds.), *GDPR and Biobanking: Individual Rights, Public Interest and Research Regulation across Europe* (Springer 2021) 187, 187–394 (hereafter Slokenberga, Tzortzatou, and Reichel (eds.), *GDPR and Biobanking*).

[35] European Commission, Data protection as a pillar of citizens' empowerment and the EU's approach to the digital transition—two years of application of the General Data Protection Regulation (Communication from the Commission to the European Parliament and the Council, 2020) 6.

[36] European Data Protection Supervisor, A Preliminary Opinion on data protection and scientific research (Policy, 2020) 23 (hereafter EDPS, A Preliminary Opinion).

[37] Gabriela Zanfir, 'Forgetting About Consent. Why the Focus Should Be on "Suitable Safeguards" in Data Protection Law', in Serge Gutwirth, Ronald Leenes, and Paul De Hert (eds.), *Reloading Data Protection* (Springer 2013) 237, 240. See also, with more specific applicability to the research context: Victoria Chico, 'The Impact of the General Data Protection Regulation on Health Research' (2018) *British Medical Bulletin* 128 109, 112 (hereafter Chico, 'The Impact of the General Data Protection Regulation'); Edward Dove and Jiahong Chen, 'Should Consent for Data Processing Be Privileged in Health Research? A Comparative Legal Analysis' (2019) *International Data Privacy Law ipz023* 1, 10 Dove and Chen also observe, however, that this is not a position they find to be normatively desirable: 'we do not support the current default data protection model in Europe, reflected in the GDPR', 13.

[38] Mark J. Taylor and Tess Whitton, 'Public Interest, Health Research and Data Protection Law: Establishing a Legitimate Trade-Off between Individual Control and Research Access to Health Data' (2019) *Laws* 9(1) 16 <https://www.mdpi.com/2075-471X/9/1/6> accessed 3 June 2020. Taylor and Whitton provide an interesting argument, from a legal theoretical perspective, as to the limitations of the 'public interest' in UK law as a justification for overriding the basic obligation to obtain consent for research. The argument they present is approximately reflected, in legal terms, in my second argument. See also: Marcello Ienca, James Scheibner, Agata Ferretti, et al., How the General Data Protection Regulation changes the rules for scientific research Study (Report, ETH Zürich Research Collection, 2019) 60.

over other legitimations. This position was recognised by the Article 29 Working Party. When discussing the relationship between consent and all other justifications for processing personal data, they observed: 'The order in which the legal grounds are cited [in the Directive] is relevant'.[39] This interpretation is given further credence by the Court of Justice of the European Union (CJEU). In their *ASNEF and FECEMD* judgment, when discussing alternative grounds to legitimate the processing of personal data, the Court specifically observed the relevance of other justifications only 'in the absence of the data subject's consent'.[40] On the one hand, this expression could be understood in a matter-of-fact manner: if consent is present, there is no need to consider other justifications. On the other hand, however, a normal reading of the statement suggests the Court intended a juxtaposition of grounds, with consent occupying prime position.

Second, consent is preferable from the perspective of the underlying rights involved. Commentators such as Beyleveld suggest that the processing of sensitive data may be seen as, by nature, an infringement of fundamental rights: 'the European Court of Human Rights has ruled that to process sensitive personal data without consent is by the very nature of the case an interference of the right to private life under Article 8(1) of the ECtHR'.[41] This statement is certainly true in relation to genetic data. In the *Marper* case, for example, the ECtHR referred to genetic samples as containing information of an 'intrinsically private character'.[42] The CJEU, in *Digital Rights Ireland*, further established that 'the persons concerned [need not be] inconvenienced in any way' by processing for an infringement with their right to privacy to be recognised.[43] In turn, the ECtHR, in *M.S. v. Sweden*, found that processing sensitive personal data with consent meant there was no infringement of privacy. Conversely, they found that processing sensitive data without consent would mean privacy had been infringed—albeit this infringement might be justified.[44] In EU fundamental rights law, if the same result can be achieved with a lower impact on an individual's rights, this option is seen as preferable and must be taken. The GDPR is a legal instrument which seeks to protect data subjects' rights. Accordingly, processing of sensitive data based on the data subject's consent under Article 9(2)(a), in principle, should be preferred to processing without consent—including via Article 9(2)(j). As Beyleveld summarises: 'this implies ... consent must be obtained unless to do so would be impracticable/involve disproportionate effort'.[45]

Third, the Regulation was designed as an instrument of general application. Accordingly, its principles were always intended to be adapted, as needed, to each

[39] Article 29 Working Party, Opinion 15/2011 on the definition of consent (n. 15) 7.

[40] *ASNEF and FECEMD v. Administración del Estado* (2011) ECLI:EU:C:2011:777, paras 39, 49, and 54.

[41] Deryck Beyleveld, 'An Overview of Directive 95/46/EC in Relation to Medical Research', in Deryck Beyleveld, David Townend, Ségolène Rouillé-Mirza, and Jessica Wright (eds.), *The Data Protection Directive and Medical Research Across Europe* (Ashgate 2004) 5, 11 (hereafter Beyleveld, 'An Overview of Directive 95/46/EC').

[42] *S. and Marper v. United Kingdom*, App nos 30562/04 and 30566/04, 4 December 2008, para. 104.

[43] *Digital Rights Ireland Ltd (C-293/12) v. Minister for Communications, Marine and Natural Resources and Others and Kärntner Landesregierung (C-594/12) and Others* (2014) ECLI:EU:C:2014:238, para. 33.

[44] *M.S. v. Sweden*, App no 74/1996/693/885, 27 August 1997, paras 34–5.

[45] Beyleveld, 'An Overview of Directive 95/46/EC' (n. 41) 12. See also, for a discussion of this argument: Hallinan, 'Broad Consent' (n. 11) 6.

sector of data processing.[46] In this regard, the Article 29 Working Party recognise that different justifications for processing may be relevant 'depending on ... context'.[47] One strong indication that a certain justification will have precedence in a certain context is the pre-existence of a clear legal or ethical norm promoting that justification. In both law and ethics relevant to biobanking, there is overwhelming agreement that, in principle, research subject consent must be sought to justify research. As Forsberg et al. observe in relation to data-based research: 'requiring informed consent [is] the default position ... for non-interventional research'.[48] This is borne out by the analysis of international and European biobanking law in previous chapters. For example, at international level, the Declaration of Helsinki states, in Article 25: 'Participation by individuals capable of giving informed consent as subjects in medical research must be voluntary', whilst at European state level the Estonian Human Genes Research Act states: 'It is prohibited to take a tissue sample and prepare a description of state of health or genealogy without... voluntary consent'.[49]

D. Biobanking and Data Subject Rights under the GDPR

When personal data are being processed, the Regulation foresees that data subjects will retain a set of eight rights over their personal data. One of these rights—concerning profiling which produces legal or other significant effects—will not be relevant in biobanking.[50] Seven rights are thus generally relevant:

1. The right to withdraw consent
2. The right to be informed
3. The twin rights to access and rectification[51]
4. The right to erasure
5. The right to restrict processing
6. The right to data portability
7. The right to object.

[46] See: European Commission, Impact Assessment Accompanying the General Data Protection Regulation (Policy, SEC(2012)72 final, 2012) 65–74.

[47] Article 29 Working Party, Opinion 06/2014 on the notion of legitimate interests of the data controller under Article 7 of Directive 95/46/EC (Policy, 844/14/EN WP 217, 2014) 16.

[48] Joanna Forsberg, Mats Hansson, and Stefan Eriksson, 'Biobank Research: Who Benefits from Individual Consent?' (2011) *British Medical Journal* 343 727, 727.

[49] See chapter 5, sections C and E; chapter 6, sections D, E, and F. See also, for a discussion of this argument: Hallinan, 'Broad Consent' (n. 11) 6–7.

[50] Article 22 relates to the right of the data subject 'not to be subject to a decision based solely on automated processing, including profiling, which produces legal effects concerning him or her or similarly significantly affects him or her'. As the biobanking process intends to produce scientific knowledge, it does not intend to produce such effects.

[51] The right to rectification generally follows as a consequence of the right to access. Accordingly, it makes sense to deal with the two rights together.

The right to withdraw consent is outlined in Article 7(3) and will apply whenever processing has been legitimised based on data subject consent under Article 9(2)(a). The biobank will be the controller which obtains the initial consent, will be the controller to whom withdrawal requests will be directed and for whom the right will be relevant.

When the right applies, Article 7(3) requires the biobank to provide the data subject with the possibility to completely withdraw consent. The Regulation does not mention the possibility to offer partial withdrawal. However, there is no reason this should be impermissible provided the data subject agrees and the conditions of consent remain valid for any continued processing. Curren and Kaye, for example, see no problem conceiving of withdrawal in terms of 'a fine-grained process that can be qualified by specific attributes, in that it might not just be a matter of "turning off" the entire consent given on a set of personal data, but there could be degrees of revocation, affecting specific data.'[52]

If the data subject chooses to exercise the right, this serves to withdraw justification for processing provided by an original consent—although not retrospectively. The consequence of this withdrawal is the activation of the Article 17 right to erasure—the substantive content of which will be discussed below.

The right to be informed about data processing is outlined in Articles 13 and 14 and will apply whenever there is an identifiable data subject.[53] As the biobank is the controller which initially collects data, the biobank will primarily be responsible for informing the data subject. The right will normally require action when data is collected.

The right requires a biobank to provide the subject with information allowing them to understand the scope and consequences of processing to be undertaken.[54] The forms of information to be provided are also outlined in Articles 13 and 14. Article 13 is relevant when personal data is collected from the data subject—recall Article 13 information requirements also serve to discharge the obligation to inform the data subject in consent under Article 9(2)(a). Article 14 is relevant when personal data is collected from a third party. Under Articles 13 and 14, four categories of information must be provided:

a. The type of data being processed: whilst this is not specifically mentioned in Article 13, the European Data Protection Board have specifically clarified that data subjects must be provided with information as to the '(type of) data will be collected and used.'[55]

[52] Liam Curren and Jane Kaye, 'Revoking Consent: A "Blind Spot" in Data Protection Law?' (2010) *Computer Law and Security Review* 26(3) 273, 274.

[53] For an extensive discussion of the relevant modalities of these rights, see: Article 29 Working Party, Guidelines on transparency under Regulation 2016/679 (Policy, 17/EN WP260 rev.01, 2017 [updated 2018]) (hereafter Article 29 Working Party, Guidelines on transparency).

[54] As the Article 29 Working Party observe: 'A central consideration of the principle of transparency outlined in these provisions is that the data subject should be able to determine in advance what the scope and consequences of the processing entails.' Article 29 Working Party, Guidelines on transparency (n. 53) 7.

[55] European Data Protection Board, Guidelines on consent (n. 15) 15. Interestingly, the Article 29 Working Party Opinion on transparency in relation to the GDPR did not mention this type of information. The Opinion, however, address the issue in one of its examples of good transparency practice. In this example, the Opinion

b. The modalities of processing being undertaken: information to be provided includes where the data came from, who the controller is, the aim of processing, and who else might be given access to the data.
c. Information on data subject rights in relation to processing: information to be provided includes the rights the data subject retains during processing and the modalities of the execution of these rights.
d. Information on the likely consequences associated with processing: whilst this type of information is not specifically mentioned in either Article 13 or 14, the Article 29 Working Party clarify that: 'as well as providing the prescribed information under Articles 13 and 14 … controllers should also separately spell out … what the most important consequences of the processing will be'.[56]

In certain cases, the Regulation foresees exceptions to obligations to inform. The obligation under Article 13 is excepted only when, according to Article 13(4), the data subject already has the information. Article 14, however, is subject to a greater number of exceptions. These are outlined in Article 14(5). The following three are particularly relevant to biobanking: first, the data subject already has the information; second, provision of information would be impossible; third, provision of information would involve disproportionate effort. The use of the second and third exceptions is subject to the presence of safeguards outlined in Article 89(1)—see section C for a discussion—as well as other necessary 'measures to protect the data subject's rights and freedoms … including making the information publicly available'.

Whilst the scope of the first exception is clear, this is not necessarily the case for the second and third exceptions. Fortunately, there is subject to some, albeit limited, guidance available. In relation to the impossibility criterion, the Article 29 Working Party observe a high threshold should be observed and suggest there are few situations in which provision of information will be truly impossible. They do, however, observe that the threshold might be met when the controller has no way to contact the data subject.[57] In this regard, Pormeister logically recognises that, in certain biobanking contexts, this situation may pertain when a biobanking controller only has access to pseudonymised data.[58] In relation to the disproportionate effort criterion, Recital 62 suggests a set of factors to be taken into account in determining disproportionate effort. These include the number of data subjects, the age of the data, and any appropriate safeguards adopted'. The Article 29 Working Party then further suggest that the decision as to whether the threshold is met, whilst being content dependent, should result from a

observed that the fact a data subject could easily tell which personal data was collected about them from a transparency notice was significant in marking the example out as good practice. Article 29 Working Party, Guidelines on transparency (n. 53) 9.

56 Article 29 Working Party, Guidelines on transparency (n. 53) 7.
57 Article 29 Working Party, Guidelines on transparency (n. 53) 29.
58 Kärt Pormeister, Transparency in relation to the data subject in genetic research: An analysis on the example of Estonia (University of Tartu Ph.D. thesis, 2019) 67–9.

balancing exercise taking into account the impact on the controller if information must be provided and the impact on the data subject if information is not provided.[59]

Rights to access and rectification are outlined in Articles 15, 16, and 19. The rights apply across the biobanking process to all biobanking controllers unless the controller , according to Article 11, cannot identify the data subject and the data subject does not provide supplemental information allowing their identification. As the biobank will be the point of contact for data subjects, the biobank will bear the burden of discharge of obligations associated with the rights. In terms of content, the rights comprise three connected sub-rights.

First, Article 15(1) permits the data subject to obtain from any biobanking controller, at any time, 'confirmation as to whether ... personal data concerning him or her are being processed'. This includes the right to be provided with information as to how personal data are being processed. The list of information to be provided by the biobanking controller following the exercise of Article 15(1) is comparable to that outlined in Articles 13 and 14.

Second, Article 15(3) permits the data subject to obtain, from a biobanking controller, at any time, 'a copy of ... personal data undergoing processing'. Significantly, the right applies to all personal data processed in a biobanking operation. The data subject may thus, in principle, request copies of each of the following types of data: the biological sample; health, lifestyle, and biographical information; sequenced genomic data; and individual research results.

Finally, if an access request under Article 15(3) reveals inaccuracics in personal data being held by a biobanking controller, Article 16 permits a subject to have the controller rectify the data. The biobanking controller responsible for rectification is also responsible, under Article 19, to inform other biobanking controllers, to whom they have given the data, about the rectification.

The right to erasure—popularly known as the right to be forgotten is outlined in Article 17 and is applicable in five situations relevant to biobanking, outlined in Articles 17(1)(a)–(e): where the biobanking controller no longer needs the data; where the data subject withdraws consent; where the data subject objects; where biobanking processing is illegitimate; or where a biobank must erase personal data to comply with a legal obligation. The right will not apply, however, when the controller , according to Article 11, cannot identify the data subject and the data subject does not provide supplemental information allowing their identification.

Where one of these situations is relevant, Article 17(3)(d) excludes applicability of the right to scientific research when erasure: 'is likely to render impossible or seriously impair the achievement of the objectives of ... processing'.[60] This exception will at least exclude applicability in biobanking to data used in ongoing or completed research.

[59] Article 29 Working Party, Guidelines on transparency (n. 53) 31.

[60] Article 17(3) includes other exceptions. Some of these may, on occasion, also be relevant. For example, biobanking actors might need to exclude, ad hoc, the applicability of the right by virtue of needing to comply with legal obligations or for reasons of public interest related to public health under Articles 17(3)(b) or (c). Usually, however, these exceptions will not be applicable and are thus not dealt with in detail.

Research requires integrity in data. Without integrity, conditions cannot be controlled or results verified. As Melham et al. observe: 'past uses of data and samples cannot be undone'.[61]

When the right applies without exception, Article 17(1) requires a biobanking controller to permanently erase the personal data in question.[62] When the right applies by virtue of the subject withdrawing consent, and where the personal data in question has been made public, Article 17(2) requires the biobank to inform any third parties known to be processing the data that they too are under an erasure obligation. Finally, Article 19 requires a biobanking controller who is subject to an erasure obligation to inform other controllers, who have access to the data, about the erasure obligation.

The right to restrict processing is elaborated in Article 18 and will be applicable in four situations potentially relevant to biobanking—although these seem unlikely to occur with any frequency. These are outlined in Articles 18(1)(a)–(d): the accuracy of data is disputed; 'processing is unlawful', but restriction is preferred to erasure by the data subject; the data subject requires the data for legal proceedings; and finally, when the data subject clearly opposes the legitimacy of processing. The right will not apply, however, when the controller , according to Article 11, cannot identify the data subject and the data subject does not provide supplemental information allowing their identification.

When the right is applicable and has been exercised, Article 18 requires the biobanking controller to do two things. First, the controller must cease any processing involving the personal data in question. Second, the controller must retain personal data in unaltered form.[63] Article 19 then requires the controller to inform other controllers, to whom they have given the data, about the restriction put in place.

The right to data portability is outlined in Article 20. The right will have only limited applicability in biobanking. In the first instance, the right will only apply to health, lifestyle, and biographical information. Article 20(1) clarifies the right applies only to data provided to the controller by the data subject. This excludes sequenced genomic data and individual research results—both of which are produced in the biobanking process. As the Article 29 Working Party observe: 'inferred data and derived data are

[61] Karen Melham, Linda Briceno Moraia, Colin Mitchell, et al., 'The Evolution of Withdrawal: Negotiating Research Relationships in Biobanking' (2014) *Life Sciences, Society and Policy* 10(16) <http://lsspjournal.springeropen.com/articles/10.1186/s40504-014-0016-5> accessed 11 December 2019.

This interpretation, in line with Pormeister, takes the conditions outlined in Article 17 as clarifications for the conditions and limits of withdrawal of consent in the Regulation—as seems logical from the text of Article 17(1). Kärt Pormeister, 'Genetic Research and Applicable Law: The Intra-EU Conflict of Laws as a Regulatory Challenge to Cross-Border Genetic Research' (2018) *Journal of Law and the Biosciences* 5(3) 706, 710. The EDPB has observed: 'the GDPR is clear that consent can be withdrawn and controllers must act upon this—there is no exemption to this requirement for scientific research. If a controller receives a withdrawal request, it must in principle delete the personal data straight away if it wishes to continue to use the data for the purposes of the research.' European Data Protection Board, Guidelines on consent (n. 15) 32. It is unclear why the Board makes no mention of Article 17(3)(d). This seems an oversight given the fact the Article obviously provides an exception to the obligation to erase following withdrawal outlined in Article 17(1)(b).

[62] Luiz Costa and Yves Poullet, 'Privacy and the Regulation of 2012' (2012) *Computer Law and Security Review* 28(3) 254, 257 (hereafter Costa and Poullet, 'Privacy and the Regulation of 2012').

[63] Restrictions may be lifted, under Article 18(2): 'with the data subject's consent or for the ... defence of legal claims or for the protection of the rights of another natural or legal person or for reasons of important public interest of the Union or of a Member State'.

created by the data controller based on the data "provided by the data subject" [will not fall within the scope of the right]'.[64] In turn, Article 20(1)(b) clarifies that the right will only apply to personal data processed by 'automated means'. This excludes applicability to biological samples—which must be processed either manually or partially automatically. Article 20(1)(a) then specifies that the right only applies when processing is legitimated by consent.[65] The right will thus not apply when processing is justified by the Article 9(2)(j) scientific research exception. Finally, the right will not apply when the controller , according to Article 11, cannot identify the data subject and the data subject does not provide supplemental information allowing their identification.

When the right applies, Costa and Poullet observe it consists of two connected sub-rights.[66] In the first instance, Article 20(1) grants: 'the right to receive the personal data . . . provided to a controller, in a structured, commonly used and machine-readable format'. In turn, Article 20(2) grants the data subject: '[the] right to have the personal data transmitted directly from one controller to another, where technically feasible'.

Where they do apply, portability rights superficially seem to place arduous burdens on biobanking controllers to ensure use of compatible processing formats. Swire, for example, has observed that such obligations may: 'impose substantial costs [and may be] difficult to achieve'.[67] The Regulation, however, clarifies that no such concrete obligations are imposed. Recital 68 states: '[the] data subject's right to transmit or receive personal data concerning him or her should not create an obligation for . . . controllers to adopt or maintain processing systems which are technically compatible'.

The right to object is outlined in Article 21. The right, in principle, applies to all biobanking processing of: 'personal data . . . which is based on point (e) or (f) of Article 6(1)'. This means the right will, in principle, apply whenever a biobanking actor engages in processing without the consent of the research subject. The applicability of the right to research activity is confirmed in Article 21(6), which states: 'Where . . . data are processed for scientific . . . research purposes . . . the data subject . . . shall have the right to object'.

Article 21(6) does elaborate an exception to applicability in relation to scientific processing: 'necessary for the performance of a task carried out for reasons of public interest'. This exception could be interpreted as meaning the right is excluded from applying to all biobank processing in the public interest. The validity of this interpretation is, however, doubtful. This interpretation would have the effect of excluding the applicability of the right in all European states in which science is generally regarded as a public interest and would thus render the first clause in Article 21(6) largely pointless.[68]

[64] Article 29 Working Party, Guidelines on the right to data portability (Policy, 16/EN WP 242, 2016) 10.

[65] Recital 68 states: '[the right to portability] should not apply where processing is based on a legal ground other than consent or contract' and 'should not apply where the processing of the personal data is necessary . . . for the performance of a task carried out in the public interest'.

[66] Costa and Poullet, 'Privacy and the Regulation of 2012' (n. 62) 257.

[67] Peter Swire and Yianni Lagos, 'Why the Right to Data Portability Likely Reduces Consumer Welfare: Antitrust and Privacy Critique' (2013) *Maryland Law Review* 72(2) 335, 379.

[68] See chapter 4, section G for a discussion of the recognition of the public interest in science in Europe.

A more plausible interpretation is that the exception applies only in relation to biobank processing legitimated under Article 6(1)(e) which specifically encompasses: 'processing ... necessary for the performance of a task carried out in the public interest'. There is limited jurisprudence concerning when Article 6(1)(e) can be used to legitimate scientific research. However, the EDPB suggest that, when processing of sensitive data for science is legitimated under Article 9(2)(j), the relevant correlating ground under Article 6 will likely be Article 6(1)(f).[69] In biobanking, as processing without consent will usually be legitimated under Article 9(2)(j), it is logical to suggest the exception will usually not apply.

When the right is exercised, the data subject is obliged to provide reasons for their objection, according to Article 21(1), concerning their: 'particular situation'. Consequently, it is not possible for research subjects, or others, to object to biobanking on general grounds—such as disagreeing with the focus of research supported. The biobanking controller may then refute the objection by elaborating, according to Article 21(1): 'compelling legitimate grounds for the processing which override the interests, rights and freedoms of the data subject'.

The consequences of an exercise of the right, when the biobanking controller cannot show an overriding legitimate interest to continue processing, is the erasure of data according to Article 17—see above for a longer discussion. Article 17(1)(c) clarifies: 'The ... subject shall have the right to obtain from the controller the erasure of personal data ... where ... the data subject objects to the processing pursuant to Article 21(1) and there are no overriding legitimate grounds for the processing'.[70]

E. Biobanking and Data Controller Obligations under the GDPR

When personal data are processed, the GDPR foresees that data controllers will be subject to nine obligations. Of these, one—the obligation to keep data in a form allowing identification no longer than necessary—will be irrelevant.[71] Accordingly, eight obligations are generally relevant:

1. Purpose specification

[69] European Data Protection Board, Opinion on Clinical Trials (n. 11) 5.

[70] The general obligation to delete may be lifted, according to Article 21(1) if the data are needed for 'for the establishment, exercise or defence of legal claims' or if an exception to the erasure obligation in Article 17 applies.

[71] Article 5(1)(e) requires that biobanking controllers keep personal data 'in a form which permits identification of data subjects for no longer than is necessary for the purposes for which the personal data are processed'. As discussed extensively in the previous chapter, genomic data cannot be effectively anonymised. Therefore, the obligation is irrelevant in biobanking. One further obligation is also outlined in Article 5(1)(a). This Article requires that all biobanking actors process personal data 'lawfully, fairly and in a transparent manner in relation to the data subject'. Despite its apparent breadth, the substantive content of this obligation is more clearly defined by reference to other Articles. To process personal data fairly and lawfully, biobanks must process data in accordance with relevant legal obligations as outlined elsewhere in the Regulation as well as to not behave in a way which would be unexpected to data subjects. The obligation to process data transparently—as clarified in Recital 39—requires biobanking actors to conduct processing in light of 'data subject' rights relating to obtaining and accessing information about processing concerning them. See, for a discussion of fairness: Damian Clifford and Jef Ausloos, 'Data Protection and the Role of Fairness' (2018) *Yearbook of European Law* 130, 130–87.

2. Compatible use
3. Data minimisation
4. Data accuracy
5. Security and confidentiality
6. Accountability
7. Data protection by design and default
8. Data breach notification.

The purpose specification obligation is outlined in Article 5(1)(b) and requires biobanking controllers, in all circumstances, to only collect and use personal data for 'specified, explicit and legitimate purposes'. The obligation can be broken down into three separate substantive criteria:

a. Specified
b. Explicit
c. Legitimate purposes.

The concept of specified is not elaborated in relation to Article 5(1)(b). However, the Article 29 Working Party observe it relates to the need to 'delimit the scope of... processing'.[72] The concept thus has a close connection with the concept of specificity in consent—defined in Recital 33 and discussed in section C, above. Accordingly, the concept permits biobanking controllers to collect data for multiple research purposes simultaneously.

The concept of explicit also lacks definition in relation to Article 5(1)(b). However, the Article 29 Working Party elaborate the concept relates to the fact that processing purposes 'must be clearly revealed, explained or expressed in some intelligible form', with the aim to 'ensure that the purposes are specified without vagueness or ambiguity as to their meaning or intent'.[73] Thus, the concept basically requires biobanking controllers to ensure that all external communication regarding approaches and aims of processing—for example, to the data subject under Articles 13—is clear and understandable to recipients.

The concept of legitimate purposes, as the Article 29 Working Party observe, simply requires biobanking controllers to make sure that the purposes of processing are 'in accordance with all provisions of applicable data protection law, and other applicable laws'.[74]

The compatible use obligation is outlined in Article 5(1)(b) and will become relevant whenever a biobanking controller wishes to use collected substances for a novel secondary, priorly unforeseen, processing purpose. The obligation requires that secondary use must not be 'incompatible' with the initial purpose of processing. Fortunately for

[72] Article 29 Working Party, Opinion 03/2013 on purpose limitation (n. 20) 12.
[73] Article 29 Working Party, Opinion 03/2013 on purpose limitation (n. 20) 17.
[74] Article 29 Working Party, Opinion 03/2013 on purpose limitation (n. 20) 15–18.

biobanking, Article 5(1)(b) clarifies, as Chico makes clear, that there is: 'a presumption that further processing of personal data for scientific research purposes will be compatible with the purpose for which they were originally collected'.[75] The Article states: 'processing for … scientific … research purposes … [will] not be considered to be incompatible with the initial purpose'.[76] Accordingly, the obligation will never constitute an obstruction to research. This is not, however, the case for any other type of secondary, non-research, uses of biobanking personal data.

In this regard, the Regulation, in Article 6(4), provides a set of criteria to be considered when evaluating whether other types of secondary processing, not legitimated by consent or Member State law, are compatible.[77] These criteria include: the similarity in aim of the original processing and proposed novel processing; the context of collection and the reasonable expectations of data subjects; the types of data involved; the possible consequences for data subjects; and the existence of appropriate safeguards. These criteria serve to exclude non-research uses of biobanking substances as compatible purposes. In the first instance, none of the possible non-research uses of biobanking substances to which this provision of the Regulation can apply—employment, insurance, and public administration—bears any similarity to biobanking. In turn, there is no reason to think individuals have a reasonable expectation their substances will be accessed for non-research purposes. In fact, Budimir et al. observe: 'a widespread concern that insurance companies and employers could access personal information [in biobanks]'.[78]

The data minimisation obligation is outlined in Article 5(1)(c) and requires biobanking controllers to ensure, at all times, that the personal data they collect are 'adequate, relevant and limited to what is necessary in relation to the purposes for which they are processed'. As the content of the obligation is tied to processing aims, the obligation applies differently to different biobanking controllers.

The obligation will impose no processing restriction on biobanks operating prospectively. These biobanks do not define specific research purposes in advance of data collection. In turn, genomic research can potentially profit from the investigation of the interplay of genomic and—almost any type of—participant lifestyle, health, or biography information.[79] There are thus no clear limitations relevant to the aims of prospective collection.

[75] Chico, 'The Impact of the General Data Protection Regulation' (n. 37) 111.

[76] Article 5(1)(b) does not, however, on its own, serve to justify processing. Recital 50 suggests this should indeed be the case. This is also the position supported by certain scholars, such as Reimer. Philipp Reimer, 'Artikel 5: Grundsätze für die Verarbeitung personenbe-zogener Daten', in Gernot Sydow (ed.), *Europäische Datenschutzgrundverordnung: Handkommentar* (Nomos 2018) 319, 326. I cannot agree with this interpretation. In the first instance, there are convincing arguments that a new legitimation for processing is required. Arguments can be built around the legislative history of the Regulation and the suggestion that Recital 50 is an editorial mistake. See, for example, Frederik Zuiderveen Borgesius and Dara Hallinan, 'Article 5', in Franziska Boehm and Mark Cole (eds.), GDPR Commentary (Elgar Forthcoming 2021). In turn, strong arguments can also be built around the contextualisation of Article 5(1)(b) in relation to the fundamental right to data protection in the Charter and the need for a legitimate basis in relation to all processing. See, for example, EDPS, A Preliminary Opinion (n. 36) 22–3.

[77] These largely build on: Article 29 Working Party, Opinion 03/2013 on purpose limitation (n. 20) 23–4.

[78] Danijela Budimir, Ozren Polašek, Ana Marušić, et al., 'Ethical Aspects of Human Biobanks: A Systematic Review' (2011) *Croatian Medical Journal* 52(3) 262, 268.

[79] 'Data minimisation' has been touted as a problem for data processing operations which function through the collection of ever-increasing amounts of data with no specific idea of its use or results. See, for example, Omer

The obligation will, however, place limits on the data which can be collected and used by biobanks operating with a specific research agenda as well as on external researchers. Agenda specific biobanks can only collect personal data relevant to the research they support. External researchers can only access and use personal data relevant to the research they intend to conduct.

The accuracy obligation is outlined in Article 5(1)(d) of the Regulation and requires biobanking controllers to take 'every reasonable step ... having regard to the purposes [of processing]' to make sure personal data are accurate. Substantively, the principle requires personal data are maintained accurately in two ways.[80]

First, data must be maintained in a factually 'accurate' manner. This form of accuracy is neither specifically defined in the Regulation, nor elsewhere in EU data protection law. Perhaps this is because the meaning of the concept has tended to be presumed to be obvious: to denote factual correlation between real-world phenomena and their data records. This is certainly the meaning ascribed to the concept by DPAs.[81] The Information Commissioner's Office (ICO)—the UK DPA—for example, confidently suggest: 'it will usually be obvious whether information is accurate or not'.[82] Under this interpretation of accuracy, to fulfil the obligation, biobanks must simply make reasonable efforts to ensure personal data are as factually accurate as possible.[83]

Second, data must be kept 'up to date'. This concept has also evaded detailed definition. Once again, perhaps the meaning was presumed to be self-explanatory: the maintenance of the factual accuracy of the data to reflect changes to real-world phenomena. This is certainly how DPAs understand the concept. The ICO, for example, observes: 'If an individual moves house from London to Manchester a record saying that they currently live in London will obviously be inaccurate'.[84] Given that Article 5(1)(d) qualifies the data accuracy obligation in relation to 'the purposes [of processing]', to fulfil the obligation, biobanking controllers need only update personal data records when current information is specifically required for research or administrative purposes.[85]

Tene and Jules Polonetsky, 'Big Data for All: Privacy and User Control in the Age of Analytics' (2013) *Northwestern Journal of Technology and Intellectual Property* 11(5) 240, 259. However, unlike other big data models, biobanks may justify vast data collection in relation to their specific and legitimate purposes of processing.

[80] Dara Hallinan and Frederik Zuiderveen Borgesius, 'Opinions Can Be Incorrect (in Our Opinion)! On Data Protection Law's Accuracy Principle' (2019) *International Data Privacy Law* 10(1) 1, 2–3.

[81] The Article 29 Working Party observe, in this regard: 'In general, "accurate" means accurate as to a matter of fact.' Article 29 Working Party, Guidelines on the Implementation of the Court of Justice of the European Union Judgment on 'Google Spain and inc v. Agencia Española de Protección De Datos (AEPD) and Mario Costeja González' C-131/12 (Policy, 14/EN WP 225, 2014), 15.

[82] See ICO guidance on accuracy: ICO, 'Principle (d): Accuracy' (ICO 2019) <https://ico.org.uk/for-organisations/guide-to-data-protection/guide-to-the-general-data-protection-regulation-gdpr/principles/accuracy/> accessed 11 December 2019 (hereafter ICO, 'Principle (d): Accuracy').

[83] An interesting question is raised: how accurate is accurate enough? For example, different sequencing options have different error rates. Could some of these fail to qualify as accurate enough for biobanking purposes? See for example, Jeffrey Wall, Ling Tang, Brandon Zerbe, et al., 'Estimating Genotype Error Rates from High-Coverage Next-Generation Sequence Data' (2014) *Genome Research* 24(11) 1734, 1736–8.

[84] ICO, 'Principle (d): Accuracy' (n. 82).

[85] Indeed, as the ICO further observe: 'if you hold personal data only for ... research reasons, updating the data might defeat that purpose'. ICO, 'Principle (d): Accuracy' (n. 82).

The security and confidentiality obligation is outlined in Articles 5(1)(f), 32, and 89 and constitutes a general obligation that all biobanking controllers, at all times, must make sure personal data are: 'processed in a manner that ensures appropriate security . . . including protection against unauthorised or unlawful processing and against accidental loss, destruction or damage using appropriate technical or organisational measures'. The obligation is then concretised, in two different ways, in Articles 32 and 89.

First, Articles 32 and 89 outline three specific technical and organisational measures which must, whenever possible, be adopted by all biobanking controllers. First, Article 32(1)(a) and Article 89(1) mandate, where possible, the pseudonymisation of data. Second, Article 32(1)(a) requires, where possible, encryption of data. Finally, Article 32(1)(d) demands biobanking controllers have systems to test 'the effectiveness of . . . [security and confidentiality] measures'.

Second, Article 32(1)—recognising that the three specific approaches may be insufficient to ensure security and confidentiality—provides a system of considerations to assist controllers in deciding which extra measures may be necessary. Biobanking controllers will need this system. Best practice guidelines for information security in biobanking already go beyond the three specific measures outlined in Articles 32 and 89. Heatherly, for example, discusses the supplemental necessity of access controls and authentication mechanisms.[86] The system requires that biobanking controllers consider the state of the art in technical and organisational measures, their cost, and their difficulty in implementation. Controllers must then weigh available options against the risks to data subjects posed by processing. The result of the consideration must be the adoption of 'appropriate security and confidentiality' measures.

The accountability obligation is outlined in Article 5(2) and Article 30. The obligation does not impose rules aimed at shaping the mechanics of processing operations. Rather, it relates to biobanking controllers' approach to ensuring compliance with data protection principles. Article 5(2) generally obliges that biobanking controllers must be 'responsible for, and be able to demonstrate compliance' with, the substantive provisions of the GDPR. The obligation can be broken down into two parts.

First, the obligation places a requirement on all biobanking controllers, at all times, to, as the Article 29 Working Party put it: 'take appropriate and effective measures to implement data protection principles'.[87] The specifics of such systems are not elaborated in the Regulation. This leaves the final decision as to how to comply with accountability with the biobanking controller. However, the Article 29 Working Party have provided examples of approaches which may be helpful. These examples include: establishing data protection procedures; privacy policies; and training programmes for staff.[88]

[86] Raymond Heatherly, 'Privacy and Security within Biobanking: The Role of Information Technology' (2016) *Journal of Law, Medicine & Ethics* 44 156, 159.

[87] Article 29 Working Party, Opinion 3/2010 on the principle of accountability (Policy, 00062/10/EN WP 173, 2010) 9 (hereafter Article 29 Working Party, Opinion 3/2010).

[88] Article 29 Working Party, Opinion 3/2010 (n. 87) 11–12.

Second, the obligation requires biobanking controllers to be able to demonstrate that their processes and actions comply with the GDPR. This allows DPAs—or other authorities—to check whether controllers fulfil their obligations. Exactly what must be demonstrated, or how this must be demonstrated, is not elaborated. Nevertheless, the obligation will, at least, as mandated by Article 30, require biobanking controllers to keep extensive documentation showing which processing they have undertaken and how data protection principles have been implemented. In this regard, the EDPS observes demonstration of compliance should include: 'adequate documentation on what personal data are processed, how, to what purpose, how long [and] documented processes and procedures aiming at tackling data protection issues at an early state when building information systems or responding to a ... breach'.[89]

Data protection by design and data protection by default obligations are outlined in Articles 25 and 89. The obligations concern the operational parameters of technical and organisational systems. Thus, they require specific action when biobanking controllers set operational parameters. As Hildebrandt and Tielemans observe, the obligations are predominantly relevant 'when developing ... technologies and the business models they ... enable or sustain'.[90] As the EDPB observes, however, the obligations remain applicable throughout the duration of processing. In this regard, the Board thus observe controllers must also: 're-evaluate their processing operations through regular reviews and assessments of the effectiveness of their chosen measures and safeguards'.[91]

In terms of substantive content, Articles 25 and 89, in principle, require biobanking controllers to design data protection principles into all technical and organisational systems. Unfortunately, neither Article is specific regarding the technical or organisational approaches necessary to discharge the obligation in the biobanking context. Article 25(1), however, does provide some general assistance.

The Article provides a decision support system which may be used to assist biobanking controllers in concretising their obligations. Under this system, biobanking controllers must first, '[take] into account the state of the art, the cost of implementation and the nature, scope, context and purposes of processing'. Available options must then be considered in light of 'the risks of varying likelihood and severity for rights and freedoms of natural persons posed by the processing'. The result of the process must be the adoption of 'appropriate' measures. The EDPB offer further assistance in their elaboration of the bounds of each of the above factors, along with the provision of a key set of considerations to be taken into account when implementing data protection by design and default in relation to the data protection principles outlined in Article 5 of the GDPR.[92]

[89] European Data Protection Supervisor, 'Accountability' (European Data Protection Supervisor 2019) <https://edps.europa.eu/data-protection/our-work/subjects/accountability_en> accessed 11 December 2019.

[90] Mireille Hildebrandt and Laura Tielemans, 'Data Protection by Design and Technology Neutral Law' (2013) *Computer Law and Security Review* 29 509, 517.

[91] European Data Protection Board, Guidelines 4/2019 on Article 25 Data Protection by Design and by Default (Policy, 2019) 10 (hereafter European Data Protection Board, Guidelines on Data Protection by Design and by Default).

[92] European Data Protection Board, Guidelines on Data Protection by Design and by Default (n. 91) 7–24.

Data breach notification obligations are outlined in Articles 4(12), 33, and 34, and become applicable when a data breach occurs. The concept of a data breach is broadly defined in Article 4(12) of the Regulation as 'a breach of security leading to the accidental or unlawful destruction, loss, alteration, unauthorised disclosure of, or access to, personal data transmitted, stored or otherwise processed'. O'Brien notes that the breadth of the definition means that breaches relate to both external interference with data and 'the wrong personnel internally' engaging and interfering with data.[93]

Even when a breach occurs, obligations will not always be applicable to biobanking controllers. Article 33(1) and Article 34(1) restrict the scope of obligations in biobanking to one type of data breach: confidentiality breaches. The Articles clarify there is no notification obligation in relation to breaches unlikely to result in, respectively, risk or significant risk to individuals.[94] As the biobanking process intends no direct effects on data subjects, other forms of breaches—destruction, loss, or alteration—are unlikely to carry risk.

When breach obligations are applicable, Article 33(1) obliges biobanking controllers to: 'without undue delay and, where feasible, not later than 72 hours after having become aware of it, notify ... the supervisory authority'. Article 34(1) on the other hand, obliges biobanking controllers to: 'communicate the ... breach to the data subject without undue delay'.

In relation to Article 34, the obligation can be waived by the biobanking controller. This is the case if the controller has, under Article 34(3)(a) and (b), taken measures to mitigate the effects of a breach or when, according to Article 34(3)(c), such communication would involve disproportionate effort. In the latter case, general public communication may substitute for individual communication. However, as the EDPB observes: 'technical arrangements [may also need to be] envisaged to make information about the breach available on demand [to individuals the controller could not contact]'.[95] Significantly, Article 34(3) exceptions eventually leave the decision as to whether appropriate measures have been taken, up to the biobanking controller.

F. Biobanking and Transfers to Third Countries under the GDPR

Chapter V of the Regulation outlines multiple options a data controller may use to transfer personal data to non-EU states. Whenever a biobanking controller wishes to transfer personal data outside Europe, they are obliged to point to one of these reasons to legitimate the transfer. Of this list of options, the majority will be of marginal

[93] Ralf O'Brien, 'Privacy and Security: The New European Data Protection Regulation and Its Data Breach Notification Requirements' (2016) *Business Information Review* 33(2) 81, 82.

[94] Article 33(1) excludes applicability when 'the ... breach is unlikely to result in a risk to the rights and freedoms of natural persons'. Article 34(1) excludes applicability when a breach will not result in a 'high risk' to natural persons.

[95] Article 29 Working Party, Guidelines on Personal data breach notification under Regulation 2016/679 (Policy, 18/EN WP250rev.01, 2017 [revised 2018]) 22.

relevance to biobanking.[96] Six options, however, present themselves as generally relevant. These options are arranged in a three-tier hierarchy:[97]

1. Tier 1: adequacy.
2. Tier 2—if adequacy is not available—a biobanking controller may choose between four types of ad hoc solution: data protection clauses; Binding Corporate Rules; codes of conduct; and certification mechanisms.
3. Tier 3—if neither adequacy nor an ad hoc solution is available—certain biobanking controllers may rely on the consent of the data subject.

The tier 1 adequacy option is outlined in Article 45 and is, as summarised by Kosseim et al. as, 'a functional concept that means the data protection regime of the importing country affords ... sufficient ... protection' to EU citizens' personal data that it may be freely—subject to adequacy conditions—transferred to that country.[98]

Adequacy decisions upon which biobanking controllers may rely exist for the following states: Andorra; Argentina; Canada—for commercial organisations; Faroe Islands; Guernsey; Isle of Man; Israel; Japan; Jersey; New Zealand; Switzerland; and Uruguay.[99] A special form of adequacy agreement previously existed for commercial

[96] The following options will be of little relevance for biobanking: 'a legally binding and enforceable instrument between public authorities or bodies'; judgments of courts and tribunals subject to a Mutual Legal Assistance Treaty; transfers necessary 'for the performance of a contract' of for pre-contractual purposes; transfers necessary for the defence of legal claims; transfers necessary for the protection of vital interests; transfers of information on public registers; transfers which serve a compelling controller interest.

One option may indeed be occasionally relevant to biobanking: the legitimation of international transfers based on 'important public interest', permitted by Article 49(1)(d). This ground may become particularly relevant in relation to transfers necessary for combatting serious public health emergencies—such as the COVID-19 pandemic. The utility of the exception in such contexts has been confirmed by the European Data Protection Board, Guidelines on processing data concerning health for scientific research in the context of COVID-19 (n. 12) 12–13. However, there are two limitations to the use of this option which will curtail its relevance. First, the option falls under Article 49(1). This means it can only be relied upon in relation to 'a transfer or a set of transfers of personal data to a third country'. Use is thus limited for biobanking controllers who require continuous flows of data or data flows to multiple countries. Second, as discussed previously, only a limited amount of biobanking research, under normal circumstances, will qualify as an 'important ... public interest'.

[97] See, for a general discussion of third-country transfer possibilities: Santa Slokenberga, Jane Reichel, Rachel Niringiye, et al. 'EU Data Transfer Rules and African Legal Realities: Is Data Exchange for Biobank Research Realistic?' (2018) *International Data Privacy Law* 9(1) 30, 30–48.

[98] Patricia Kosseim, Edward Dove, Carman Baggaley, et al., 'Building a Data Sharing Model For Global Genomic Research' (2014) *Genome Biology* 15(430) <https://genomebiology.biomedcentral.com/articles/10.1186/s13059-014-0430-2> accessed 11 December 2019 (hereafter Kosseim, Dove, Baggaley, et al., 'Building a Data Sharing Model').

The adequacy of a third state is decided by the Commission. According to Article 45(2), the Commission must conduct an in-depth investigation of the applicable law in a third state—or territory or sector within a state. This investigation will consider applicable data protection laws and the general legal context in which these laws exist. See, for a more detailed discussion of Adequacy criteria: Article 29 Working Party, Adequacy Referential (Policy, 18/EN WP 254 rev.01, 2017 [revised 2018]).

[99] European Commission, 'Adequacy decisions' (European Commission 2019) <https://ec.europa.eu/info/law/law-topic/data-protection/international-dimension-data-protection/adequacy-decisions_en> accessed 11 December 2019. Slokenberga, however, also highlights: 'However, this small number of decisions is the tip of the iceberg in regard to work that has been done in assessing third countries ... the European Commission has outsourced studies to review the state of art of data protection in the countries considered for adequacy but these reports have not been made public.' Santa Slokenberga, 'Biobanking and Data Transfer between the EU and Cape Verde, Mauritius, Morocco, Senegal, and Tunisia: Adequacy Considerations and Convention 108' (2020) *International Data Privacy Law Advance Publication* 1, 6.

organisations in the United States under the Privacy Shield agreement.[100] It should be noted, however, that the Privacy Shield agreement was recently struck down by the CJEU in the *Schrems II* case.[101] The decision came as little surprise to those familiar with the agreement. Warning bells were sounded prior to its adoption and had continued to ring ever since.[102] At the moment of writing, there is thus now no functional adequacy agreement in place between the EU and the United States.[103]

The tier 2 data protection clauses option is outlined in Articles 46(2)(c), (d), and 46(3)(a). Data protection clauses are bilateral agreements between EU actors and non-EU actors which guarantee EU data protection standards in bilateral exchanges of data.[104] The GDPR provides for two types of data protection clause upon which biobanking controllers may rely.

First, Article 46(2)(c) and (d) permit biobanking controllers to use 'standard data protection clauses' adopted by the Commission, or adopted by a DPA and subsequently approved by the Commission. Under the Directive, the Commission has already produced two sets of clauses potentially relevant for biobanking—both sets relate to transfers between EU data controllers and non-EU data-controllers.[105] Article 46(5) confirms that these clauses continue to remain valid under the Regulation until specifically revoked.[106]

[100] In a recent case, the CJEU found the prior transfer agreement—the Safe Harbor agreement—invalid owing to the scale of US intelligence services access to EU citizens' personal data. *Maximillian Schrems v. Data Protection Commissioner* (2015) ECLI:EU:C:2015:650. In 2016, the Privacy Shield agreement was reached as its successor. Commission Implementing Decision (EU) 2016/1250 of 12 July 2016 pursuant to Directive 95/46/EC of the European Parliament and of the Council on the adequacy of the protection provided by the EU–US Privacy Shield (2016) OJ L 207/1.

[101] *Data Protection Commissioner v. Facebook Ireland Ltd, Maximillian Schrems* (2020) ECLI:EU:C:2020:559, paras 199–202 (hereafter *Schrems II*).

[102] See: Article 29 Working Party, Opinion 01/2016 on the EU–US Privacy Shield draft adequacy decision (Policy, 16/EN WP 238, 2016). See also: Article 29 Working Party, EU–US Privacy Shield—First annual Joint Review (Policy, 17/EN WP 255, 2017) 4; Franziska Boehm, 'Assessing the New Instruments in EU–US Data Protection Law for Law Enforcement and Surveillance Purposes' (2016) *European Data Protection Law Review* 3 178, 190; European Data Protection Board, EU– US Privacy Shield—Third Annual Joint Review (Policy, 2019) 7.

[103] Reliance on adequacy will, for the foreseeable future, be limited by two factors. First, there are only very few adequacy decisions currently in force. Second, it is unlikely that many new countries will be found adequate in the near future. The process for reaching an adequacy decision is lengthy. Kuner observes: 'A finding of adequacy . . . typically takes several years.' Christopher Kuner, *Transborder Data Flows and Data Privacy Law* (Oxford University Press 2013) 65 (hereafter Kuner, *Transborder Data Flows*). Second, the proceedings are open to political machinations. Kuner observes: 'it can be difficult . . . to pass judgement on a foreign regulatory system without political considerations playing some role'. Kuner, *Transborder Data Flows* 66. See, for an example, Peter Laurence, 'Ireland Delays EU Deal with Israel on Data Transfers' (BBC News, 3 September 2010) <http://www.bbc.com/news/world-europe-11176926> accessed 11 December 2019.

[104] In this regard, and with applicability to all other tier 2 mechanisms, it should be noted that, as the CJEU confirmed in the *Schrems II* case, any bilateral agreements must be capable of providing the relevant level of protection for EU citizens' personal data in a third country. Accordingly, if the legal system of a third country is such that this protection cannot be provided by the bilateral agreement, transfers under the agreement will not be legitimate under EU data protection law. See: *Schrems II* (n. 101) paras 122–49.

[105] See: European Commission, 'Standard Contractual Clauses' (European Commission, 2019) <https://ec.europa.eu/info/law/law-topic/data-protection/international-dimension-data-protection/standard-contractual-clauses-scc_en> accessed 11 December 2019. A third set of clauses has been produced which relates to transfers between data controllers and data processors. This may occasionally be useful for biobanking actors who wish to contract non-EU processing services—for example, genome sequencing facilities.

[106] It should be noted that model contract clauses are not necessarily applicable to all biobanking activity. See the discussion of the inadequacy of the initial set of clauses even for all business purposes. European Commission, Frequently Asked Questions Relating to Transfers of Personal Data from The EU/EEA to Third Countries (FAQs, 2009) 30. See also, Peloquin et al.'s discussion of the difficulties for US public actors to rely on these clauses: Peloquin, DiMaio, Bierer, et al., 'Disruptive and Avoidable' (n. 22) 702.

Second, Article 46(3)(a) permits biobanking controllers to use ad hoc contractual clauses. As Kuner observes, these are 'clauses, which are custom-drafted in each specific case by the parties' involved in the transfer.[107] To be valid, all biobanking ad hoc clauses must fulfil two conditions. First, the content of the clause must, according to Recital 108, 'ensure compliance with data protection requirements and the rights of the data subjects ... including the availability of enforceable data subject rights and of effective legal remedies'. Second, biobanking controllers must ensure clauses are authorised, prior to use, by the responsible DPA.

The tier 2 binding corporate rules (BCR) option is outlined in Article 46(2)(b) and Article 47. BCRs are sets of data protection rules permitting transfers within: 'A group of undertakings, or ... enterprises engaged in ... joint economic activity'. As the Article 29 Working Party observe, BCRs are essentially internal 'codes of conduct for international transfers'.[108] With regard to the applicability of BCRs to biobanking, Kosseim et al. observe: 'Although BCRs have only been approved for certain multinationals, the concept could, in theory, be applied to other entities, such as ... international research consortia'.[109]

BCRs relied upon by a biobanking consortium would need to fulfil several conditions. Four are significant: first, Article 47(1)(a) requires that all BCRs must be legally binding for all members of the group; second, Article 47(1)(b) requires BCRs must provide research subjects with enforceable rights; third, Article 47(2) requires that BCRs contain all relevant information allowing data subjects to understand their structure, function, and content; fourth, Article 47(1) requires that BCRs must have advance approval from the responsible DPA.[110]

The tier 2 codes of conduct option is outlined in Articles 46(2)(e) and 40 of the Regulation. Codes of conduct are specific sets of data protection rules outlining obligatory behaviour on the part of an EU controller, and by a transferee. This behaviour ensures that EU data protection principles are adhered to even when data are transferred abroad.[111]

A European biobanking controller may rely on a code of conduct provided several conditions are fulfilled. Four are particularly relevant: first, Article 40(2) requires that

[107] Kuner, *Transborder Data Flows* (n. 103) 43.

[108] Article 29 Working Party, Working Document: Transfers of personal data to third countries: Applying Article 26 (2) of the EU Data Protection Directive to Binding Corporate Rules for International Data Transfers (Policy, 11639/02/EN WP 74, 2003) 5.

[109] Kosseim, Dove, Baggaley, et al., 'Building a Data Sharing Model' (n. 98).

With certain trepidation, however, Kosseim et al. also note: 'From a regulatory perspective, the BCR approval process can be lengthy despite the mutual-recognition scheme and is not easily scalable to handle many applications at once.'

[110] See, for a more extensive discussion of the requirements of BCR schemes: Article 29 Working Party, Working Document setting up a table with the elements and principles to be found in Binding Corporate Rules (Policy, 18/EN WP 256 rev.01, 2017 [revised 2018]) 5–19.

[111] Codes of conduct are appealing in principle. Indeed, efforts have already been made to put codes together which outline principles biobanking controllers must follow when transferring data internationally—for example, the International Charter of principles for sharing biospecimens and data. See, for example, Deborah Mascalzoni, Edward Dove, Yaffa Rubinstein, et al., 'International Charter of Principles for Sharing Bio-Specimens and Data' (2015) *European Journal of Human Genetics* 23 721, 721–8. However, none of these currently have DPA or EDPB approval.

the code be originally produced by an organisation representing biobanking controllers; second, Article 40(2) obliges that the code must contain provisions which ensure the application of the principles of the Regulation; third, Article 46(2)(e) requires that any transferee give a 'binding and enforceable' guarantee that they will adhere to the code's provisions;[112] and finally, Articles 40(5) and (7), require, respectively, that the code has been approved either by a DPA or by the EDPB.[113]

The tier 2 certification mechanism option is outlined in Articles 46(2)(f) and 42 of the Regulation. These are testing procedures designed to confirm that a data controller's international transfer processes and safeguards are stringent enough to maintain EU data protection standards.

EU biobanking controllers may rely on certification for international transfers if certain conditions are fulfilled. Two deserve mention: first, Article 42(5) requires that a certification mechanism must have been put together by a DPA, the EDPB—the European Data Protection Seal—or an accredited body. Article 43 requires that only bodies which have been approved by the DPA and fulfil a series of conditions related to their expertise and certification procedures can qualify as accredited.[114] Second, Article 46(2)(f) requires that the biobanking controller must ensure that all transferees make enforceable commitments to abide by certification standards.[115]

Finally, the tier 3 data subject consent option is outlined in Article 46(2)(f) and Article 42. As opposed to each of the options discussed above, consent under Article 49(1)(a) may only be used for specific, discrete quantities of biobanking transfers: 'a transfer or a set of transfers of personal data to a third country'. As the EDPB clarify: 'These terms indicate that such transfers may happen more than once, but not regularly, and would occur outside the regular course of actions, for example, under random, unknown circumstances and within arbitrary time intervals'.[116] Accordingly, the mechanism cannot be used when biobanking controllers require continuous flows of data abroad, when controllers require different transfers to a range of third states, or when destination states are unknown when consent is sought. This excludes the option for biobanks operating prospectively—as these will not know the intended recipients or their countries at the moment of consent.

[112] Article 40(3) clarifies such a guarantee may be made 'via contractual or other legally binding instruments'.

[113] If the body behind the code represents biobanking actors in only one Member State, approval will be required only from the DPA. When the body in question represents biobanking actors in multiple Member States, approval will be required from the DPA, the EDPB and finally, also from the Commission. The code may then be used by biobanking controllers EU wide.

[114] Specifically, in order to be accredited, a body: must have been approved by the DPA or by the national certification authority; it must undertake to adhere to the criteria for certification provided by the accrediting authority; it must show an 'appropriate level of expertise in relation to data protection'; it must prove its independence and expertise; it must have systems for issuing, reviewing, and withdrawing certification; it must provide systems for addressing infringements of certification provisions by those processing entities it certifies; and finally, it must make these systems transparent to data subjects. See, for a further, more detailed discussion: European Data Protection Board, Guidelines 1/2018 on certification and identifying certification criteria in accordance with Articles 42 and 43 of the Regulation (Policy, 2019).

[115] According to Article 42(2) such guarantees may be made 'via contractual or other legally binding instruments'.

[116] European Data Protection Board, Guidelines 2/2018 on derogations of Article 49 under Regulation 2016/679 (Policy, 2018) 4.

If the option can be relied upon, for consent to be legitimate, it must meet the criteria elaborated in Article 4(11)—see section C, above. The meaning of the conditions freely given and unambiguous remains as discussed. The definition of specificity follows from the limitations on the use of the option in Article 49(1)(a)—consent can only justify a transfer, or set of transfers, to one state. Concerning the condition that consent must be informed, however, Article 49(1)(a) lays down special rules. Specifically, Article 49(1)(a) requires biobanking controllers to provide the data subject with information as to the 'possible risks of such transfers ... due to the absence of an adequacy decision and appropriate safeguards'.

G. Biobanking and Sanctions under the GDPR

When a biobanking controller processes personal data in violation of the principles of the Regulation, two key types of sanctions are foreseen:[117]

1. Liability and compensation sanctions, outlined in Articles 79, 80, and 82
2. Administrative sanctions, outlined in Articles 57, 77, 83, and 84.

To begin a liability and compensation claim, a complaint must be lodged before a relevant national court. A complaint may be lodged by two entities:

a. The data subject may directly approach the courts under Article 79(1).[118]
b. The data subject may also, under Article 80(1), 'mandate a not-for-profit body, organisation or association which has been properly constituted in accordance with the law of a Member State ... to lodge the complaint'.

A biobanking controller will be liable to pay compensation if, under Article 82(1), 'material or non-material damage' has resulted from 'an infringement of [the] Regulation'. Recital 75 clarifies that immaterial harms may include, but are not limited to, instances 'where data subjects might be deprived of their rights and freedoms or prevented from exercising control over their personal data' or where sensitive data are illegitimately processed. Laurie et al. observe that previously, the law on immaterial damage and compensation claim was unclear and 'damage [was] equated with financial loss'.[119] Article 82(1) removes this lack of clarity. This is significant in the biobanking context.

[117] See, for an extended discussion of the two sanctions mechanisms: Hallinan, 'Biobank Oversight and Sanctions' (n. 1) 131-136.
[118] The Article specifically provides 'the right to an effective judicial remedy'.
[119] Graeme Laurie, Kerina Jones, Leslie Stevens, et al., A Review of Evidence Relating to Harm Resulting from the Uses of Health and Biomedical Data (Technical Report prepared for the Nuffield Council on Bioethics Working Party on Biological and Health Data and the Wellcome Trust's Expert Advisory Group on Data Access, 2015) 37.

As biobanking does not aim at having any direct effects on individuals, infringements are unlikely to result in material harm.

Biobanking usually involves a complex chain of processing. Accordingly, fault for infringements may be spread across multiple controllers. Articles 82(4) and (5) provide a system for clarifying how compensation may be claimed and subsequently apportioned. Article 82(4) ensures the data subject does not suffer by having to chase multiple biobanking controllers and may hold each 'liable for the entire damage'. Article 82(5) then ensures that disproportionately penalised controllers may seek restitution from other responsible controllers for 'compensation corresponding to their part of responsibility for the damage'.

The initiation of the administrative sanctions procedure will begin with an investigation into a biobanking controller's practices. The investigation may be launched in three ways:

a. The DPA may launch an independent investigation under Article 57(1)(a) and 58(1)(b).
b. A data subject may lodge a complaint with a DPA under Article 77(1)—in which case Article 57(1)(f) obliges a DPA to investigate.[120]
c. A data subject may, under Article 80(1), mandate an organisation to complain to a DPA on their behalf, in which case Article 57(1)(f) requires the DPA to investigate.

If an investigation into a biobanking controller finds an infringement, the DPA may impose a range of sanctions. These include temporary or permanent bans on processing—discussed above, in section B. More importantly, these include administrative sanctions in the form of a fine. There are multiple levels of fine relevant to biobanking. Each is, as Wybitul observes, 'drastic'.[121]

At the lower level, Article 83(4) provides for a fine of up to '10,000,000 EUR, or in the case of an undertaking, up to 2 % of the total annual turnover'. This level of fine may be levied for an infringement by a controller of, for example, data controller obligations under Articles 25–39 or certification obligations under Articles 42 and 43. At the higher level, Article 83(5) provides for a fine of up to '20,000,000 EUR, or in the case of an undertaking, up to 4 % of the total worldwide annual turnover'. This level of fine may be levied for violations of, for example, principles of processing under Articles 5, 7, and 9; data subject rights in Articles 13–20; international transfer principles in Articles 44–49; and a refusal to cooperate with a DPA under Article 58.

[120] The complaint may be lodged either in the place of residence or work of a data subject, or where the infringement is alleged to have been committed.

[121] Tim Wybitul, 'Was ändert sich mit dem neuen EU-Datenschutzrecht für Arbeitgeber und Betriebsräte? Anpassungsbedarf bei Beschäftigtendatenschutz und Betriebsvereinbarungen' (2016) *Zeitschrift für Datenschutz* 5 203, 203. Translation by the author of 'drastisch'.

Whilst fines are in principle huge, in practice, they need not necessarily be imposed at maximum levels on biobanking controllers. The Regulation gives national DPAs considerable leeway in tailoring fines to suit the specific facts and context of a case. For minor infringements, Recital 148 permits the DPA to waive the fine altogether. Even when a DPA concludes that a fine is deserved by a biobanking controller, the GDPR, in Recital 150, gives DPAs discretion in defining the level of the fine.[122]

H. Biobanking and Derogations under the GDPR

The GDPR is designed, in principle, to be directly applicable in states in which it applies. The law, however, also contains several possibilities for these states to derogate, in national law, from the GDPR's default standard of protection. Roßnagel and Nebel count seventy such possibilities in total.[123] Whilst such derogation provisions do not themselves elaborate substantive conditions on processing, they can be key in defining the degree to which the default standard of protection outlined by the GDPR will apply in any given case of biobanking. Two derogation provisions are particularly relevant to biobanking and deserve further discussion—although other provisions may become relevant in specific situations, such as the possibility under Article 84 and Recital 149 concerning the ability for states to pass criminal sanctions for violations of the Regulation:[124]

1. Derogations relating to scientific research under Article 89(2)
2. Derogations relating to genetic data and data concerning health under Article 9(4).

Article 89(2) clarifies derogations are possible, in relation to processing for 'scientific purposes', from the rights outlined in Articles 15, 16, 18, and 21. Recital 156 also

[122] To assist the DPA in deciding, Article 83(2) of the Regulation provides a set of considerations for the calculation of administrative fines, including: the seriousness and duration of infringement; the degree of intent or fault; steps taken to mitigate harm; the willingness of the biobanking controllers to cooperate with the DPA; and finally, the data protection track record of the responsible controllers. These factors have also been subject to helpful Article 29 Working Party clarification: Article 29 Working Party, Guidelines on the application and setting of administrative fines for the purposes of the Regulation 2016/679 (Policy, 17/EN WP 253 2017). These Guidelines, however, fall far short of providing a framework through which fines can be standardised across the EU. In consequence, there is, in practice, considerable divergence. See: Diana Dimitrova and Dara Hallinan, 'Bulgarian DPA Issues Multi-Million Euro Fine' *Data Protection Insider* (Karlsruhe, 5 September 2019). A standardised model has been proposed by German Data Protection Authorities. Take-up of the model to date, however—at least at European level—seems limited. Konferenz der unabhängigen Datenschutzaufsichtsbehörden des Bundes und der Länder, Konzept der unabhängigen Datenschutzaufsichtsbehörden des Bundes und der Länder zur Bußgeldzumessung in Verfahren gegen Unternehmen (Policy, 2019).

[123] Alexander Roßnagel and Maxi Nebel, Die Neue Datenschutzgrundverordnung: Ist das Datenschutzrecht nun für heutige Herausforderungen gerüstet? (Policy Paper Forum Privatheit, 2016) 4.

[124] Article 85(2) also permits Member States the possibility to derogate from virtually all of the GDPR's substantive provisions for the purpose of protection the freedom of expression and information in relation to 'academic' activities. There is no clear definition for the concept of academic activities provided. As Pötters observes, however, the concept may encompass certain scientific activity and the exception may thus, in principle, have some relevance for biobanking. The significance of Article 85(2) for biobanking, however, has scarcely been discussed. Stephan Pötters, 'Artikel 89', in Peter Gola (ed.), *DS-GVO Datenschutz-Grundverordnung VO (EU) 2016/679 Kommentar* (Beck 2017) 781, 785.

suggests the scope of Article 89(2) may also include Article 20: 'Member States should be authorised to provide ... derogations with regard to data portability ... for scientific ... research purposes'.[125] The term 'scientific research' as used in the Regulation is broad. As I have observed elsewhere: 'Recital 159 clarifies that the concept [of scientific research] must be interpreted in a broad manner and [may include]: 1. processing for the purposes of technological development or demonstration; 2. fundamental and applied research; 3. publicly and privately funded research'.[126] Given the breadth of the definition, it is hard to imagine circumstances in which the concept will not, in principle, apply to biobanking.

Derogations under Article 89(2), however, are only legitimate under two conditions. First, derogations must be provided for in EU or Member State law which takes into account the conditions outlined in Article 89(1). In particular, the law must foresee the presence of adequate alternative safeguards which protect subjects' rights. These safeguards should include technical and organisational measures—in particular ensuring the principle of data minimisation—and must require that processing should not require the use of personal data for any longer than necessary. Second, derogations may only be applicable in as far as the exercise of the rights derogated from would 'render impossible or seriously impair' the conduct of research and the derogation is necessary to facilitate research.

Article 9(4) does not elaborate the possibility to derogate from a specific set of provisions, but rather permits: 'Member States [to] maintain or introduce further conditions, including limitations, regarding the processing of genetic data, biometric data or data concerning health'. As discussed in the previous chapter, all biobanking substances qualify as either genetic data or data concerning health. Accordingly, the Article provides states with a broad possibility to implement conditions and limitations, in national law, relevant for biobank processing.[127]

There is a significant question which emerges as to the scope of the concept of 'limitations' in Article 9(4). On the one hand, the concept could be understood to encompass only limitations on processing supplemental to the conditions already outlined in the Regulation—i.e. limitations on processing which serve to increase the standard of protection. On the other hand, however, the concept could be understood to also encompass substantive limitations to the protection offered under the Regulation—i.e. limitations which would serve to limit the standard of protection already available. Unfortunately, the text of the Regulation does not provide a clear answer as to which interpretation is correct.

A contextual reading of the provision, however, suggests the former interpretation to be more logical. Under the latter interpretation, Article 9(4) would function to permit

[125] Given the assertion is only in a Recital, jurisprudential confirmation of this interpretation would be welcome.

[126] Dara Hallinan, 'Article 89', in Franziska Boehm and Mark Cole (eds.), *GDPR Commentary* (Elgar Forthcoming 2021).

[127] See chapter 10, section 3.

national derogations from all of the Regulation's provisions, to all processing of sensitive personal data, without stipulating any conditions on derogating laws. This seems unlikely for at least two reasons. First, such a general possibility to derogate from protection under the GDPR does not fit the mold of any other derogation provision—these tend to apply only in specific instances and always subject to conditions aimed at ensuring data subject protection. In turn, such a broad derogation possibility would serve to render all other provisions permitting the adoption of specific national laws in relation to sensitive personal data, and the supplemental conditions these outline—including Articles 9(2)(j) and Article 89(2)—pointless. It seems highly unlikely the legislator would have intended such redundancy in key provisions.[128]

The GDPR itself provides little further clarification of the conditions under which Article 9(4) may be used. The EDPS, however, has given the issue brief consideration in their Preliminary Opinion on Scientific Research. Specifically, the Supervisor observes that Article 9(4) is a: 'new area and requires adoption of EU or Member State law before the use of special categories of data for research purposes can become fully operational'.[129] The reasoning of the EDPS in requiring the adoption of specific new law to legitimate derogations under Article 9(4) is, however, not clear. The position is especially curious, given that the text of Article 9(4) specifically refers to the possibility for states to maintain existing legislation.

European states have already passed laws, relevant to biobank processing, which derogate from the default standard of protection outlined in the GDPR.[130] For example, in Germany, the Bundesdatenschutzgesetz 2018—the German national implementing law for the GDPR—in Article 27, outlines research exemptions from the rights in Articles 15, 16, 18, and 21 of the GDPR.[131] In Ireland, the Data Protection Act 2018, in Article 61(2), foresees limitations to Articles 15, 16, 18, and 21 for scientific processing.[132] In the UK, the Data Protection Act 2018, in Article 15 and Schedule 2, Part 6(27), outlines exemptions from Articles 15, 16, 18, and 21 for scientific research.

I. Conclusion

The GDPR exhibits an impressive array of protection for rights engaged by biobanking. In the first instance, a multifaceted supervision and oversight system is evident. The system kicks in prior to the start of a biobank processing operation, with the obligation that a biobanking actor conduct a DPIA. The system then continues to operate at all stages throughout a processing operation, providing DPOs and DPAs with an ongoing

[128] In turn, should it have been the intention of the legislator to enact a derogation of such breadth, and such potential to undermine subject rights, surely this would have been the subject of greater attention during, and subsequent to, the legislative process. In fact, the Article has hitherto received little attention.

[129] EPDS, *A Preliminary Opinion* (n. 36) 17.

[130] It is beyond the scope of this book to consider each of these national derogations in detail. See, for a discussion of national law: Slokenberga, Tzortzatou, and Reichel (eds.), *GDPR and Biobanking* (n. 34).

[131] Bundesdatenschutzgesetz 2018.

[132] Data Protection Act 2018 (Ireland), Article 61(2).

supervision mandate relevant for all biobanking processing. The system finally operates at a general level, providing the facility for DPAs and the EDPB to supervise the activities of the biobanking sector as a whole.

In turn, the GDPR outlines an extensive set of substantive provisions concerning the procedurally correct processing of personal data in biobanking. In the first instance, the GDPR outlines a set of conditions for the legitimation of biobank processing. These include the possibility of legitimate processing by obtaining data subject consent, as well as alternative possibilities where consent is not suitable. In turn, the GDPR outlines an extensive set of data subject rights—including, for example, the right to withdraw consent—and data controller obligations—including, for example, the obligation to maintain data accurately. Finally, the GDPR outlines provisions dealing with the transfer of biobanking substances outside Europe, ensuring that rights are protected even when biobanking substances are processed abroad.

The GDPR then ensures substantive provisions are respected by biobanking actors via a consequential sanctions mechanism. The mechanism foresees the possibility for data subjects, or their representatives, to chase biobanking actors in front of national courts for damages. The mechanism also, and perhaps more importantly, grants DPAs the power to levy administrative sanctions on biobanking actors found in violation of the law. The range of sanctions DPAs may levy is broad. Without doubt the most significant of these sanctions, however, are the administrative fines, which may stretch to 20,000,000 EUR, or 4 per cent of a biobanking actor's annual turnover.

The protection offered by the substantive provisions of the GDPR, however, is liable, in relation to certain types of biobanking processing, to vary between European states. Although the GDPR is, in principle, intended to be directly applicable in all states in which it applies, the law does contain several derogation possibilities relevant for biobanking—for example, in relation to data subject rights. European states have already taken advantage of these possibilities to pass national laws, applicable to biobanking, outlining provisions which deviate from the default standard of protection.

10

A Critical Analysis of the Efficacy of the GDPR as a Framework for the Protection of Genetic Privacy in Biobanking

A. Introduction

The previous three chapters provided an extensive look at how the General Data Protection Regulation (GDPR) applies to biobanking. Whilst these chapters appear to show that the GDPR offers an extensive system of protection, the chapters were descriptive rather than analytical. This final chapter thus moves to provide a critical analysis of the efficacy of the GDPR as a framework for the protection of genetic privacy in biobanking. In this regard, the chapter identifies problems with the approach of the GDPR. The chapter also, however, provides an analysis of the degree to which each identified problem casts doubt on the utility and suitability of the GDPR—including a consideration of the degree to which each problem in fact requires a solution as well as a consideration of the availability of solutions. Through this analysis, the chapter shows that, whilst the GDPR exhibits numerous problems, none of these casts serious doubt on its efficacy as a framework for the protection of genetic privacy in biobanking.

The chapter begins by outlining a framework to identify, and evaluate the severity of, problems with the GDPR (section B). Using this framework, the chapter then proceeds to describe twenty-three problems with the GDPR and, for each problem, to discuss the degree to which the problem casts doubt on the efficacy of the GDPR as a framework for the protection of genetic privacy in biobanking. Two problems concern the suitability of the structure of the GDPR for biobanking (section C). Two problems concern the range of research subject genetic privacy rights protected (section D). Two problems concern the range of genetic relatives' and groups' genetic privacy rights protected (section E). Six problems concern the standard of substantive protection provided (section F). Three problems concern the technical suitability of the GDPR's provisions to biobanking (section G). Three problems concern the disproportionate impact of the GDPR's provisions on other legitimate interests in biobanking (section H). Three problems concern the practical applicability of the GDPR's provisions to biobanking (section I). Two problems concern the degree to which the GDPR harmonises protection across European states (section J).

Protecting Genetic Privacy in Biobanking through Data Protection Law. Dara Hallinan, Oxford University Press (2021). © Dara Hallinan.
DOI: 10.1093/oso/9780192896476.003.0010

B. A Framework for the Critical Analysis of the GDPR

I propose a framework for the critical analysis of the GDPR as an instrument for the protection of genetic privacy in biobanking consisting of two parts. The first part constitutes a scheme for the identification of problems with the GDPR. This scheme consists of eight questions:

1. Is the GDPR suitably structured to provide optimal protection for genetic privacy in biobanking—in particular, is the GDPR applicable to the range of biobanking activity engaging genetic privacy rights and does it offer a cogent system of protection?
2. Does the GDPR provide protection for the full range of genetic privacy rights engaged by biobanking in relation to the research subject on the transactional axis? [1]
3. Does the GDPR provide protection for the full range of genetic privacy rights engaged by biobanking in relation to genetic relatives and genetic groups on the relational axis? [2]
4. Does the GDPR, where it provides protection for genetic privacy rights and genetic privacy rights holders, provide adequate substantive protection—measured against the baseline standard provided by international law and against European state protection?[3]
5. Where the GDPR's provisions are applicable, are they technically suited for the specifics of biobanking?
6. Does the protection provided by the GDPR disproportionately impact on other legitimate interests in biobanking—in particular, interests tied up with the conduct and outcome of research?[4]
7. Are there practical obstructions to the use of the GDPR as a framework for the protection of genetic privacy in biobanking?
8. Given biobanking is an increasingly international endeavour, are there problems with the degree to which the GDPR provides harmonised protection in Europe?

The second part of the framework then constitutes a scheme for the evaluation of the severity of each identified problem. This scheme considers both the basic severity of a

[1] See chapter 4, section D.

[2] See chapter 4, sections E and F.

[3] Recall there is no generally applicable EU law, apart from data protection, in place to consider—see chapter 6, section C. See, for a similar approach concerning international standards and the GDPR—albeit not focused specifically on genetic privacy: Ciara Staunton, Santa Slokenberga, and Deborah Mascalzoni, 'The GDPR and the Research Exemption: Considerations on the Necessary Safeguards for Research Biobanks' (2019) *European Journal of Human Genetics* 27, 1159, 1159.

[4] This consideration focuses on interests tied up with the research process, as third-party non-research interests in biobanking are not as relevant for the GDPR to support as research interests. Certain non-research interests—law enforcement interests—are not covered by the GDPR at all. The case for the remainder to be specifically recognised and protected is weak.

problem—how serious consequences flowing from the problem will be—and the potential for its resolution. In this regard, the scheme consists of three questions:

1. How far do the negative impacts of the problem—on genetic privacy, or other interests—mandate the GDPR to facilitate a solution to be regarded as an efficacious instrument for the protection of genetic privacy in biobanking? The answer to this question, in each case, will not be monolithic, but will rather lie on a spectrum. In this regard, it is helpful to divide problems into one of three groups: i) problems so significant that they absolutely require resolution—problems, the consequences of which are so severe that, if no approach for resolution is available, this would constitute grounds to rethink the GDPR as a framework for the protection of genetic privacy in biobanking; ii) problems, the consequences of which are not prohibitive to the utility of the GDPR, but which would nevertheless benefit from resolution; and iii) problems which do not require a resolution under the GDPR at all—e.g. problems displaying mitigating factors which will, in practice, render the consequences of the problem negligible.
2. If a resolution is necessary or desirable, can this be delivered through the Regulation's internal interpretation and adaptation mechanisms? The Regulation foresees that both national DPAs—at European state level—and the European Data Protection Board (EDPB)—at European level—will have broad powers to interpret and adapt the Regulation.[5] This question thus relates to the capacity for these powers to be deployed to resolve problems. Simply as DPAs and the EDPB have broad interpretation and adaptation powers, however, does not mean these powers do not have limits. Four types of limiting factor are notable. First, limitations appear when solutions to problems would require divergence from the conceptual rationale of the Regulation: conceptual limitations. Second, limitations appear when solutions would require a legal approach antithetical to that of the GDPR: legal structural limitations. In particular, in this regard, with its aim of facilitating the legitimate processing of personal data, the GDPR is well suited to incorporating procedural provisions, but not necessarily to incorporating

[5] See chapter 9, section A.

The GDPR provides national DPAs with, under Articles 40(5) and (6), and Article 42(5), the power to adopt, respectively, sector-specific codes of conduct and certification mechanisms. In turn, as discussed in the previous chapter, the GDPR, in Article 58(3)(b), provides national DPAs with discretionary powers to: 'issue ... opinions ... on any issue related to the protection of personal data'.

The EDPB may directly provide adaptations and interpretations applicable across the EU. The GDPR, in Article 40(7)–(11) tasks the Board—with the assistance of the Commission—with adopting EU-wide codes of conduct and in Article 42(6) with the adoption of EU-wide certification mechanisms. In turn, the GDPR grants the Board, as discussed in the previous chapter, broad and authoritative interpretation powers.

The EDPB's powers will also, likely, be interpreted with a wide scope. First, given the pace of technological change, a broad interpretation of powers seems necessary. Second, the EDPB is the successor to the Article 29 Working Party. The Working Party had a broad appreciation of its interpretation function. This appreciation even extended to the introduction of novel data protection principles. For example, in relation to international transfers, Moerel observes: 'The BCR [Binding Corporate Rules] regime [was]set by the Working Party 29.' Lokke Moerel, *Binding Corporate Rules: Corporate Self-Regulation of Global Data Transfers* (Oxford University Press 2012) 23.

bright-line normative prohibitions.[6] Third, limitations appear when solutions to problems would require DPAs or the EDPB to act outside the scope of their powers: technical limitations. Technical limitations become relevant in relation to solutions which would require novel legal approaches to the processing of data completely absent from the GDPR, in relation to solutions which would require a contravention of data protection principles, and in relation to solutions which would require DPAs or the EDPB to act in relation to data processing over which they have no jurisdiction. Fourth, limitations appear when solutions would need to be focused on national level: geographical limitations. Whilst national DPAs do have the power to provide national interpretations and can thus provide solutions to national-level problems, if these conflict across Member States they are liable to be overridden by EDPB harmonised interpretations.[7]

3. If a solution through the Regulation is unavailable or undesirable, does the Regulation permit a solution through other legal approaches operating in parallel? In this regard, recall, as discussed in the previous chapter, that the Regulation elaborates two key derogation possibilities significant for biobanking which facilitate parallel solutions. First, Article 89(2) clarifies derogations are possible, in relation to processing for 'scientific purposes', from Articles 15, 16, 18, and 21. Second, Article 9(4) offers the possibility for European states to derogate from the protection offered by the Regulation in relation to processing involving genetic data and data concerning health: 'Member States may maintain or introduce further conditions, including limitations, with regard to the processing of genetic data ... or data concerning health.' The Regulation also foresees specific derogation possibilities which may be relevant to biobanking in specific situations—such as the possibility under Article 84 and Recital 149 for states to pass criminal sanctions for violations of the Regulation.

Considering the GDPR against the first part of this framework reveals twenty-three problems.[8] In the following, each of these twenty-three problems will be elaborated, followed by a discussion of each problem's severity.

[6] Legislative approaches might be split into two groups: opacity approaches and transparency approaches. Opacity approaches are relevant when the normative illegitimacy of an action has been clarified and clear prohibitions—bright-line rules—are needed. As De Hert and Gutwirth observe, such approaches: 'tend to guarantee non-interference in individual matters'. Paul De Hert and Serge Gutwirth, 'Privacy, Data Protection and Law Enforcement: Opacity of the Individual and Transparency of Power', in E. Claes, A. Duff, and S. Gutwirth (eds.), *Privacy and the Criminal Law* (Intersentia 2006) 61, 66 (hereafter De Hert and Gutwirth, 'Privacy, Data Protection and Law Enforcement'). Transparency approaches, in contrast, as Gutwirth et al. observe, '[come] into play after normative choices have been made, in order to channel the normatively accepted exercise of power'. Serge Gutwirth, Raphael Gellert, Rocco Bellanova, et al., Legal, Social, Economic and Ethical Conceptualisations of Privacy and Data Protection (PRESCIENT Project Deliverable, 1, 2011) 8.

[7] DPA solutions can be overridden, for example, by EDPB guidance—in line with consistency procedures outlined in Articles 63–67. National DPA interpretations may thus only be temporary solutions.

[8] Among these problems, the reader may notice the absence of a discussion of the GDPR's provisions on international transfers. Transfer provisions have certainly been problematised in literature. Peloquin et al., for example, observe the difficulty in securing certain transfers to the United States David Peloquin, Michael DiMaio, Barbara Bierer, et al., 'Disruptive and Avoidable: GDPR Challenges to Secondary Research Uses of Data' (2020) *European Journal of Human Genetics* 28 697, 702. The fact that transfers may be difficult under the GDPR, however, need not necessarily be seen as a problem concerning the protection of genetic privacy. The general approach of the GDPR to transfers is to secure protection of EU citizens' personal data outside the EU. This is not an unreasonable

C. Problems Concerning the Structure of the GDPR

1. The Regulation Cannot Protect Genetic Privacy Rights Engaged by the Processing of Scientific Conclusions (Problem 1)

a) Problem

As discussed, the concept of personal data cannot encompass scientific conclusions.[9] Scientific conclusions are impersonal information. They therefore cannot fulfil two requisite criteria—relating to or natural person—of personal data. Scientific conclusions therefore cannot currently fall within the scope of applicability, *rationae materiae*, of the Regulation.

Yet, as discussed, genetic privacy rights are engaged by the processing of scientific conclusions. Recall the observation that genetic groups—both genetic classes and categories—may have genetic privacy rights separate from single group members.[10] Thus, whilst no single member of a genetic group may have their genetic privacy rights engaged by the processing of scientific conclusions, a genetic group as a whole may still claim genetic privacy rights. Even in impersonal, abstract form, scientific conclusions may constitute information—even sensitive information—about a genetic group. For example, knowledge that an extra chromosome is indicative of Down's Syndrome in humans constitutes abstract scientific information.[11]

b) Severity and Resolution

The lack of applicability of the Regulation to scientific conclusions does not have negative consequences for the protection of genetic privacy. Accordingly, no solution is strictly necessary. In the first instance, as the Regulation does not apply to scientific conclusions, it cannot diminish protection otherwise available in relation to scientific conclusions. Even if it could, the Regulation's approach would still not diminish protection in Europe, as there is none otherwise available. It is clear, from previous analyses of international and alternative European law, that other relevant legal approaches have

or disproportionate approach. Equally, it is not the case that biobanks cannot technically or practically use the mechanisms already in place—although further work must be done in this regard. Problems rather come down to the fact that jurisdictions do not always align in the requirements they place on actors. There is nothing that could be done within the GDPR itself to address this—failing dropping EU standards. This is recognised in many of the texts dealing with biobanking and international transfers under the GDPR. See, for example, Santa Slokenberga, Jane Reichel, Rachel Niringiye, et al. 'EU Data Transfer Rules and African Legal Realities: Is Data Exchange for Biobank Research Realistic?' (2018) *International Data Privacy Law* 9(1) 30, 30–48; Michael Morrison, Jessica Bell, Carol George, et al., 'The European General Data Protection Regulation: Challenges and Considerations for iPSC Researchers And Biobanks' (2017) *Regenerative Medicine* 12(6) 693, 699 (hereafter Morrison, Bell, George, et al., 'The European General Data Protection Regulation: Challenges and Considerations').

[9] See chapter 7, section D.

[10] See chapter 4, sections E and F.

[11] See: Genetic and Rare Diseases Information Center, 'Down Syndrome' (Genetic and Rare Diseases Information Center, 2019) <https://rarediseases.info.nih.gov/diseases/10247/down-syndrome#diseaseCauseSection> accessed 11 December 2019.

not been designed with the intention of extending protection to scientific conclusions.[12] Normatively, such a lack of protection is, to a degree, defensible. As discussed previously, there are legitimate policy reasons put forward supporting limiting protection for genetic groups in scientific conclusions. Recall, in particular, objections regarding the difficulty that protection for scientific conclusions might have for the conduct and dissemination of research.[13]

Nevertheless, a solution would be desirable. In the first instance, from a normative perspective, protection for scientific conclusions is desirable. Recall the theoretical arguments put forward in previous chapters supporting the legitimacy of both types of genetic groups' genetic privacy rights.[14] Recall, for example, the justification of genetic privacy rights on the basis of the horrific history of genetic profiling in Europe—continuing even into this millennium, as evidenced by the 2011 European Court of Human Rights (ECtHR) case of *V.C. v. Slovakia* in which a Roma woman, allegedly based on her ethnicity, was forcibly sterilised.[15] Whilst the legitimacy of policy reasons mitigating against extending protection to genetic groups is unquestioned, recall also the observation that these cannot account for a complete lack of protection for genetic groups and therefore, by extension, to scientific conclusions.[16] In turn, an argument can be put forward that the Regulation is a relevant forum through which to provide protection. That the Regulation does not apply to scientific conclusions is a difficult obstacle to overcome in making this claim. Yet, data protection under the Regulation generally aims to provide comprehensive protection for rights—in particular, privacy rights—impacted by the use of data. Accordingly, the fact the Regulation does not apply might simply be argued to be a flaw in its approach to be legitimately addressed.

Solutions to the lack of applicability to scientific conclusions are arguably facilitated through the Regulation's internal mechanisms.[17] Superficially, a conceptual objection to any extension of protection to scientific conclusions presents itself. As discussed in the previous chapter, the concept of the data subject is key to defining the target of protection of the Regulation. As also discussed, genetic groups cannot be data subjects.[18] It might thus be argued that extending protection to scientific conclusions would represent a conceptual break with the aims and goals of the Regulation.

However, the idea of including protection for scientific conclusions within the scope of the Regulation finds some justification on the back of the history of data protection principles' applicability to group data. As Bygrave observes: 'there was a fairly strong trend during the 1970s to propose and/or enact data protection laws expressly covering

[12] See chapters 5 and 6.
[13] See chapter 5, section I.
[14] See chapter 4, sections E and F.
[15] *V.C. v. Slovakia*, App no 18968/07, 8 November 2011. The case charts a long history of such practices in Eastern Europe.
[16] See chapter 5, section I.
[17] The discussion of genetic groups in this chapter—in this section as well as in section E—relies on reworked argumentation from: Dara Hallinan and Paul De Hert, 'Genetic Classes and Genetic Categories: Protecting Genetic Groups Through Data Protection Law', in Linnet Taylor, Luciano Floridi, and Bart van der Sloot (eds.), *Group Privacy* (Springer 2017) 175 175–96 (hereafter Hallinan and De Hert, 'Genetic Classes and Genetic Categories').
[18] See chapter 8, section C.

data on [certain types of groups]'.[19] The possibility to protect group data was recognised, for example, in the Council of Europe's (CoE's) Convention 108. Article 3(2)(b) clarified that states were granted derogatory discretion to apply the Convention: 'relating to groups of persons, associations, foundations, companies, corporations and any other bodies consisting directly or indirectly of individuals'. This strand of thought even remains visible in recent history. For example, certain states' implementations of Directive 95/46—for instance, Austria's—aimed to provide protection to certain types of group data.[20]

In terms of the content of a solution, the EDPB could issue guidelines suggesting alternative interpretations of the problematic applicability criteria in the concept of personal data—relate to and natural person—to encompass scientific conclusions. This may, however, be inadvisable. Such a broadening of the concept would involve rewriting applicability criteria which have long constituted core definitions of European data protection law. This approach would also run up against the problem that the Regulation currently treats all subjects of protection as data subjects and treats all data subjects the same. Yet, the structure of the Regulation cannot handle multiple data subjects simultaneously—this obstacle will be discussed at length below, in relation to problem 6. Alternatively, and much less problematically, the EDPB might extend protection to scientific conclusions by introducing new applicability criteria relating solely to group data. The question of the substantive content of protection to be granted to scientific conclusions then raises its own problems. Possible approaches to this issue will be discussed in relation to problem 5, concerning the protection of genetic groups generally, below.

The Regulation does not, however, facilitate the adoption of alternative approaches to the lack of applicability to scientific conclusions via other law. The Regulation provides no derogation which might be relied on to facilitate the extension, or provisions of protection, to scientific conclusions via other law. It cannot thus facilitate a solution to the problem. The lack of applicability of the Regulation to scientific conclusions means, however, that this is a moot point. As the Regulation does not apply to scientific conclusions, it has no impact on the adoption of external legislation concerning scientific conclusions.

2. The Regulation Cannot Protect Genetic Privacy Rights Engaged by Law Enforcement Processing (Problem 2)

a) Problem

The Regulation clearly excludes law enforcement processing from its scope despite this type of processing engaging genetic privacy rights. The Regulation's exclusion of law enforcement processing is explicit. Article 2(2) excludes: 'the processing of personal

[19] Lee Bygrave, *Data Protection Law: Approaching Its Rationale, Logic and Limits* (Kluwer 2002) 296.
[20] Bundesgesetz über den Schutz personenbezogener Daten 2000.

data ... by competent authorities for the purposes of the prevention, investigation, detection or prosecution of criminal offences or the execution of criminal penalties, including the safeguarding against and the prevention of threats to public security'.

Yet, as clarified previously, law enforcement authorities have an interest in accessing research subjects' biological samples and sequenced genomic information for use in criminal investigations.[21] Recall Kaye's observation that biobanks are: 'attractive to the police, because they will be an easy entry into a comprehensive and useful body of information'.[22] As further clarified in previous analysis, this type of use would be in direct conflict with research subjects', genetic relatives', and genetic groups' genetic privacy rights. Law enforcement agencies' access to biobanking would almost invariably happen without prior consent, perhaps without prior expectations of rights holders and with the intention of making potentially negative judgments about rights holders.[23]

The significance of this gap is exacerbated by the fact that law enforcement use of biobanking substances is not merely a theoretical possibility. Law enforcement agencies have already successfully accessed biobanks in Europe. Swedish police use of biobank samples in the murder of Anna Lindh has been discussed multiple times in this book.[24] This is, however, not a one-off. Dranseika et al., for example, also note the UK case of Stephen Kelley. They observe: 'The scientific evidence that led to the conviction was derived from an earlier biological sample, obtained from ... researchers by a police warrant.'[25]

b) Severity and Resolution

The lack of applicability to law enforcement processing is not a problem which requires resolution for the efficacy of the Regulation as a tool for the protection of genetic privacy in biobanking. In the first instance, as the Regulation does not apply to law enforcement processing, it cannot impact or diminish protection already available regarding law enforcement.

In turn, the Regulation should not be expected to provide protection in relation to law enforcement processing. On the one hand, the significance of law enforcement processing for genetic privacy in biobanking is unquestioned. This has been shown in the analysis of interest conflicts in biobanking in previous chapters.[26] This is also shown, in practice, by the significance the issue has been attributed by the Deutscher Ethikrat, which took it as a core issue around which to build a concept for biobank regulation.[27] A comprehensive system of protection should thus doubtlessly deal with law

[21] See chapter 4, section H.

[22] Jane Kaye, 'Police Collection and Access to DNA Samples' (2006) *Genomics, Society and Policy* 2(1) 16, 23 (hereafter Kaye, 'Police Collection and Access to DNA Samples').

[23] See chapter 4, section I.

[24] Kaye, 'Police Collection and Access to DNA Samples' (n. 22) 17.

[25] Vilius Dranseika, Jan Piaseck, and Marcin Waligora, 'Forensic Uses of Research Biobanks: Should Donors Be Informed?' (2016) *Medicine, Health Care and Philosophy* 19 141, 141–2.

[26] See chapter 4, section I.

[27] Deutscher Ethikrat, Humanbiobanken für die Forschung: Stellungnahme (Position Paper, 2010) 34–8.

enforcement processing. Judged against the measure of an ideal system, the Regulation thus appears problematic.

On the other hand, however, as the Regulation was specifically designed not to deal with law enforcement processing, it is not legitimate to consider it as a legal tool to deal with issues of law enforcement processing. Certain types of law enforcement involving national security fall outside the scope of EU law altogether and cannot be dealt with by any EU organ or law. Whilst ordinary police and law enforcement processing falls within the scope of EU law, this activity was deliberately excluded from the Regulation's scope in the legislative process. This decision reflects the idea that law enforcement requires special consideration and cannot be dealt with through legislation ostensibly designed for commerce and bureaucracy. There is a thus separate piece of data protection legislation specifically designed for police and law enforcement processing: Directive 2016/680.[28]

Historically, as Boehm observes, law enforcement processing was deliberately 'excluded from the scope of Directive 95/46'.[29] The logic of separation then played a significant role in the process of data protection law reform leading to the adoption of the Regulation. From the outset, issues of both national divergence and substance mediated against the use of the Regulation in the law enforcement context. In relation to national divergence, as De Hert and Papakonstantinou observe: 'a Directive was the instrument of choice [as] ... law enforcement processing practices differ widely among EU Member States, ultimately being connected to issues of history and culture'.[30] In terms of substance, the need to balance security against privacy—and other rights—required a different calculus in relation to law enforcement than in relation to other sectors. As De Hert and Papakonstantinou further observe: 'special security-related needs have to be accommodated'.[31]

Even if a solution were necessary, the lack of applicability to law enforcement is not a problem which can be solved through the Regulation's interpretation and adaptation mechanisms. There is a clear technical objection which can be put forward. The exclusion of law enforcement from the scope of the Regulation has both deep roots and, following in this tradition, was a clear political choice made by the legislator in drafting the Regulation. The clarity and pedigree of this political choice mean this is not an issue in relation to which national DPAs and the EDPB have jurisdiction and which thus cannot be circumvented by administrative interpretation.

[28] Directive (EU) 2016/680 of the European Parliament and of the Council of 27 April 2016 on the protection of natural persons with regard to the processing of personal data by competent authorities for the purposes of the prevention, investigation, detection or prosecution of criminal offences or the execution of criminal penalties, and on the free movement of such data, and repealing Council Framework Decision 2008/977/JHA [2016] OJ L119/89.

[29] Franziska Boehm, 'Information Sharing in the Area of Freedom, Security and Justice: Towards a Common Standard for Data Exchange Between Agencies and EU Information Systems', in Serge Gutwirth, Ronald Leenes, Paul De Hert, and Yves Poullet (eds.), *European Data Protection: In Good Health?* (Springer 2012) 143, 146.

[30] Paul De Hert and Vagelis Papakonstantinou, 'The New Police and Criminal Justice Data Protection Directive: A First Analysis' (2016) *New Journal of European Criminal Law* 7(1) 7, 8–10 (hereafter De Hert and Papakonstantinou, 'The New Police and Criminal Justice Data Protection Directive').

[31] De Hert and Papakonstantinou, 'The New Police and Criminal Justice Data Protection Directive' (n. 30) 9.

Even if a solution were necessary, the Regulation does not facilitate the adoption of a solution via other law. The derogations in the Regulation only apply in relation to activities falling within the scope of the Regulation. Accordingly, they cannot apply to facilitate the adoption of solutions to the lack of applicability to law enforcement. This is, of course, irrelevant. As the Regulation does not apply to law enforcement processing, it has no impact on the maintenance, or future enactment, of genetic privacy relevant provisions relating to law enforcement via other law.

D. Problems Concerning the Protection of Research Subjects' Genetic Privacy Rights on the Transactional Axis

1. The GDPR Cannot Protect the Research Subject's Information Privacy Right to Choose Not to Know Their Own Genetic Data (Problem 3)

a) Problem

The Regulation contains no provisions concerned with data subjects' information privacy rights to choose not to know their genetic data. It is true that the Regulation contains several provisions relating to data subject control over the communication of their genetic data by biobanking actors. In relation to communication of personal data to third parties, Article 9, for example, in principle requires that data subject consent, where possible, be obtained before collection and processing of their data. Even more poignantly, Article 15 concerns when and how a data subject might require a biobanking actor to reveal to them their genetic data produced in the course of research. These provisions, however, are unconcerned with data subjects' abilities to decide not to have information returned.[32]

A close reading of the text of the Regulation suggests the omission of recognition for the right is an oversight. It appears the legislator designed the Regulation with a model of data mediated relationships in mind in which data subjects would already know the factual content of their personal data. Under such a model, the data subject would have no need to ever be protected from feedback. Evidence for the fact the legislator relied on such a model is reflected in the Regulation's transparency provisions.[33] Article 13, for example, concerns the obligation to inform the data subject about proposed processing

[32] There are certain suggestions that indicate the right may already exist to some degree under data protection law. Such assertions are, however, hard to directly discern from text of the GDPR. See, for example, Deutsche Gesellschaft für Medizinische Informatik, Biometrie und Epidemiologie e. V., Gesellschaft für Datenschutz und Datensicherheit e. V., Datenschutzrechtliche Anforderungen an die medizinische Forschung unter Berucksichtigung der EU Datenschutz-Grundverordnung (DS-GVO) (Policy, 2018) 14 (hereafter GMDS and GDD, Datenschutzrechtliche Anforderungen an die medizinische Forschung).

[33] See, for a more extensive discussion: Dara Hallinan and Raphaël Gellert, 'The Concept of "Information": An Invisible Problem in the GDPR' (2020) *Scripted* 17(2), 269, 297–300 (hereafter Hallinan and Gellert, 'The Concept of "Information"').

when personal data have been collected from that subject. To understand processing, the data subject would need to know the content of personal data to be processed.[34] Yet, Article 13 omits any requirement that data controllers explain which personal data have been collected or could be processed. This omission only makes sense under the presumption that the data subject already knows the socially relevant content of their data.

b) Severity and Resolution

The lack of protection will not have significant negative consequences for genetic privacy protection. There is thus no strict need for a solution. In most cases, the approach of the Regulation mirrors the status quo. The right is not identifiable as an international principle.[35] Nor is the right protected in all European states' legal systems—German law, for example, contains no provisions protecting the right.[36] Even in those cases in which the right was protected in European state law—notably in Estonian law—the Regulation is scarcely a practical obstacle to the ongoing protection of the right.[37] In principle, protection for the right could be challenged in data protection on the basis—under Article 1(3) of the Regulation—that it constitutes an obstacle to 'free movement of personal data within the Union … connected with the protection of natural persons'. It is, however, hard to see how biobanking feedback would ever, in practice, constitute a serious problem for cross-border data flows and be subject to challenge.

Nevertheless, a solution would be desirable. There are strong normative arguments supporting the idea that this type of genetic privacy right should be given some degree of protection. In the first instance, previous analysis recognised the legitimacy of the research subject's right to choose not to know their genetic data.[38] On top of this, previous analysis highlighted that comprehensive legal systems could, and should, protect the right.[39] Indeed, analysis also highlighted that there is little clear justification as to why a legal system would not protect the right to some degree. In turn, where the right is currently protected, it would be odd that its protection should—albeit perhaps only technically—be placed in jeopardy by existence of the Regulation.

Solutions to the lack of protection are arguably facilitated through the Regulation's internal interpretation and adaptation mechanisms. There are no conceptual, legal structural, or technical objections evident. From a conceptual and legal structural perspective, the right is proximate to the aims and approach of the Regulation. The right can be regarded as simply constituting an extension of concepts of informational self-determination already firmly embedded in the Regulation. As Andorno observes: 'the right not to know is widely recognised … by the German legal literature as a part of the "right to informational self determination"'.[40] From a technical perspective, there are

[34] Article 29 Working Party, Opinion 15/2011 on the definition of consent (Policy, 01197/11/EN WP187, 2011) 17 (hereafter Article 29 Working Party, Opinion 15/2011).

[35] See chapter 5, sections C and E.

[36] See chapter 6, section H.

[37] See chapter 6, section H.

[38] See chapter 4, section D.

[39] See chapter 5, section H.

[40] Roberto Andorno, 'The Right Not to Know: An Autonomy Based Approach' (2004) *Law, Ethics and Medicine* 30 435, 436.

no existing data protection provisions which would necessarily need to be ignored or significantly altered to ensure the right's inclusion in the Regulation. Indeed, the idea that internal mechanisms might be used to amend the Regulation's approach to informational self-determination has already been demonstrated. The Article 29 Working Party, for example, have issued extensive guidance on the conditions of consent under Directive 95/46.[41]

In terms of the content of a solution, in introducing the right to the Regulation, the EDPB might adopt a strategy focusing on the conditions of consent. The moment of consent is a reasonable point at which a data subject might be given the chance to choose not to know their genetic data. In this regard, the EDPB could issue interpretative guidance requiring, in the consent process, that relevant biobanking actors do two things:

1. Provide data subjects with a prior explanation of their feedback procedures
2. Allow data subjects to give a clear declaration as to whether they would prefer not to receive research results—which could be overridden at a later stage.

The Regulation also facilitates the adoption of approaches addressing the lack of protection through other law. If protection through the Regulation does not eventuate, the Regulation still permits the adoption of supplementary rules at national level. Such national rules would be legitimate as supplemental conditions, under Article 9(4), relating to the processing of genetic data and data concerning health. For example, the Regulation would not preclude the Estonian government from retaining protection for the right already granted under Article 11(1) of the Human Genes Research Act.[42]

2. The GDPR Cannot Protect the Research Subject's Spatial Privacy Right Not to Be Informed of Potentially Harmful Genetic Information (Problem 4)

a) Problem

The Regulation contains no provisions concerned with the research subject's spatial privacy right not to be informed. As discussed in the previous problem, the Regulation contains provisions relating to the return of information to data subjects. The example of Article 15 data subject access rights is again relevant. However, none of these provisions concern limitations on feeding personal data back to a data subject.

Once again, the lack of recognition of the right seems likely a result of oversight as opposed to design. If—as discussed in relation to the previous problem—it is correct that the regulator presumed that the data subject would generally know the factual

[41] Article 29 Working Party, Opinion 15/2011 (n. 34) 8–9.

[42] There are suggestions, for example from the EDPS, that legislation under 9(4) is only legitimate following specific announcement. This suggestion is not, however, mirrored in the text of the Regulation. European Data Protection Supervisor, A Preliminary Opinion on data protection and scientific research (Policy, 2020) 17.

content of their personal data being processed, then, in the drafting process, the legislator is unlikely to have considered the need to address scenarios of harm resulting from the feedback of novel personal data produced in the course of research.

b) Severity and Resolution

The lack of protection will not have any significant negative consequences for the protection of genetic privacy. There is thus no strict need for a solution. The approach of the Regulation simply mirrors the dominant approach of other lawmakers to date. It thus does nothing to diminish protection otherwise available. From previous analyses, it is clear there is no international principle, or clear European state law, protecting the right.[43] In turn, as observed previously, there are also important policy arguments mediating against protecting the right. In particular, recall concerns around the unsuitability of researchers as arbiters of what research subjects should and should not know—biobanking researchers may not, for example, have the relevant relationship with research subjects allowing them to make such decisions.[44]

Nevertheless, a solution remains desirable. Despite the lack of negative consequences in relation to the current standard of protection, there are strong normative arguments supporting the idea that the right should be protected. Recall, in the first instance, previous analysis supporting the recognition of the legitimacy of the right in principle.[45] Recall, in turn, previous arguments highlighting that comprehensive legal systems should, and indeed could, provide some protection for the right without falling foul of legitimate policy objections.[46]

Unfortunately, the Regulation is not suited to facilitate solutions to the lack of protection through its internal mechanisms. In the first instance, there is a clear conceptual objection evident. The aim of the right is arguably antithetical to the aims of the Regulation. Whilst the right serves to obscure information from the research subject, the Regulation predominantly seeks to make processing transparent.

In turn, a legal structural problem is evident. The right relates to a type of harm-causing act against which the research subject cannot act to place any kind of obstacle—because they are in no position to. Accordingly, protection for the right would involve, as Laurie observes, a 'paternalistic' element in which choice is taken away from the individual and information is deliberately hidden from them.[47] This is indicative of a prohibitive approach. As De Hert and Gutwirth have observed, such solutions are characterised by the fact that: 'the legislator takes the place of the individual as the prime arbiter of desirable or undesirable acts'.[48] This approach is quite distinct from that found in the other substantive provisions in the Regulation, which are procedural in nature.

[43] See chapter 5, section H and chapter 6, section H.
[44] See chapter 5, section H.
[45] See chapter 5, section H.
[46] See chapter 5, section H.
[47] Graham Laurie, 'A Response to Andorno' (2004) *Law, Ethics and Medicine* 30 439, 440.
[48] De Hert and Gutwirth, 'Privacy, Data Protection and Law Enforcement' (n. 6) 66.

Fortunately, the Regulation facilitates the adoption of approaches addressing the lack of protection through other law. European state legislation placing restrictions on the feedback of certain types of personal data to research subjects would constitute conditions applicable to the processing of genetic data and data concerning health. Such conditions would thus fall within the scope of Article 9(4). There is no reason, for example, that the German government could not enshrine personality rights-based arguments supporting the right in law, and for this act to be compatible with the Regulation.[49]

E. Problems Concerning the Protection of Genetic Relatives' and Genetic Groups' Genetic Privacy Rights on the Relational Axis

1. The Regulation Cannot Protect Genetic Groups (Problem 5)

a) Problem

No genetic group—either class or category—can qualify as a data subject. No genetic group is a target of protection for the Regulation. The concept of the data subject defines the type of actor protected by the Regulation.[50] The concept functions not only as a practical technical tool serving to allocate rights and obligations but also as a philosophical keystone defining the Regulation's aims. The concept is entrenched in data protection law and is far older than the Regulation, with a history stretching to the genesis of EU data protection law and beyond. In turn, through the course of its use in EU law, there has been little jurisprudential reassessment of its core defining criteria. Accordingly, if an actor cannot qualify as a data subject, it becomes difficult indeed to make an argument that they may constitute a target of protection under the Regulation.

Unfortunately, as discussed previously, in relation to problem 1, all genetic groups—both classes and categories—are excluded from being able to qualify as data subjects.[51] No group, whether genetic or not, can be a natural person and thus no group can be a data subject. Indeed, the clear exclusion of groups as subjects of data protection has been observed by commentators such as Mantelero and Vaciago: 'the traditional notions of ... data protection are mainly based on the model of individual rights ... [and that] the right holder has remained the data subject and the rights have mainly been exercised by individuals'.[52] Floridi expresses the same sentiment: 'the concept of "data subject" [constitutes] an "atomistic" ontology ... at the roots of current European [data protection] legislation'.[53]

[49] See chapter 6, section H.
[50] See chapter 8, section B.
[51] See chapter 8, section C.
[52] Alessandro Mantelero and Giuseppe Vaciago, 'Data Protection in a Big Data Society: Ideas for a Future Regulation' (2015) *Digital Investigation* 15 104, 107.
[53] Luciano Floridi, 'Open Data, Data Protection and Group Privacy' (2014) *Philosophy and Technology* 27(1) 1, 2.

b) Severity and Resolution

The lack of protection provided by the Regulation will not have significant negative consequences for the protection of genetic privacy. There is thus no strict need for a solution. The approach of the Regulation follows the status quo and thus does not imply any diminished standard of protection for genetic groups. Previous analysis highlighted there is no identifiable international principle—common or emerging—for the protection of genetic groups.[54] Previous analysis also showed that no European state law provides protection for genetic groups either.[55] It should further be recalled that there are legitimate policy reasons put forward mediating against protecting genetic groups. Recall, in particular, objections highlighting that protecting genetic groups could negatively impact other legitimate rights and interests engaged by the biobanking process—both research subjects' rights and interests connected with the conduct and outcome of research.[56]

Nevertheless, a solution would be desirable. There are normative arguments supporting the idea that genetic groups should receive some degree of protection. In the first instance, as pointed out in previous chapters, there are persuasive normative arguments supporting the legitimacy of both types of genetic groups'—classes' and categories'—genetic privacy rights.[57] In turn, it was observed that, whilst policy objections against extending protection were both legitimate and compelling, they lacked subtlety. Eventually, it was observed that a comprehensive legal system could, and should, provide some form of protection for genetic groups.[58]

Solutions to the lack of protection are arguably facilitated through the Regulation's internal interpretation and adaptation mechanisms. The key objection which could be put forward is that the Regulation was designed only as a system for the protection of individuals. This objection, however, has already been addressed above—in relation to problem 1—concerning the possibility that the Regulation might be used to protect genetic privacy rights engaged by the processing of scientific conclusions.

In terms of the substance of a resolution, the EDPB would need to address three key issues. First, the EDPB would need to provide a cogent definition for which types of genetic groups qualify for protection. As discussed previously, each genome could relate to an almost infinite number of genetic groups.[59] Yet, it would not make sense to give all possible genetic groups protection in relation to each genome. In this regard, most genetic groups will have such a tenuous relationship with the data in question as to be irrelevant from a privacy perspective. Thus, a functional delineation of relevant genetic groups might focus on, as I have observed elsewhere, the aim of processing.[60] Such an approach could build on considerations of the intention and capacity of processing to produce information with significance for a genetic group.

[54] See chapter 5, section I.
[55] See chapter 6, section I.
[56] See chapter 6, section I.
[57] See chapter 4, sections E and F.
[58] See chapter 5, section I.
[59] See chapter 4, section E.
[60] Hallinan and De Hert, 'Genetic Classes and Genetic Categories' (n. 17) 192.

Second, the EDPB would need to introduce genetic groups as a separate category of subject of protection. The Regulation currently treats all subjects of protection as data subjects and treats all data subjects the same. Yet, the structure of the Regulation cannot handle multiple data subjects simultaneously—this point will be discussed at greater length later in relation to the next problem. Only by treating genetic groups as a separate category of subject of protection could this problem be avoided.

Third, the EDPB would need to carefully consider the substantive protection granted to genetic groups. As discussed previously, a red line for the provision of protection might be that protection for genetic groups should not disrupt the existing balance of interests in biobanking.[61] With this in mind, the EDPB might begin with a conservative approach and consider which of the Regulation's substantive provisions might be extended without causing such disruption. In this regard, three data controller obligations spring immediately to mind.[62] Significantly, none of these obligations requires communication between groups and data controllers, or relates to rights to know and not know. Accordingly, all are suitable to protect both types of genetic group—genetic classes and genetic categories:

1. The obligation to take genetic groups into account in the DPIA
2. The obligation to hold group data accurately
3. The obligation to hold group data securely

The Regulation also facilitates the adoption of approaches addressing the lack of protection through other law. Were European states to have a change of heart as to the logic of protecting genetic groups in biobanking, the Regulation would permit protection under other approaches. National law introduced to protect genetic groups would consist of supplemental conditions relating to the processing of genetic data and data concerning health. Justification for such national conditions would be provided by derogation possibilities under Article 9(4).

2. The Regulation Cannot Protect Genetic Relatives (Problem 6)

a) Problem

Unlike genetic groups, genetic relatives can qualify as data subjects.[63] Superficially, then, there seems to be no problem—relatives fall within the class of actors the Regulation protects. However, thinking through the consequences of using the Regulation as a system for the protection of genetic relatives reveals a different story.

[61] See chapter 5, section I.

[62] The extension of data subject rights and most data controller obligations to genetic groups would pose significant issues. The extension of research subject rights would unquestionably impact research subject rights. The extension of most data controller obligations—in particular, data controller obligations related to limitations on processing possibilities—would place limitations on the conduct and diffusion of research.

[63] See chapter 8, section C.

The Regulation makes no facility for differentiation of application according to the subject of protection—all are simply data subjects and all data subjects are treated equally. Accordingly, considering the Regulation as a tool for the protection of genetic relatives would mean all relatives would be treated in exactly the same way as research subjects. This is problematic. The provisions of the Regulation cannot, and should not, be applied to genetic relatives in the same way as to research subjects. As a result, the Regulation cannot be regarded as providing a framework capable of protecting genetic relatives. Three specific problems deserve discussion.

First, the Regulation offers no *rationae personae* capable of defining which genetic relatives would constitute subjects of protection. The Regulation provides only one concept aimed at determining the actors subject to its protection—its *rationae personae*: the concept of the data subject. Whilst genetic relatives can technically qualify as data subjects, when used in relation to genetic relatives, the concept has little cogency as either a philosophical or practical tool for the delineation of targets of protection. Unfortunately, the concept, as it currently appears, offers no way in which to determine a cut-off point between relevant and irrelevant genetic relatives.

Scientifically, the concept of the genetic relative is broad. The idea of a genetic relative extends far beyond the nuclear family. It includes more distant genetic relatives—such as cousins, second cousins, third cousins etc. Eventually, moving degrees of genetic separation from an original genomic research subject, the concept will include all humans—we are all genetically related. In fact, the difference in genetic architecture between any two individuals is minimal. As Jorde puts it: 'The average proportion of nucleotide differences between a randomly chosen pair of humans ... is consistently estimated to lie between 1 in 1,000 and 1 in 1,500.'[64]

However, as genetic relatives become more distant, the individual significance of shared genetic architecture decreases. For example, much unique may be assumed about a research subject's biological child from that subject's genome, whilst almost nothing unique could be assumed about a fifteenth cousin. As McGuire et al. comment: 'The generation of whole-genome data significantly increases the ability to reveal predictive information about [*close*] relatives'... health risks [emphasis added]'.[65]

Accordingly, whilst all people are theoretically genetic relatives, it is not the case that all genetic relatives have recognisable genetic privacy rights in any given genome. As Taylor comments, a genome is only relevant for genetic relatives if the genome concerns them 'in a relevant fashion because of its ... implications ... in terms of architecture or significance'.[66] It thus makes no sense to suggest that all genetic relatives should be considered as subjects of protection of the Regulation. After all, if a genetic relative has no discernible rights engaged by the processing of genomic data, what is there

[64] Lynn Jorde and Stephen Wooding, 'Genetic Variation, Classification and "Race"' (2004) *Nature Genetics* 36 28, 28.

[65] Amy McGuire, Timothy Caulfield, and Mildred Cho, 'Research Ethics and the Challenge of Whole-Genome Sequencing' (2008) *Nature Reviews Genetics* 9(2) 152, 154.

[66] Mark Taylor, *Genetic Data and the Law: A Critical Perspective on Privacy Protection* (Cambridge University Press 2012) 106 (hereafter Taylor, *Genetic Data and the Law*).

for the Regulation to protect? It thus makes no sense that all genetic relatives should qualify as data subjects.

Second, provisions which rely on active data subject-data controller engagement lack the subtlety to apply to genetic relatives. Such provisions are numerous and include two types of provision which arguably constitute, as Beyleveld puts it, 'the core of protection provided' by European data protection law.[67] First, these include provisions aiming to provide information allowing the data subject to understand processing—transparency provisions. Such provisions include the Article 4(11) rights to be informed in consent, Article 13 and 14 rights to information, and Article 15 rights to access. Second, these include provisions allowing data subjects to control the processing of their personal data—self-determination provisions. These include the Article 9(2)(a) right to give consent, the Article 7(3) right to withdraw consent, and the Article 17 right to erasure.

Looking across these provisions, they have been designed to deal with bilateral relationships between one data subject and one data controller. For example, the Article 9(2)(a) consent procedure requires that a legitimate consent be given by one data subject to one data controller. Treating genetic relatives as data subjects, however, would mean the recognition of multiple data subjects in relation to one genome—the research subject plus each genetic relative.

This changes the relevant relationship constellation significantly. The bilateral relationship around which the provisions were designed is no longer relevant. Rather, a much more complex, multilateral, relationship constellation becomes relevant. The research subject's relationship with the biobanking controller remains, and mimics, that in the one data subject–one data controller model. This relationship, however, is joined by three new types of relationship: the research subject's relationship with their genetic relatives; genetic relatives' relationships with each other; and genetic relatives' relationships with the biobanking controller.

As I have observed elsewhere, transparency and self-determination provisions 'lack the complexity to deal with this new dynamic'.[68] In the first instance, they provide no answers to several questions arising regarding the exercise of provisions. For example: from which data subject should the biobanking controller ask for consent under Article 9(2)(a)—all possible data subjects, any single data subject, or one specific data subject? In turn, as Taylor observes: 'Raising the possibility of multiple data subjects raises the possibility of conflict between those subjects.'[69] The Regulation provides no scheme for the resolution of such conflicts. Which data subject's rights should be given higher importance than other data subjects' rights?

Finally, the privacy rights of the research subject and those of genetic relatives are not equal and should not be treated as such. If the Regulation were to be used as an instrument for the protection genetic relatives, genetic relatives would occupy the same

[67] Deryck Beyleveld, 'An Overview of Directive 95/46/EC in Relation to Medical Research', in Deryck Beyleveld, David Townend, Ségolène Rouillé-Mirza, and Jessica Wright (eds.), *The Data Protection Directive and Medical Research Across Europe* (Ashgate 2004) 5, 11 (hereafter Beyleveld, 'An Overview of Directive 95/46/EC').

[68] Hallinan and De Hert, 'Genetic Classes and Genetic Categories' (n. 17) 190.

[69] Taylor, *Genetic Data and the Law* (n. 66) 116.

legal position as the research subject. This would be akin to recognising that the functional protection deserved by both parties is the same. This, in turn, would be akin to recognising parity between the parties' underlying genetic privacy rights. Yet, there is no justification for recognising such parity. This can be argued from two perspectives.

In the first instance, as discussed previously, a research subject's privacy right is much stronger than a genetic relative's equivalent right.[70] For example, the strength of a privacy right can be considered as a function of the form and content of connection between information and rights holder. This is the justification for the category of sensitive personal data in the Regulation. This has also been repeatedly recognised in ECtHR case law—for example, in the case of *I v. Finland*.[71] In terms of the form of connection, recall the genome acts as a unique biometric identifier only for a research subject. Whilst a research subject's genome can be used to identify genetic relatives, the process is arduous and subject to greater inaccuracy. In terms of the content of connection, a large quantity of socially significant information can be extracted about a research subject from their genome.[72] Whilst significant information can also be extracted about genetic relatives from a research subject's genome, this is quantitatively and qualitatively incomparable with that extractable about the subject.

In turn, the idea of considering genetic relatives as being entitled to the same level of privacy protection as research subjects runs contrary to ethical and legal norms hitherto relevant in biobanking. In fact, to elevate the interests of genetic relatives to the level of those of research subjects would be equivalent to turning the last century—a century in which the research subject alone stood as the focus of protection—of bioethics and biomedical law on its head. The primacy of the research subject is evident in previous analyses of international and EU law relevant to biobanking.[73] Not one instrument considered came close to recognising a parity of interests. As the Declaration of Helsinki states, for example, in Article 8: 'While the primary purpose of medical research is to generate new knowledge, this goal can never take precedence over the rights and interests of individual research subjects.'

b) Severity and Resolution

The lack of protection will not have any significant negative consequences for the protection of genetic privacy. There is thus no strict need for a solution. The approach of the Regulation is simply the equivalent of that adopted by other legal approaches relevant in Europe. It thus does not represent a drop in the standard of protection otherwise available. Recall that no concrete international principles relating to the protection of genetic relatives were identifiable.[74] Recall also that alternative European state approaches do not provide protection for genetic relatives.[75] In turn, it was previously

[70] See chapter 5, section I.
[71] *I. v. Finland*, App. no. 20511/03, 17 October 2008, para. 38.
[72] See chapter 2, section F.
[73] See chapters 5 and 6.
[74] See chapter 5, sections D and F.
[75] See chapter 6, section I.

observed that there were legitimate policy arguments supporting not extending protection to genetic relatives. Convincing arguments were put forward outlining the disruption such protection might cause to carefully struck balances between research subject rights and legitimate interests in the research process.[76]

Nevertheless, a solution remains desirable. As discussed previously, there are strong normative arguments recognising the legitimacy of genetic relatives' genetic privacy rights in biobanking. Indeed, the basic justification for these is largely the same as the justification for research subjects' genetic privacy rights in biobanking.[77] However, although policy arguments against the protection of genetic relatives' rights are convincing, recall that these do not constitute a complete obstacle to providing some protection to relatives. In this regard, it was argued that the extension of certain types of protection to relatives would be possible without significantly impacting other rights and interests. On the back of the above, recall the normative conclusion that a comprehensive legal system could, and should, provide some degree of protection for genetic relatives.[78]

Solutions to the lack of protection are arguably facilitated through the Regulation's internal mechanisms. There are no objections to the use of the Regulation's internal interpretation and adaptation mechanisms to protect genetic relatives. From conceptual and legal structural perspectives, not only is the logic of genetic relatives' privacy claims similar to that of research subjects' privacy claims, but genetic relatives can, themselves, even qualify as data subjects.[79] From a technical perspective, the suitability of the Regulation's internal interpretation and adaptation mechanisms as a forum for the provision of protection for genetic relatives has already been demonstrated. Certain DPAs have already interpreted data protection principles to the benefit of genetic relatives. The Italian DPA, for example—the Garante—has used its powers to allow a woman to exercise data subject access rights in relation to her genetic father's genetic data.[80] Equally, the Article 29 Working Party, in their consideration of genetic data speculated that: 'other family members could also be considered as "data subjects" with all the rights that follow ... this'.[81]

In terms of the content of a solution, the EDPB would need to address three key issues. First, the Board would need to delineate which degree of genetic relative should constitute a subject of protection. As a starting point, an effective delineation might consider the accuracy with which information extracted from a genome could be used to predict significant information about genetic relatives: only relatives about whom extracted information could be used to generate socially significant information should be considered as subjects of protection.

[76] See chapter 5, section I.
[77] See chapter 4, section E.
[78] See chapter 5, section I.
[79] See chapter 8, section C.
[80] Garante, Cittadini e società dell'informazione (Policy, no. 8, 1999) 13–15.
[81] Article 29 Working Party, Opinion 15/2011 (n. 34) 8–9.

Second, the EDPB would need to introduce genetic relatives as a separate category of protection to research subjects—for example, as an alternative type of data subject. As discussed, the Regulation only recognises one category of protected entity, yet it cannot effectively function if multiple entities occupy this role at once. Only by introducing genetic relatives as a separate category of protected entity could the Regulation remain functional.

Third, the EDPB would need to consider the substantive protection given to genetic relatives. As argued previously, a red line for protection for genetic relatives should be the disruption of the existing balance of interests in biobanking.[82] In this regard, it would seem extension of the majority of data controller obligations would be possible without impacting other rights or interests. The following obligations could each be owed to research subjects and genetic relatives simultaneously—without impacting research subject rights—and may be executed by biobanking actors with little extra effort, and may thus be used as an initial approach to protection:

1. The obligation to take genetic relatives into account in the DPIA
2. The obligation to hold genetic relatives' data accurately
3. The obligation to hold relatives' data in as unidentifiable a state as possible
4. The obligation to hold relatives' data securely.

The Regulation also facilitates the adoption of approaches addressing the lack of protection for genetic relatives through other law. If European states were to change their current stance and recognise the need to extend protection to genetic relatives, any such protection would constitute supplemental obligations related to the processing of genetic data or data concerning health. Legislation outlining such protection would thus fall within the scope of Article 9(4).

F. Problems Concerning the Substantive Protection Offered by the GDPR

1. The Regulation Imposes No Obligation to Seek Prior Approval from a DPA (Problem 7)

a) Problem

The obligation to obtain prior approval from a supervisory authority is a common international principle.[83] In turn, where oversight is required in EU Member State approaches, advance review and evaluation of biobanking by Research Ethics Committees (RECs) is often mandatory. Article 15 of the German Musterberufsordnung für Ärzte

[82] See Chapter 5, section I.
[83] See chapter 5, section C.

2015, for example, states: 'Physicians who participate in a research project . . . must ensure that advice on questions of professional ethics and professional conduct associated with the project is obtained from an Ethics Committee.'[84]

There is no mandatory obligation to obtain prior authorisation and approval under the Regulation. Oversight is discussed at length in the Regulation and Article 36 foresees, in certain cases, the need for prior consultation by a DPA. However, Article 36 only applies: '[when] a data protection impact assessment . . . indicates that processing would result in a high risk in the absence of measures taken by the controller.'[85] As De Hert and Papakonstantinou observe, deciding whether the Article's thresholds have been met is eventually left to the data controller.[86]

b) Severity and Resolution

The absence of this obligation from the Regulation is unlikely to have significant negative impact on genetic privacy rights. This minimises the strict need for a solution. This is true for two reasons. First, the Regulation does, in Article 36, foresee the obligation to engage in prior consultation in high-risk cases, and the significance of this obligation should not be discounted.

Second, oversight by other types of body—for example, RECs—will not be impacted by the Regulation. These bodies are not legitimated by data protection law and have co-existed with European data protection law for many years. For example, the Regulation will have no impact on German Physicians' REC prior consultation obligation in line with the requirements of Article 15 of the Musterberufsordnung für Ärzte 2015. Arguments have been put forward highlighting the insufficiency of these bodies in engaging in genetic privacy oversight. Dove, for example, observes: 'the misalignment of data privacy laws and ethics review boards and committees is an ongoing challenge . . . [T]hese entities may impose higher standards of privacy protection than privacy laws require . . .Moreover, there is an inconsistent level or lack of privacy expertise, training, and oversight of many REC members.'[87] Their general suitability to perform the oversight function, however, is undoubted.

Nevertheless, a solution would be ideal. Despite mitigating factors, the lack of obligation to seek prior approval remains a clear gap in the protection offered by the Regulation. In failing to require advance oversight by the DPA, the Regulation may be argued to fail to live up to the minimum standard of genetic privacy protection required of a legal system outlined by the international framework.

[84] See chapter 6, section E. See, also, for a discussion of the problem in question: Dara Hallinan, 'Biobank Oversight and Sanctions Under the General Data Protection Regulation', in Santa Slokenberga, Olga Tzortzatou, and Jane Reichel (eds.), *GDPR and Biobanking: Individual Rights, Public Interest and Research Regulation across Europe* (Springer 2021) 121, 138–139. (hereafter Hallinan, 'Biobank Oversight and Sanctions').

[85] See chapter 9, section B.

[86] Paul De Hert and Vagelis Papakonstantinou, 'The New General Data Protection Regulation: Still a Sound System for the Protection of Individuals?' (2016) *Computer Law and Security Review* 32(2) 179, 192.

[87] Edward Dove, 'Biobanks, Data Sharing, and the Drive for a Global Privacy Governance Framework' (2015) *Journal of Law, Medicine & Ethics* 44(4) 675, 682.

Solutions to the lack of prior consultation obligation are certainly facilitated through the Regulation's internal mechanisms. The problem revolves around the details of obligations already present in the Regulation—Articles 35 and 36(d) already foresee the need for oversight in some form. From conceptual and legal structural perspectives, there are thus no doubts concerning the compatibility of prior authorisation obligations with the general aims and approach of the Regulation. From a technical perspective, whilst it is true that any solution would require alterations to the Regulation's specific approach to prior oversight, the extent and type of alteration required need not require broad diversion from, or contradiction of, existing data protection principles.

In terms of content of a solution, the EDBP could simply provide straightforward guidance suggesting that biobanking actors ought to consult with, and seek prior approval from, a DPA prior to engaging in processing.

The Regulation also facilitates the adoption of approaches addressing the lack of prior approval obligation through other law. The Regulation, by virtue of Article 9(4), imposes no restrictions on European states imposing requirements on biobanking actors to consult, and gain approval from, national DPAs prior to engaging in processing. Such national provisions would constitute supplemental requirements relating to the processing of genetic data and data concerning health and would thus be legitimate under Article 9(4).

2. The Regulation Imposes No Strict Consent Obligation (Problem 8)

a) Problem

The strict obligation to obtain consent appears in certain European state laws. In the case that research subject consent cannot be obtained under these laws, research is simply prohibited from proceeding altogether. Estonia provides an example of such an approach. Article 9(1) of the Estonian Human Genes Research Act states: 'It is prohibited to take a tissue sample and prepare a description of state of health or genealogy without the specific knowledge and voluntary consent of the person.'

There is no comparable protection available in the Regulation—exceptions to consent are always technically available. The Regulation does require that research subject consent, if possible, should be sought by biobanking actors. However, the Regulation also provides alternatives to legitimate processing where, for whatever reason, research subject consent cannot reasonably be obtained. For example, biobanking controllers may legitimate processing based on the scientific research exception in Article 9(2)(j).[88]

b) Severity and Resolution

In most cases, the position taken by the Regulation will not have any negative impact on genetic privacy protection. In these cases, no solution is necessary. The previous

[88] See Chapter 9, section C.

analysis of international principles showed that exceptions to a general consent obligation are, in principle, normatively acceptable.[89] In turn, the analysis of European national approaches foresee such exceptions—for example, the UK.[90] There is also a firm policy argument supporting this position. It is a fact that not all biobanking operations can rely on consent as a legitimation. Should all substances whose donors are impossible to trace, for example, simply be discarded regardless of their potential scientific utility for research?

In those European states with a strict consent obligation, however, the applicability of the Regulation could lead to a significant negative impact on the available standard of protection for genetic privacy. In these cases, an argument might be put forward that a solution is indeed necessary. It has also been argued that the choice between legitimation grounds in the Regulation is highly context-dependent.[91] From a privacy perspective, it would be highly unfortunate if the Regulation—with its aim to provide a high standard of protection for rights in personal data—were to diminish protection by overriding context-specific state legislation requiring consent. It seems an absurd proposition, for example, that European data protection law should take away Estonian research subjects' rights to self-determine in biobank research.

Whilst solutions to the lack of strict consent provisions are available through the Regulation's internal mechanisms, these may not be ideal. The problem of the lack of strict consent obligations relates to the details of application of obligations already present in the Regulation. There are thus no conceptual, legal structural, or technical issues with the use of the Regulation's internal mechanisms. From conceptual and legal structural perspectives, the idea that consent may be required in certain cases is nothing new or strange to data protection law. As the Article 29 Working Party observe: 'The use of consent "in the right context" is crucial.'[92] From a technical perspective, both the Article 29 Working Party and the EDPB have already seen fit to provide guidance on consent in EU data protection law. This serves as a demonstration of the ability and willingness of supervisory authorities to use their powers in this context.[93] The problem, however, emerges in relation to geographical specificity. As discussed, the Regulation's interpretation and adaptation mechanisms are not best suited to providing solutions to specific national problems. Action by the EDPB, at European level, would be geographically too broad—forcing states which currently, legitimately, allow exceptions, to abide by strict consent requirements. Interpretation by individual national DPAs in affected EU Member States would be possible, but would be subject to being overridden by European-level decisions.

Should relevant national DPAs nevertheless choose to act, they might provide solutions by simply recognising that the obligation to obtain consent, in certain biobanking

[89] See chapter 5, section E.
[90] See chapter 6, section F.
[91] See chapter 9, section C.
[92] Article 29 Working Party, Opinion 15/2011 (n. 34) 14.
[93] Article 29 Working Party, Opinion 15/2011 (n. 34); European Data Protection Board, Guidelines 05/2020 on consent under Regulation 2016/679 (Policy, 2020) (hereafter European Data Protection Board, Guidelines 05/2020 on consent under Regulation).

processes, was a strict necessity. In their guidance, there is no reason they could not refer to other existing national legislation as providing guiding criteria for the decision.

Fortunately, the Regulation also facilitates the adoption of approaches addressing the lack of strict consent obligation through other law. Parallel legislation in affected European states imposing a strict requirement to obtain consent would qualify as legislation imposing supplemental conditions on the processing of genetic data and data concerning health. Such legislation would thus fall within the scope of Article 9(4). For example, Estonia could legally retain the applicability of the strict consent obligation in Article 9 of the Human Genes Research Act relevant to the operation of the Estonian Biobank.

3. The Regulation Provides No Support for Disclosures in the form of Genetic Counselling (Problem 9)

a) Problem

In certain cases in which the research subject's right to choose to know their genetic data is recognised, European state laws provide a supplemental supporting right to genetic counselling. The aim of this genetic counselling right is to mitigate the consequences of surprising or harmful genetic information disclosure. Estonia is an example. Article 11(4) of the Human Genome Research Act states: 'Gene donors have the right to genetic counselling upon accessing their data stored in the Gene Bank.'[94]

There is no right to genetic counselling in the Regulation. Article 15(3) does provide research subjects with extensive rights of access—both to pre- and post-sequence genomic data and individual research results.[95] Yet these access rights are unconcerned with the informational content of disclosure. There are thus no supporting provisions relating to harm mitigation following from disclosure. As discussed previously in this chapter—in relation to problems 3 and 4—the Regulation is largely blind to the possibility that disclosure could be unexpected, unpleasant, or could have negative consequences for subjects.

b) Severity and Resolution

This is not a problem which requires a solution for the efficacy of the Regulation as an instrument for the protection of genetic privacy in biobanking. In the first instance, the lack of genetic counselling provisions in the Regulation will not imply a diminished standard of protection for genetic privacy. The scope of the Regulation does not stretch to cover activities such as genetic counselling and will thus have no effect on existing genetic counselling provisions already in force. A genetic counselling service accompanying feedback relates to the processing of genetic data. It does not, however, specifically concern the processing, or mode of processing, of data. Rather, genetic

[94] See chapter 6, section D.
[95] See chapter 9, section D.

counselling services are better understood as mental health services to ensure the well-being of research subjects.

In turn, this is not a form of privacy protection which one would look to the Regulation to provide. It is true that certain states provide for genetic counselling in national law. It could thus be argued that an ideal comprehensive system of protection would include such provisions—at least in those states in which they are already present. Against this measure, the Regulation can be regarded to be deficient. However, the Regulation was never designed to be a completely comprehensive system for the protection of all possible privacy rights in all contexts. The rationale behind the Regulation is to protect privacy rights by ensuring that personal data processing happens fairly in relation to those whose rights might be impacted. Genetic counselling provisions do not deal with the fair processing of personal data. They are engaged only after choices have been made by individuals relating to the use of their data. It would thus be unreasonable to expect the presence of such provisions in the Regulation, or to see their absence as a problem to be resolved.

Even if a solution to the lack of genetic counselling provisions were necessary, the Regulation's internal adaptation and interpretation mechanisms would not be a suitable forum for its integration. Conceptual and technical objections might be put forward. From a conceptual perspective, there is no justification for the Regulation to include conditions which have, as a primary goal, the health and well-being of individuals rather than the processing of personal data of individuals. From a technical perspective, such obligations are technically very different from anything currently present in the Regulation. It is hard to see that the Regulation's internal mechanisms could stretch to the integration of such distant provisions.

Nor could the Regulation facilitate a solution through other law. The derogations in the Regulation only apply in relation to activities falling within the scope of the Regulation. Accordingly, they cannot apply to facilitate the adoption of solutions to the lack of genetic counselling provisions. This is, however, a moot point. As the Regulation does not apply to genetic counselling, it has no impact on the retention or adoption of genetic counselling provisions via other law.

4. The Regulation Provides No Strict Prohibitions on Third-Party Non-Research Access (Problem 10)

a) Problem

Certain European states provide strict prohibitions on all third-party non-research access to biobank substances. Once again, Estonia provides an example. The Estonian Human Genes Research Act prohibits all third-party non-research access to substances in the Estonian Biobank. This prohibition encompasses both substances stored within the biobank and certain types of access to information fed-back to research subjects. Article 26, for example, prohibits the use of biobank data in insurance.[96]

[96] See chapter 6, section D.

The Regulation provides no explicit prohibitions on third-party non-research access possibilities. The compatible use principle in Article 5(1)(b) prohibits biobanking controllers from allowing third parties to engage in certain types of unforeseen non-research use of substances.[97] This is not, however, a strict prohibition—for example, if third-party non-research use was announced in advance in a consent procedure, it would not be regarded as incompatible and the principle would not apply. Equally, once information has been fed-back to subjects, biobanking actors are no longer controllers, and restrictions are no longer relevant.

b) Severity and Resolution

The lack of protection provided by the Regulation does not have significant negative consequences for the protection of genetic privacy in most instances. In most cases, the Regulation simply mirrors the existing legal status quo. Recall that the lack of strict prohibition on third-party non-research access is the norm in the international framework on biobanking.[98] The lack of strict third-party non-research prohibitions is also the approach taken in several European states—Germany, for example.[99]

This is not true, however, in all European states. Estonia, for example, includes such strict requirements in Article 16 of the Human Genes Research Act.[100] In these states, the applicability of the Regulation may override this obligation. This will lead to a considerable decrease in the standard of protection available. In relation to these states, a solution is required.

Recall that the Regulation has been designed as an instrument of general application to provide a high standard of protection for rights engaged by the processing of personal data in all instances.[101] Recall also that the conflicts between third-party non-research access interests and genetic privacy rights are particularly pronounced—not least as these parties may use such information to inform judgements about data subjects with negative effects.[102] In this regard, it would be unfortunate if the effect of the Regulation would be to open up possibilities for third-party non-research access which were previously impossible. Consider, for example, the counter-intuitive idea that EU data protection law could open up legal possibilities for Estonian insurance companies to access research subjects' genetic data.

Unfortunately, the Regulation is not suited to incorporate solutions to the lack of strict prohibitions on third-party non-research access through internal mechanisms. Two types of objection are evident. First, from a legal structural perspective, strict prohibitions on third-party non-research access would represent bright-line normative prohibitions. As discussed above, data protection law is generally not the ideal forum for the enactment of such solutions. Second, the above discussion shows the problem

97 See chapter 9, section E.
98 See chapter 5, sections C and E.
99 See chapter 6, section E.
100 See chapter 6, section D.
101 See chapter 6, section L.
102 See chapter 4, section I.

to be geographically defined. This is thus a problem in relation to which action by the EDPB, at European level, would be too broad. Whilst national DPAs could, in principle, enact national solutions, these would be liable to be overridden by subsequent EU-level decisions.

Fortunately, the Regulation facilitates the adoption of approaches addressing the lack of strict prohibition on third-party non-research access through other law. Adoption or retention of legislation in affected states imposing strict prohibitions on third-party non-research access to biobanks would constitute supplemental conditions concerning the processing of genetic data and data concerning health. Accordingly, such legislation would fall within the scope of Article 9(4). There is no reason, for example, that Estonia cannot retain the strict prohibitions listed in Article 16 of the Human Genes Research Act.

5. The Regulation Does Not Require Public and Accessible Access Policies (Problem 11)

a) Problem

An emerging international principle is identifiable regarding the obligation on biobanking actors to make access policies public and accessible. The emerging international principle was visible in two of three biobank-specific international instruments.[103] CoE Recommendation CM/Rec(2016)6 provides an example. It states, in Article 18(3): 'Transparent access policies should be developed and published'.

The Regulation contains no comparable obligation. The Regulation does contain transparency provisions serving somewhat equivalent ends. As discussed, transparency provisions in Articles 13 and 14 relate to advance communication to data subjects concerning who might gain access to personal data in biobanking operations, and data subject access provisions in Article 15 require provision of information concerning who has been given access.[104] There is also a suggestion, in Recital 58, that transparency could mean making relevant processing information '[available] to the public, through a website'.

These provisions, however, do not equate to a clear obligation to make access policies public and accessible. In the first instance, the Regulation's provisions do not completely mimic the obligation's function. The obligation allows frictionless access to information for data subjects and prospective data subjects. The Regulation's provisions, however, require devoted effort by subjects to realise—requiring instigating and following up communication with data controllers—and are only realisable for current data subjects—not prospective data subjects. Recital 58, whilst conceptually proximate to the obligation, does not itself impose an obligation.

103 See chapter 5, section E.
104 See chapter 9, section D.

b) Severity and Resolution

The lack of the obligation in the Regulation will have only a minor impact on genetic privacy. Accordingly, no solution is strictly necessary. In this regard, potential impact is mitigated by alternative provisions serving similar functions. The genetic privacy value in the obligation to publish access policies is in the ability for current and future data subjects to know who might have access to their data. As discussed, Articles 13, 14, and 15 mandate that biobanking data subjects are informed as to which third parties might access their substances at the moment of collection and can be informed of third-party access throughout processing.

Nevertheless, a solution is desirable. Two reasons are evident. First, whilst there are comparable provisions in the Regulation which serve to mitigate the consequences of the absence of the provision, as discussed above, these principles cannot completely substitute for the obligation. Second, the obligation to make access policies public and accessible is an international principle. It therefore constitutes a minimum standard of genetic privacy protection the Regulation should reach as an instrument of biobanking regulation.

Solutions to the lack of obligation are arguably facilitated through the Regulation's internal mechanisms. There are no conceptual, legal structural, or technical objections identifiable to the integration of the obligation into the Regulation. From conceptual and legal structural perspectives, the missing obligation aims at providing increased data subject transparency and is thus perfectly aligned with the aims and approach of the Regulation. From a technical perspective, it is true the idea of making data access policies public and transparent has not played, to date, a significant role in EU data protection law discussions. Scratch the surface, however, and one does find provisions, already available in the Regulation, which recognise the utility of public communication for transparency. For example, Article 34(3)(c) permits that, in instances where a data breach cannot reasonably be communicated to specific individual data subject: 'there shall instead be a public communication or similar measure whereby the data subjects are informed in an equally effective manner'. Equally, as discussed above, Recital 58 explicitly recognises the value in making certain types of data processing policies publicly available and offers encouragement for this practice.[105]

In terms of substance, the integration of the obligation would be unproblematic. EDPB guidance could simply outline a general principle obliging biobanking controllers to make access policies public and accessible.

The Regulation also facilitates the adoption of approaches addressing the lack of obligation through other law. Article 9(4) again comes into play. National-level provisions outlining the obligation to publicise access policies would constitute supplemental conditions concerning the processing of genetic data and data concerning health. Such obligations would thus constitute legitimate derogations from the conditions of the Regulation under Article 9(4).

[105] See chapter 9, section E.

6. The Regulation Fails to Outline Criminal Sanctions (Problem 12)

a) Problem

Previous analysis showed criminal sanctions to be omnipresent in European state law.[106] In Estonia, for example, Articles 138^1 to 140 of the Penal Code criminalise the imposition of certain types of involuntary participation in research.

The Regulation's sanctions provisions unfortunately fall short of outlining criminal sanctions. In this regard, the Regulation only provides compensation and administrative sanctions in the case of infringement. These sanctions are indeed impressive—consider the potential fines of up to 20,000,000 EUR on biobanking actors available under Article 83.[107] Administrative sanctions, however, do not carry the same normative weight—they do not denote normative wrongs as clearly—as criminal sanctions, and cannot be regarded as equivalent.

b) Severity and Resolution

This absence of criminal sanctions implies a considerable reduction in protection for genetic privacy. Accordingly, the issue requires resolution. The provision of criminal sanctions is a staple in European state law. As the Regulation, in principle, overrides national law, the fact that it does not include criminal sanctions suggests a significant drop in the level of protection available. This would be no problem if the drop were normatively justifiable. It is not.

In outlining criminal sanctions, Member States laid down clear normative markers as to right and wrong in biomedical research. The administrative sanctions in the Regulation are no substitute. They do not demonstrate the same significance placed on compliance with principles aimed at the protection of genetic privacy. As De Hert observes in relation to the distinction between administrative and criminal sanctions: 'Turning wrongs into administrative law wrongs rather than criminal crimes... is transforming the social into the commercial ... By simply paying an administrative fine, [a biobank actor] can solve its problem with no criminal public record to remind society about the wrong done.'[108] In this regard, the Regulation, as omnibus legislation, should not be in the position to be converting context-specific criminal wrongs into administrative wrongs.

Unfortunately, the Regulation cannot facilitate solutions to this absence through its internal adaptation and interpretation mechanisms. Both legal structural and technical objections might be highlighted. From a legal structural perspective, criminal sanctions sit uneasily with the legislative approach of the Regulation. Criminal sanctions are the embodiment of the bright-line normative solutions—the marking of clear boundaries of right and wrong. As De Hert specifically observes: 'Data protection

[106] See chapter 6, sections D, E, and F.
[107] See chapter 9, section G.
[108] Paul De Hert, 'The Future of Privacy: Addressing Singularities to Identify Bright-Line Rules That Speak to Us' (2016) *European Data Protection Law Review* 2(4) 461, 466 (hereafter De Hert, 'The Future of Privacy').

law ... with its ... preference for administrative enforcement, is not well suited for this much needed demarcation of good and bad.'[109] From a technical perspective, if criminal sanctions represent the elaboration of such bright-line rules, then the definition of such rules should be the result of social deliberation. The result of decision making in democratically elected parliaments. This is beyond the competence of the EDPB and national DPAs.

Fortunately, the Regulation does facilitate the adoption of approaches addressing the absence through other law. Article 84, read in conjunction with Recital 149, permits states to law down criminal sanctions for violations of the Regulation. Recital 149 specifically states: 'Member States should be able to lay down the rules on criminal sanctions for infringements of this Regulation, including for infringements of national rules adopted pursuant to and within the limits of this Regulation.' Thus criminal sanctions, such as, for example, those outlined in UK law for the illegitimate use of biological samples and analysis of DNA—Sections 5 and 45 respectively, of the Human Tissue Act 2004—could be legitimately retained, or passed in future, under the Regulation.

G. Problems Concerning the Technical Applicability of the GDPR's Provisions to Biobanking

1. Transparency Provisions Are Technically Unsuited to the Broad Analytical Potential of Genomic Data (Problem 13)

a) Problem

The goal of transparency provisions—specifically Articles 4(11), 13, 14, and 15—is to provide the data subject with the information needed to understand and quantify the scope of processing being undertaken, and the potential consequences of this processing.[110] These provisions currently aim to do this by following a specific informational model. This model consists of four key types of information a controller must give to a subject. One of these is the type of personal data being processed.

In this model, knowledge of the type of personal data being processed is key in allowing the data subject to quantify factors significant to the consequences of processing. Only with this knowledge can a subject, for example, evaluate the social significance of the content of data—who might wish to process it and what they might do with it. Accordingly, the information model will only work when the type of personal data processed is in a form which allows data subjects to quantify such factors. This is only possible when the personal data is in the form of social facts about the data subject—clearly socially quantifiable information.

[109] De Hert, 'The Future of Privacy' (n. 108) 466.

[110] See: Article 29 Working Party, Guidelines on transparency under Regulation 2016/679 (Policy, 17/EN WP260 rev.01, 2017 (updated 2018)) 7 (hereafter Article 29 Working Party, Guidelines on transparency).

In biobanking, however, the key type of personal data processed is genomic data. Genomic data, however, is not in the form of social facts about a subject.[111] Rather, genomic data is raw data. In biological form, genomic data consists of a string of nucleotides along a DNA molecule. In sequenced form, genomic data consists of alphanumeric (or other forms of) representations of nucleotides. These have no quantifiable social significance. As Albers observes: 'data are not meaningful per se, but rather as "potential information"'.[112] A string of nucleotides itself, for example, reveals nothing about its potential socially significant informational content, nor about who might benefit from access to it. Accordingly, alone, these data do not provide the data subject with the relevant information which would allow them to understand the scope of consequences of processing.

b) Severity and Resolution

The problem will only have limited impact on genetic privacy rights. Accordingly, a solution is not strictly necessary. The severity of impact of the problem is diminished by two mitigating factors. These mean the problem is not a complete obstruction to research subject understanding of biobanking and its potential consequences. First, under the current approach, the data subject will be aware that genomic data will be processed. It is true that these, as raw data, are not in the form of social facts. They are not, however, a complete black box either. There is certain common knowledge of the analytical potential of genomic data. It is common knowledge, for example, that health information—even if the precise form of such information is unclear—can be extracted from a genome.

Second, the problem impacts only one aspect of the Regulation's transparency mechanisms. The Regulation's transparency approach in fact requires much more information to be communicated to the subject than just information concerning the type of personal data being processed.[113] The accuracy of these other forms of information is largely unaffected by the fact that genomic data constitutes raw data rather than social facts. For example, information relating to the aim of biobank processing can be communicated irrespective of this problem.[114]

Nevertheless, the problem would ideally be resolved. Communication of the social significance of personal data being processed is an important aspect of the Regulation's transparency mechanisms' approach to making sure data subjects are informed of processing involving them. In turn, transparency provisions are central to the model of protection offered by the Regulation.[115] Not only is transparency itself a goal the

[111] This problem should come as no surprise. As Manson observes: '[data protection law] came into being as a way of regulating communicative information'—facts intended for exchange between humans. Neil Manson, 'The Medium and the Message: Tissue Samples, Genetic Information and Data Protection Legislation', in Heather Widdows and Caroline Mullen (eds.), *The Governance of Genetic Information: Who Decides?* (Cambridge University Press 2009) 15, 27 (hereafter Manson, 'The Medium and the Message').

[112] Marion Albers, 'Realizing the Complexity of Data Protection', in Serge Gutwirth, Ronald Leenes, and Paul De Hert (eds.), *Reloading Data Protection* (Springer 2014) 213, 222.

[113] See chapter 9, section D.

[114] See also, for a discussion: Hallinan and Gellert, 'The Concept of "Information"' (n. 33) 297-300.

[115] Beyleveld, 'An Overview of Directive 95/46/EC' (n. 67) 11.

Regulation seeks to achieve, but it is a prerequisite for the effective function of other aspects of protection—for example, self-determination provisions, such as consent.

Solutions to this problem are facilitated via the Regulation's internal adaptation and interpretation mechanisms. This is a problem connected with the technical function of certain provisions already present in the Regulation. It thus raises no difficult conceptual or legal structural questions regarding the suitability of the Regulation as a regulatory forum to accommodate a legislative response. In turn, there are no obvious technical obstacles. Indeed, as discussed, the utility of internal systems for the clarification of transparency provisions has already been demonstrated. Recall the Article 29 Working Party's clarification of the effective function of transparency under the Regulation.[116]

In terms of the content of a solution, the EDPB could issue guidance asserting that biobanking transparency protocols include extra information allowing the research subject to understand the parameters of the analytical potential of their genetic data. This would put them in the position to understand the potential social significance of the data as well as the unknowns associated with this potential. As a start, three types of extra information might be provided:[117]

1. Information outlining the mechanisms through which further socially significant information about the data subject might be produced from their genomic sequence
2. Information about the types of socially significant information about the data subject which can already be produced from their genomic sequence
3. Information as to uncertainties surrounding which information about the data subject might eventually be produced from their genomic sequence: emerging due to uncertainties as to the form of genetic analyses which will be applied to their sequence and due to the future development of genetic science and the novel analyses this may eventually permit—this latter form of uncertainty will be discussed in more detail in relation to the subsequent problem.

Concerns have been enunciated that average citizens 'might face a knowledge deficit relating to genetics', making effective communication of these types of information difficult.[118] Indeed, certain genomic research projects have taken action based on these concerns. For example, in relation to the Personal Genomes Project (PGP),

[116] See: Article 29 Working Party, Opinion 15/2011 (n. 34); Article 29 Working Party, Guidelines on transparency (n. 110).

[117] A more extensive elaboration of the problem, and of the substantive content of a solution, is provided here: Dara Hallinan, 'The Genomic Data Deficit: On the Need to Inform Research Subjects of the Informational Content of their Genomic Sequence Data in Consent for Genomic Research' (2020) *Computer Law and Security Review* 37 <https://www.sciencedirect.com/science/article/pii/S0267364920300327> accessed 23 June 2020 (hereafter Hallinan, 'The Genomic Data Deficit').

[118] Dara Hallinan and Michael Friedewald, 'Open Consent, Biobanking and Data Protection Law: Can Open Consent be "Informed" under the Forthcoming Data Protection Regulation?' (2015) *Life Sciences, Society and Policy* 11(1) 32 <https://lsspjournal.springeropen.com/track/pdf/10.1186/s40504-014-0020-9?site=lsspjournal.springeropen.com> accessed 29 November 2019 (hereafter Hallinan and Friedewald, 'Open Consent, Biobanking and Data Protection Law').

Lunshof et al. observed: 'In the PGP we strive to ensure that the consent process is as fully informed as possible ... Therefore, the participants of the ... study cohort were requested ... to have a master's degree in genetics or equivalent.'[119] Whilst the argument is appreciated, it surely overstates the necessity of understanding specific scientific underpinnings of genome analysis. Information in each of the three categories need not be communicated such that an individual can understand the underlying science. Information must only be communicated such that it allows the subject to generally understand which, and how, relevant information about them might be produced from their genomic data.

The Regulation also facilitates the adoption of approaches addressing the issue through other law. Article 9(4) once again comes into play. European states could pass law placing supplemental obligations on biobanking actors which relate to transparency provisions andalleviate the information deficit—for example, law including informational obligations equivalent to those outlined in the paragraph above. Such obligations would constitute supplementary conditions relevant to the processing of genetic data and data concerning health and would thus be legitimate under Article 9(4).

2. Transparency Provisions Are Technically Unsuited to the Uncertain Future Analytical Potential of Genomic Data (Problem 14)

a) Problem

Each transparency provision—specifically those outlined in Articles 4(11), 13, 14, and 15 —mandates a one-off interaction between data subject and data controller. For example, Articles 4(11) and 13 provide for a single engagement in obtaining informed consent, whilst Article 15 provides for a one-time provision of information in access requests—although multiple invocations are possible.[120] This single interaction must provide the data subject with all information relevant to understand the scope and consequences of processing through the life-cycle of processing. Thus, the approach can only work if all information given to a subject remains both factually accurate, and accurate in relation to the consequences of processing, throughout the life-span of processing.

The potential to interpret and use genomic data, however, changes over time. As a result, the potential consequences of allowing the processing of genomic data in biobanking also changes over time. This is true for two reasons. First, the type of

[119] Jeantine Lunshof, Ruth Chadwick, Daniel Vorhaus, et al., 'From Genetic Privacy to Open Consent' (2008) *Nature Reviews Genetics* 9(5) 406, 409.

[120] See chapter 11, section D. It is true the Article 29 Working Party highlight the need for changes in processing to be accompanied by new information being provided to data subjects. Thus far, however, they have only referred to concrete changes in the processing operation, or the organisational context in which processing is embedded—as opposed to the interpretative potential of personal data—as mandating new information provision. They state, for example: 'Changes ... that should always be communicated to data subjects include inter alia: a change in processing purpose; a change to the identity of the controller; or a change as to how data subjects can exercise their rights in relation to the processing.' Article 29 Working Party, Guidelines on transparency (n. 110) 17.

information which can be extracted from a genome will change. As genetic science delves deeper into the genome and its reaction to external stimuli, the mechanisms of genotype–phenotype translation become clearer. The result is that: 'the content and amount of information capable of being extracted from the genome at any given time, is dependent on the state of genetic science at that time'.[121]

Second, the more information which can be extracted from genomic data, the greater the number of contexts in which genomic data is likely to be used. For example, research into the interaction between pharmaceutical drugs and the genome plays a role in the growth of personalised medicine. This research has made genome collection and analysis more widespread in European healthcare systems. As Offit observes: 'Personalized genomics builds on principles established by the integration of genetics into medical practice.'[122]

The issue of change over time would be mitigated if developments in genetics were linear and predictable. They are not. This is shown by the sea changes and unexpected developments permeating the last decade of genetics. As Pontin observed in 2010: 'taken as a whole, it was a long, hard decade for genomics ... no one will contest that the genome has turned out to be bafflingly complex'.[123] Nobody knows when the next breakthrough in understanding the genome will come, and nobody knows what form this breakthrough will take.

b) Severity and Resolution

The problem will have a limited impact on the protection of genetic privacy rights. Accordingly, a solution is not strictly necessary. The severity of impact is mitigated by two factors—comparable to those outlined in relation to the previous problem. First, the lack of updated information on the potential of genomic analyses will be mitigated by general knowledge and publicly available information regarding the analytical potential of genomic data. Second, transparency provisions require more information to be communicated to a subject than just concerning the type of personal data processed. The accuracy of other required information is not impacted by changes in the analytical potential of genomic data.

Nevertheless, a solution would be desirable. Despite mitigating factors, as discussed above, the ability to understand the social significance of personal data processed is central to a data subject's ability to paint a picture of biobanking and the consequences of biobanking. In turn, also discussed above, transparency provisions are central to the function of the Regulation—both in achieving the goal of transparency and as instrumental in relation to the effective function of other provisions.

Solutions to the problem are facilitated through the Regulation's internal adaptation and interpretation mechanisms. The logic for the applicability of the Regulation's

121 Hallinan and Friedewald, 'Open Consent, Biobanking and Data Protection Law' (n. 118) 16.

122 Kenneth Offit, Personalized Medicine: New Genomics, Old Lessons [2011] *Human Genetics* 130(1) 3, 3.

123 Jason Pontin, 'A Decade of Genomics: On the 10th Anniversary of the Human Genome Project, We Ask: Where Are the Therapies?' *MIT Technology Review* (21 December 2010) <https://www.technologyreview.com/s/422130/a-decade-of-genomics/> accessed 11 December 2019.

internal mechanisms is the same as outlined in relation to the previous problem. From a conceptual and legal structural perspective, this is a problem concerning the assumptions the Regulation makes as to the nature of data. There are no thus problematic issues concerning any possible solution's alignment with the rationale of the Regulation. From a technical perspective, as discussed above, the ability of the Regulation's internal mechanisms to address issues of transparency has already been demonstrated. Recall the Article 29 Working Party's existing clarifications of transparency under the Regulation.[124]

In terms of the content of a solution, one option might be for the EDPB to issue guidance advocating a shift from a one-off communication model to an ongoing communication model in biobanking. Such a shift would not be a novel idea. Grady et al., for example, highlight the need for 'ongoing communication with donors' as a prerequisite to certain types of biobanking.[125] Under this ongoing communication model, significant information regarding relevant changes in the analytical and interpretative potential of genomic data could be communicated as they become available.

The EDPB might suggest that ongoing communication could take the form of a platform accessible by data subjects providing continually updated information. Such a system might be general to all data subjects or tailored for individual subjects considering the research projects their substances are involved in.[126] The feasibility of ongoing communication systems has been demonstrated in practice. One example is the system of dynamic consent.[127] As Kaye et al. observe: 'using a technology-based platform, the [dynamic consent] process is not locked in time to the beginning of the research process'.[128] Rather, the system allows ongoing communication between biobanking actors and research subject and 'interactions over time'.[129]

The Regulation also facilitates the adoption of approaches addressing the problem through other law. European states could implement legislation outlining supplemental transparency obligations alleviating the issues described—for example, those outlined in the paragraph above. Such obligations would constitute additional requirements relating to the processing of genetic data and data concerning health. They would thus be legitimate under Article 9(4).

[124] See: Article 29 Working Party, Opinion 15/2011 (n. 34); Article 29 Working Party, Guidelines on transparency (n. 110).

[125] Christine Grady, Lisa Eckstein, Ben Berkman, et al., 'Broad Consent for Research with Biological Samples: Workshop Conclusions' [2015] *American Journal of Bioethics* 15(9) 34, 43.

[126] A more extensive elaboration of the problem, and of the substantive content of a solution, is provided here: Hallinan, 'The Genomic Data Deficit' (n. 117).

[127] See, for a discussion of the utility of the dynamic consent mechanism for fufilling the requirements of the GDPR: Megan Prictor, Harriet J. A. Teare, Jessica Bell, et al., 'Could "Dynamic Consent" Be a Useful Tool for Researchers?' (2019) *Journal of Data Protection and Privacy* 3(1) 93, 93–112.

The utility of dynamic consent in biobanking has even been recognised by certain national DPAs. See: Konferenz der unabhängigen Datenschutzbehörden des Bundes und der Länder, Beschluss der 97. Konferenz der unabhängigen Datenschutzaufsichtsbehörden des Bundes und der Länder zu Auslegung des Begriffs „bestimmte Bereiche wissenschaftlicher Forschung" im Erwägungsgrund 33 der DS-GVO (Policy, 2019) 2.

[128] Jane Kaye, Edgar Whitley, David Lund, et al, 'Dynamic Consent: A Patient Interface for Twenty-First Century Research Networks' (2015) *European Journal of Human Genetics* 23(2) 141, 142 (hereafter Kaye, Whitley, Lund, et al., 'Dynamic consent').

[129] Kaye, Whitley, Lund, et al., 'Dynamic consent' (n. 128) 142.

3. Self-Determination Provisions Are Technically Unsuited to Genomic Data (Problem 15)

a) Problem

The Regulation's self-determination provisions function with the aim of giving the data subject the possibility to exercise self-determination over whether, and how, personal data are processed—in particular consent under Article 9(2)(a), and the right to withdraw under 7(3).[130] However, they do not foresee all decisions as being constitutive of adequate self-determination. Rather, they work on the established legal principle that the individual making the choice must be informed. As the Court of Appeals of the District of Columbia put it in the famous *Canterbury v. Spence* case: 'True consent to what happens to oneself is the informed exercise of a choice.'[131]

This quality of effective self-determination is made explicit in the Regulation. For example, Article 4(11) elaborates that consent under Article 9(2)(a) is only legitimate provided the subject has been effectively 'informed' about processing. Accordingly, self-determination provisions only work if transparency provisions—the provisions aimed at informing the subject about processing—work.

It is true there is nothing about biobanking process which prevents a research subject from exercising self-determination rights. Neither institutional constellations, nor aims of processing, nor the types of personal data processed prevent a research subject from making and communicating a consent decision.

However, the previous two problems highlighted that the Regulation's transparency provisions will not function effectively in biobanking. Self-determination provisions are thus also undermined. As Pormeister observes: 'an essential precondition for the exercise of any rights [including self-determination rights] is transparency within the context in which these rights are to be exercised'.[132]

b) Severity and Resolution

The lack of technical suitability of transparency provisions will not have a significant impact on genetic privacy rights in biobanking. Accordingly, no solution is strictly necessary. As the issue stems from the above two underlying problems with transparency provisions, the same two factors mitigating the severity of the impact of these problems will also serve to mitigate the severity of impact of the problem at hand. First, the information deficits undermining the ability to self-determine will be mitigated by general knowledge, and publicly available information, concerning the analytical potential of genomic data. Second, information deficits will be mitigated by the fact that other information provided under transparency provisions will remain accurate irrespective of uncertainties around genomic analysis.

[130] See chapter 9, sections C and D.

[131] *Canterbury v. Spence* [1972] 464 F 2d 772, para. 28.

[132] Kärt Pormeister, Transparency in relation to the data subject in genetic research—an analysis on the example of Estonia (University of Tartu Ph.D. thesis, 2019) 29.

Nevertheless, this is a problem which would ideally be resolved. Despite mitigating factors, data subjects working under an information deficit have diminished abilities to exercise self-determination. In turn, self-determination provisions—in particular consent and the right to withdraw—are highly significant for the function of the Regulation generally and, more specifically, to the legitimation of biobanking under the Regulation.

The Regulation certainly facilitates the adoption of solutions via internal interpretation and adaptation mechanisms. As the self-determination problem results from transparency problems, the problem will be resolved as transparency problems are resolved. The arguments supporting the utility of the Regulation's internal mechanisms to solve transparency problems are thus also relevant for the self-determination problem.

In terms of the content of a solution, EDPB guidance in relation to transparency problems would resolve the issue. EDPB guidance requiring a data subject to be informed of the mechanisms and uncertainties of the analytical potential of genetic data at the moment of consent would furnish the data subject with adequate information to make an informed decision—to exercise effective self-determination—as to whether they want to consent to biobanking. EDPB guidance requiring ongoing communication between biobanking actors and the data subject would provide the data subject with the informational resources to make an informed decision, at any moment, as to whether they wish to withdraw from association with a biobank.

The Regulation also facilitates the adoption of solutions to the problem through other law. As discussed in relation to the previous two problems: European state legislators can adopt or retain supplemental measures ensuring the adequate communication of information on the analytical potential of genetic data to the data subject. Such provisions would constitute additional requirements on the processing of genetic data and data concerning health and would be legitimate under Article 9(4). Such provisions would also resolve the self-determination problem.

H. Problems Concerning the Disproportionate Impact of the GDPR on Research

1. Disproportionate Impact Associated with the Right to Obtain a Copy of Personal Data Applied to the Biological Sample (Problem 16)

a) Problem

The Article 15 right to obtain a copy of one's personal data is not senseless in relation to biobanking.[133] The right may be argued to protect data subject rights in two separate

[133] There are two other data controller obligations which seem difficult or illogical when applied to biological samples. In the biobanking context, however, there is no consequence of note associated with this difficulty. First, data minimisation as outlined in Article 5(1)(c). The concept functions on the back of the presumption that a data controller can make choices as to which data they collect. This is not possible in relation to a biological sample as each cell contains the complete genome. Second, data accuracy—as outlined in Article 5(1)(d). The idea of

ways. In the first instance, the right may function to allow the data subject insight into which personal data is being processed and thereby aid in allowing the data subject to understand processing and the consequences of processing. In turn, and more specifically to the processing of genomic data and individual research results, the right may facilitate the information genetic privacy right to choose to know one's own genome—furnishing, as it does, data subjects with the ability to gain access to their genetic data from biobanking actors.

When applied to the biological sample, however, the right fulfils neither of these purposes. In this case then, generally speaking, the right thus plays no role in privacy protection. The provision of a copy of a sample will not allow a data subject to understand biobank processing. The sample is not in a form which allows an ordinary subject to better understand what information is being processed about them. Only with special equipment and training would this become possible. Equally, receipt of a sample will not aid a subject's right to choose to know their genetic data. The right to know only sensibly relates to the sequenced genome. Prainsack, for example, outlines seven different manifestations of the right, each of which relates to the sequenced genome.[134] Subjects already have copious amounts of their own genetic material—every cell in a subject's body contains a copy of their genome.

Despite its lack of function in the protection of privacy in relation to samples, the right, in principle, applies to the processing of all personal data and therefore also to the sample.[135] It will thus, in principle, thus impose burdens on biobanking actors. This is true for two reasons. First, any infringements of the right would be subject to sanction. In terms of administrative fines, for example, infringements will fall under the strict regime under Article 83(5) and will be punishable, in principle, with a fine of up to 20,000,000 EUR.[136]

Second, the right will impose burdens whenever it is exercised. Both the copying and transfer of the sample will impose burdens. Copying the sample is possible. Dove observes that 'researchers have identified numerous ways to transform primary tissues from humans and animals into immortalized cell lines'.[137] However, this is

inaccuracy relates to discrepancies between real-world phenomena and the data record. Inaccuracy may occur as a result of the recording process, or as the result of changes in the real-world phenomena. Genomic data stored in a biological sample cannot be regarded, however, as 'inaccurate' in either of these regards. As Hashiyada observes in relation to the stability of DNA over an individual's lifetime: 'DNA provides the most reliable personal identification ... unchangeable while the person is alive, and even after his/her death.' Masaki Hashiyada, 'Development of Biometric DNA Ink for Authentication Security' (2004) *Tohoku Journal of Experimental Medicine* 204 109, 109. Although it should be noted that the genome as a whole is susceptible to change. Epigenetic marks are chemical traces left on the non-DNA structures—such as the nucleosomes around which the DNA is coiled—which make up the genome. These do change over time as a result of non-DNA factors such as environmental influence. See: Hans Bjornsson, Martin Sigurdsson, M. Daniele Fallin, et al., 'Intra-Individual Change over Time in DNA Methylation with Familial Clustering' (2009) *Journal of the American Medical Association* 299(24) 2877, 2877–83.

[134] Barbara Prainsack, 'DIY Genetics: The Right to Know Your Own Genome', in Ruth Chadwick, Mairi Levitt, and Darren Shickle (eds.), *The Right to Know and the Right Not to Know: Genetic Privacy and Responsibility* (Cambridge University Press 2014) 100, 102.

[135] See chapter 9, section D.

[136] See chapter 9, section G.

[137] Alan Dove, 'The Art of Culture: Developing Cell Lines' (2014) *Science* 346(6212) 1013, 1013.

resource-intensive.[138] It will require special materials—such as enzymes—time and labour. As Manson observes: 'the data subject could be given a sample of "relevant" genetic material amplified by polymerase chain reaction (though at disproportionate cost!)'.[139] Transferring the sample is also possible. Samples can be moved from place to place. This too, however, will be resource-intensive. The transport of many types of biological sample requires bespoke and expensive equipment. Kunkel et al. observe, for example, that cryopreserved biospecimens would require the 'maintenance of ultra-low conditions at all stages during transport ... obtained with high-quality packaging and dry ice or liquid nitrogen in quantities sufficient to last during unforeseen delivery delays'.[140]

b) Severity and Resolution

The problem is unlikely to have significant negative consequences for biobanking actors' interests. This fact removes the strict need for a solution. In practice, there is likely to be a significant mitigating factor minimising the resources which will need to be invested in the right: it is hard to see that data subjects will often actually exercise the right. As discussed, in most cases, data subjects will have little to gain through obtaining a copy of their own sample. Why then, would they go to the trouble of exercising the right? Indeed, that data subjects are unlikely to exercise the right has been demonstrated in practice. Recall that certain European states already apply data protection principles to samples—Estonia, for example.[141] To my knowledge, in no such State have sample access requests been problematic for biobanks.

Nevertheless, this is a problem that would ideally be resolved. Despite the mitigating factor, the existence of the right may still potentially negatively impact biobanking actors. As long as the right exists, the possibility of use exists, and with it the possibility of sanctions and the possible need to divert resources towards effective realisation. The lack of justification for the right means this represents an unnecessary and disproportionate impact.

Solutions to the problem are certainly facilitated through the Regulation's internal mechanisms. From conceptual and legal structural perspectives, the problem concerns obligations imposed by the Regulation which are too strict. There are thus no awkward questions about whether the introduction of novel substantive principles is feasible. From a technical perspective, the idea of circumvention of the Regulation's principles via internal adaptation mechanisms superficially seems problematic. Recall, however, as discussed above—in section B—the Regulation's internal interpretation and adaptation mechanisms can be used to read principles into the Regulation if this is justifiable in relation to the context. The opposite is also true: internal mechanisms can be used to

[138] In turn, the process is not infallible and results will not always be perfect. See: Gurvinder Kaur and Jannette Dufour, 'Cell Lines: Valuable Tools or Useless Artefacts' (2012) *Spermatogenesis* 2(1) 1, 1.

[139] Manson, 'The Medium and the Message' (n. 111) 29.

[140] Eric Kunkel and Rolf Ehrhardt, 'Frozen Assets: An Expert Guide to Biobanking' *Select Science* (23 December 2014) <http://www.selectscience.net/editorial-articles/frozen-assets--an-expert-guide-to-biobanking/?artID=35743> accessed 11 December 2019.

[141] See chapter 6, section L.

disapply principles which make no sense in a processing context. This position has jurisprudential support. The Article 29 Working Party has explicitly recognised the principle that: 'where processing of personal data within the scope of the [law] is involved, not all the rules ... may be applicable in the particular case'.[142]

In terms of the content of a solution, the EDPB could simply provide guidance clarifying that Article 15(3) does not provide the data subject with an automatic right to a copy of their biological sample in biobanking.[143]

The Regulation also facilitates the adoption of solutions to the problem through other law. EU or state law could rely on the derogation possibilities afforded by Article 89(2) to pass law voiding the applicability of the Article 15 right to a copy of the sample, wherever the exercise of the right would be likely to impair the conduct of biobanking or biobank-based research—including where this would constitute an absurd, or disproportionate, burden.

2. Disproportionate Impact Associated with Data Portability Rights (Problem 17)

a) Problem

Swire summarises the problem dealt with by the right to data portability as follows: 'users start to use one service, such as Facebook, and then find it costly or technically difficult to shift to another service'.[144] This practice was regarded as an affront to the ability of users to control their own personal data—in particular in light of the significant role such information could play in users' social lives. Accordingly, as Zanfir observes: 'data portability appeared as a way that would enable the widespread sharing of social information between websites'.[145]

In the biobanking context, however, the problem underlying the justification for the right is not present and thus, the right fulfils little function.[146] Biobanking controllers do not usually impose unique data formats to prevent research subjects from migrating their data. Indeed, there would normally be no point in such an imposition. Computerised personal data provided by participants—the only personal data to which the right applies—is not solely held by biobanks. The data is simultaneously

[142] Article 29 Working Party, Opinion 4/2007 on the concept of personal data (Policy, 01248/07/EN WP 136, 2007) 5.

[143] Exceptions could be imagined in relation to those requests relating to circumstances in which data subjects can demonstrate the necessity and feasibility of their request for a copy—for example, regarding rare disease samples.

[144] Peter Swire and Yianni Lagos, 'Why the Right to Data Portability Likely Reduces Consumer Welfare: Antitrust and Privacy Critique' (2013) *Maryland Law Review* 72(2) 335, 338.

[145] Gabriela Zanfir, 'The Right to Data Portability in the Context of the EU Data Protection Reform' (2012) *International Data Privacy Law* 2(3) 149, 149.

[146] As with the right to access associated with the biological sample, there may be certain, limited exceptions to the general assertion that the right has no function in the biobanking context. Certain biobanking substances may have limited availability—for example, rare disease data. Data subjects may indeed benefit from the right to require a return or direct transfer of such data to facilitate specific research. This does not, however, justify the imposition of the right to data portability across the biobanking spectrum.

retained by participants—for example, certain types of health, lifestyle, or biographical information—or by third parties—for example, healthcare providers in the case of medical records. Even if lock-in did exist, there would be little restriction to research subjects flowing from it. A social media profile may be significant to an individual's social life, a research subject's biobank profile is not.

Yet, the right applies to the processing of all personal data and therefore still functions to place burdens on biobanking controllers. It is true that the Regulation imposes limitations on the obligations associated with the right. Recall that the right will have limited applicability in biobanking—applying only to health, lifestyle, or biographical information when processed with consent—and does not require compatible formats to be adopted solely for compliance.[147]

However, limitations do not preclude the right from being associated with any obligations at all. Where possible, biobanks must endeavour to provide personal data in a common, interoperable, format. As the Article 29 Working Party observe: 'The most appropriate format ... should always be chosen to achieve the purpose of being interpretable.'[148] In turn, failure to fulfil obligations can result in potentially high sanctions. In terms of administrative sanctions, infringements of the right fall under Article 83(5) and are thus subject to fines of up to 20,000,000 EUR.[149]

b) Severity and Resolution

The problem is unlikely to have significant negative consequences on biobanking actors' interests. There are both legal and practical mitigating factors evident. These serve to remove the strict need for a solution. Legally, the limited applicability of the right in biobanking restricts the possible scope of burdens. Indeed, regarding the extent of exceptions, Diker Vanberg et al. argue: 'Article 20 of the GDPR limits the scope of the right to data portability to a great extent.'[150] Practically, as with the right to a copy in relation to biological samples, it is hard to see data subjects often exercising the right. It is hard to see many instances in which subjects could need the data in question returned to them—information they will either already have or which will be accessibly held by health providers. It is equally hard to imagine the actors to whom they would need information transferred.

Nevertheless, this is a problem which would ideally be addressed. Despite mitigating factors, the existence of the right may require biobanks to take action to make sure it can, in principle, be exercised. In turn, any actual exercise of Article 20 will require specific action by biobanking actors. Finally, any need to engage in specific action comes with the potential for large fines and sanctions. Given the lack of justification for the right, these constitute undesirable disproportionate impacts.

147 See chapter 9, section D.

148 Article 29 Working Party, Guidelines on the right to data portability (Policy, 16/EN WP 242, 2016) 13.

149 See chapter 9, section G.

150 Aysem Diker Vanberg and Mehmet Ünver, 'The Right to Data Portability in the GDPR and EU Competition Law: Odd Couple or Dynamic Duo?' (2017) *European Journal of Law and Technology* 8(1), 3 <http://ejlt.org/article/view/546/727> accessed 11 December 2019.

Solutions to the problem are certainly facilitated through the Regulation's internal mechanisms. The Regulation's internal mechanisms doubtless provide a forum for a solution. The problem concerns the fact that one of the Regulation's provisions is too strict in relation to the specifics of biobanking. From conceptual and legal structural perspectives, considering a solution raises no awkward questions around the limitations of approaches which may be integrated into the Regulation. From a technical perspective, argumentation supporting the idea that the Regulation's internal mechanisms may disapply unsuitable provisions in a given context has already been outlined in relation to the previous problem.

In terms of the substantive content of a solution, the EDPB could simply provide interpretative guidance to the Regulation clarifying the inapplicability of Article 20 in relation to biobanking.

The Regulation also facilitates the adoption of solutions to the problem through other law. EU or European state law could be passed, under Article 89(2), voiding the applicability of the Article 20 right to portability in relation to the sample, wherever the exercise of the right would be likely to impair the conduct of biobanking or biobank-based research—including where this would constitute an absurd, or disproportionate, burden. Whilst Article 89(2) does not directly reference the possibility to derogate from Article 20, recall that Recital 156 clarifies the scope of Article 89(2) in relation to Article 20, and states: 'Member States should be authorised to provide, under specific conditions ... derogations with regard to data portability ... for scientific ... research purposes.'[151]

3. Disproportionate Impacts Associated with the Size of Administrative Fines (Problem 18)

a) Problem

Articles 83(4) and (5) of the Regulation foresee the possibility to levy administrative fines of '10,000,000 EUR, or up to 2 % of ... total ... turnover' for lower-tier infringements or '20,000,000 EUR, or ... up to 4 % of ... total ... turnover' for higher-tier infringements. As testament to their magnitude, Faust et al. observe their form and content as being taken straight directly from EU anti-trust legislation.[152] The apparent reason for the scale of these fines was the legislator's desire to give the Regulation teeth in the face of infringements by large multinational companies. It was believed that only massive fines would be dissuasive to multinationals against the background of their enormous resources. Jan Philipp Albrecht, for example—the European Parliament's Rapporteur on the Regulation—specifically commented on fines in relation to multinational companies.[153]

[151] Given the assertion is only in a Recital, jurisprudential confirmation of the interpretation would be ideal.

[152] Sebastain Faust, Jan Spittika, and Tim Wybitul, 'Milliardenbußgelder nach der DS-GVO: Ein überblick über die neuen Sanktionen bei Verstößen gegen den Datenschutz' (2016) *Zeitschrift für Datenschutz* 120, 120. See, also, for a discussion of the problem in question: Hallinan, 'Biobank Oversight and Sanctions' (n. 84) 139-141.

[153] As Albrecht observed: 'Companies which violate the new rules must pay fines of up to four per-cent of their yearly turnover. That could be billions for the global internet companies.' Author translation of: 'Unternehmen, die

Yet, the vast majority of biobanking actors will not remotely compare in size to the organisations which might be considered as the targets of EU anti-trust legislation. Indeed, the majority of biobanking actors will not even be set-up with the direct intention of making profit—but rather with the intention of furthering scientific research. For example, Zika et al. observed that only a tiny 3 per cent of respondent biobanks were completely under private ownership.[154]

Accordingly, it is hard to see how such large fines are necessary or proportionate for biobanking. Biobanking actors will rarely, if ever, have such resources such that fines of this size would be necessary to dissuade them from infringements. Can it be proportionate that, for example, the tiny Daccò Center rare disease biobank is subject to the same sanction regime as Google?[155] The disproportionate nature of the approach has been observed in relation to other processing sectors as well. Christensen et al., for example, draw similar conclusions concerning the sanctions regime and small and medium-sized enterprises (SMEs): 'the proposed system of administrative sanctions implies a homogenous application to all [processing entities: this may create unfair and disproportionate burdens'.[156]

b) Severity and Resolution

In practice, the problem is unlikely to have a significant impact on biobanking actors' interests. This minimises the strict need for a solution. Specifically, the scale of administrative fines will almost certainly be mitigated by DPAs' discretion—as foreseen in Recital 148. For a DPA to insist on imposing high fines would potentially be perilous for the future conduct of biobanking in their jurisdiction. Taking into account the socially beneficial aims of biobanking, and the characteristics of biobanking actors—provided actors' violations are not wilful, severe, or repeated—it is hard to see why a sensible and reasonable DPA would impose fines at a disproportionate level.[157]

Nevertheless, this remains a problem which would ideally be solved. Despite the significance of DPA discretion as a mitigating factor, in any given instance of a violation, theoretically, a DPA might choose to enforce full-scale maximum fines on biobanking

gegen die neuen Regeln verstoßen, müssen Strafen von bis zu vier Prozent ihres Jahresweltumsatzes zahlen, das können für die großen globalen Internetkonzerne Milliarden sein.' Jan Philipp Albrecht, *Starke Verbraucherrechte und mehr Wettbewerb: EU-Datenschutzreform* (Jan Phillip Albrecht, 21 December 2015) <https://www.janalbrecht.eu/2015/12/2015-12-21-starke-verbraucherrechte-und-mehr-wettbewerb/> accessed 11 December 2019.

[154] Eleni Zika, Daniele Paci, Tobias Schulte in den Bäumen, et al., Biobanks in Europe: Prospects for Harmonisation and Networking (European Commission Report, 2010) 19.

[155] Instituto di Recerche Farmacologiche Mario Negri, 'Biological Resources Centre' (Instituto di Recerche Farmacologiche Mario Negri, 2019) <https://www.marionegri.it/eng/biological-resources-center> accessed 11 December 2019.

[156] L. Christensen, A. Colciago, F. Etro, et al., The Impact of the Data Protection Regulation in the EU (International Think-tank on Innovation and Competition INTERTIC Report, 2013) 4.

[157] See, for a further discussion of the rationale behind DPAs' likelihood to be lenient on biobanking actors: Dara Hallinan, 'Broad Consent under the GDPR: An Optimistic Perspective on a Bright Future' [2020] *Life Sciences, Society and Policy* 16(1) 13–16 <https://lsspjournal.biomedcentral.com/track/pdf/10.1186/s40504-019-0096-3> accessed 19 June 2020 (hereafter Hallinan, 'Broad Consent under the GDPR').

actors. This is a sword of Damocles hanging over biobanking actors' heads. This is undesirable given that such a level of fine is, *a priori*, disproportionate for biobanking.

Solutions to the problem are certainly facilitated through the Regulation's internal mechanisms. There is little question that the scale of administrative fines is an issue which might be addressed through internal mechanisms. From conceptual and legal structural perspectives, the issue concerns the optimisation and calibration of provisions already embedded in the Regulation and raises no issues. From a technical perspective, the Regulation is clear that guidance on the scale of administrative fines falls within the power of internal mechanisms. Article 70(k) explicitly refers to one of the EDPB's key tasks as being to: 'draw up guidelines for supervisory authorities concerning the application of ... and the setting of administrative fines pursuant to Article 83'.

In terms of content, it would seem logical for the EDPB to issue guidance to Member State DPAs outlining generally applicable upper limits, or criteria for determining upper limits, for fines to be levied on biobanks and biobanking actors. Naturally, exceptions could be foreseen for particularly willful, repeated, or malicious abuses.

The Regulation does not, however, facilitate the adoption of solutions to the problem through other law. Article 84 foresees the possibility for states to enact bespoke penalties for violations of the Regulation—including, as clarified in Recital 149—criminal penalties. There is no derogation provision in the Regulation, however, which permits European states to set specific limits on the administrative fines system in relation to biobanking.

I. Problems Concerning the Practical Applicability of the GDPR to Biobanking

1. The Conditions of Consent Remain Uncertain for Biobanking (Problem 19)

a) Problem

The significance of the conditions of consent cannot be understated in biobanking. The narrower these are defined, the fewer activities biobanking controllers may engage in with a research subject's personal data—and vice versa. Recital 33 and its associated jurisprudence have provided some clarity on the conditions of consent in relation to research. In this regard, there are also scholars, such as Morrison et al. and Rumbold and Pierscionek, who consider Recital 33 clear in what it permits. Rumbold and Pierscionek, for example, assert: 'the agreed text permits broad consent'.[158] Yet, closer

[158] Morrison, Bell, George, et al., 'The European General Data Protection Regulation: Challenges and Considerations' (n. 8) 697; John Rumbold and Barbara Pierscionek, 'The Effect of the General Data Protection Regulation on Medical Research' (2017) *Journal of Medical Internet Research* 19(2) <https://www.ncbi.nlm.nih.gov/pmc/articles/PMC5346164/> accessed 11 December 2019.

inspection reveals, as Dove observes, 'confusion ... based on the language of Recital 33'.[159] Two types of uncertainty are notable.

First, the scope of consent remains unclear. The statement, in Recital 33, that 'data subjects may give their consent to certain areas of scientific research' remains unclear. This statement puts it beyond question that consent in biobanking may justify multiple types of research processing.[160] However, the concept of 'certain areas of scientific research' does not necessarily map to any specific scope of consent.[161] There is a wide range of interpretations which might be equally legitimately applied to the concept. The concept could be interpreted narrowly to mean consent may only permit specific types of genomic research—for example, research relating only to Charcot-Marie-Tooth disease.[162] The concept could just as easily be interpreted broadly, to refer to any and all types of biological research.[163]

Second, the substantive criteria under which broader types of consent are permissible remain unclear. Two issues present. First, the suggestion, in Recital 33, that research subjects may only give consent to 'areas of scientific research' when 'in keeping with recognized ethical standards for scientific research' is unclear. There is a wide range of interpretations of the concept of 'recognized ethical standards' including: international standards; national standards; and ad hoc standards imposed by RECs. It is not immediately apparent which interpretation is meant. Second, the role of the safeguards outlined by the EDPB connected with Recital 33 is unclear. It is unclear how these safeguards relate to the obligation to obtain consent in line with 'recognized ethical standards'. Are the safeguards listed intended to be an elaboration of the requirement, to sit on top of the requirement, or to be unconnected with the requirement? It is also unclear to which degree safeguards are intended to be obligatory across biobanking contexts. Are safeguards intended as obligatory in all cases, only in specific cases, or only meant as helpful suggestions?[164]

159 Edward Dove, 'The EU General Data Protection Regulation: Implications for International Scientific Research in the Digital Era' (2018) *Journal of Law Medicine & Ethics* 46 1013, 1022 (hereafter Dove, 'The EU General Data Protection Regulation').

160 The Article 29 Working Party, for example, stated the previous position as follows: '"Specific" consent must relate to a well-defined, concrete situation in which the processing of ... data is envisaged.' Article 29 Working Party, Opinion 15/2011 (n. 34) 1.

161 See chapter 3, section K for a discussion of the varieties of consent in biobanking.

162 See: US National Library of Medicine, 'Charcot Marie Tooth Disease' (Genetics Home Reference, 10 December 2019) <https://ghr.nlm.nih.gov/condition/charcot-marie-tooth-disease> accessed 11 December 2019.

163 The EDPB refers to this issue, stating: 'Recital 33 allows as an exception that the purpose may be described at a more general level.' Their consideration, however, does not address the underlying uncertainty. European Data Protection Board, Guidelines 05/2020 on consent under Regulation (n. 93) 30. See also: Katharina Ó Cathaoir, Eugenijus Gefenas, Mette Hartlev, et al., Legal and ethical review of in silico modelling (EU-STANDS4PM Project Deliverable, 3.1, 2020) 24.

The range of third parties to whom a consent permits a data subject's personal data to be given is also unclear. Article 13(1)(e) obliges biobanking actors to provide the research subject with information related to future recipients or categories of recipients of information. However, the scope of 'categories of recipients' is not further defined. In relation to Directive 95/46, the Article 29 Working Party, when discussing direct marketing, suggested that personal data may be given to undefined third parties in the future if 'the information provided to the data subject ... indicate[s] the purpose(s), the goods and services ... for which those parties would send e-mails'. Article 29 Working Party, Opinion 5/2004 on unsolicited communications for marketing purposes under Article 13 of Directive 2002/58/EC, 11601/EN WP 90, 2004) 5 <https://ec.europa.eu/justice/article-29/documentation/opinion-recommendation/files/2004/wp90_en.pdf> accessed 11 December 2019. This guidance, however, only serves to tie the scope of recipients to the scope of purpose.

164 European Data Protection Board, Guidelines 05/2020 on consent under Regulation (n. 93) 30–2.

b) Severity and Resolution

The lack of clarity will not have significant negative effects on genetic privacy rights or other interests in biobanking. This serves to remove the strict need for a solution. The lack of clarity does not represent a deterioration in the current situation. Rather, the lack of clarity mirrors a situation already prevalent in biobanking law. The analysis of international instruments showed a lack of clarity at this level. In terms of scope, for example, whilst the legitimacy of broader forms of consent is an emerging international principle, this is not endorsed by all relevant instruments—there remains no full consensus.[165] The analysis of European state law also showed uncertainty around the conditions of consent. In terms of scope, the limits of legitimate consent remain unclear in certain states—Germany, for example.[166]

It is true there are European states in which the conditions of consent have been defined in more detail—in Estonia, for example.[167] In these states, however, the breadth of possible interpretations of the relevant provisions in the Regulation, and of associated jurisprudence, means there is no conflict. Broad consent in Estonia, for example, can easily be regarded as legitimate within possible interpretations of the conditions of consent under the Regulation.

Nevertheless, a clarification of uncertainty is desirable. No lack of clarity in relation to consent is ideal. Recall the significance of consent as one of the key legitimating factors for biobanking activities.[168] In this regard, in order for research subjects to understand the limits of their interaction with biobanks, they ideally need to be clear as to the bounds of legitimate consent. Equally, for biobanking actors to plan operating practices and research programmes, and to legitimately collect and use substances, they too need clarity as to the conditions of consent they work with.

Solutions to the lack of clarity are facilitated through the Regulation's internal adaptation and interpretation mechanisms. There is no doubt the Regulation's interpretation and adaptation mechanisms are suited to address the problem. From conceptual and legal structural perspectives, the problem merely concerns the calibration of a concept already present in the Regulation and, accordingly, no issues as to the relevance of the Regulation's internal mechanisms as fora for a solution present themselves. Technically, specifying the scope and conditions of consent are activities which have already been shown to fall within the scope of internal mechanisms. Indeed, the European Data Protection Board have already used their powers to provide guidance on the scope and conditions of consent under the Regulation.[169]

In terms of the content of a solution, The EDPB may start by providing a clarification of the legitimate scope of consent. Here, I would strongly suggest the EDPB offer a general endorsement for broad consent. In the first instance, this would align the approach of data protection law with the dominant ethical position concerning the scope

165 See chapter 5, sections C and E.
166 See chapter 6, section E.
167 See chapter 6, section D.
168 See chapter 9, section C.
169 European Data Protection Board, Guidelines 05/2020 on consent under Regulation (n. 93).

of consent in biobanking—recall that all international biobank-specific international instruments already endorse broad consent.[170]

In turn, broad consent represents a legitimate balance between the need to protect research subjects' privacy and the needs of research. From a research perspective, the more uses to which biobanking substances can be put, the more research that can be done. In this regard, broad consent facilitates the range of research for which biobanking substances may be needed. As Sheehan summarises: 'a broader model of consent is often ... justified by ... reference to the potential benefits brought by the research it will facilitate'.[171]

From a privacy perspective, it is true there is some opposition to broader forms of consent. This opposition focuses on the idea that broad consent may not ensure adequate self-determination. The argument runs: as broad consent does not communicate to a research subject-specific intended uses of their substances, the research subject is not informed and cannot exercise self-determination. As Caulfield et al. argue: 'Consent law is concerned with providing research participants with relevant information in order to allow autonomous decision-making. Withholding or tailoring the provision of information ... to meet a broader ... agenda, conflicts directly with the ethical principles that underlie much consent jurisprudence.'[172]

A close look at this opposition, however, reveals flaws. In principle, any narrowing, or specification, of the scope of consent is a restriction on the liberty of a data subject to decide what to do with their personal data—a restriction of self-determination. Such limitations are, in principle, undesirable in relation to personal data unless they are supported by clear normative justification. As Taupitz and Weigel put it, the data subject has, in principle, the 'right to take a risk'.[173] It is true there are circumstances in which restrictions may be justified to protect data subjects. In particular, where:

1. The interests of subjects do not align with those processing their data.
2. The lack of specificity in the scope of consent may be used as a vehicle to obscure relevant knowledge and unfairly prejudice subjects' interests.

Justifications supporting the introduction of limitations on the basis of these circumstances are relevant for most personal data transactions covered by the Regulation,

[170] See chapter 5, section E. See, for a more extensive discussion of this, and subsequent arguments supporting broad consent: Hallinan, 'Broad consent under the GDPR' (n. 157) 10–15.

[171] Mark Sheehan, 'Can Broad Consent Be Informed Consent?' (2011) *Public Health Ethics* 4(3) 226, 226. Equally, van Veen suggests: 'broad consent ... has been the norm in biobanking and data sharing based on the FAIR ... principles'. Evert-Ben van Veen, 'Observational Health Research in Europe: Understanding the General Data Protection Regulation and Underlying Debate' (2018) *European Journal of Cancer* 104 70, 74.

[172] Timothy Caulfield, Ross Upshure, and Abdallah Daar, 'DNA Databanks and Consent: A Suggested Policy Option Involving an Authorization Model' (2003) *BMC Medical Ethics* 4(1) <https://bmcmedethics.biomedcentral.com/articles/10.1186/1472-6939-4-1> accessed 11 December 2019.

[173] Jochen Taupitz and Jukka Weigel, 'The Necessity of Broad Consent and Complementary Regulations for the Protection of Personal Data in Biobanks: What Can We Learn from the German Case' (2012) *Public Health Genomics* 15 263, 265–6.

both commercial and bureaucratic.[174] These limitations, however, are largely inapplicable to biobanking. In the first instance, in biobanking, as discussed in previous chapters, the interests of data subjects can be seen to be much more aligned with those of biobanking actors than is the case in ordinary commercial or bureaucratic transactions.[175] In turn, the breadth of consent in a broad consent transaction is necessary precisely as, as Ienca et al. put it because: 'at the beginning of a scientific research project, it may be impossible ... to fully identify the reasons for which the data [will be] processed'.[176] It is not a gap for sneaky, unscrupulous data controllers to obscure important information.[177]

The EDPB might then go on to clarify the substantive criteria under which broad consent is permissible. In this regard, the EDPB could provide clarification of the content of the requirement that consent only be obtained 'in keeping with recognized ethical standards for scientific research'. Here, bearing in mind the lack of overarching normative clarity regarding the conditions of consent, as well as the range of different types of biobanking activity, I would suggest the EDPB takes a light touch.

In this respect, the EDPB might highlight that there is a range of instruments outlining ethical principles concerning research subject rights and consent in biobanking—at both international and national level. The EDPB might also highlight, however, that the applicability of principles outlined in instruments may need to be adapted to the specifics of the case at hand. In this regard, in line with scholars such as Marelli and Testa, the EDPB should point to RECs, and other institutionalised ethics organs, as the arbiters of 'relevant ethical standards' in any specific case.[178] Building on this recognition, the EDPB might go on to highlight that the safeguards outlined in their previous guidance should not be understood as mandatory in any given case, but rather should be taken as generally helpful suggestions which may, depending on context, serve to support transparency and self-determination.

The Regulation also facilitates the adoption of solutions to the problem through other law. National-level law clarifying the scope of consent would be permissible under Article 9(4). All relevant clarifications—for example, explicit recognition of the legitimacy of broad consent—would constitute supplemental conditions relating to the processing of genetic data and data concerning health and would be legitimate under Article 9(4).

[174] See, for example, Frederik Zuiderveen Borgesius, Consent to Behavioural Targeting in European Law: What are the Policy Implications of Insights from Behavioural Economics? (Amsterdam Law School Legal Studies Research Paper, No. 2013-43, 2013) 28.

[175] See chapter 4, section J.

[176] Marcello Ienca, James Scheibner, Agata Ferretti, et al., How the General Data Protection Regulation changes the rules for scientific research (Report, ETH Zürich Research Collection, 2019) 61 (hereafter Ienca, Scheibner, Ferretti, et al., How the General Data Protection Regulation changes the rules for scientific research).

[177] See for a more complete elaboration of the argument: Hallinan and Friedewald, 'Open Consent, Biobanking and Data Protection Law' (n. 118) 19–22. Hallinan, 'Broad consent under the GDPR' (n. 157) 10–12.

[178] Indeed, Marelli and Testa propose the Recital already implies looking to: 'institutionalized ethics ... that is, ethics committees'. Luca Marelli and Giuseppe Testa, 'Scrutinizing the EU General Data Protection Regulation: How Will New Decentralized Governance Impact Research?' (2018) *Science* 360(6388) 496, 497.

2. The DPIA Obligation Is Unclear for Biobanking (Problem 20)

a) Problem

The Data Protection Impact Assessment (DPIA) obligation for biobanking is elaborated in Article 35. Whilst the Regulation does devote considerable space to elaborating the obligation, provisions concretising the practical conduct of the DPIA are currently, as Wright puts it, 'rather sketchy'.[179] This sketchiness manifests in relation to the biobanking processing context in four significant ways. Whilst the Article 29 Working Party has provided guidance on the obligation, the guidance remains rudimentary and, as a result, fails to adequately address these issues.[180]

First, the range of biobanking processing operations a single DPIA might cover is unclear. As discussed previously, Article 35(1) is explicit that multiple processing operations may be covered by one DPIA.[181] Yet, there remains no clear information as to how diverse different processing operations subsumed in one DPIA may be.[182] As a result, biobanking controllers cannot currently be sure when separate DPIAs will be required.

Second, there remains a lack of specificity concerning the DPIA methodology. Whilst Article 35(7) does provide methodological instructions, these are limited and, eventually, insufficient to provide controllers with clarity as to how to effectively conduct a DPIA.[183] There are more complete DPIA methodologies which have been proposed by significant European data protection bodies—for example, the Commission Nationale de l'Informatique et des Libertés (CNIL) and the ICO.[184] Unfortunately, it is not clear these are Regulation compatible or that they are suitable for biobanking.[185]

179 David Wright, 'Making Privacy Impact Assessment More Effective' (2013) *Information Society* 29 307, 307. See, also, for a discussion of the problem in question: Hallinan, 'Biobank Oversight and Sanctions' (n. 84) 136-138.

180 Article 29 Working Party, Guidelines on Data Protection Impact Assessment (DPIA) and determining whether processing is 'likely to result in a high risk' for the purposes of Regulation 2016/679 (Policy, 17/EN WP 248, 2017) (hereafter Article 29 Working Party, Guidelines on Data Protection Impact Assessment).

181 See chapter 9, section B.

182 See: R. Fears, H. Brand, R. Frackowiak, et al., 'Data Protection Regulation and the Promotion of Health Research: Getting the Balance Right' (2014) *QJM: An International Journal of Medicine* 107 3, 4.

183 See chapter 9, section B. In particular, uncertainty remains as to the precise normative reference point which should be taken as the core of this methodology. See, for a discussion: Dara Hallinan and Nicholas Martin, 'Fundamental Rights, the Normative Keystone of DPIA' (2020) *European Data Protection Law Review* 6(2) 178, 178–93 (hereafter Hallinan and Martin, 'Fundamental Rights, the Normative Keystone of DPIA').

184 Commission Nationale de l'Informatique et des Libertés, Privacy Impact Assessment (PIA): Methodology (Policy, 2018); Information Commissioner's Office, 'Data protection impact assessments' (Information Commissioner's Office) <https://ico.org.uk/for-organisations/guide-to-data-protection/guide-to-the-general-data-protection-regulation-gdpr/accountability-and-governance/data-protection-impact-assessments/> accessed 11 December 2019.

185 The need for specificity in DPIA methodologies has been recognised. See, for example, European Commission's Community Research and Development Information Service, Privacy and Data Protection Impact Assessment Framework for RFID Applications (Policy, 2011) (hereafter European Commission's Community Research and Development Information Service, Privacy and Data Protection Impact Assessment Framework for RFID). See also, for a discussion: Hallinan and Martin, 'Fundamental Rights, the Normative Keystone of DPIA' (n. 183) 184–6.

Third, the consequences of a change in processing operation for the DPIA are unclear. In the case of a change, Article 35(11) requires that 'the controller ... review whether the processing is still compliant with the findings of the DPIA.' There remains a lack of guidance, however, clearly outlining what should happen when a process is no longer in accordance with the results of an original DPIA. Does a new DPIA need to be conducted, engaging the same effort as the first? Would this DPIA have the same consequences as the first—might the controller, for example, potentially need to re-seek DPA approval?

Finally, it remains unclear as to the resources which must be invested in order to conduct an effective DPIA. As Wright et al. observe: '[resource investment is central to how] credible the ... assessment [will] be.'[186] On the one hand, a DPIA conducted with minimal resource investment will be futile. This will not allow any kind of thorough consideration of risks or mitigation strategies. On the other hand, biobanking controllers cannot be expected to conduct endless DPIAs. How is a biobanking controller to know when they have done, and invested, enough?

b) Severity and Resolution

The lack of clarity is unlikely to have significant negative impacts on genetic privacy rights or other interests. This renders the strict need for a solution moot. In terms of genetic privacy rights, the DPIA has only limited significance in ensuring protection. Most importantly, it does not itself consist of substantive safeguards. Rather it constitutes an information production process allowing substantive obligations to be better met. As Gellert, for example, observes: 'DPIA [is an] obligation to describe the data processing life cycle [and] ... provide for ... meaningful information [to be produced].'[187] Accordingly, even if a biobanking actor failed to effectively fulfil their DPIA obligations—provided compliance is otherwise assured—this would not cause data subjects any specific problems.

In terms of other interests in biobanking—particularly those of actors under the obligation to conduct DPIAs—the DPIA requirement is novel in data protection. It is thus novel for biobanking actors and DPAs alike. Consequently, it would seem most likely that, at first, DPAs will be lenient regarding the specifics of DPIAs—provided effort is made to comply with the obligation. This may change over time as the details of DPIA execution crystalise. Following crystallisation, however, uncertainty should also become less problematic.

Nevertheless, a clarification of uncertainty is desirable. Despite mitigating factors, uncertainty in relation to the DPIA is not ideal. Regarding genetic privacy, this uncertainty undermines the optimal function of a useful tool in ensuring protection.

[186] David Wright, Inga Kroener, Monica Lagazio, et al., A guide to surveillance impact assessment — How to identify and prioritise risks arising from surveillance systems (SAPIENT Project Deliverable, 4.4, 2014) 10.

[187] Raphaël Gellert, 'The Article 29 Working Party's Provisional Guidelines on Data Protection Impact Assessment' (2017) *European Data Protection Law Review* 3(2) 212, 216.

Regarding biobanking actors' interests, dealing with uncertainty may require a diversion of resources which could otherwise be invested in research.

Solutions to the lack of clarity are facilitated through the Regulation's internal adaptation and interpretation mechanisms. There is no doubt that the lack of clarity concerning the DPIA obligation can be solved by the Regulation's internal mechanisms. From a conceptual and legal structural perspective, the problem concerns the clarification of provisions already present in the Regulation. Thus, no awkward questions about the Regulation's internal mechanisms as suitable fora for a solution are raised. Technically, the Regulation is explicit that its internal mechanisms should provide clarity to the DPIA obligation. Article 64(1)(a) highlights that the EDPB should offer an opinion when a national DPA 'aims to adopt a list of the processing operations subject to the requirement for a [DPIA]'. The competence of such mechanisms has been further proven by the Article 29 Working Party, which recently saw fit to publish guidance on the obligation.[188]

In terms of the content of a solution, the EDPB should ideally adopt guidance specifying a DPIA methodology adapted solely to biobanking, ideally addressing each of the four key areas of uncertainty identified in the section above:

1. The range of processing operations a DPIA might address
2. The DPIA methodology
3. The consequences of a change in processing
4. The resources which should be invested.

The idea of a sector-specific DPIAs is not novel or impossible. Such specific frameworks have already been developed for, for example, Radio Frequency Identification (RFID) technologies.[189] As an alternative, however, the EDPB could adopt a scalable elaborated general framework applicable and adaptable to biobanking. Frameworks of this form have already been proposed. One such promising and extensive framework, for example, has recently been proposed by Martin et al.[190]

The Regulation also facilitates the adoption of solutions to the problem through other law. In this regard, European states could act under Article 9(4). Specific clarifications, in national laws, for the conduct of a DPIA in biobanking would count as supplementary conditions related to the processing of genetic data and data concerning health. They would thus be legitimate under Article 9(4).

[188] Article 29 Working Party, Guidelines on Data Protection Impact Assessment (n. 180).

[189] European Commission's Community Research and Development Information Service, Privacy and Data Protection Impact Assessment Framework for RFID (n. 185).

[190] Nicholas Martin, Michael Friedewald, Ina Schiering, et al., *The Data Protection Impact Assessment According to Article 35 GDPR: A Practitioner's Manual* (Fraunhofer Press 2020).

3. The Data Protection by Design and Default Obligation Is Unclear for Biobanking (Problem 21)

a) Problem

The data protection by design and default obligation is outlined in Article 25. This is, however, as Spiekermann puts it, 'barely specified'.[191] The consequence is, as Koops and Leenes observe, that 'it is not . . . clear what the obligation . . . would entail' in practice.[192] These conclusions hold true for biobanking.

The Regulation does provide a decision support system—outlined in Article 25(1)—which is designed to assist biobanking controllers in concretising the obligation.[193] Unfortunately, this decision support system is also vague. The EDPB also provides clarification. This clarification provides a more granular consideration of the content of the factors in the decision support system in Article 25 and even provides a set of key data protection by design and default considerations in relation to each data protection principle.[194] Even this clarification, however, does not provide a clear blueprint for biobanking controllers to implement the obligation. Two important practical questions, in particular, remain unanswered.

First, how should the costs and risks referred to in the decision support system be balanced? The decision support system can be described as a balancing exercise—the costs borne by the biobanking controller must be balanced against the risks to the research subject. Yet, there is no clarity provided as to how to do this balancing. When, for example, is an available approach too expensive? When is a potential impact so significant as to require a response? How are these things to be weighed against each other to produce an 'appropriate' result?

Second, what level of flexibility does a biobanking controller have in implementing the obligation? This question is particularly significant in a processing sector as dynamic as biobanking. If a controller begins with a specific research purpose in mind, do they need to design processing operations strictly for this purpose? To do so would restrict the ability to subsequently change. This will limit the biobanking actor's capacity to adapt to change. If not, what flexibility is permissible?

There are firm policy arguments for a general and flexible approach. Two are noteworthy. First, data protection by design and default requirements for each processing context will be unique. This means, as Gürses et al. observe, 'it is not possible to reduce ... privacy by design principles to a checklist'.[195] Second, such specification of

[191] Sarah Spiekermann, 'The Challenges of Privacy by Design' (2012) *Communications of the ACM* 55(7) 38, 38.

[192] Bert-Jaap Koops and Ronald Leenes, 'Privacy Regulation Cannot Be Hardcoded: A Critical Comment on the "Privacy by Design" Provision in Data-Protection Law' (2014) *International Review of Law, Computers & Technology* 28(2) 159, 162.

[193] See chapter 9, section E.

[194] European Data Protection Board, Guidelines 4/2019 on Article 25 Data Protection by Design and by Default (Policy, 2019) (hereafter European Data Protection Board, Guidelines 4/2019 on Article 25 Data Protection by Design and by Default).

[195] Seda Gürses, Carmela Troncoso, and Claudia Diaz, 'Engineering Privacy by Design' (Research Paper, 2011) <https://securewww.esat.kuleuven.be/cosic/publications/article-1542.pdf> accessed 11 December 2019, 21.

technical standards in the Regulation could have been awkward. As Kosta and Stuurman observe: '[This is] because the development of too detailed or too specific standards may result in undermining the objective of technology neutrality'.[196] The legitimacy of these arguments notwithstanding, the fact that the lack of clarity in the Article leaves biobanking controllers largely in the dark as to its practical implementation, is not ideal.

b) Severity and Resolution

The lack of clarity is unlikely to have significant negative impacts on genetic privacy rights or other interests. This renders the strict need for a solution moot. In terms of genetic privacy rights, the lack of clarity does not render the obligation meaningless. In principle, it remains clear that biobanking actors must seek to integrate data protection principles into technical and organisational systems. Accordingly—provided a biobanking actor makes a legitimate effort to adhere to the obligation—the concrete impact of the lack of clarity on protection will be limited.

In terms of other interests in biobanking—namely those interests of biobanking actors obliged to fulfil the obligation—the obligation may be regarded as novel to the Regulation. Bygrave, for example, asserts: 'The provisions of GDPR Article 25 are amongst the most innovative and ambitious norms of the EU's newly reformed data protection regime.'[197] This novelty means uncertainty exists on the part of biobanking actors and DPAs. Accordingly, at first at least, it would seem unlikely that DPAs will be strict regarding adherence to some specific uncodified or esoteric conceptualisation of the obligation. Indeed, as Bygrave generally states: 'Invoking stiff sanctions for breach of Article 25(1) will not be easy given the very general ... way in which its obligations are formulated.'[198] It is true that the specifics of the privacy by design and default obligation will crystalise for biobanking over time. Along with the process of crystallisation, it also seems likely that DPA leniency will diminish. Such crystallisation, however, will likely also be accompanied by a parallel decrease in uncertainty.

Nevertheless, a clarification of uncertainty is desirable. Despite mitigating factors, the lack of clarity will have negative impacts. Concerning genetic privacy rights, the lack of clarity will undermine the optimal function of one of the Regulation's protective provisions. Concerning biobanking actors' interests, the lack of clarity is undoubtedly irritating and may require a diversion of time and resources to address—resources which would ideally be invested in research.

Solutions to the lack of clarity are certainly facilitated through the Regulation's internal adaptation and interpretation mechanisms. There is no doubt the clarification of vague principles in Article 25 falls within the ambit of the Regulation's internal

[196] Eleni Kosta and Kees Stuurman, 'Technical Standards and the Draft General Data Protection Regulation', in Panagiotis Delimatsis (ed.), *The Law, Economics and Politics of International Standardization* (Cambridge University Press 2015) 434, 444.

[197] Lee Bygrave, 'Data Protection by Design and by Default: Deciphering the EU's Legislative Requirements' (2017) *Oslo Law Review* 4(2) 105, 106 (hereafter Bygrave, 'Data Protection by Design and Default').

[198] Bygrave, 'Data Protection by Design and Default' (n. 197) 117.

mechanisms to solve. From a conceptual and legal structural perspective, the problem relates to the lack of optimisation of one of the Regulation's existing principles and thus raises no awkward questions as to the relevance of the Regulation's internal mechanisms. Technically, the problem concerns the lack of clarity in an existing provision. There thus seems little reason to doubt the Regulation's internal mechanisms' power to act. This is especially true as the obligation is one of the most novel and uncertain in the Regulation. Indeed, the relevance of the Regulation's internal mechanisms has already been demonstrated by the EDPB's decision to produce guidance on the obligation.[199]

In terms of the content of a solution, the EDPB would ideally build on its existing guidance.[200] In this regard, the Board would ideally offer sector-specific biobanking clarification. Building on observations as to key uncertainties above, this guidance should ideally seek to clarify the following questions:

1. What constitutes a cost, and what a risk, in biobanking?
2. How should costs and risks be effectively balanced?
3. What might model approaches to data protection by design and default look like in biobanking?
4. To what degree might biobanking actors be flexible in implementing data protection by design and default?

If the production of such a biobank-specific approach is not feasible, as an alternative, the EDPB might adopt further general, scalable, and adaptable clarification. Such clarification might build on the body of academic work already available on the conversion of the data protection by design and default obligation from legal principle into technical practice. Danezis et al., for example, conducted a detailed study into: '[how to bridge] the gap between the legal framework and the available technological implementation measures'.[201] Such clarification might elaborate catalogues of existing technical and organisational measures to take in response to different types of data protection by design and default considerations. Existing catalogues of this sort, built by DPAs, might be useful as a template on which to build.[202]

The Regulation also facilitates the adoption of solutions to the lack of clarity through other law. The broad construction of Article 9(4) provides legitimacy for European

[199] European Data Protection Board, Guidelines 4/2019 on Article 25 Data Protection by Design and by Default (n. 19).

[200] European Data Protection Board, Guidelines 4/2019 on Article 25 Data Protection by Design and by Default (n. 194).

[201] George Danezis, Josep Domingo-Ferrer, and Marit Hansen, Privacy and Data Protection by Design—from policy to engineering (ENISA Report, 2015) 3.

[202] See, for example, Commission Nationale de l'Informatique et des Libertés, Privacy Impact Assessment (PIA): Knowledge Bases (Policy, 2018); Konferenz der unabhängigen Datenschutzbehörden des Bundes und der Länder, Das Standard Datenschutzmodell: Eine Methode zur Datenschutzberatung und -prüfung auf der Basis einheitlicher Gewährleistungsziele, (Policy, Version 2.0b, 2018) 31–8; Der Landesbeauftragte für Datenschutz und Informationsfreiheit Mecklenburg-Vorpommern 'Erste Bausteine des SDM-Maßnahmenkatalogs' (Der Landesbeauftragte für Datenschutz und Informationsfreiheit Mecklenburg-Vorpommern) <https://www.datenschutz-mv.de/datenschutz/publikationen/Erste-Bausteine-des-SDM%E2%80%93Ma%C3%9Fnahmenkatalogs/>accessed 23 June 2020.

state law outlining specific rules clarifying data protection by design and default obligations for biobanking. Such rules would qualify as conditions relating to the processing of genetic data or data concerning health, and would thus fall under the scope of Article 9(4).

J. Problems Concerning the Degree to Which the GDPR Harmonises Protection

1. National Interpretations of Generally Applicable Provisions Diverge (Problem 22)

a) Problem

The GDPR is, in principle—where no derogation is possible, or no derogation has been used—meant to be directly applicable in all European states in which it applies. However, the GDPR outlines only top-level rules applicable across a range of different contexts in which personal data are processed. Consequently, the GDPR does not always provide clear answers as to how its substantive provisions should be applied in biobanking—the cause of several problems listed above.[203] In certain cases, jurisprudence fills the gap.

In other cases, however, differing interpretations of directly applicable principles relevant to biobanking have emerged between European states. In practice, these differing interpretations can give rise to differing obligations on biobanking processing and serve to place different types of burdens on biobanking actors. Eventually, such different interpretations can fragment the way in which the Regulation is understood, and functions, across European states and, as a consequence, can undermine the degree to which the Regulation is capable of providing a harmonised European approach to biobanking.

For example, in the UK, the dominant position is that consent, under 9(2)(a), will not be the relevant grounds for processing in scientific research—including biobanking—wherever a public authority is involved. As the UK NHS Health Research Authority observes: 'The GDPR sets out the expectation that consent would not be appropriate as a legal basis under this legislation where there is an imbalance of power in the relationship between the controller and the data subject, eg where the controller is a public authority . . . the legal basis for processing data for health and social care research should NOT be consent. This means that requirements in the GDPR relating to consent do NOT apply to health and care research.'[204]

[203] As Lattanzi observes: 'Before embarking on a search for the peculiarities of genetic research and biobanks, it may be helpful to recall that [the Directive and the Regulation, are] omnibus regulation [and do] not provide detailed guidance.' Roberto Lattanzi, 'Data Protection Principles and Research in the Biobanks Age', in Deborah Mascalzoni (ed.), *Ethics, Law and Governance of Biobanking* (Springer 2015) 79, 85.

[204] NHS Health Research Authority, 'Consent in Research' (NHS Health Research Authority, 2018) <https://www.hra.nhs.uk/planning-and-improving-research/policies-standards-legislation/

This position, however, is not reflected in dominant German understandings of the role of consent under Article 9(2)(a) in relation to scientific research—including biobanking. For example, Schaar, in discussing the position of the GDPR on consent and scientific research, highlights a general 'maxim of informed consent' relevant across all types of research involving personal data.[205] Equally, the Deutsche Gesellschaft für Medizinische Informatik, Biometrie und Epidemiologie e. V. et al. recognise the relevance of consent under Article 9(2)(a) for all types of medical research.[206]

b) Severity and Resolution

It is hard to determine, with precision, the severity of consequences this lack of confluence in interpretations will have for the degree to which the Regulation can provide a harmonised approach to biobanking in Europe. This is true for two reasons. First, the degree to which divergence exists between national interpretations of provisions relevant to biobanking is not yet completely clear. Second, the degree to which divergences in interpretation give rise to practical issues for the conduct of cross-border European biobanking activity also remains unclear.

Nevertheless, there are strong arguments to suggest that the existence of divergent interpretations is unlikely to have significant negative effects on the harmony of European approaches to the regulation of biobanking. Consequently, the issue does not strictly require a solution. Three arguments support this position. First, from a legal technical perspective, there is no reason to think that divergent interpretations of the Regulation will lead to a diminished level of harmony compared to that which existed prior to the Regulation. In this regard, there is no indication that differences in interpretations of the Regulation's provisions are more pronounced than national divergences which pertained in relation to provisions of Directive 95/46.[207]

Second, from a practical perspective, there is no indication—although this may yet be proven wrong—that diverging interpretations of the Regulation's provisions are causing significant novel problems for the practical conduct of cross-border European biobanking. In the first instance, there is little evidence that divergent interpretations of the Regulation's provisions are posing barriers to biobanking processing which did not exist prior to the Regulation. In turn, currently, it would seem the majority of differing national interpretations take the form of technical differences, which simply require administrative effort by biobanking actors—in the identification of relevant interpretations and obligations, and in the adaptation of procedures—to address.

data-protection-and-information-governance/gdpr-guidance/what-law-says/consent-research/> accessed 19 June 2020.

205 Translation by the author of: 'Maxime des Informed Consent'. Katrin Schaar, 'Anpassung von Einwilligungserklärungen für wissenschaftliche Forschungsprojekte: Die informierte Einwilligung nach der DS-GVO und den Ethikrichtlinien' (2017) *Zeitschrift für Datenschutz* 5/2017 213, 219.

206 GMDS and GDD, Datenschutzrechtliche Anforderungen an die medizinische Forschung (n. 32) 14.

207 Gibbons, for example, describes the: 'notoriously inconsistent interpretation and implementation of the Data Protection Directive 95/46/EC'. Susan Gibbons, 'Mapping the Regulatory Space', in Jane Kaye, Susan M. C. Gibbons, Catherine Heeney, Michael Parker, and Andrew Smart (eds.), *Governing Biobanks: Understanding the Interplay between Law and Practice* (Hart 2012) 51, 53.

Third, from a temporal perspective, the range and breadth of different national interpretations will likely diminish over time. Prior to the Regulation, data protection law in Europe had a distinctly national flavour—Directive 95/46 required full implementation in national law, whilst prior to Directive 95/46, data protection was a matter for national law alone.[208] Prior to the Regulation, many European states thus already had extensive national data protection traditions, including *sui generis* understandings of the role and function of data protection law in society and *sui generis* interpretations of provisions now present in the Regulation. Where European-level guidance is not available under the Regulation, actors naturally continue to apply legacy approaches. The Regulation, however, foresees an extensive harmonisation apparatus—including strong European-level interpretation mechanisms and extensive DPA co-operation systems.[209] Over time, it is to be expected that this apparatus will work to resolve differing interpretations relevant for biobanking, in favour of harmonised interpretations.[210]

Nevertheless, a solution would still be welcome. In the first instance, the fact that there are divergent interpretations of the Regulation's provisions means that the Regulation cannot fulfil its promise in offering a harmonised approach to biobanking in Europe. In turn, even if the practical consequences of this unfulfilled promise are merely higher administrative burdens on biobanking actors, the discharge of such administrative burden still requires resources. There is no guarantee that such resources will always be available to biobanking actors. Even when resources are available, resources devoted to incidental administrative problems are resources unnecessarily diverted from research.

Resolution through the Regulation's internal adaptation and interpretation mechanisms is evidently possible. The issue concerns the harmonised interpretation of provisions which are, in principle, intended to be directly applicable in EU Member States. Consequently, there are no conceptual, legal structural, or technical obstacles to the utility of the Regulation's internal mechanisms in addressing the issue. Indeed, recall that, according to Article 70(1), one of the key tasks of the EDPB is to: 'ensure the consistent application of [the] Regulation'. In turn, the EDPB has already used this power several times in providing harmonising guidance on the interpretation of the Regulation.[211]

Resolution of the issue through alternate law operating in parallel with the GDPR is not, however, possible. The issue concerns the fragmentation of the legal framework set by the GDPR through diverse national interpretations. Accordingly, the codification

[208] See, for a discussion of national data protection histories and traditions leading into the development of European data protection law: Viktor Mayer-Schönberger, 'Generational Development of Data Protection in Europe', in Phillip Agre and Marc Rotenberg (eds.), *Technology and Privacy: The New Landscape* (MIT Press 1997) 219, 219–41; Gloria González Fuster, *The Emergence of Personal Data Protection as a Fundamental Right of the EU* (Springer 2014) 55–252.

[209] Including, for example, the EDPB as discussed above and the cooperation and consistency procedure outlined in Chapter VII of the Regulation.

[210] The EDBP plans to produce further guidance on the interpretation of the GDPR in relation to scientific research. European Data Protection Board, Guidelines 03/2020 on the processing of data concerning health for the purpose of scientific research in the context of the COVID-19 outbreak (Policy, 2020) 4.

[211] Consider, for example, European Data Protection Board, Guidelines 4/2019 on Article 25 Data Protection by Design and by Default (n. 194).

of national positions, in national law, would scarcely provide an answer—indeed, this would likely exacerbate the problem. Whilst there may, theoretically, be the possibility to pass EU law which would harmonise approaches in relation to specific issues, the idea of passing EU law, to operate in parallel with the GDPR, to codify harmonised interpretations of the provisions of the GDPR, would be illogical.

2. National Laws Derogating from the GDPR Diverge (Problem 23)

a) Problem

As discussed in the previous chapter, the Regulation permits states, in certain cases, to derogate from its—otherwise directly applicable—provisions. Three provisions permitting such derogations are particularly significant in relation to biobanking processing: the Article 9(2)(j) possibility to legitimate processing for scientific research purposes subject to specific national safeguards; the Article 89(2) possibility to derogate from data subject rights under Articles 15, 16, 18, and 21; and the Article 9(4) possibility to impose additional conditions on the processing of genetic data and data concerning health.

The problem is that states, in using these derogation powers, have passed laws, the scope and conditions of which do not necessarily align. This has the impact of fragmenting the legal framework in Europe, in principle set by the Regulation, for biobanking processing. For example, in relation to Article 9(2)(j), the German Bundesdatenschutzsgesetz, in Article 27, outlines a legitimation applicable to all types of research. In relation to Article 9(2)(j), the UK Data Protection Act, however, according to Schedule 1, Part 4(c), only legitimates research 'in the public interest'.

Equally, in relation to Article 89(2), Article 27 of the German Bundesdatenschutzgesetz limits the applicability of exemptions to listed rights to the degree that the exercise of these rights would prevent, or seriously impair research, and the restriction on the right is necessary to facilitate research. The UK Data Protection Act, however, not only elaborates the conditions outlined in the German law but also elaborates supplemental conditions—including, for example, that processing must not, according to Article 19 of the Act, cause significant damage or distress to a subject.

b) Severity and Resolution

As with the previous problem, it is hard to pinpoint with certainty the degree to which divergence in the scope and content of national derogations from the GDPR's provisions are problematic from the perspective of the harmony of European approaches to the regulation of biobanking. As with the previous problem, this lack of clarity stems both from the fact that the range in scope and content of derogations under the Regulation is not yet completely clear, as well as from the fact that the practical consequences of these divergences for cross-border biobanking practice are not yet completely clear.

Nevertheless, there is reason to believe the consequences of divergent derogations are unlikely to have significant negative effects on the harmony of the regulation of biobanking in Europe. There are two reasons for this—both of which were also relevant in relation to the previous problem. First, from a legal technical perspective, there is no reason to think that the degree of divergence between national derogations under the Regulation does, or will, supersede the degree of national legislative divergence exhibited under Directive 95/46.

In this regard, not only did Directive 95/46 require national implementation of all its provisions—which the Regulation does not, and which itself led to significant divergence in national approaches—but it also included broad possibilities for states to derogate from its provisions for scientific research. Many of the possibilities for states to derogate under the Regulation are thus not new, but rather already existed under the Directive. For example, all but one of the rights—the right to object—from which states are explicitly allowed to derogate under Article 89(2) of the Regulation, were also derogable under Directive 95/46. Equally, the possibility to pass supplemental conditions on the processing of genetic data and data concerning health under Article 9(4) of the Regulation, had an equivalent in Article 8(4) of the Directive.

Second, from a practical perspective, there remains little evidence that differences in the scope and content of national laws derogating from the Regulation are causing significant novel obstructions to the conduct of cross-border European biobanking. In the first instance, there is little indication that divergent national derogations constitute consequential obstacles to the conduct of European biobanking which did not exist prior to the Regulation. In turn—as is the case regarding the previous problem—it would appear most differences between national derogating laws only pose legal technical hurdles, requiring only administrative effort to address.

The problem ideally, however, would benefit from resolution. In the first instance, the fact that national laws exhibit divergent derogations from the Regulation means that the Regulation cannot optimally function to harmonise the regulation of biobanking across Europe. As Dove observes: 'There is ... a potential for national divergence and regulatory fragmentation, undermining the very purpose of an EU Regulation.'[212] In turn, even if the practical consequences of divergent national derogations only take the form of administrative hurdles for biobanking, such administrative hurdles still require resources to address. Such resources may not always be available to biobanking actors, and, in such cases, administrative hurdles may act as deterrents to cross-border activity. In turn, even when the requisite resources are available, resources devoted to administrative hurdles are resources diverted from research.

The problem cannot be substantively addressed through the Regulation's internal interpretation and adaptation systems. An obvious technical problem emerges. The problem concerns national laws legitimately derogating from the Regulation's provisions. The Regulation's internal mechanisms cannot function to substantively alter the scope or conditions of the Regulation's provisions permitting such derogations. Nor can the Regulation's internal mechanisms directly intervene to adapt the content of the national laws at issue. Both activities would go beyond the interpretation and

[212] Dove, 'The EU General Data Protection Regulation' (n. 159) 1014.

Table 10.1: Overview of the necessity and availability of solutions by problem

	Gaps in Member State Approaches without Data Protection	How Necessary is a Solution?			Is a Solution Possible through the GDPR's Internal Mechanisms?		Does the GDPR Facilitate a Solution through Other Law?	
		Necessary	Not Strictly Necessary	Not Necessary	Yes	No	Yes	No
Type of Problem	Lack of Applicability to Scientific Conclusions (Problem 1)		•		•		•	
	Lack of Applicability to Law Enforcement Processing (Problem 2)			•	N.A.	N.A.	N.A.	N.A.
	Lack of Protection for the Information Privacy Right not to Know (Problem 3)		•		•		•	
	Lack of Protection for the Spatial Privacy Right not to Know (Problem 4)		•			•	•	
	Lack of Protection for Genetic Groups (Problem 5)		•		•		•	
	Lack of Protection for Genetic Relatives (Problem 6)		•		•		•	
	Lack of Obligation to Seek Prior Approval (Problem 7)		•		•		•	
	Lack of Strict Consent Obligation (Problem 8)	•				•	•	
	Lack of Genetic Counselling Provisions (Problem 9)			•	N.A.	N.A.	N.A.	N.A.
	Lack of Strict Prohibitions on Third-Party Access (Problem 10)	•				•	•	
	Lack of Obligation to Make Access Policies Public and Accessible (Problem 11)		•		•		•	
	Lack of Criminal Sanctions (Problem 12)	•				•	•	

Gaps in Member State Approaches without Data Protection		How Necessary is a Solution?			Is a Solution Possible through the GDPR's Internal Mechanisms?		Does the GDPR Facilitate a Solution through Other Law?	
		Necessary	Not Strictly Necessary	Not Necessary	Yes	No	Yes	No
Type of Problem	Transparency Provisions' Unsuitability for the Broad Interpretative Potential of Genomic Data (Problem 13)		•		•		•	
	Transparency Provisions' Unsuitability fot the Uncertain Future Interpretative Potential of Genomic Data (Problem 14)		•		•		•	
	Self-Determination Provisions' Unsuitability for Genomic Data (Problem 15)		•		•		•	
	Disproportionate Impact of the Right to a Copy of Personal Data in relation to the Sample (Problem 16)		•		•		•	
	Disproportionate Impact of the Right to Data Portability (Problem 17)		•		•		•	
	Disproportionate Impact of the Scale of Administrative Fines (Problem 18)		•		•			•
	Vague Consent Provisions (Problem 19)		•		•		•	
	Vague DPIA Provisions (Problem 20)		•		•		•	
	Vague Data Protection by Design and Default Provisions (Problem 21)		•		•		•	
	Deviating National Interpretations (Problem 22)		•		•			•
	Deviating National Derogating Laws (Problem 23)		•			•	•	

adaptation powers of the EDPB or national DPAs. The Regulation's internal adaptation and interpretation mechanisms may nevertheless assist resolution in a supporting context: in providing clarifications concerning the unclear scope of possible derogations and in collating information as to the use and extent of derogations.

Resolution is, however, certainly possible under parallel law. The problem emerges because of procedurally legitimate, albeit substantively divergent, European state laws. The Regulation thus facilitates a resolution via the same procedures which led to the problem. States could minimise issues of divergence by adopting legislation aimed at making sure national derogations diverge as little as possible and, if they must diverge, are at least consistent and compatible as far as possible. As Ienca et al. observe: 'as a policy option, the national legislators of member states should attempt to define consistent national exceptions as soon as possible'.[213]

K. Conclusion

A critical analysis of the protection offered to genetic privacy in biobanking by the GDPR initially reveals a plethora of problems: twenty-three in total. These problems take a variety of different forms, including: limitations in scope; a lack of protection for the full range of research subject's genetic privacy rights; a lack of protection for the full range of genetic privacy rights holders—specifically genetic relatives and genetic groups; inadequacies in the standard of protection offered—in relation to those genetic privacy rights and rights holders which are protected; the technical unsuitability of provisions—when they do apply; the disproportionate impact of provisions on other interests in the biobanking process; the practical inapplicability of provisions; and the degree to which the GDPR harmonises protection across European states.

Yet, a deeper consideration reveals that none of these problems critically calls into question the utility of the GDPR as a framework for the protection of genetic privacy in biobanking. In the first instance, most problems reveal themselves to either not require a solution at all, or to not, strictly speaking, require a solution. For example, certain problems concern aspects of biobank processing, or genetic privacy, in relation to which the GDPR need not provide protection. For example, there is no reason the GDPR should be looked to as a framework to resolve problems concerning the lack of protection for genetic privacy rights in relation to law enforcement. Equally, other problems display mitigating factors which will significantly ameliorate their eventual impact and limit the strict need for a solution. For example, problems relating to the huge size of administrative fines will, likely, be mitigated through DPA discretion in deciding the level of fines.

In turn, all problems which either require, or would benefit from, resolution, are amenable to resolution. Options for resolution invariably present themselves either

[213] Ienca, Scheibner, Ferretti et al., How the General Data Protection Regulation changes the rules for scientific research (n. 176) 25.

through the GDPR's internal interpretation and adaptation mechanisms or through other national legislation operating in parallel with the GDPR. For example, the fact that the GDPR does not impose an obligation to make access policies public and accessible could easily be resolved through the Regulation's internal mechanisms—specifically through EDPB guidance. Equally, the fact that the Regulation imposes no obligation to seek approval from a DPA prior to processing could be addressed by national laws, legitimately derogating from the provisions of the GDPR under Article 9(4).

11
Conclusion

Over the past two decades, biobanks have become key aspects of medical research infrastructure. With this growth in importance, however, has come increased ethical and legal scrutiny. In this regard, one of the most discussed issues is the protection of privacy. Privacy has been the subject of such discussion for two reasons. First, as biobanking involves the processing of genomic data, novel questions appear as to precisely which privacy rights should be protected in research: questions of genetic privacy. For example, novel questions appear as to whether privacy rights to know, and not know, information produced during research should be protected, and as to whether other possible rights holders in genomic data, apart from research subjects—particularly genetic relatives and groups—also deserve protection. Second, biobanking is a novel practice in medical research and engages novel institutional and actor constellations. This novelty raises questions as to how the protection of genetic privacy rights should be effectively and proportionately balanced against other legitimate interests.

Since 25 May 2018, the General Data Protection Regulation (GDPR) has applied and now forms the keystone of European data protection law. There is no doubt the GDPR occupies a key place in the legal landscape relevant for the regulation of biobanking in Europe. At first glance, it may seem obvious that the GDPR should thus play a significant role in the protection of genetic privacy in biobanking. Closer scrutiny, however, reveals uncertainties as to what this role can, and should, be. Three forms of uncertainty appear. First, uncertainty appears as to the relationship between data protection law and the protection of privacy. Accordingly, it remains unclear as to the degree to which the GDPR can be looked at to protect privacy. Second, even if the function of the GDPR in relation to privacy generally were clear, uncertainty appears in relation to the degree to which the GDPR can function to protect genetic privacy. Finally, uncertainty appears as to whether the GDPR can provide a suitable framework for the protection of genetic privacy in biobanking.

Against this background, this book engaged in a detailed consideration of the function, problems and opportunities presented by the GDPR as a framework for the protection of genetic privacy in biobanks and biobanking in Europe. In doing so, the book presented the following argument: European data protection law, under the GDPR, can and ought to be looked at to play a central role in the protection of genetic privacy in biobanking in Europe. In the first instance, the substantive framework presented by the GDPR already offers an impressive baseline level of protection for genetic privacy. In turn, whilst numerous problems with this baseline standard of protection

Protecting Genetic Privacy in Biobanking through Data Protection Law. Dara Hallinan, Oxford University Press (2021). © Dara Hallinan.
DOI: 10.1093/oso/9780192896476.003.0011

are identifiable, the GDPR offers the normative flexibility to accommodate solutions to these problems, as well as the procedural mechanisms to facilitate the realisation of solutions.

The argument began with the identification of the range of legitimate genetic privacy rights and other interests in biobanking. At a fundamental level, five different types of legitimate genetic privacy right held by research subjects are identifiable. These include: an information privacy right to restrict states of access in relation to the biological sample; an information privacy right to restrict states of access in relation to associated data—genomic data as well as other forms of data; an information privacy right to choose to know one's own genetic data produced during research; an information privacy right to choose not to know one's own genetic data produced during research; and a spatial privacy right to not be informed of potentially harmful genetic information produced during research. In turn, each of these rights might legitimately be claimed by two other rights holders: genetic relatives and genetic groups. These genetic privacy rights occupy space alongside a series of other types of legitimate interest engaged by biobanking. These include a range of interests tied up with the conduct and outcome of research—such as the interests of researchers—as well as third-party non-research interests connected with access to biobanking substances—such as the interests of law enforcement.

A baseline standard of protection for genetic privacy in biobanking—against which other laws could be compared and evaluated—was then established by considering the protection provided to genetic privacy in biobanking under the international framework. There is a vibrant international regulatory landscape, consisting of numerous relevant instruments, from several different organisations. Across these instruments, a range of substantive principles of genetic privacy protection is identifiable. This includes seven common principles—principles identifiable in a majority of international instruments—and six emerging principles—principles identifiable in a majority of biobank specific instruments. Although the set of identifiable principles is impressive, however, a close look at the international framework reveals weaknesses with the protection it provides. Accordingly, whilst the set of identified principles might certainly be regarded as providing a baseline standard of protection, these principles should not be considered as outlining a flawless system of protection.

Following the analysis of the international framework, one key question remained to be answered prior to looking at the GDPR in detail: is there any need to consider EU data protection law as a framework for the protection of genetic privacy in biobanking in Europe at all? In the first instance, a thought experiment was conducted in which the European legal landscape regarding the protection of genetic privacy in biobanking *excluding* data protection law was analysed—including an analysis of EU, Estonian, German, and UK law. This analysis shows a landscape riddled with inadequacies and problems—each system analysed, for example, fails, on multiple counts, to deliver the baseline standard of protection as outlined by the international framework. In turn, a superficial look at the scope and function of EU data protection law under the GDPR highlights its relevance in providing a resolution to each of the problems identified with other approaches.

The argument then moved forward with an in-depth look at the applicability of the GDPR in relation to biobanking. In terms of scope, the GDPR will apply to almost all types of biobanking activity. The sole exception is its inapplicability to law enforcement efforts to access and use biobanking substances. The GDPR will also apply to almost all substances used in biobanking—including biological samples—regardless of the form of link these retain with a research subject. The sole exception is its inapplicability to scientific conclusions. In terms of classification, the GDPR will regard both biobanks and external researchers as data controllers and will regard research subjects and their genetic relatives—although not genetic groups—as data subjects. The GDPR will also regard all types of substances processed in biobanking, which can qualify as personal data, as sensitive personal data—as either genetic data, or as data concerning health, or as both.

In terms of substance, the GDPR outlines an extensive and impressive system of protection—at first glance easily more extensive than anything evident in the international framework or in alternative EU or European state approaches. This system can be usefully broken down into seven types of substantive principle: oversight principles—including ongoing oversight of biobanking actors by DPAs; legitimate processing principles—including an obligation on biobanking actors, where possible and relevant, to obtain consent from research subjects prior to engaging in processing; data subject rights—including rights to withdraw consent and rights to access personal data processed by biobanking actors; data controller obligations—including obligations to process data only for specified purposes and obligations to process personal data accurately; international transfer provisions—including obligations on biobanking controllers to only transfer personal data outside the EU when adequate protection in third countries is ensured; sanctions provisions—including the possibility for DPAs to hand down huge administrative fines; and derogation provisions—including broad possibilities for European states to deviate from aspects of protection foreseen under the GDPR.

Simply as the GDPR appears to offer an extensive system of protection, however, does not mean that the GDPR should immediately be accepted as a legal panacea for the protection of genetic privacy in biobanking in Europe. Accordingly, a detailed critical analysis of the GDPR's approach to the protection of genetic privacy in biobanking was conducted. A first step in this analysis revealed a daunting set of twenty-three different problems, of eight different types, with the GDPR's approach. Problems are identifiable in relation to: the structure of the GDPR—in particular regarding the scope of the GDPR; the range of research subject genetic privacy rights protected; the protection offered to genetic relatives and genetic groups; the standard of substantive protection offered—to rights and rights holders which are protected; the technical suitability of the GDPR's substantive provisions to biobanking; the disproportionate impact the GDPR's provisions may have on other legitimate interests in biobanking—in particular, interests tied up with the conduct and outcome of research; the practical applicability of the GDPR's provisions to biobanking; and the degree to which the GDPR harmonises protection across European states.

The number and range of problems identifiable appear ominous indeed for the prospects of the GDPR as a framework for the protection of genetic privacy in biobanking. However, it is not the case that any specific number, or form, of problems need constitute a critical issue for the utility of the GDPR. In this regard, the argument concluded with a subsequent analysis of the severity of each problem. The analysis shows that most identifiable problems also exhibit features which will ameliorate the severity of their impact. As a result, there are only very few problems identifiable which, strictly speaking, require resolution for the GDPR to be regarded as a suitable framework for the protection of genetic privacy in biobanking. In turn, all problems which would either strictly require resolution, or would ideally be resolved, are subject to resolution. In all cases, the GDPR presents options for the resolution of problems either through its internal interpretation and adaptation mechanisms, or through EU or national law operating in parallel, or through both approaches.

This book presented the case for the GDPR as a viable and useful framework for the protection of genetic privacy in biobanking. We are, however, still in the early stages of the interaction between the GDPR and biobanking. Whether this potential is realised will now depend on the decisions and actions of stakeholders in the biobanking space. In the first instance, the choices regulators—particularly DPAs, the EDPB, and governments—make in adapting, and derogating from, the GDPR will be definitive as to how the law functions moving forward. Their choices—perhaps following some of the advice in this book—have the potential to optimise, or undermine, the GDPR as a system for the protection of genetic privacy in biobanking. In turn, the biobanking community have choices as to how they perceive, and operationalise, the GDPR. They may choose to embrace the GDPR, and establish a healthy culture of compliance in which the potential of the law may best be realised, or they may choose to oppose the GDPR, and establish a culture of resistance in which realisation of potential is impossible. Time will tell.

References

Albers, M., 'Rechtsrahmen und Rechtsprobleme bei Biobanken' (2013) *Medizinrecht* 31(8) 483.

Albers, M., 'Realizing the Complexity of Data Protection', in Serge Gutwirth, Ronald Leenes, and Paul De Hert (eds.), *Reloading Data Protection* (Springer 2014) 213.

Albrecht, J. P., *Starke Verbraucherrechte und mehr Wettbewerb: EU-Datenschutzreform* (Jan Phillip Albrecht, 21 December 2015) <https://www.janalbrecht.eu/2015/12/2015-12-21-starke-verbraucherrechte-und-mehr-wettbewerb/> accessed 11 December 2019.

Allen, J., 'Group Consent and the Nature of Group Belonging: Genomics, Race and Indigenous Rights' (2010) *Journal of Law, Information and Science* 20(2) 28.

Almqvist, E., Bloch, M., Brinkman, R., et al., 'A Worldwide Assessment of the Frequency Of Suicide, Suicide Attempts, or Psychiatric Hospitalisation after Predictive Testing for Huntington Disease' (1999) *American Journal of Human Genetics* 64(5) 1293.

Andorno, R., 'The Right Not to Know: An Autonomy Based Approach' (2004) *Law, Ethics and Medicine* 30 435.

Andorno, R., 'The Oviedo Convention: A European Legal Framework at the Intersection of Human Rights and Health Law' (2005) *Journal of International Biotechnology Law* 2 133.

Andorno, R., 'Global Bioethics at UNESCO: In Defence of the Universal Declaration on Bioethics and Human Rights' (2007) *Journal of Medical Ethics* 33(3) 150.

Annas, G., 'Genetic Prophecy and Genetic Privacy: Can We Prevent the Dream from Becoming a Nightmare?' (1995) *American Journal of Public Health* 85(9) 1196.

Annas, G., 'The Legacy of the Nuremberg Doctors' Trial to American Bioethics and Human Rights' (2009) *Journal of Law, Science and Technology* 10(1) 19.

Anthony, S., 'Harvard Cracks DNA Storage, Crams 700 Terabytes of Data into a Single Gram' *Extremetech* (17 August 2012) <http://www.extremetech.com/extreme/134672-harvard-cracks-dna-storage-crams-700-terabytes-of-data-into-a-single-gram> accessed 11 December 2019.

Arampatzis, A., Papagiouvanni, I., Anestakis, D., et al., 'A Classification and Comparative Study of European Biobanks: An Analysis of Biobanking Activity and Its Contribution to Scientific Progress' (2016) *Archives of Medicine* 8(3:6) <http://www.archivesofmedicine.com/medicine/a-classification-and-comparative-study-of-european-biobanks-an-analysis-of-biobanking-activity-andits-contribution-to-scientific-p.pdf> accessed 29 November 2019.

Arnason, G., Icelandic Biobank: A Report for GenBenefit (Report, 2007).

Article 29 Working Party, Working Document: Transfers of personal data to third countries: Applying Article 26 (2) of the EU Data Protection Directive to Binding Corporate Rules for International Data Transfers (Policy, 11639/02/EN WP 74, 2003).

Article 29 Working Party, Opinion 5/2004 on unsolicited communications for marketing purposes under Article 13 of Directive 2002/58/EC, 11601/EN WP 90, 2004).

Article 29 Working Party, 'Working Document on Genetic Data' (Working Document, WP 91, 2004).

Article 29 Working Party, Working document on a common interpretation of Article 26(1) of Directive 95/46/EC of 24 October 1995 (Policy, 2093/05/EN WP 114, 2005).

Article 29 Working Party, Opinion 4/2007 on the concept of personal data (Policy, 01248/07/EN WP 136, 2007).

Article 29 Working Party, Working Document on the Processing of Personal Data Relating to Health in Electronic Health Records (EHR) (Policy, 00323/07/EN WP 131, 2007).

Article 29 Working Party, Opinion 1/2010 on the concepts of "controller" and "processor" (Policy, 00264/10/EN WP 169, 2010).

Article 29 Working Party, Opinion 3/2010 on the principle of accountability (Policy, 00062/10/EN WP 173, 2010).

Article 29 Working Party, Opinion 15/2011 on the definition of consent (Policy, 01197/11/EN WP187, 2011).

Article 29 Working Party, Opinion 03/2013 on purpose limitation (Policy, 00569/13/EN WP 203, 2013).

Article 29 Working Party, Guidelines on the Implementation of the Court of Justice of the European Union Judgment on 'Google Spain and inc v. Agencia Española de Protección De Datos (AEPD) and Mario Costeja González' C-131/12 (Policy, 14/EN WP 225, 2014).

Article 29 Working Party, Opinion 05/2014 on Anonymisation Techniques (Policy, 0829/14/EN WP 216, 2014).

Article 29 Working Party, Opinion 06/2014 on the notion of legitimate interests of the data controller under Article 7 of Directive 95/46/EC (Policy, 844/14/EN WP 217, 2014).

Article 29 Working Party, 'Health Data in Apps and Devices', Annex to Communication between the Article 29 Working Party and DG Connect (Policy, 2015).

Article 29 Working Party, Opinion 01/2016 on the EU–US Privacy Shield draft adequacy decision (Policy, 16/EN WP 238, 2016).

Article 29 Working Party, Guidelines on Data Protection Officers ('DPOs') (Policy, 16/EN WP 243 rev.01, 2016 (revised 2017)).

Article 29 Working Party, Guidelines for Identifying a Controller or Processor's Lead Supervisory Authority (Policy, 16/EN WP 244, 2016).

Article 29 Working Party, Guidelines on the right to data portability (Policy, 16/EN WP 242, 2016).

Article 29 Working Party, Adequacy Referential (Policy, 18/EN WP 254 rev.01, 2017 (revised 2018)).

Article 29 Working Party, EU–US Privacy Shield: First annual Joint Review (Policy, 17/EN WP 255, 2017).

Article 29 Working Party, Guidelines on the application and setting of administrative fines for the purposes of the Regulation 2016/679 (Policy, 17/EN WP 253 2017).

Article 29 Working Party, Guidelines on Data Protection Impact Assessment (DPIA) and determining whether processing is 'likely to result in a high risk' for the purposes of Regulation 2016/679 (Policy, 17/EN WP 248, 2017).

Article 29 Working Party, Guidelines on transparency under Regulation 2016/679 (Policy, 17/EN WP260 rev.01, 2017 (updated 2018)).

Article 29 Working Party, Guidelines on Personal data breach notification under Regulation 2016/679 (Policy, 18/EN WP250rev.01, 2017 (revised 2018)).

Article 29 Working Party, Working Document setting up a table with the elements and principles to be found in Binding Corporate Rules (Policy, 18/EN WP 256 rev.01, 2017 (revised 2018)).

Asslaber, M., and Zatloukal, K., 'Biobanks: Transnational, European and Global Networks' (2007) *Briefings in Functional Genomics and Proteomics* 6(3) 193.

BBMRI-ERIC, *About Us* (Information Sheet, 2019) <http://www.bbmri-eric.eu/BBMRI-ERIC/about-us/> accessed 28 November 2019.

BBMRI-ERIC, *Home Page* (Home Page, 2019) <http://www.bbmri-eric.eu/> accessed 10 June 2020.

BBMRI-ERIC, Material Transfer Policy and Agreement (Policy, 2012) <http://www.bbmri-eric.eu/wp-content/uploads/Sample-Data-and-Material-Transfer-Agreement.pdf> accessed 28 November 2019.

BBMRI-ERIC, The European Research Infrastructure for BioBanking and Biomolecular Resources Partner Charter (Policy, 2014) <http://www.bbmri-eric.eu/wp-content/uploads/2016/08/Partner-Charter-approved-AoM2.pdf> 29 November 2019.

Beier, K., and Lenk, C., 'Biobanking Strategies and Regulative Approaches in the EU: Recent Perspectives' (2015) *Journal of Biorepository Science for Applied Medicine* 3 69.

Bentzen, H.B., and Høstmælinge, N., 'Balancing Protection and Free Movement of Personal Data: The New European Union General Data Protection Regulation' (2019) *Annals of Internal Medicine* 170(5) 335.

Beyleveld, D., 'An Overview of Directive 95/46/EC in Relation to Medical Research', in Deryck Beyleveld, David Townend, Ségolène Rouillé-Mirza, and Jessica Wright (eds.), *The Data Protection Directive and Medical Research Across Europe* (Ashgate 2004) 5.

Beyleveld, D., 'The Duty to Provide Information to the Data Subject: Articles 10 and 11 of Directive 95/46/EC', in Deryck Beyleveld, David Townend, Ségolène Rouillé-Mirza and Jessica Wright (eds.), *The Data Protection Directive and Medical Research Across Europe* (Ashgate 2004) 68.

Beyleveld, D., and Brownsword, R., *Consent in the Law* (Hart 2007).

Beyleveld, D., and Histed, E., 'Betrayal of Confidence in the Court of Appeal' (2000) *Medical Law International* 4(3&4) 277.

Beyleveld, D., Grubb, A., Townend, D., et al., 'The UK's Implementation of Directive 95/46/EC', in Deryck Beyleveld, David Townend, Ségolène Rouillé-Mirza, and Jessica Wright (eds.), *Implementation of the Data Protection Directive in Relation to Medical Research in Europe* (Ashgate 2004) 403.

Biobank Act 2012. Unofficial English Translation <http://www.finlex.fi/fi/laki/kaannokset/2012/en20120688.pdf> accessed 4 December 2019.

Bjornsson, H., Sigurdsson, M., Fallin, M. D., et al, 'Intra-Individual Change over Time in DNA Methylation with Familial Clustering' (2009) *Journal of the American Medical Association* 299(24) 2877.

Bledsoe, M., Wright, E., and McGuire, A., 'Return of Research Results from Genomic Biobanks: Cost Matters' (2013) *Genetic Medicine* 15(2) 103.

Boehm, F., 'Information Sharing in the Area of Freedom, Security and Justice: Towards a Common Standard for Data Exchange Between Agencies and EU Information Systems', in Serge Gutwirth, Ronald Leenes, Paul De Hert, and Yves Poullet (eds.), *European Data Protection: In Good Health?* (Springer 2012) 143.

Boehm, F., 'Assessing the New Instruments in EU–US Data Protection Law for Law Enforcement and Surveillance Purposes' (2016) *European Data Protection Law Review* 3 178.

Bovenberg, J., Meulenkamp, T., Smets, E., et al., 'Your Biobank, Your Doctor? The Right to Full Disclosure of Population Biobank Findings' (2009) *Genomics, Society and Policy* 5(1) 55.

Budimir, D., Polašek, O., Marušić, A., et al., 'Ethical Aspects of Human Biobanks: A Systemic Review' (2011) *Croatian Medical Journal* 52(3) 262.

Branicki, W., Liu, F., van Duijn, K., et al., 'Model-Based Prediction of Human Hair Color Using DNA Variants' (2011) *Human Genetics* 129 453.

Brown, I., Brown, L., and Korff, D., 'Using NHS Patient Data for Research Without Consent' (2010) *Law Innovation and Technology* 2(2) 219.

Brownsword, R., and Wale, J., 'The Right to Know and the Right Not to Know Revisited: Part One' (2017) *Asian Bioethics Review* 9 3.

Bundesärztekammer, Musterberufsordnung für die in Deutschland tätigen Ärztinnen und Ärzte (Policy, 1997 (updated 2018)).

Bygrave, L., *Data Protection Law: Approaching Its Rationale, Logic and Limits* (Kluwer 2002).

Bygrave, L., 'The Body as Data? Biobank Regulation via the "Back Door" of Data Protection Law' (2010) *Law, Innovation and Technology* 2(1) 1.

Bygrave, L., 'Data Protection by Design and by Default: Deciphering the EU's Legislative Requirements' (2017) *Oslo Law Review* 4(2) 105.

Cadigan, J., '"That's a Good Question": University Researchers' Views on Ownership and Retention of Human Genetic Specimens' (2011) *Genetics in Medicine* 13 569.

Cambon-Thomsen, A., Rial-Sebbag, E., and Knoppers, B., 'Trends in Ethical and Legal Frameworks for the Use of Human Biobanks' (2007) *European Respiratory Journal* 30 373.

Canavan Foundation, 'How Canavan Disease Is Inherited' (Canavan Foundation, 2019) <http://www.canavanfoundation.org/how_canavan_disease_is_inherited> accessed 11 December 2019.

Caulfield, T., Upshure, R., and Daar, A., 'DNA Databanks and Consent: A Suggested Policy Option Involving an Authorization Model' (2003) *BMC Medical Ethics* 4(1) <https://bmcmedethics.biomedcentral.com/articles/10.1186/1472-6939-4-1> accessed 11 December 2019.

Cave, E., 'The Ill-Informed: Consent to Medical Treatment and the Therapeutic Exception' (2017) *Common Law World Review* 46(2) 140.

Chadwick, R., Levitt, M., and Shickle, D., 'The Right to Know and the Right Not to Know: The Emerging Debate', in Ruth Chadwick, Mairi Levitt, and Darren Shickle (eds.), *The Right to Know and the Right Not to Know: Genetic Privacy and Responsibility* (Cambridge University Press 2014).

Chassang, G., 'The Impact of the EU General Data Protection Regulation on Scientific Research' (2017) *Ecancermedicalscience* 11(709) <https://www.ncbi.nlm.nih.gov/pmc/articles/PMC5243137/> accessed 11 December 2019.

Chico, V., 'The Impact of the General Data Protection Regulation on Health Research' (2018) *British Medical Bulletin* 128 109.

Christensen, L. , Colciago, A., Etro, F., et al., The Impact of the Data Protection Regulation in the EU (International Think-tank on Innovation and Competition INTERTIC Report, 2013).

Church, G., Gao, Y., and Kosuri, S., 'Next Generation Digital Information Storage in DNA' (2012) *Science* 337(6102) 1628.

Cierniak, J., and Niehaus, H., 'StGB § 203 Verletzung von Privatgeheimnisse', in Wolfgang Joecks and Klaus Miebach (eds.), *Münchener Kommentar zur Strafprozessordnung* (3rd edn, Beck 2012) <https://beck-online.beck.de/?vpath=bibdata/komm/MuekoStGB/cont/MuekoStGB%2Ehtm> accessed 11 December 2019.

Clifford, D., and Ausloos, J., 'Data Protection and the Role of Fairness' (2018) *Yearbook of European Law* 1.

Cobb, M., '1953: When Genes Became "Information"' (2013) *Cell* 153(1) 503.

Cohen, I., Atlan, H., and Efroni, S., 'Genetics as Explanation: Limits to the Human Genome Project' (2016) *eLS* <http://onlinelibrary.wiley.com/doi/10.1002/9780470015902.a0005881.pub3/full> accessed 28 November 2019.

Collins, F., 'What We Do and Don't Know About "Race", "Ethnicity", Genetics and Health at the Dawn of the Genome Era' (2004) *Nature Genetics* 36 513.

Collins, F., Morgan, M., and Patrinos, A., 'The Human Genome Project: Lessons from Large-Scale Biology' (2003) *Science* 300 286.

Commission of the European Communities, Amended proposal for a Council Directive on the protection of individuals with regard to the processing of personal data and on the free movement of such data (Policy, COM (92) 422 final – SYN 287, OJ C311/03, 1992).

Commission Nationale de l'Informatique et des Libertés, Privacy Impact Assessment (PIA): Knowledge Bases (Policy, 2018).

Commission Nationale de l'Informatique et des Libertés, Privacy Impact Assessment (PIA): Methodology (Policy, 2018).

Costa, L., and Poullet, Y., 'Privacy and the Regulation of 2012' (2012) *Computer Law and Security Review* 28(3) 254.

Craig, J., 'Complex Diseases: Research and Applications' (2008) *Nature Education* 1(1) 184.

Curren, L., and Kaye, J., 'Revoking Consent: A "Blind Spot" in Data Protection Law?' (2010) *Computer Law and Security Review* 26(3) 273.

Custers, B., van der Hof, S., Schermer, B., et al., 'Informed Consent in Social Media: The Gap between User Expectations and EU Personal Data Protection Law' (2013) *SCRIPTed* 10(4) 435.

D'Abramo, F., 'Biobank Research, Informed Consent and Society: Towards a New Alliance?' (2015) *Journal of Epidemiology and Community Health* 69(11) Online First: doi:10.1136/jech-2014-205215 1.

Dammann, U., 'Artikel 3', in Spiros Simitis (ed.), *Bundesdatenschutzgesetz* (Nomos 2014) 315.

Danezis, G., Domingo-Ferrer, J., and Hansen, M., Privacy and Data Protection by Design—from policy to engineering (ENISA Report, 2015).

De Hert, P., 'The Future of Privacy: Addressing Singularities to Identify Bright-Line Rules That Speak to Us' (2016) *European Data Protection Law Review* 2(4) 461.

De Hert, P. and Gutwirth, Serge, 'Privacy, Data Protection and Law Enforcement: Opacity of the Individual and Transparency of Power', in E. Claes, A. Duff, and S. Gutwirth (eds.), *Privacy and the Criminal Law* (Intersentia 2006) 61.

De Hert, P., and Papakonstantinou, V., 'The New General Data Protection Regulation: Still a Sound System for the Protection of Individuals?' (2016) *Computer Law and Security Review* 32(2) 179.

De Hert, P., and Papakonstantinou, V., 'The New Police and Criminal Justice Data Protection Directive: A First Analysis' (2016) *New Journal of European Criminal Law* 7(1) 7.

Der Landesbeauftragte für Datenschutz und Informationsfreiheit Mecklenburg-Vorpommern 'Erste Bausteine des SDM-Maßnahmenkatalogs' (Der Landesbeauftragte für Datenschutz und

Informationsfreiheit Mecklenburg-Vorpommern) <https://www.datenschutz-mv.de/datenschutz/publikationen/Erste-Bausteine-des-SDM%E2%80%93Ma%C3%9Fnahmenkatalogs/> accessed 23 June 2020.

Deutsche Gesellschaft für Medizinische Informatik, Biometrie und Epidemiologie e. V., and Gesellschaft für Datenschutz und Datensicherheit e. V., Datenschutzrechtliche Anforderungen an die medizinische Forschung unter Beru cksichtigung der EU Datenschutz-Grundverordnung (DS-GVO) (Policy, 2018).

Deutscher Ethikrat, Humanbiobanken für die Forschung: Stellungnahme (Position Paper, 2010).

Dimitrova, D. and Hallinan, D., 'Bulgarian DPA Issues Multi-Million Euro Fine' *Data Protection Insider* (Karlsruhe, 5 September 2019).

Dove, A., 'The Art of Culture: Developing Cell Lines' (2014) *Science* 346(6212) 1013.

Dove, E., 'Biobanks, Data Sharing, and the Drive for a Global Privacy Governance Framework' (2015) *Journal of Law, Medicine and Ethics* 43(4) 675.

Dove, E., 'The EU General Data Protection Regulation: Implications for International Scientific Research in the Digital Era' (2018) *Journal of Law Medicine & Ethics* 46 1013.

Dove, E., and Chen, J., 'Should Consent for Data Processing Be Privileged in Health Research? A Comparative Legal Analysis' (2019) *International Data Privacy Law* 10(2) 117.

Dove, E., Chico, V., Fay, M., et al., 'Familial Genetic Risks: How Can We Better Navigate Patient Confidentiality and Appropriate Risk Disclosure to Relatives?' (2019) *Journal of Medical Ethics* 45 504.

Down's Syndrome Association, 'Home Page' (Down's Syndrome Association, 2019) <http://www.downs-syndrome.org.uk/> accessed 4 December 2019.

Dranseika, V., Piaseck, J., and Waligora, M., 'Forensic Uses of Research Biobanks: Should Donors Be Informed?' (2016) *Medicine, Health Care and Philosophy* 19 141.

Drepper, J., 'Data Protection in Biobanks from a Practical Point of View: What Must Be Taken into Account during Set-up and Operation?' (2019) *Journal of Laboratory Medicine* 43(6) 301.

Duster, T., 'A Post-Genomic Surprise. The Molecular Re-Inscription of Race in Science, Law and Medicine' (2015) *British Journal of Sociology* 66(1) 1.

Eensaar, R., 'Estonia: Ups and Downs of a Biobank Project', in Herbert Gottweis and Alan Petersen (eds.), *Biobanks: Governance in Comparative Perspective* (Routledge 2008).

Elger, B., and Caplan, A., 'Consent and Anonymisation in Research Involving Biobanks: Differing Terms and Norms Present Serious Barriers to an International Framework' (2006) *EMBO reports* 7(7) 661.

Estonian Genome Centre, Estonian Genome Centre 2001–2011 (Report, 2011) <https://www.geenivaramu.ee/sites/default/files/geenivaramu/estoniangenomecenter.pdf> 29 November 2019.

European Commission, Frequently Asked Questions Relating to Transfers of Personal Data from The EU/EEA to Third Countries (FAQs, 2009) .

European Commission, 'Adequacy decisions' (European Commission, 2019) <https://ec.europa.eu/info/law/law-topic/data-protection/international-dimension-data-protection/adequacy-decisions_en> accessed 11 December 2019.

European Commission, 'Standard Contractual Clauses' (European Commission, 2019) <https://ec.europa.eu/info/law/law-topic/data-protection/international-dimension-data-protection/standard-contractual-clauses-scc_en> accessed 11 December 2019.

European Commission, Impact Assessment Accompanying the General Data Protection Regulation (Policy, SEC(2012)72 final, 2012).

European Commission, Data protection as a pillar of citizens' empowerment and the EU's approach to the digital transition—two years of application of the General Data Protection Regulation (Communication from the Commission to the European Parliament and the Council, 2020).

European Commission's Community Research and Development Information Service, Privacy and Data Protection Impact Assessment Framework for RFID Applications (Policy, 2011).

European Data Protection Board, Guidelines 1/2018 on certification and identifying certification criteria in accordance with Articles 42 and 43 of the Regulation (Policy, 2018).

European Data Protection Board, Guidelines 2/2018 on derogations of Article 49 under Regulation 2016/679 (Policy, 2018).

European Data Protection Board, EU–US Privacy Shield—Third Annual Joint Review (Policy, 2019).

European Data Protection Board, Guidelines 4/2019 on Article 25 Data Protection by Design and by Default (Policy, 2019).

European Data Protection Board, Opinion 3/2019 concerning the Questions and Answers on the interplay between the Clinical Trials Regulation (CTR) and the General Data Protection regulation (GDPR) (art. 70.1.b)) (Policy, 2019).

European Data Protection Board, Guidelines 03/2020 on the processing of data concerning health for the purpose of scientific research in the context of the COVID-19 outbreak (Policy, 2020).

European Data Protection Board, Guidelines 05/2020 on consent under Regulation 2016/679 (Policy, 2020).

European Data Protection Supervisor, 'Accountability' (European Data Protection Supervisor, 2019) <https://edps.europa.eu/data-protection/our-work/subjects/accountability_en> accessed 11 December 2019

European Data Protection Supervisor, A Preliminary Opinion on data protection and scientific research (Policy, 2020).

Expert Group on Dealing with Ethical and Regulatory Challenges of International Biobank Research, Biobanks for Europe: A Challenge for Governance (European Commission Report, 2012).

Falkingbridge, S., *The Future of Biobanks: Regulation, Ethics, Investment and the Humanization of Drug Discovery* (Business Insight 2009).

Faundez-Zanuy, M., 'Privacy Issues on Biometric Systems' (2005) *IEEE Aerospace and Engineering Systems Magazine*, 13 February.

Faust, S., Spittika, Jan, and Wybitul, Tim, 'Milliardenbußgelder nach der DS-GVO: Ein überblick über die neuen Sanktionen bei Verstößen gegen den Datenschutz' (2016) *Zeitschrift für Datenschutz* 120.

Fears, R., Brand, H., Frackowiak, R., et al., 'Data Protection Regulation and the Promotion of Health Research: Getting the Balance Right' (2014) *QJM: An International Journal of Medicine* 107 3.

Feng, Y., Zhang, Y., Ying, C., et al., 'Nanopore-B Fourth-Generation DNA Sequencing Technology' *Genomics Proteomics Bioinformatics* 13(4), 4.

Fernández-Cañón, J. M., Granadino, B., Beltrán-Valero de Bernabé, D., et al., 'The Molecular Basis of Alkaptonuria' (1996) *Nature Genetics* 14(1) 19.

Floridi, L., 'Open Data, Data Protection and Group Privacy' (2014) *Philosophy and Technology* 27(1) 1.

Fondazione Telethon, Telethon Network of Genetic Biobanks (Information Sheet, 2019) <http://biobanknetwork.telethon.it/> accessed 28 November 2019.

Ford, D., Easton, D. F., Stratton, M., et al., 'Genetic Heterogeneity and Penetrance Analysis of the BRCA1 and BRCA2 Genes in Breast Cancer Families' (1998) *American Journal of Human Genetics* 62(3) 676.

Forsberg, J., Hansson, M., and Eriksson, S., 'Biobank Research: Who Benefits from Individual Consent?' (2011) *British Medical Journal* 343 727.

Francis, C., 'What We Do and Don't Know About"Race", "Ethnicity", Genetics and Health at the Dawn of the Genome Era' (2004) *Nature Genetics* 36 513.

Fuster, G. G., *The Emergence of Personal Data Protection as a Fundamental Right of the EU* (Springer 2014).

Gabel, J., 'Probable Cause from Probable Bonds: A Genetic Tattle Tale Based on Familial DNA' (2010) *Hasting's Women's Law Journal* 21(1) 3.

Garante, Cittadini e società dell'informazione (Policy, no. 8, 1999).

Gellert, R., 'The Article 29 Working Party's Provisional Guidelines on Data Protection Impact Assessment' (2017) *European Data Protection Law Review* 3(2) 212.

Genetic and Rare Diseases Information Center, 'Down Syndrome' (Genetic and Rare Diseases Information Center, 2019) <https://rarediseases.info.nih.gov/diseases/10247/down-syndrome#diseaseCauseSection> accessed 11 December 2019.

Genetic and Rare Diseases Information Center, 'Huntington Disease' (*Genetic and Rare Disease Center*) <https://rarediseases.info.nih.gov/diseases/6677/huntington-disease#ref_8727> accessed 27 November 2019.

Genetic and Rare Diseases Information Center 'Tay-Sachs Disease' (*Genetic and Rare Disease Center*) <https://rarediseases.info.nih.gov/diseases/7737/tay-sachs-disease/cases/50741> accessed 27 November 2019.

Genetics Home Reference, 'Down Syndrome' <https://ghr.nlm.nih.gov/condition/down-syndrome#genes> accessed 27 November 2019.

Gerards, J., 'General Issues Concerning Genetic Information', in Janneke Gerards, Aalt Heringa, and Heleen Janssen (eds.), *Genetic Discrimination and Genetic Privacy in a Comparative Perspective* (Intersentia 2005) 5.

German Ethics Council, Human Biobanks for Research: Opinion (Opinion, 2010).

Gibbons, S., 'Mapping the Regulatory Space', in Jane Kaye, Susan M. C. Gibbons, Catherine Heeney, Michael Parker, and Andrew Smart (eds.), *Governing Biobanks: Understanding the Interplay between Law and Practice* (Hart 2012), 51.

Global Alliance for Genomics and Health, Framework for Responsible Sharing of Genomic and Health-Related Data (Policy, 2014).

Goers, M., 'StPO § 81e Molekulargenetische Untersuchung', in Jürgen-Peter Graf (ed.), *Beck'scher Online-Kommentar StPO mit RiStBV und MiStra* (29th Edition, Beck 2018) <https://beck-online.beck.de/?vpath=bibdata/komm/beckok_29_BandStPO/cont/beckok.StPO%2Ehtm> accessed 11 December 2019.

Goisauf, M., Martin, G., and Bentzen, H. B., 'Data in Question: A Survey of European Biobank Professionals on Ethical, Legal and Societal Challenges of Biobank Research' (2019) *PLOS ONE* 14(9) <https://journals.plos.org/plosone/article/file?id=10.1371/journal.pone.0221496&type=printable> accessed 5 June 2020.

Gostin, L., 'Genetic Privacy' (1995) *Journal of Law, Medicine and Ethics* 23 320.

Gottweis, H., and Lauss, G, 'Biobank Governance: Heterogenous Modes of Ordering and Democratization' (2012) *Journal of Community Genetics* 3(2) 61.

Government of Australia, Full Australian Government Response to ALRC Report 96 (Policy, 2005)

Grady, C., Eckstein, L., Berkman, B., et al., 'Broad Consent for Research with Biological Samples: Workshop Conclusions' (2015) *American Journal of Bioethics* 15(9) 34.

Green, P. 'Against a Whole-Genome Shotgun' (1997) *Genome Research* 7 410.

Griffiths, P., and Stotz, K., *Genetics and Philosophy: An Introduction* (Cambridge University Press 2013).

Gronek, P., Wieliński, D., and Gronek, J., 'Genetic and Non-Genetic Determinants of Aggression in Combat Sports' (2015) *Open Life Sciences* 10 7.

Grubb, A., 'Breach of Confidence: Anonymised Information' (2000) *Medical Law Review* 8(1) 115.

Gürses, S., Troncoso, C., and Diaz, C. (2011) *Engineering Privacy by Design* (Research Paper, 2011) <https://securewww.esat.kuleuven.be/cosic/publications/article-1542.pdf> accessed 11 December 2019.

Gutwirth, S., Gellert, R., Bellanova, Rocco, et al., Legal, social, economic and ethical conceptualisations of privacy and data protection (PRESCIENT Project Deliverable, 1, 2011).

Gymrek, M., McGuire, A. L., Golan, D., et al., 'Identifying Personal Genomes by Surname Inference' (2013) *Science* 339(6117) 321.

Haier, J., 'Gegenwärtige rechtliche Rahmenbedingungen für den Betrieb und die Nutzung von Biobanken. Teil 1: Rechtsgrundlage' (2013) *Der Chirurg* 84(9) 785.

Haier, J., 'Gegenwärtige rechtliche Rahmenbedingungen für den Betrieb und die Nutzung von Biobanken. Teil 2: Datenschutz und Informierte Einwiligung' (2013) *Der Chirurg* 84(10) 892.

Haier, J., 'Gegenwärtige rechtliche Rahmenbedingungen für den Betrieb und die Nutzung von Biobanken. Teil 3: Eigentum und Nutzungsrechte' (2013) *Der Chirurg* 85(10) 918.

Hallinan, D., 'Broad Consent under the GDPR: an Optimistic Perspective on a Bright Future' (2020) *Life Sciences, Society and Policy* 16(1) 1 <https://lsspjournal.biomedcentral.com/track/pdf/10.1186/s40504-019-0096-3> accessed 19 June 2020.

Hallinan, D., 'The Genomic Data Deficit: On the Need to Inform Research Subjects of the Informational Content of their Genomic Sequence Data in Consent for Genomic Research' (2020) *Computer Law and Security Review* 37 <https://www.sciencedirect.com/science/article/pii/S0267364920300327> accessed 23 June 2020.

Hallinan, D, 'Biobank Oversight and Sanctions Under the General Data Protection Regulation', in Santa Slokenberga, Olga Tzortzatou, and Jane Reichel (eds.), *GDPR and Biobanking: Individual Rights, Public Interest and Research Regulation across Europe* (Springer 2021) 121.

Hallinan, D., 'Article 89', in Franziska Boehm and Mark Cole (eds.), *GDPR Commentary* (Elgar Forthcoming 2021).

Hallinan, D., and De Hert, P., 'Many Have It Wrong: Samples Do Contain Personal Data: The Data Protection Regulation as a Superior Framework to Protect Donor Interests in Biobanking and Genomic Research', in Brent Mittelstadt and Luciano Floridi (eds.), *The Ethics of Biomedical Big Data* (Springer, 2016) 119.

Hallinan, D., and De Hert, P., 'Genetic Classes and Genetic Categories: Protecting Genetic Groups Through Data Protection Law', in Linnet Taylor, Luciano Floridi, and Bart van der Sloot (eds.), *Group Privacy* (Springer 2017) 175.

Hallinan, D., and Friedewald, M., 'Open Consent, Biobanking and Data Protection Law: Can Open Consent be "Informed" under the Forthcoming Data Protection Regulation?' (2015) *Life Sciences, Society and Policy 11*(1) <https://lsspjournal.springeropen.com/track/pdf/10.1186/s40504-014-0020-9?site=lsspjournal.springeropen.com> accessed 29 November 2019.

Hallinan, D., and Gellert, R., 'The Concept of "Information": An Invisible Problem in the GDPR' (2020) *Scripted* 17(2) 269.

Hallinan, D., and Martin, N., 'Fundamental Rights, the Normative Keystone of DPIA' (2020) *European Data Protection Law Review* 6(2) 178.

Hallinan, D., and Zuiderveen Borgesius, F., 'Opinions Can Be Incorrect (In Our Opinion)! On Data Protection Law's Accuracy Principle' (2019) *International Data Privacy Law* 10(1) 1.

Harbinja, E., 'Does the EU Data Protection Regime Protect Post-Mortem Privacy and What Could Be the Potential Alternatives?' (2013) *Scripted* 10(1) 19.

Hashiyada, M., 'Development of Biometric DNA Ink for Authentication Security' (2004) *Tohoku Journal of Experimental Medicine* 204 109.

Heeney, C., 'Dynamic Networks of Practice', in Jane Kaye, Susan M. C. Gibbons, Catherine Heeney, Michael Parker, and Andrew Smart (eds.), *Governing Biobanks: Understanding the Interplay between Law and Practice* (Hart 2012) 94.

Health and Social Care, NHS Research Scotland, Health and Care Research Wales, NHS Health Research Authority, Governance arrangements for research ethics committees: 2020 edition (Policy, 2020).

Heatherly, R., 'Privacy and Security within Biobanking: The Role of Information Technology' (2016) *Journal of Law, Medicine & Ethics* 44 156.

Her Majesty's Government and the Association of British Insurers, Code on Genetic Testing and Insurance (Code of Practice, 2018).

Hewitt, R., and Watson P., 'Defining Biobank' (2013) *Biopreservation and Biobanking* 11(5) 309.

Hewitt, R., 'Biobanking: The Foundation of Personalized Medicine' (2011) *Current Opinion in Oncology* 23 112.

Hildebrandt, M., and Tielemans, L., 'Data Protection by Design and Technology Neutral Law' (2013) *Computer Law and Security Review* 29 509.

Hirtzlin, I., Dubreuil, C., Préaubert, N., et al., 'An Empirical Survey on Biobanking of Human Genetic Material and Data in Six EU Countries' (2003) *European Journal of Human Genetics* 11 475.

Hoppe, N., 'Privacy Laws and Biobanking in Germany' (2016) *Journal of Law, Medicine & Ethics* 44(4) 35.

Hu, F., 'Globalization of Diabetes' (2011) *Diabetes Care 34* 1249.

Human Genes Research Act 2000 list of amendments unofficial English translation <https://www.riigiteataja.ee/en/eli/531102013003/consolide> accessed 11 December 2019.

Human Genome Organisation, 'Summary of Principles Agreed at the First International Strategy Meeting on Human Genome Sequencing' (1996) <http://www.casimir.org.uk/storyfiles/64.0.summary_of_bermuda_principles.pdf> accessed 28 November 2019.

Human Tissue Authority, Code of Practice 5: Disposal of human tissue (Policy, 2014).

Human Tissue Authority, Guidance on Relevant Material (Policy, 2014).

Human Tissue Authority, Code of Practice 8: Import and export of human bodies, body parts and tissue (Policy, 2014).

Human Tissue Authority, Code of Practice A: Guiding principles and the fundamental principle of consent (Policy, 2017).

Human Tissue Authority, Code of Practice B: Post-Mortem Examination (Policy, 2017).

Human Tissue Authority, Code of Practice E: Research (Policy, 2017).

HumGen International, 'GenBiblio: Database of Laws and Policies' (*HumGen International,* 2019) <http://www.humgen.org/> accessed 5 December 2019

Hummel, M., and Krawczak, M., 'Biobanken im Spannungsfeld zwischen Forschung und Gesellschaft' (2007) *Information Technology* 49(6) 335.

Husa, J., 'Classification of Legal Families Today: Is It Time for a Memorial Hymn?' (2004) *Revue Internationale de Droit Comparé* 1 11.

Ienca, M., Scheibner, J., Ferretti, A. et al., How the General Data Protection Regulation changes the rules for scientific research Study (Report, ETH Zürich Research Collection, 2019).

IGSR, 'IGSR and the 1000 Genomes Project' <http://www.1000genomes.org/> accessed 28 November 2019.

Ilkilic, I. 'Coming to Grips with Genetic Exceptionalism: Roots and Reach of an Explanatory Model' (2009) *Medicine Studies* 1 131.

Illumina, HiSeq X Ten Specification Sheet (Information Sheet, 2016) <http://www.illumina.com/content/dam/illumina-marketing/documents/products/datasheets/datasheet-hiseq-x-ten.pdf> accessed 28 November 2019.

Information Commissioner's Office, 'Data protection impact assessments' (Information Commissioner's Office) <https://ico.org.uk/for-organisations/guide-to-data-protection/guide-to-the-general-data-protection-regulation-gdpr/accountability-and-governance/data-protection-impact-assessments/> accessed 11 December 2019.

Information Commissioner's Office, 'Principle (d): Accuracy' (ICO, 2019) <https://ico.org.uk/for-organisations/guide-to-data-protection/guide-to-the-general-data-protection-regulation-gdpr/principles/accuracy/> accessed 11 December 2019.

Instituto di Recerche Farmacologiche Mario Negri, 'Biological Resources Centre' (Instituto di Recerche Farmacologiche Mario Negri, 2019) <https://www.marionegri.it/eng/biological-resources-center> accessed 11 December 2019.

International Standards Organisation, Information Technology—Vocabulary—Part 1: Fundamental Terms (Policy, ISO 2382-1, 1993 (Revised by ISO/IEC 2382-1, 2015)).

Jain, A., Ross, A. and Prabhakar, S., 'An Introduction to Biometric Recognition' (2004) *IEEE Transactions on Circuits and Systems for Video Technology* 14(1) 4.

Johnston, C., and Kaye, J., 'Does the UK Biobank Have a Legal Obligation to Feedback Individual Findings to Participants?' (2004) *Medical Law Review* 12(3) 239.

Joint Committee on Medical Genetics, Consent and confidentiality in clinical genetic practice: Guidance on genetic testing and sharing genetic information (Policy, 2nd edn, 2011) viii.

Jorde, L., and Wooding, S., 'Genetic Variation, Classification and "Race"' (2004) *Nature Genetics* 36 28.

Joyce, K., Mammo, D., Siegel, M., et al., 'Policy Implications for Familial Searching' (2011) *Investigative Genetics* 2(22) <https://www.ncbi.nlm.nih.gov/pmc/articles/PMC3253037/pdf/2041-2223-2-22.pdf> accessed 5 December 2019.

Juengst, E., 'Groups as Gatekeepers to Genomic Research: Conceptually Confusing, Morally Hazardous and Practically Useless' (1998) *Kennedy Institute of Ethics Journal* 8 183.

Karsten, J., Reinert, S., Helge, J., et al., 'Ethical Endgames: Broad Consent for Narrow Interests; Open Consent for Closed Minds' (2011) *Cambridge Quarterly of Healthcare Ethics* 20 572.

Kaur, G., and Dufour, J., 'Cell Lines: Valuable Tools or Useless Artefacts' (2012) *Spermatogenesis* 2(1) 1.

Kaye, J., 'Do We Need a Uniform Regulatory System for Biobanks across Europe?' (2006) *European Journal of Human Genetics* 14 245.

Kaye, J., 'Police Collection and Access to DNA Samples' (2006) *Genomics, Society and Policy* 2(1) 16.

Kaye, J., 'Embedding Biobanks in a Changing Context', in Jane Kaye, Susan M. C. Gibbons, Catherine Heeney, Michael Parker, and Andrew Smart (eds.), *Governing Biobanks: Understanding the Interplay between Law and Practice* (Hart 2012).

Kaye, J., Bell, J, Briceno, L., et al., 'Biobank Report: United Kingdom' (2016) *Journal of Law, Medicine & Ethics* 44(4, pt 2) 96.

Kaye, J., Helgason, H., Nõmper, A., et al. 'Population Genetic Databases: A Comparative Analysis of the Law in Iceland, Sweden, Estonia and the UK' (2004) *TRAMES: A Journal of the Humanities and Social Sciences* 8(1/2) 15.

Kaye, J., Whitley, E., Lund, D., et al, 'Dynamic Consent: A Patient Interface for Twenty-First Century Research Networks' (2015) *European Journal of Human Genetics* 23(2) 141.

Kayser, M., and Schneider, P. M., 'DNA-Based Prediction of Human Externally Visible Characteristics in Forensics: Motivations, Scientific Challenges, and Ethical Considerations' (2009) *Forensic Science International Genetics* 3(3) 154.

Keis, A., 'Biobanking in Estonia' (2016) *Journal of Law, Medicine & Ethics* 44(4, pt 1) 20.

Kellis, M., Wold, B., Snyder M., et al., 'Defining Functional DNA Elements in the Human Genome' (2014) *Proceedings of the National Academy of Sciences of the United States of America* 111(17) 6131.

Kersten, J., 'Biobanken sind zu wichtig, um nicht geregelt zu sein' (LMU Medizinrecht Blog Interview, 13 April 2015) <https://www.uni-muenchen.de/forschung/news/2015/kersten_interview_biobanken.html> accessed 11 December 2019.

Knoppers, B. M., Joly, Y., Simard, J., et al., 'The Emergence of an Ethical Duty to Disclose Genetic Research Results: International Perspectives' (2006) *European Journal of Human Genetics* 14 1170.

Konferenz der unabhängigen Datenschutzaufsichtsbehörden des Bundes und der Länder, Konzept der unabhängigen Datenschutzaufsichtsbehörden des Bundes und der Länder zur Bußgeldzumessung in Verfahren gegen Unternehmen (Policy, 2019).

Konferenz der unabhängigen Datenschutzbehörden des Bundes und der Länder, Das Standard Datenschutzmodell: Eine Methode zur Datenschutzberatung und -prüfung auf der Basis einheitlicher Gewährleistungsziele (Policy, Version 2.0b, 2018).

Koops, B., and Leenes, R., 'Privacy Regulation Cannot Be Hardcoded: A Critical Comment on the "Privacy by Design" Provision in Data-Protection Law' (2014) *International Review of Law, Computers & Technology* 28(2) 159.

Koops, B., and Schellekens, M., 'Forensic DNA Phenotyping: Regulatory Issues' (2008) *Columbia Science and Technology Law Review* 9 158.

Kosseim, P., Dove, E., and Baggaley, C., 'Building a Data Sharing Model for Global Genomic Research' (2014) *Genome Biology* 15(430) <https://genomebiology.biomedcentral.com/track/pdf/10.1186/s13059-014-0430-2?site=genomebiology.biomedcentral.com> accessed 5 December 2019.

Kosta, E., *Consent in European Data Protection Law* (Martinus Nijhoff 2013).

Kosta, E., and Stuurman, K., 'Technical Standards and the Draft General Data Protection Regulation', in Panagiotis Delimatsis (ed.), *The Law, Economics and Politics of International Standardization* (Cambridge University Press 2015) 434.

Kukk, P., and Hüsing, B., 'Privacy, Data Protection and Policy Implications in Whole Genome Sequencing', in Rinie van Est and Dirk Stemerding (eds.), *Making Perfect Life: European Governance Challenges in 21st Century Bio-Engineering* (European Commission 2012).

Kuner, C., 'The European Commission's Proposed Data Protection Regulation: A Copernican Revolution in European Data Protection Law' (2012) *Bloomberg BNA Privacy and Security Law Report February* 6 1.

Kuner, C., *Transborder Data Flows and Data Privacy Law* (Oxford University Press 2013).

Kunkel, E., and Ehrhardt, R., 'Frozen Assets: An Expert Guide to Biobanking' *Select Science* (23 December 2014) <http://www.selectscience.net/editorial-articles/frozen-assets--an-expert-guide-to-biobanking/?artID=35743> accessed 11 December 2019.

Lander, E. S., Linton, L. M., Birren, B., et al., 'Initial Sequencing and Analysis of the Human Genome' (2001) *Nature* 409 860.

Lattanzi, R., 'Processing of Personal Data and Medical/Scientific Research within the Framework of Italy's Legal System', in Deryck Beyleveld, David Townend, Ségolène Rouillé-Mirza, and Jessica Wright (eds.), *Implementation of the Data Protection Directive in Relation to Medical Research in Europe* (Ashgate 2004) 193.

Lattanzi, R., 'Data Protection Principles and Research in the Biobanks Age', in Deborah Mascalzoni (ed.), *Ethics, Law and Governance of Biobanking* (Springer 2015) 79.

Laurence, P., 'Ireland Delays EU Deal with Israel on Data Transfers' (BBC News, 3 September 2010) <http://www.bbc.com/news/world-europe-11176926> accessed 11 December 2019.

Laurie, G. 'Challenging Medical-Legal Norms: The Role of Autonomy, Confidentiality and Privacy in Protecting Individual and Familial Group Rights in Genetic Information' (2001) *Journal of Legal Medicine* 22 1.

Laurie, G., *Genetic Privacy: A Challenge to Medico-Legal Norms* (Cambridge University Press 2002).

Laurie, G., 'A Response to Andorno' (2004) *Law, Ethics and Medicine* 30 439.

Laurie, G., 'Privacy and the Right Not to Know: A Plea for Conceptual Clarity', in Ruth Chadwick, Mairi Levitt, and Darren Shickle (eds.), *The Right to Know and the Right Not to Know: Genetic Privacy and Responsibility* (Cambridge University Press 2014) 38.

Laurie, G., and Harmon, S., Through the Thicket and Across the Divide: Successfully Navigating the Regulatory Landscape in Life Sciences Research (Edinburgh School of Law Research Paper, No. 2013/30, 2013).

Laurie, G., Jones, K., Stevens, L., et al., A Review of Evidence Relating to Harm Resulting from the Uses of Health and Biomedical Data (Technical Report prepared for the Nuffield Council on Bioethics Working Party on Biological and Health Data and the Wellcome Trust's Expert Advisory Group on Data Access, 2015).

Leitsalu, L., Alavere, H., Tammesoo, M., et al., 'Linking a Population Biobank with National Health Registries: The Estonian Experience' (2015) *Journal of Personalized Medicine* 5(2) 96.

Leitsalu, L., Haller, T., and Esko, T., 'Cohort Profile: Estonian Biobank of the Estonian Genome Center, University of Tartu' (2015) *International Journal of Epidemiology* 44(4) 1137.

Lemke, A., Wolf, Hebert-Beirne, W. J., et al., 'Public and Biobank Participant Attitudes toward Genetic Research Participation and Data Sharing' (2010) *Public Health Genomics* 13(6) 368.

Locke, A., Kahali, B., and Berndt, S., 'Genetic Studies of Body Mass Index Yield New Insights for Obesity Biology' (2015) *Nature* 518 197.

Lowe, A. L., Urquhart, A., Foreman, L. A., et al., 'Inferring Ethnic Origin by Means of an STR Profile' (2001) *Forensic Science International* 119 17.

Lucassen, A., and Parker, M., 'Confidentiality and Serious Harm in Genetics: Preserving the Confidentiality of One Patient and Preventing Harm to Relatives' (2004) *European Journal of Human Genetics* 12 93.

Lunshof, J., Chadwick, R., Vorhaus, D., et al., 'From Genetic Privacy to Open Consent' (2008) *Nature Reviews Genetics* 9(5) 406.

Lynch, E., Doherty, R., Gaff, C. et al., 'Cancer in the Family and Genetic Testing: Implications for Life Insurance' (2003) *Medical Journal of Australia* 179 480.

Lynsky, O., *The Foundations of EU Data Protection Law* (Oxford University Press 2015).

MacDonald, M., Ambrose, C., Duyao, M., et al., 'A Novel Gene Containing a Trinucleotide Repeat That Is Expanded and Unstable on Huntington's Disease Chromosomes' (1993) *Cell* 72(6) 971.

Manilo, T., Collins, F., Cox, N., et al., 'Finding the Missing Heritability of Complex Diseases' (2009) *Nature* 461 747.

Manson, N., 'The Medium and the Message: Tissue Samples, Genetic Information and Data Protection Legislation', in Heather Widdows and Caroline Mullen (eds.), *The Governance of Genetic Information: Who Decides* (Cambridge University Press 2009) 15.

Mantelero, A., and Vaciago, G., 'Data Protection in a Big Data Society: Ideas for a Future Regulation' (2015) *Digital Investigation* 15 104.

Marelli, L. and Testa, G., 'Scrutinizing the EU General Data Protection Regulation: How Will New Decentralized Governance Impact Research?' (2018) *Science* 360(6388) 496.

Margulis, S., 'Conceptions of Privacy: Current Status and Next Steps' (1977) *Journal of Social Issues* 33(3) 5.

Martin, N., Friedewald, M., Schiering, I., et al., *The Data Protection Impact Assessment according to Article 35 GDPR: A Practitioner's Manual* (Fraunhofer Press 2020).

Mascalzoni, D., Bentzen, H. B., Budin-Ljøsne, I. S., et al., 'Are Requirements to Deposit Data in Research Repositories Compatible with the European Union's General Data Protection Regulation?' (2019) *Annals of Internal Medicine* 170(5) 332.

Mascalzoni, D., Dove, E., Rubinstein, Y., et al., 'International Charter of Principles for Sharing Bio-Specimens and Data' (2015) *European Journal of Human Genetics* 23 721.

Mayer-Schönberger, V., 'Generational Development of Data Protection in Europe', in Phillip Agre and Marc Rotenberg (eds.), *Technology and Privacy: The New Landscape* (MIT Press 1997) 219.

Maynard Smith, J., 'The Concept of Information in Biology' (2000) *Philosophy of Science* 67(2) 177.

McGregor, J., 'Racial, Ethnic, and Tribal Classifications in Biomedical Research with Biological and Group Harm' (2010) *American Journal of Bioethics* 10 23.

McGuire, A., Caulfield, T., and Cho, M., 'Research Ethics and the Challenge of Whole-Genome Sequencing' (2008) *Nature Reviews Genetics* 9(2) 152.

McPherson, K., Steel, C. M., and Dixon, J. M. 'Breast Cancer: Epidemiology, Risk Factors and Genetics' (2000) *British Medical Journal* 321(7261) 624.

Melham, K., Moraia, L. B., Mitchell, C., et al., 'The Evolution of Withdrawal: Negotiating Research Relationships in Biobanking' (2014) *Life Sciences, Society and Policy* 10(16) <https://lsspjournal.springeropen.com/track/pdf/10.1186/s40504-014-0016-5?site=lsspjournal.springeropen.com> accessed 5 December 2019.

Mengel-From, J., Wong, T., Morling, N., et al., 'Genetic Determinants of Hair and Eye Colours in the Scottish and Danish Populations' (2009) *BMJ Genetics* 10 88.

METADAC, 'How to Apply' (Information sheet, 2015) <https://www.metadac.ac.uk/data-access-through-metadac/> accessed 28 November 2019.

Metspalu, A., 'The Estonian Genome Project' (2004) *Drug Development Research* 62 97.

Ministerial Ordinances 2019. Unofficial English translations of all documents <https://genomics.ut.ee/en/access-biobank/legislation> accessed 23 April 2020.

Moerel, L., *Binding Corporate Rules: Corporate Self-Regulation of Global Data Transfers* (Oxford University Press 2012).

Molnár-Gábor, F., 'Germany: A Fair Balance between Scientific Freedom and Data Subjects' Rights?' (2018) *Human Genetics* 137 618.

Monateri, P. G., 'Methods in Comparative Law: An Intellectual Overview', in Pier Giuseppe Monateri (ed.), *Methods of Comparative Law* (Elgar 2012).

Morozova, T., Goldman, D., Mackay, T., et al., 'The Genetic Basis of Alcoholism: Multiple Phenotypes, Many Genes, Complex Networks' (2012) *Genome Biology* 13(239) <http://genomebiology.com/content/pdf/gb-2012-13-2-239.pdf> accessed 27 November 2019.

Morrison, M., Bell, J., George, C., et al., 'The European General Data Protection Regulation: Challenges and Considerations for iPSC Researchers and Biobanks' (2017) *Regenerative Medicine* 12(6) 693.

Mourby, M., Mackey, E., Elliot, M., et al., 'Are "Pseudonymised" Data Always Personal Data? Implications of the GDPR for Administrative Data Research in the UK' (2018) *Computer Law and Security Review* 34 222.

Murphy, J., Scott, J., Kaufman, D., et al., 'Public Expectations for Return of Results from Large-Cohort Genetic Research' (2009) *American Journal of Bioethics* 8(11) 36.

National Health and Medical Research Council, Biobanks Information Paper (Information Paper, 2010).

National Human Genome Research Institute, DNA Sequencing Costs: Data from the NHGRI Genome Sequencing Program (GSP) (Fact Sheet, 2016) <https://www.genome.gov/sequencingcostsdata/> accessed 29 November 2019.

National Institutes of Health, NIH Genomic Data Sharing Policy (Policy, 2014).

NCBI, 'NCBI Retiring HapMap Resource' <http://hapmap.ncbi.nlm.nih.gov/> accessed 28 November 2019.

Newcastle Brain Tissue Resource, Material Transfer Agreement for the Provision of Human- Tissue for (Non-Commercial) Academic Research (Material Transfer Agreement, 2014) <https://nbtr.ncl.ac.uk/uploads/MTA%20-%20NBTR%20standard.pdf> accessed 11 December 2019.

Ngwena, C., and Chadwick, R., 'Genetic Diagnostic Information and the Duty of Confidentiality: Ethics and Law' (1993) *Medical Law International* 1 73.

NHS, Manchester Allergy, Respiratory and Thoracic Surgery Biobank (Information sheet, 2019) <https://www.hra.nhs.uk/planning-and-improving-research/application-summaries/

research-summaries/manchester-allergy-respiratory-thoracic-surgery-biobank/> accessed 28 November 2019.

NHS Health Research Authority, 'The Health Service (Control of Patient Information) Regulations 2002: regulation 5 decision procedure for research applications' (NHS Health Research Authority, 2017) <https://www.hra.nhs.uk/about-us/committees-and-services/confidentiality-advisory-group/guidance-confidentiality-advisory-group-applicants/health-service-control-patient-information-regulations-2002-regulation-5-decision-procedure-research-applications/> accessed 16 June 2020.

NHS Health Research Authority, 'Consent in Research' (NHS Health Research Authority, 2018) <https://www.hra.nhs.uk/planning-and-improving-research/policies-standards-legislation/data-protection-and-information-governance/gdpr-guidance/what-law-says/consent-research/> accessed 19 June 2020.

Nicholas, N., 'Risk Management: Confidentiality, Disclosure and Access to Medical Records' (2007) *The Obstetrician and Gynaecologist* 9 257.

Niedringhaus, T., Milanova, D., Kerby, M., et al., 'Landscape of Next-Generation Sequencing Technologies' (2012) *Analytical Chemistry* 83(12) 4327.

Nuffield Council of Bioethics, The Forensic Use of Bioinformation: Ethical Issues (Report, 2007).

Nys, H., 'Report on the Implementation of Directive 95/46/EC in Belgian Law', in Deryck Beyleveld, David Townend, Ségolène Rouillé-Mirza, and Jessica Wright (eds.), *Implementation of the Data Protection Directive in Relation to Medical Research in Europe* (Ashgate, 2004) 29.

Nys, H., Dreezen, I., Vinck, I., et al., Genetic Testing: Patients' Rights, Insurance and Employment: A Survey of Regulations in the European Union (European Commission Report, 2002).

O'Brien, R., 'Privacy and Security: The New European Data Protection Regulation and Its Data Breach Notification Requirements' (2016) *Business Information Review* 33(2) 81.

Ó Cathaoir, K., Gefenas, E., Hartlev, M., Mourby, M., and Lukaseviciene, V., Legal and ethical review of in silico modelling (EU-STANDS4PM Project Deliverable, 3.1, 2020).

O'Doherty, K., Christofides, E., Yen, J., et al., 'If You Build It, They Will Come: Unintended Future Uses of Organised Health Data Collections' (2016) *BMC Medical Ethics* 17(54) <https://www.ncbi.nlm.nih.gov/pmc/articles/PMC5011895/pdf/12910_2016_Article_137.pdf> accessed 11 December 2019.

OECD, Guidelines Governing the Protection of Privacy and Transborder Flows of Personal Data (Policy, 1980).

OECD, Best Practice Guidelines for Biological Resource Centres (Policy, 2007).

OECD, Principles and Guidelines for Access to Research Data from Public Funding (Policy, 2007).

OECD, Guidelines on Human Biobanks and Genetic Research Databases (Guidelines, 2009).

OECD, Biological Resource Centres: Underpinning the Future of Life Sciences and Biotechnology (Position Statement, 932001041E1, 2011).

OECD, 'OECD Legal Instruments' (OECD) <http://www.oecd.org/legal/legal-instruments.htm> accessed 5 December 2019.

Ohshiro, T., Msutsui, M., Matsubara, K., et al., 'Single-Molecule Tunnel-Current Based Identification of DNA/RNA towards Sequencing by Using Nano-MCBJ' (2012) *16th International Conference on Miniaturized Systems for Chemistry and Life Sciences* 204.

Office of the Press Secretary, Remarks Made by the President, Prime Minister Tony Blair of England (via satellite), Dr Francis Collins, Director of the National Human Genome Research Institute, and Dr Craig Venter, President and Chief Scientific Officer, Celera Genomics Corporation, on the Completion of the First Survey of the Entire Human Genome Project (Press Conference Report, 2000).

Offit, K., 'Personalized Medicine: New Genomics, Old Lessons' (2011) *Human Genetics* 130(1) 3.

O'Hara, K., and Shadbolt, N., *The Spy in the Coffee Machine: The End of Privacy as We Know it* (Oneworld 2008).

Olson, M., 'The Human Genome Project: A Player's Perspective' (2002) *Journal of Molecular Biology* 319 931.

O'Neil, O., and Manson, C., *Rethinking Informed Consent in Bioethics* (Cambridge University Press 2007).

openSNP, 'Welcome to openSNP' (openSNP, 2019) <https://opensnp.org/> accessed 11 December 2019.

Oxford Nanopore Technologies, 'MinION' (Oxford Nanopore Technologies, 2019) <https://nanoporetech.com/products/minion> accessed 11 December 2019.

Peloquin, D., DiMaio, M., Bierer, B., et al., 'Disruptive and Avoidable: GDPR Challenges to Secondary Research Uses of Data' (2020) *European Journal of Human Genetics* 28 697.

Penasa, S., Miguel Beriain, I., Barbosa, C., et al., 'The EU General Data Protection Regulation: How Will It Impact the Regulation of Research Biobanks? Setting the Legal Frame in the Mediterranean and Eastern European Area' (2018) *Medical Law International* 18(4) 241.

Pennisi, E., 'ENCODE Project Writes Eulogy for Junk DNA' (2012) *Science* 337(6099) 1159.

Phillips, A. M., and Hervey, T. K., 'Brexit and Biobanking: GDPR Perspectives', in Santa Slokenberga, Olga Tzortzatou, and Jane Reichel (eds.), *GDPR and Biobanking: Individual Rights, Public Interest and Research Regulation across Europe* (Springer 2021) 145.

Ples, L., 'The Implementation in Domestic Law of Directive 95/46/EC in Romania', in Deryck Beyleveld, David Townend, Ségolène Rouillé-Mirza, and Jessica Wright (eds.), *Implementation of the Data Protection Directive in Relation to Medical Research in Europe* (Ashgate, 2004) 341.

Ploem, M., Essink-Bot, M. L., and Stronks, K., 'Proposed EU Data Protection Regulation Is a Threat to Medical Research: A Suggested Amendment Would Make Most Epidemiological and Health Research Impossible' (2013) *British Medical Journal* 346 1.

Polašek, O., 'Future of Biobanks: Bigger, Longer, and More Dimensional' (2013) *Croatian Medical Journal* 54(5) 496.

Pollack, A., 'Building a Face, and a Case, on DNA' *New York Times* (New York, February 23, 2015) <http://www.nytimes.com/2015/02/24/science/building-face-and-a-case-on-dna.html> accessed 27 November 2019.

Pontin, J., 'A Decade of Genomics: On the 10th Anniversary of the Human Genome Project, We Ask: Where Are the Therapies?' *MIT Technology Review* (21 December 2010) <https://www.technologyreview.com/s/422130/a-decade-of-genomics/> accessed 11 December 2019.

Pormeister, K., 'Genetic Research and Applicable Law: The Intra-EU Conflict of Laws as a Regulatory Challenge to Cross-Border Genetic Research' (2018) *Journal of Law and the Biosciences* 5(3) 706.

Pormeister, K., Transparency in relation to the data subject in genetic research: An analysis on the example of Estonia (University of Tartu Ph.D. thesis, 2019).

Pötters, S., 'Artikel 89', in Peter Gola (ed.), *DS-GVO Datenschutz-Grundverordnung VO (EU) 2016/679 Kommentar* (Beck 2017) 781.

Prainsack, B., 'DIY Genetics: The Right to Know Your Own Genome', in Ruth Chadwick, Mairi Levitt, and Darren Shickle (eds.), *The Right to Know and the Right Not to Know: Genetic Privacy and Responsibility* (Cambridge University Press 2014) 100.

Price, D., 'The Human Tissue Act 2004' (2005) *Modern Law Review* 68(5) 798.

Prictor, M., Teare, H. J. A, Bell, J., et al., 'Could "Dynamic Consent" Be a Useful Tool for Researchers?' (2019) *Journal of Data Protection and Privacy* 3(1) 93.

Quinn, P., 'The Anonymisation of Research Data: A Pyric Victory for Privacy that Should Not Be Pushed Too Hard by the EU Data Protection Framework?' (2017) *European Journal of Health Law* 24 1.

Raab, C., 'Privacy, Social Values and the Public Interest', in Andreas Busch and Jeanette Hofmann (eds.), *Politik und die Regulierung von Information* (Nomos 2012) 129.

Rees, J., 'Genetics of Hair and Skin Color' (2003) *Annual Review Genetics* 37 67.

Reimer, P. 'Artikel 5: Grundsätze für die Verarbeitung personenbezogener Daten', in Gernot Sydow (ed.), *Europäische Datenschutz-grundverordnung: Handkommentar* (Nomos 2018) 319.

Research Ethics Committee of the University of Tartu, Continuous Review Document Requirements (Policy, 2009) <http://www.ut.ee/sites/default/files/ut_files/CONTINUOUS%20REVIEW%20DOCUMENT%20REQUIREMENTS%20of%20UT%20REC%202012.pdf> accessed 11 December 2019.

Rial-Sebbag, E., 'The Emergence of Biobanks in the Legal Landscape: Towards a New Model of Governance' (2012) *Journal of Law and Society* 39(1) 113.

Riegman, P. H, Morente, M. M., Betsou, F., et al., 'Biobanking for better healthcare' (2008) *Molecular Oncology* 2 213.

Roche, *Roche Position on Human Specimen Resources (Biobanks)* (Position Statement, 2017) <https://www.roche.com/dam/jcr:5aa0f3e7-fa20-4153-a8b8-38df4477712f/10_Position%20on%20Human%20Specimen%20Resources%20(Biobanks)_reviewed_4_2017.pdf> accessed 28 November 2019.

Rohlfs, R., Murphy, E., Song, Y., et al., 'The Influence of Relatives on the Efficiency and Error Rate of Familial Searching' (2013) *PLOS One* 9(1) 1 <https://journals.plos.org/plosone/article?id=10.1371/journal.pone.0070495> accessed 5 December 2019.

Romeo Casabona, C. M., and Nicolás, P., 'The Implementation of Directive 95/46/EC in Spain', in Deryck Beyleveld, David Townend, Ségolène Rouillé-Mirza, and Jessica Wright (eds.), *Implementation of the Data Protection Directive in Relation to Medical Research in Europe* (Ashgate 2004) 357.

Roßnagel, A., and Nebel, M., Die Neue Datenschutzgrundverordnung: Ist das Datenschutzrecht nun für heutige Herausforderungen gerüstet? (Policy Paper Forum Privatheit, 2016).

Rothstein, M., 'Genetic Exceptionalism and Legislative Pragmatism' (2007) *Journal of Law, Medicine and Ethics* 2(Suppl.) 59.

Rouillé-Mirza, S., and Wright, J., 'Comparative Study on the Implementation and Effect of Directive 95/46 on Data Protection in Europe: Medical Research', in Deryck Beyleveld, David Townend, Ségolène Rouillé-Mirza, and Jessica Wright (eds.), *The Data Protection Directive and Medical Research Across Europe* (Ashgate 2004) 189.

Rouvroy, A., *Human Genes and Neoliberal Governance: A Foucauldian Critique* (Routledge-Cavendish 2008).

Rumbold, J., and Pierscionek, B., 'The Effect of the General Data Protection Regulation on Medical Research' (2017) *Journal of Medical Internet Research* 19(2) <https://www.ncbi.nlm.nih.gov/pmc/articles/PMC5346164/> accessed 11 December 2019.

Sándor, J., and Bárd, P. The Legal Regulation of Biobanks: National Report: Estonia (CELAB Paper Series, No. 5, 2009).

Santos, F., Machado, H., Silva, S., 'Forensic DNA Databases in European Countries: Is Size Linked to Performance?' (2013) *Life Sciences, Society and Policy* 9(12) <http://www.lsspjournal.com/content/9/1/12> accessed 28 November 2019.

Sarata, A., Genetic Exceptionalism: Genetic Information and Public Policy (Congressional Research Service Report, 2008).

Schaar, K., 'Anpassung von Einwilligungserklärungen für wissenschaftliche Forschungsprojekte: Die informierte Einwilligung nach der DS-GVO und den Ethikrichtlinien' (2017) *Zeitschrift für Datenschutz* 5/2017 213.

Schaeffer, C., C-A3-04: Project Collaboration, 'The Kaiser Permanente Research Program on Genes, Environment and Health: A Resource for Genetic Epidemiology in Adult Health and Aging' (2011) *Clinical Medicine and Research* 9(3–4) 177.

Schmidt, H. and Callier, S., 'How Anonymous Is "Anonymous"? Some Suggestions Towards a Coherent Universal Coding System for Genetic Samples' (2012) *Journal of Medical Ethics* 38(5) 304.

Shabani, M., and Borry, P., 'Rules for Processing Genetic Data for Research Purposes in View of the New EU General Data Protection Regulation' (2018) *European Journal of Human Genetics* 26 149.

Shabani, M., and Marelli, L., 'Re-identifiability of Genomic Data and the GDPR: Assessing the Re-identifiability of Genomic Data in Light of the EU General Data Protection Regulation' (2019) *EMBO Reports* 20 4 <https://www.embopress.org/doi/epdf/10.15252/embr.201948316> accessed 1 June 2020.

Sheehan, M., 'Can Broad Consent Be Informed Consent?' (2011) *Public Health Ethics* 4(3) 226.

Simm, K., 'Biobanks and Feedback', in Ruth Chadwick, Mairi Levitt, and Darren Shickle (eds.), *The Right to Know and the Right Not to Know: Genetic Privacy and Responsibility* (Cambridge University Press 2014).

Simon, C., L'Heureux, J., Murray, J., et al., 'Active Choice But Not Too Active: Public Perspectives on Biobank Consent Models' (2011) *Genetics in Medicine* 13(9) 821.

Singh, K., *Biotechnology and Intellectual Property Rights: Legal and Social Implications* (Springer 2015).

Slokenberga, S., 'Biobanking and Data Transfer between the EU and Cape Verde, Mauritius, Morocco, Senegal, and Tunisia: Adequacy Considerations and Convention 108'. (2020) *International Data Privacy Law Advance Publication* 1.

Slokenberga, S., Reichel, J., Niringiye, R., et al. 'EU Data Transfer Rules and African Legal Realities: Is Data Exchange for Biobank Research Realistic?' (2018) *International Data Privacy Law* 9(1) 30.

Slokenberga, S., Tzortzatou, O., Reichel, J. (eds.), *GDPR and Biobanking: Individual Rights, Public Interest and Research Regulation across Europe* (Springer 2021).

Sobradillo, P., Pozo, F., and Agustí, Á., 'P4 Medicine: The Future Around the Corner' (2011) *Archivos de Bronconeumologia* 47(1) 35.

Sperry, B., Allyse, M., and Sharp, R., 'Genetic Fingerprints and National Security' (2017) *American Journal of Bioethics* <https://www.tandfonline.com/doi/full/10.1080/15265161.2017.1316627> accessed 27 November 2019.

Spiekermann, S., 'The Challenges of Privacy by Design' (2012) *Communications of the ACM* 55(7) 38.

Staunton, C., Slokenberga, S., and Mascalzoni, D., 'The GDPR and the Research Exemption: Considerations on the Necessary Safeguards for Research Biobanks' (2019) *European Journal of Human Genetics* 27 1159.

Stein, R., 'Found on the Web, with DNA: A Boy's Father' *Washington Post* (Washington 13 November 2005) available at <http://www.washingtonpost.com/wp-dyn/content/article/2005/11/12/AR2005111200958.html> accessed 27 November 2019.

Stirton, R., 'Insurance, Genetic Information and the Future of Industry Self-Regulation in the UK' (2012) *Law, Innovation and Technology* 4(2) 212.

Sudlow, C., Gallacher, J., Allen, N. et al., 'UK Biobank: An Open Access Resource for Identifying the Causes of a Wide Range of Complex Diseases of Middle and Old Age' (2015) *PLoS Med* 12(3) <http://journals.plos.org/plosmedicine/article/file?id=10.1371/journal.pmed.1001779&type=printable> accessed 11 December 2019.

Suter, S. 'All in the Family: Privacy and DNA familial searching' (2010) *Harvard Journal of Law & Technology* 23(2) 309, 319.

Swire, P., and Lagos, Y. 'Why the Right to Data Portability Likely Reduces Consumer Welfare: Antitrust and Privacy Critique' (2013) *Maryland Law Review* 72(2) 335.

Taupitz, J., and Schreiber, M., 'Biobanken – zwischen Forschungs- und Spenderinteressen' (2016) *Bundesgesundheitsblatt – Gesundheitsforschung – Gesundheitsschutz* 59 304.

Taupitz, J., and Weigel, J., 'Biobanken – das Regelungskonzept des Deutschen Ethikrates' (2012) *Wissenschaftsrecht* 45 35.

Taupitz, J. and Weigel, J., 'The Necessity of Broad Consent and Complementary Regulations for the Protection of Personal Data in Biobanks: What Can We Learn from the German Case' (2012) *Public Health Genomics* 15 263.

Taylor, M., *Genetic Data and the Law: A Critical Perspective on Privacy Protection* (Cambridge University Press 2012).

Taylor, M., 'Genetic Discrimination and the Draft European Union General Data Protection Regulation', in Gerard Quinn, Aisling de Paor, and Peter Blanck (eds.), *Genetic Discrimination: Transatlantic perspectives on the case for a European-level legal response* (Routledge 2015) 211.

Taylor, M. J., and Whitton, T. 'Public Interest, Health Research and Data Protection Law: Establishing a Legitimate Trade-Off between Individual Control and Research Access to Health Data' (2019) *Laws* 9(1) 1 <https://www.mdpi.com/2075-471X/9/1/6> accessed 3 June 2020.

Tene, O., and Polonetsky, J., 'Big Data for All: Privacy and User Control in the Age of Analytics' (2013) *Northwestern Journal of Technology and Intellectual Property* 11(5) 240.

Thorogood, A., and Zawati, M., 'International Guidelines for Privacy in Genomic Biobanking (or the Unexpected Virtue of Pluralism)' (2015) *Journal of Law, Medicine and Ethics* 43(4) 690.

Tomova, S., 'Implementation of Directive 95/46/EC in Relation to Medical Research in Bulgaria', in Deryck Beyleveld, David Townend, Ségolène Rouillé-Mirza, and Jessica Wright (eds.), *Implementation of the Data Protection Directive in Relation to Medical Research in Europe* (Ashgate, 2004), 43.

Toronto International Data Release Workshop Authors, 'Prepublication Data Sharing' (2009) *Nature* 461(7261) 168.

Townend, D., 'EU Laws on Privacy in Genomic Databases and Biobanking' (2016) *Journal of Law, Medicine & Ethics* 44(4, pt 1) 128.

Tyler-Smith, C., Yang, H., Landweber, L., et al., 'Where Next for Genetics and Genomics?' (2015) *PLOS Biology* 13(7) <http://journals.plos.org/plosbiology/article/asset?id=10.1371%2Fjournal.pbio.1002216.PDF> accessed 11 December 2019

UK Biobank, About UK Biobank (Information Sheet, 2019) <http://www.ukbiobank.ac.uk/about-biobank-uk/> accessed 28 November 2019.

UK Biobank, Access Procedures: Application and Review Procedures for Access to the UK Biobank Resource (Policy, 2011) Article B4.5 <http://www.ukbiobank.ac.uk/wp-content/uploads/2012/09/Access-Procedures-2011.pdf> accessed 28 November 2019.

UK Biobank, Consent Form: UK Biobank (Policy, 2011) <http://www.ukbiobank.ac.uk/wp-content/uploads/2011/06/Consent_form.pdf> accessed 11 December 2019.

UK Biobank, 'FAQs' (UK Biobank, 2019) <https://www.ukbiobank.ac.uk/all-faqs/> accessed 4 December 2019.

UK Biobank, Information Leaflet (Information Leaflet, 2011) <http://www.ukbiobank.ac.uk/wp-content/uploads/2011/06/Participant_information_leaflet.pdf?phpMyAdmin=trmKQlYdjjnQIgJ%2CfAzikMhEnx6> accessed 11 December 2019.

UK Biobank, UK Biobank Ethics and Governance Framework (Policy, 2007).

UK Biobank, Withdrawal Protocol (Policy, 2012) <http://www.ukbiobank.ac.uk/wp-content/uploads/2012/04/Withdrawal-protocol-030412.pdf> accessed 29 November 2019.

UK Government, 'Get a DNA test' (UK Government 2019) <https://www.gov.uk/get-dna-test> accessed 5 December 2019.

UK Parliament, Human Tissue Act 2004 Explanatory Note (Policy, 2004).

University of Tartu Act 1995. Unofficial English translation <https://www.riigiteataja.ee/en/eli/ee/Riigikogu/act/522082014009/consolide> accessed 11 December 2019.

University of Tartu Institute of Genomics, 'Estonian Genome Centre' (University of Tartu Institute of Genomics) <https://genomics.ut.ee/en/about-us/estonian-genome-centre> accessed 16 June 2020.

University of Tartu Institute of Genomics, 'Issuing of Data and/or Biological Samples' (University of Tartu Institute of Genomics) <http://www.geenivaramu.ee/en/biobank.ee/data-access> accessed 11 December 2019.

University of Tartu Institute of Genomics, *Annex 1 to the Ministry of Social Affairs Decree No 36* (Policy, 2007) <http://www.geenivaramu.ee/sites/default/files/gene_donor_consent_form.pdf> accessed 11 December 2019.

US National Library of Medicine, 'Charcot Marie Tooth Disease' (*Genetics Home Reference*, 10 December 2019) <https://ghr.nlm.nih.gov/condition/charcot-marie-tooth-disease> accessed 11 December 2019.

Van Assche, K., Gutwirth, S., and Sterckx, S., 'Protecting Dignitary Interests of Biobank Research Participants: Lessons from Havasupai Tribe v Arizona Board of Regents' (2013) *Law, Innovation and Technology* 5(1) 54.

Vanberg, A. D., and Ünver, M., 'The Right to Data Portability in the GDPR and EU Competition Law: Odd Couple or Dynamic Duo?' (2017) *European Journal of Law and Technology* 8(1) 1 <http://ejlt.org/article/view/546/727> accessed 11 December 2019.

Van Dijk, N., Gellert, R., and Rommetveit, K., 'A Risk to a Right? Beyond Data Protection Risk Assessments' (2016) *Computer Law and Security Review* 32(2) 286.

Van Eijken, H., 'European Citizenship and the Competence of Member States to Grant and to Withdraw the Nationality of their Nationals' (2010) *Utrecht Journal of International and European Law* 27(72) 65.

van Veen, E. 'Observational Health Research in Europe: Understanding the General Data Protection Regulation and Underlying Debate' (2018) *European Journal of Cancer* 104 70.

Van Veen, E.-B, Riegman, P. H., Dinjens, W. N., et al., 'TuBaFrost 3: Regulatory and Ethical Issues on the Exchange of Residual Tissue for Research across Europe' (2006) *European Journal of Cancer* 42 2914.

Venter, C., Mark Adams, Granger Sutton, et al., 'Shotgun Sequencing of the Human Genome' (1998) *Science* 280(5369) 1540.

Venter, J. C., Adams, M. D., Myers, E. W., et al., 'The Sequence of the Human Genome' (2001) *Science* 291 1304.

Visscher, P., Brown, M., McCarthy, M. et al., 'Five Years of GWAS Discovery' (2012) *American Journal of Human Genetics* 90(1) 7.

Visscher, P., Wray, N., Zhang, Q., et al., '10 Years of GWAS Discovery: Biology, Function, and Translation' (2017) *American Journal of Human Genetics 101*(1) 5.

Wall, J., Tang, L., Zerbe, B., et al., 'Estimating Genotype Error Rates from High-Coverage Next-Generation Sequence Data' (2014) *Genome Research* 24(11) 1734.

Wallace, S., *P3G Sample and Data Access: Core Elements* (Position Statement, 2008).

Wallace, S., and Knoppers, B., 'The Role of P3G in Encouraging Public Trust in Biobanks', in Peter Dabrock, Jochen Taupitz, and Jens Ried (eds.), *Trust in Biobanking* (Springer 2012) 189.

'War Crimes Tribunal at Nuremberg, The Nuremberg Code (1947)' (1996) *British Medical Journal* 313 1448.

Wellcome Trust, *Policy on Data Management and Sharing* (Policy, 2017).

Wellcome Trust, *Sharing Data from Large-Scale Biological Research Projects: A System of Tripartite Responsibility* (Report, 2003).

Widdows, H., and Cordell, S., 'The Ethics of Biobanking: Key Issues and Controversies' (2011) *Health Care Analysis* 19 207.

Wilkinson, R., 'Genetic Information: Important But Not "Exceptional"' (2010) *Identity in the Information Society 3*(3) 457.

William, R., Watson, G., Kaye, E. W., et al., 'Integrating Biobanks: Addressing the Practical and Ethical Issues to Deliver a Valuable Tool for Cancer Research' (2010) *Nature Reviews Cancer* 10 646.

Williams, G. *Natural Selection: Domains, Levels and Challenges* (Oxford University Press 1992).

Williams, J., 'The Declaration of Helsinki and Public Health' (2008) *Bulletin of the World Health Organisation* 86(8) <http://www.scielosp.org/scielo.php?pid=S0042-96862008000800022&script=sci_arttext> accessed 5 December 2019.

Wjst, M., 'Caught You: Threats to Confidentiality Due to the Public Release of Large-Scale Genetic Data Sets' (2010) *BMC Medical Ethics 11*(21) <http://bmcmedethics.biomedcentral.com/articles/10.1186/1472-6939-11-21> accessed 11 December 2019.

World Medical Association, Declaration of Helsinki: Ethical Principles for Medical Research Involving Human Subjects (Policy, 1964 (updated 2013)).

World Medical Association, Declaration of Taipei on Ethical Considerations regarding health databases and biobanks (Policy, 2002 (updated 2016)).

Wright, D., 'Making Privacy Impact Assessment More Effective' (2013) *Information Society* 29 307.

Wright, D., Kroener, I., Lagazio, M., et al., A guide to surveillance impact assessment — How to identify and prioritise risks arising from surveillance systems (SAPIENT Project Deliverable, 4.4, 2014).

Wybitul, T., 'Was ändert sich mit dem neuen EU-Datenschutzrecht für Arbeitgeber und Betriebsräte? Anpassungsbedarf bei Beschäftigtendatenschutz und Betriebsvereinbarungen' (2016) *Zeitschrift für Datenschutz* 5 203.

Yassin, R., Lockhart, N., González del Riego, M., et al., 'Custodianship as an Ethical Framework for Biospecimen-Based Research' (2010) *Cancer, Epidemiology, Biomarkers and Prevention 19*(4) 1012.

Yuille, M., Dixon, C., Platt, A., et al., 'The UK DNA Banking Network: A "Fair Access" Biobank' (2010) *Cell Tissue Bank 11* 241.

Zanfir, G., 'The Right to Data Portability in the Context of the EU Data Protection Reform' (2012) *International Data Privacy Law* 2(3) 149.

Zanfir, G., 'Forgetting About Consent: Why the Focus Should Be on "Suitable Safeguards" in Data Protection Law', in Serge Gutwirth, Ronald Leenes, and Paul De Hert (eds.), *Reloading Data Protection* (Springer 2013) 237.

Ziętkiewicz, E., Witt, M., Daca, P. et al., 'Current Genetic Methodologies in the Identification of Disaster Victims and in Forensic Analysis' (2012) *Journal of Applied Genetics* 54 41.

Zika, E., Paci, D., Schulte in den Bäumen, T., et al., *Biobanks in Europe: Prospects for Harmonisation and Networking* (European Commission 2010).

Zins, C., 'Conceptual Approaches for Defining Data, Information and Knowledge' (2007) *Journal of the Association for Information Science and Technology* 58(4) 479.

Zuiderveen Borgesius, F., Consent to Behavioural Targeting in European Law: What are the Policy Implications of Insights from Behavioural Economics? (Amsterdam Law School Legal Studies Research Paper, No. 2013-43, 2013).

Zuiderveen Borgesius, F., and Hallinan, D., 'Article 5', in Franziska Boehm and Mark Cole (eds.), GDPR Commentary (Elgar Forthcoming 2021).

Zuiderveen Borgesius, F., Kruikemeier, S., Boerman, S., et al., 'Tracking Walls, Take-It-Or-Leave-It Choices, the GDPR, and the ePrivacy Regulation' (2017) *European Data Protection Law Review* 3 353.

Index

For the benefit of digital users, indexed terms that span two pages (e.g., 52–53) may, on occasion, appear on only one of those pages.